W9-ACN-201

WITHDRAWN

STAGING DEPTH

Cultural Studies of the United States | Alan Trachtenberg, editor

Staging Depth

The

University

of North

Carolina

Press

Chapel Hill

and

London

Joel Pfister

EUGENE O'NEILL

AND THE POLITICS

OF PSYCHOLOGICAL

DISCOURSE

99 98 97 96 95

5   4   3   2   1

Library of Congress Cataloging-in-Publication Data

Pfister, Joel. Staging depth : Eugene O'Neill and the
politics of psychological discourse / by Joel Pfister.

p. cm. — (Cultural studies of the United States)

Includes bibliographical references and index.

ISBN 0-8078-2186-1 (cloth : alk. paper). —

ISBN 0-8078-4496-9 (pbk. : alk. paper) 1. O'Neill,

Eugene, 1888–1953—Knowledge—Psychology.

2. Literature and society—United States—History—

20th century. 3. Domestic drama, American—

History and criticism. 4. Middle class in literature.

5. Psychology in literature. 6. Family in literature.

I. Title. II. Series.

PS3529.N5Z7742   1995   812'.52—dc20

94-26336 CIP

CONTENTS

ILLUSTRATIONS

Staging Depth undertakes something radically new in the study of Eugene O'Neill: an interpretation of his works from the perspective of the fictions that sustained them. Formal experimentation and thematic obsession make up the usual stuff of O'Neill criticism, but Joel Pfister seeks to break that conventional mold. He practices a skeptical criticism here, one that refuses to take the author at his own word and looks instead under and beyond the author's words and the mentality they project in search of cultural sources and historical causes. Pfister re-places O'Neill within the history of a precise segment of middle-class desire, aspiration, and self-doubt, joins O'Neill not only to a social history of shifting fortunes in the early twentieth century but also to an intellectual history of shifting values and outlooks during the period (the 1910s and 1920s especially) when corporate capitalism consolidated its domain of control within U.S. culture. Without ever allowing O'Neill to slip from sight, *Staging Depth* offers an acutely conceived and richly documented brief history of cultural changes in twentieth-century America.

The main issue in both the history and the literary criticism here is the concept of "depth"—and the category of the "psychological," of which it partakes. A literary critic in the first instance, Pfister takes his historicism seriously enough actually to become a historian, and a very good one. He does not just gesture at history; he digs into sources, scours the archives, reads widely in recent monographs. The result is a well-packed and nuanced argument that ties the emergence of a distinct middle-class stratum of managers and professionals to changes in family life and sexual expectations; political movements among "new women," intellectuals, and artists; the Harlem Renaissance; and experimental modernism in personal life and art. O'Neill centers this wide-ranging undertaking, and the historical discourse in *Staging Depth* in turn recenters O'Neill for us as a figure more than anecdotally linked to the forces that shaped his era.

It is the fusion of its author's two roles as scholarly historian and ideological critic that makes *Staging Depth* such a stunning achievement. One feature of the book deserves special mention for its courage and its finesse. The deconstructive historicist criticism that Pfister practices with great skill often takes the form of a kind of scandalmongering, exposing the complicity of established writers in bad discourses of gender, race, and class and reducing them (in a form of retro-punishment) to mere reflexes of contingent need. This is not the case here. Instead, Pfister undertakes what might even be called a rescue operation on O'Neill. Not that his motive is to refurbish a reputation or repolish a tarnished greatness. Pfister manages to steer a fine course between the reigning motive of criticism to *understand* even at the expense of compromised literary reputation and an older motive to *evaluate*, to judge literary value. Because it engages so openly with the push and pull of cross-purposes—the strictly historicist and the evaluative—and because it stays its subtle course where the work of another critic might well veer to one side or the other, *Staging Depth* performs a significant feat in the field of cultural studies. Literary intelligence as much as historicist dexterity informs the book. Close readings of many plays share space with detailed readings of cultural and ideological discourses. Pfister manages to put O'Neill, a literary icon, through the familiar deconstructive wringer and yet salvage a sense of importance in the very works submitted to political criticism.

Not by trimming or pulling punches does Pfister accomplish the rescue of his subject. By stripping away the image attached to the writer— O'Neill's aura of "depth"—Pfister discloses a figure struggling with his history, often blindly but also often with startling insight. Even as Pfister persuades us that the "depth" that made O'Neill famous was something staged, fabricated, clabbered together like a stage set to seem real, true to an assumed transhistorical "human nature," he shows O'Neill himself caught in the agon of his culture, as much captive and victim of the illusion of "depth" as perpetrator of the myth, often-mordant critic as much as swaggering impresario of the depthless sense of illusory depth.

Does *Staging Depth* herald a turn in historicist criticism, a swerve from the neat little piles of bones picked clean that has seemed the major delight of critics bent on exposing writers for their complicity in bad discourses of gender, race, class? Pfister takes the project of historicism as seriously as anyone: antiformalism is clear on every page of his book. The experience of O'Neill's plays is recoverable not in the lines of the plays themselves marching undisturbed across a printed page, but in the echoes and resonances of other texts of cultural belief and behavior recuperated by critical scholarship within those lines. There is the insight that "depth"—the notion that inward, private subjectivity is more true to personhood than public actions and networks of collective relations—is a historical effect, appearing when and how it does for definable reasons. It is an invention, something constructed to answer needs. From pop psychology to high-blown Freudian analysis it appears in conjunction with the rise into social prominence and cultural power of a new class of white-collar workers, professionals and managers, a new outcropping of salaried middle-class people beholden on the one hand to corporate hierarchies and on the other to their perhaps compensatory illusions of depth and inwardness.

Pfister treats the central O'Neill trope of the autonomous, tortured artist (the more tortured, the more depth) with thorough research and impressive insight. The remarkable fact is that *Staging Depth* produces a more interesting, cogent, complex, and genuinely tortured O'Neill than we have had—an artist whose private demons are revealed to be the tormented forms of cultural change and historical process. Pfister gives us an O'Neill we can see dimensionally, caught up in the dialectical swings of his era, fighting at once with and against the current. There is no other work on O'Neill quite like this one. Pfister remakes the play-wright's tortured fictions into the culture's own barely acknowledged bad dreams.

Alan Trachtenberg

Staging Depth builds on the critical framework and historical approaches I developed in *The Production of Personal Life: Class, Gender, and the Psychological in Hawthorne's Fiction*. The same American Council of Learned Societies Fellowship (1990–91) that permitted me to put the finishing touches on my Hawthorne book enabled me to do a good deal of the research for the first draft of my O'Neill book. I am indebted to the ACLS for its support. A one-term Wesleyan sabbatical that directly followed this fellowship year gave me the opportunity to complete my first draft. I thank Wesleyan's administration not only for this well-timed sabbatical but for helping to fund both the publication of photographs and the proofreading.

My primary debt is to Alan Trachtenberg, whose deft historical and editorial criticisms, and enthusiasm, strengthened several drafts. It is an honor to have my book appear in his Cultural Studies of the United States series. Sarah Winter, whose historical critiques of Freud have advanced my thinking about the politics of psychological discourse, commented on my initial draft. Another friend, Lianna Cleland Kalmar, a great admirer of O'Neill, also read and tightened the earliest version of my manuscript. Nancy Schnog's smart suggestions improved rough drafts of Chapter 1 and the Afterword. Our collaboration on the volume of essays we are editing, *Inventing the Psychological: Toward a Cultural History of Emotional Life in America*, has consistently helped me clarify the historical and theoretical issues at stake in my O'Neill project. Thomas J. Ferraro also read one of my earliest drafts and offered perceptive comments. David Lubin's attentive reading contributed to my appreciation of the complexity of the theoretical issues I raise in my introduction and Chapter 2.

Wesleyan is a hothouse for cultural studies debate, research, and writing; its rare intellectual climate has nourished the growth of this book. My colleague Richard Ohmann, director of the Center for the Humanities, read several drafts of my manuscript; his own pathbreaking work on the turn-of-the-century formation of the professional-managerial class has sharpened my understanding of the role O'Neill played in the articulation of the "psychological" identity of his class in the 1920s. I am also grateful to Richard Slotkin for reading my work and for insisting that I not soften my ideological critique of pop psychology and psychoanalysis. Another brilliant colleague, Indira Karamcheti, read several chapters and offered discerning comments on my arguments pertaining to gender and race. Al Turco provided me with meticulous and generous criticisms of some of my interpretations of O'Neill's plays; I have benefited from his readings of O'Neill. Jill Morawski's extraordinary expertise in the history of psychology informed her very helpful comments on Chapter 2.

Michael Denning's knowledge of the American Left opened up subjects to investigate in Chapter 3, and his shrewd editorial suggestions influenced me to restructure the flow of argument in the chapter. Historians Jean-Christophe Agnew, James Fisher, and Susan Pennybacker directed me to some seminal primary and secondary sources on issues of Irishness and race. Lois McDonald, associate curator of the Monte Cristo Cottage in New London, not only gave me and my students fabulous tours of O'Neill's summer home (where I was allowed to teach *Long Day's Journey Into Night* and *Ah, Wilderness!*), she made useful observations on how the O'Neills did not (or would not) fit in to the social life in New London. The cottage itself yielded fascinating insights into the themes of O'Neill's plays.

My work on O'Neill dates back to the late 1970s, while I was an M.A. student at the University of London. This work was in part sparked by an insightful production of *Long Day's Journey* staged by the students of the Royal Academy of Dramatic Art. My thinking about the class politics of "depth" originated in a chapter of my 1985 Yale dissertation that did not find its way into my book on Hawthorne. Two friends who aided in my early efforts to unite these dual concerns—O'Neill and the politics of the construction of "depth"—are Nancy Armstrong and Leonard Tennenhouse, whose scholarship, conversation, and dinner parties provided rich food for thought.

I have given talks on every chapter of this book and have learned much from the questions I have fielded. I particularly appreciated the criticisms and comments made by Alan Sinfield, Rachel Bowlby, Lindsay Smith, and my good friend Elizabeth Allen at the Critical Theory Seminar, University of Sussex. Clive Bush and his graduate students made my talks at the Institute of United States Studies and King's College, University of London, a delight. Shamoon Zamir gave me extensive feedback both during and after my talk at the Cultural Studies Faculty Seminar, University of York. The faculty and graduate students at the Commonwealth Center for the Study of American Culture, the College of William and Mary, provided me with intellectual excitement and great hospitality when I gave my talk there. Chandos Brown, the director, did me a favor by letting the question-and-answer session run so long. I am grateful to Janice Radway both for arranging my talk at the 1993 Modern Language Association Convention in Toronto (Sociology of Literature panel) and for her comments. A paper I delivered at the 1994 Hawthorne Society meeting in Concord, Massachusetts, gave me the opportunity to discuss how both Hawthorne and O'Neill contributed to the making of the cultural category of "the individual." T. Walter Herbert's comments on my paper and on the panel I chaired were stimulating.

The librarians at Yale University and Wesleyan University accelerated the pace of my research. I am especially thankful for the assistance of Patricia Willis, curator of American literature at Yale's Beinecke Library and for the advice of the many learned librarians who work there. On more than one occasion they told me what I did not know I needed to know about their magnificent O'Neill and Theatre Guild holdings. Judith Schiff, chief research archivist of Yale's Manuscripts and Archives, put me on to the fascinating George Pierce Baker–Eugene O'Neill correspondence. The librarians at New York University's Tamiment library (which houses materials pertaining to labor history and left-wing movements) also helped open up my research on the American Left and its thought-provoking criticisms of O'Neill. I feel privileged to have been the first scholar to use the splendid Louis Sheaffer–Eugene O'Neill collection at Connecticut College Library, and I thank Brian Rogers for his assistance. Pamela Jordan, librarian of the Yale Drama School library, has always given me good research suggestions.

Again, as with the Hawthorne book, my most significant critical exchanges have been those I have established with my students. I began teaching O'Neill in a seminar on Modern American Political Theatre at Yale, and I hope that Minouche Kandel, Richard Malley, and Sonya Baker will stand for the students who influenced my thinking in those classes. I continued teaching this seminar when I accepted my position at Wesleyan and was stimulated by the research and critical perspectives produced by students like Glenn Decker, Jason Lindsay, and Meesha Halm. In another seminar on the social and ideological origins of Freud's cultural theory, I taught several plays by O'Neill and received superb exploratory essays by Rebecca Rossen and Sophie Bell. More recently, I have taught an O'Neill seminar entitled, "The Cultural Production of the Psychological Self," and I am lucky to have had Whitney Bolden and Natalie Stone write such fine papers on O'Neill and his race plays. Many other students in these O'Neill seminars shaped my thinking and energized me; they include Keather Kehoe, Kelly Quinn, Arthur ("Trace") Smith, Claire Weinraub, Emily Halderman, Dylan Leiner, Adam Hirsch, Carolyn Barth, Doni Gewirtzman, and Lee Armitage. Special thanks goes to my cultural studies student Kate Gordon, who read and commented on the final draft of the manuscript.

Everyone at the University of North Carolina Press has been supportive, enthusiastic, and creative. My editor, Barbara Hanrahan, has constantly given me sage advice.

My greatest debt remains to my family, not least of all to Redmond (six) and Jeremy (three), my explosive nephews who love to ambush me and help keep me playful.

1888   Eugene Gladstone O'Neill born October 16 in a New York City hotel, the son of James O'Neill, a famous melodramatic actor and the star of *The Count of Monte Cristo*, and Mary Ellen ("Ella") Quinlan O'Neill.

1895–1900   Sent to Catholic boarding school, Saint Aloysius, at the Academy of Mount St. Vincent, Riverdale, New York.

1900–1902   Attends another Catholic boarding school, De La Salle Institute, New York City.

1902–6   Studies at nonsectarian Betts Academy, Stamford, Connecticut. Discovers his mother's morphine addiction (1903), undergoes a crisis of religious faith, begins drinking and "whoring," develops a strong interest in radical literature as well as anarchist and socialist theory (Emma Goldman, Benjamin Tucker, Max Stirner, Karl Marx).

1906–7   Matriculates at Princeton University. Devotes little attention to his courses and is expelled after wrecking some railroad property. Continues to study radical literature, social theory, and philosophy, especially the works of Nietzsche and Schopenhauer.

1909   Weds Kathleen Jenkins. Deserts her to go on a gold prospecting trip to Honduras.

1910   Kathleen gives birth to Eugene Gladstone O'Neill Jr. The new father sails to Buenos Aires, where, when he is not destitute, he is employed in a Singer sewing machine factory, in a Swift meatpacking plant, and on the city's docks.

1911   Returning to the States, O'Neill is influenced by productions of Dublin's Abbey Theatre, which is on tour in New York City.

1912–13   Divorces Kathleen Jenkins (O'Neill will get to know his son only beginning in the early 1920s). Works as a reporter for the *New London Telegraph*. Treated for tuberculosis, mainly at Gaylord Farm Sanatorium, Wallingford, Connecticut. Assiduously reads drama from the Greeks to the moderns (especially Strindberg) and experiments with writing plays, including *The Web* and *Thirst*. Votes for Eugene V. Debs, Socialist party candidate for president.

1914–15   James O'Neill pays for the publication of five of Eugene's one-act plays in a volume entitled *Thirst*. Eugene enrolls as a special student in Professor George Pierce Baker's Harvard University course in playwriting, Workshop 47, and writes a full-length play about anarchists, *The Personal Equation*. Publishes some radical poetry, including an antiwar poem, "Fratricide" ("All workers of the earth / Are brothers and WE WILL NOT FIGHT!"). Consumes great quantities of alcohol in the "Hell Hole" (The Golden Swan) in Greenwich Village and consorts with a range of characters, including artists, intellectuals, social dropouts, and an Irish American gang, the Hudson Dusters. Persists in his refusal to perform the role of proper middle-class son, despite the fact that Ella O'Neill is cured of her morphine addiction after she enters a convent.

1916   Leaves Greenwich Village for the artists' colony of Provincetown, Massachusetts, with anarchist Terry Carlin. Carlin introduces O'Neill to Susan Glaspell, who, with her husband, George Cram ("Jig") Cook, has organized the Provincetown Players, a collective dedicated to the production of new American plays. In the Players, he works with radical bohemians such as John Reed, Louise Bryant, Mary Heaton Vorse, Max Eastman, and Floyd Dell. The Players migrate to Macdougal Street in Greenwich Village in the fall. O'Neill has a steamy affair with Bryant, who is Reed's lover. The Players stage *Bound East for Cardiff*, originally in Provincetown's Wharf Theatre and a few months later in the Playwrights' Theatre on Macdougal Street; O'Neill's flair for the dramatic, his characters' working-class accents, and his subject matter (seamen) create quite a stir. O'Neill appears in blackface as the mulatto sailor (playing opposite Bryant and Cook) in the Wharf production of *Thirst*.

1917   The Players produce several other one-act dramas belonging to what O'Neill would later call his *Glencairn* cycle (the sea plays). O'Neill receives much critical praise, but reviewers generally regard Glaspell as the premier playwright in the Provincetown group.

1918   O'Neill marries Agnes Boulton. The newlyweds move to Peaked Hill Bar, a former coast guard station, on the beach outside Provincetown.

1919   A black cast appears in the Provincetown Players' production of *The Dreamy Kid*. Eugene's first child with Agnes, Shane, is born.

1920   James O'Neill dies, and his death is followed by Ella's passing (1922) and his brother Jamie's demise (1923). The Provincetown Players make *The Emperor Jones* their most ambitious production. They recruit the talented and proud black actor Charles Gilpin to play the lead. The play's extraordinary success secures O'Neill's reputation (and commercial future). The Players also produce a play about sexual repression, *Diff'rent*. O'Neill wins his first Pulitzer Prize, for *Beyond the Horizon*.

1922–23   O'Neill receives his second Pulitzer Prize for *"Anna Christie."* He purchases Brook Farm in Ridgefield, Connecticut—a thirty-acre estate—for his winter residence. The Provincetown Players produce *The Hairy Ape*, another hit that moves to Broadway. O'Neill forms the Triumvirate with his good friends critic Kenneth Macgowan and set designer Robert Edmond Jones. They manage the Provincetown Players and establish Experimental Theatre, Inc., which places a greater emphasis on the professional quality of productions. O'Neill consults psychoanalyst Dr. Smith Ely Jelliffe for advice concerning his alcoholism and marital conflicts (Jelliffe and Louise Brink published *Psychoanalysis and the Drama* in 1922).

1924   The Provincetown Players stage the psychodrama *Welded*, which receives poor notices; a controversial drama about a doomed interracial marriage, *All God's*

Chillun Got Wings, for which O'Neill and the stars, Paul Robeson and Mary Blair, receive threatening hate mail; and the sexually charged *Desire Under the Elms,* which is banned in Boston but profits from charges of "indecency" in New York. In the mid-1920s, O'Neill reassesses realism as an aesthetic value (he equates it with surface) and embraces pop psychological notions of "depth": he aims to write "deep" plays, with "deep" characters who are driven by their "deep," "primitive" instincts.

1925–26   Oona, Eugene and Agnes's second child, is born in 1925. The next year, O'Neill becomes a subject in Dr. Gilbert V. Hamilton's psychosexual research project, the results of which are later published as *A Research in Marriage* (1929) and then popularized—mostly thanks to the compositional efforts of Hamilton's coauthor, Kenneth Macgowan—as *What Is Wrong with Marriage* (also 1929). Hamilton analyzes O'Neill in extra sessions and helps rid him of his alcoholism. The Triumvirate produces *The Great God Brown,* a spiritual-psychological crisis play that experiments with masks. O'Neill buys and begins to renovate Spithead, an old mansion in Bermuda. He receives an honorary doctorate from Yale University; urged by Professor George Pierce Baker (then at Yale) to attend the commencement, O'Neill complies on the condition that he get tickets to a Yale baseball game. O'Neill becomes romantically involved with Carlotta Monterrey, who had played Mildred, the bored heiress, in the 1922 production of *The Hairy Ape.*

1928   The Theatre Guild produces O'Neill's satire of the American business ethos, *Marco Millions,* and his pop psychological hit *Strange Interlude;* the latter, which is banned in Boston, nets a third Pulitzer Prize for O'Neill.

1929   Divorces Agnes Boulton and marries Carlotta Monterrey; takes up residence in France, eventually moving to Château Le Plessis in St. Antoine-du-Rocher.

1931   The Theatre Guild produces O'Neill's oedipal trilogy, *Mourning Becomes Electra.* O'Neill contributes funds to the Group Theatre's first production, *The House of Connelly.*

1932   Moves with Carlotta to Casa Genotta, their newly built mansion in the wealthy community of Sea Island, Georgia. Writes "Memoranda on Masks" for *American Spectator* (which he coedits with George Jean Nathan, Theodore Dreiser, and James Branch Cabell).

1933   A film version of *The Emperor Jones*, starring Paul Robeson, is released. The Theatre Guild produces *Ah, Wilderness!*, featuring George M. Cohan. O'Neill's popular comedy is skewered by critics on the Left as "meaningless," "an ocean of whipped cream," "a new-fascist glorification of the American home and American idealism." The year after, Virgil Geddes would assert: "O'Neill is individualism out of control."

1935   O'Neill starts to outline his cycle of plays that would be entitled *A Tale of Possessors, Self-dispossessed* (a never-completed project that would ultimately involve eleven plays, the cycle would range over the history of the American family from 1775 to the early 1930s).

1936   Wins the Nobel Prize for Literature. Criticized by commentators on the Left for having sold out to the individualistic, "neuroticized" bourgeoisie.

1937–38   Revises drafts of *A Touch of the Poet* (begun in 1936) and *More Stately Mansions* (begun in 1938) for his cycle. Eugene and Carlotta move to Tao House, in the hills of Danville, California.

1939–40   In 1939, frustrated with his friend Sean O'Casey's *The Stars Turn Red* (a product of "the sociological propaganda mill"), O'Neill writes: "When an artist starts saving the world, he starts losing himself. . . . The interesting thing about people is the obvious fact that they don't really want to be saved—the tragic idiotic ambition of self-destruction in them." Takes a break from the unceasing labor of drafting his cycle and writes *The Iceman Cometh* (1939) and *Long Day's Journey Into Night* (1940– 41). Preoccupied with news of impending world war.

1942–43   Polishes drafts of *A Touch of the Poet* (1942) and *A Moon for the Misbegotten* (1943). Stricken by a neurological tremor and literally unable to hold a pen in order to write, O'Neill gives up on completing his cycle and destroys some of his drafts and notes.

1946–47 The Theatre Guild produces *The Iceman Cometh*, and O'Neill's return to the stage (his last new play theretofore, *Days Without End*, had been produced in 1934) is heralded by an elaborate publicity campaign. Nonetheless the production receives a mixed response. In a 1946 interview, O'Neill launches a verbal assault on the American (Pipe) Dream, suggesting that if a true American history were ever written and taught, the portraits of "our great national heroes" would have to be "taken out and burned." *A Moon for the Misbegotten* generates controversy and some negative reviews on its midwestern tour and never makes it to New York. The Theatre Guild announces plans to produce *A Touch of the Poet*, but O'Neill—whose reputation has declined somewhat, along with his health—withdraws the play.

1952 The remaining cycle plays (except for *A Touch of the Poet* and *More Stately Mansions* in draft), including many, but not all, of his outlines, notes, and scenarios, are destroyed by Eugene and Carlotta.

1953 O'Neill dies of pneumonia, having suffered terribly from his neurological tremor (a rare, perhaps familial, disease of the cerebellum).

1956–57 José Quintero's productions of *The Iceman Cometh* (May 1956) and *Long Day's Journey* (November 1956) are instrumental in the revival of O'Neill's national and international reputation as America's "greatest" dramatist. The latter play wins the tragedian his fourth Pulitzer Prize.

The Profession of "Depth"

I have looked at hundreds of photographs of Eugene O'Neill, ranging from relaxed, informal snapshots of him on the beach and at home, to formal, posed, carefully lighted professional portraits.[1] Of all these photos, there is one genre I enjoy viewing more than the others, for it so interestingly brings into focus fundamental issues at stake in my title: *Staging Depth*. From 1929 to the early 1940s, O'Neill chose to pose before the camera at work in a business suit—often pinstriped. One such photograph (Figure 1) shows the playwright seemingly at work revising his oedipal trilogy, *Mourning Becomes Electra* (1931). Sitting at his desk, O'Neill faces the camera with his head tilted to his left, ciga-

Figure 1. O'Neill revising *Mourning Becomes Electra*. Sheaffer-O'Neill Collection, Connecticut College Library.

rette in left hand, pencil in right, conspicuously well tailored in his business suit, silk tie, and collar clip. Concentrated on his creative enterprise, the dramatist's brow is furrowed and his mouth is clenched tight. The cigarette smoke ascending from hand to head seems to symbolize the smoldering artistic nervousness that finds expression in the heated-up subjectivities O'Neill is dramatizing on paper.

Another aspect of this photograph is more pronounced in a similar shot taken in 1939 (Figure 2), apparently showing O'Neill's minute scrawl bringing to life *The Iceman Cometh* (1940). In this more professional-looking photograph, O'Neill sits closer to the camera at a diagonal rather than opposite it; again he is impeccably groomed in his pinstripe business suit and tasteful silk tie. O'Neill's artistic "depth" here is communicated visually by a semiotic of shadows, arranged artfully so that a bright light—inspiration perhaps—appears on his left forehead, atop his furrowed brow. Again his lips are clenched, on the verge of a disdainful pout. Both photographs of O'Neill-at-work aim to evoke the intensity, introspection, and "depth" that were integral to the cultural image of the man heralded since the early 1920s as America's greatest dramatist.

Figure 2. O'Neill in 1939. Yale Collection of American Literature Photographs, Beinecke Rare Book and Manuscript Library, Yale University. Louis Sheaffer suggests in *O'Neill: Son and Artist* (p. 496) that O'Neill is writing *The Iceman Cometh*.

But it was O'Neill's sartorial elegance that first aroused my curiosity as a cultural historian, especially when I reminded myself that at that very moment he was ostensibly writing a play about the down-and-out "moochers" of Harry Hope's saloon, men who have withdrawn from the bourgeois system of prestige symbolized by their creator's Madison Avenue threads. If such Depression era photographs were meant to exhibit O'Neill's smoldering subjectivity and shadowy depths, they also, revealingly, frame him as a successful member of the professional class.[2]

Another intriguing series of photographs of O'Neill by novelist and critic Carl Van Vechten, taken in September 1933, makes more obvious one element of the playwright-as-professional portraits described above. In the Van Vechten photos (Figure 3), O'Neill appears (from the shoulders up) draped in black against a dark background. Like many of O'Neill's photographers, Van Vechten arranges shadows so that one experiences the emotional intensity of O'Neill's depth; but it is the blending of the black covering into the backdrop that creates the illusion of a floating head. Another pose in this series shows O'Neill's head with eyes closed—a suspended death mask,[3] perhaps a depth mask (Figure 4). Van Vechten's photographs, more patently than the playwright-as-professional shots, display a posed interiority, an artfully lighted sense of depth. In each of the photographs I have described, this depth is

Figure 3. O'Neill in 1933, photographed by Carl Van Vechten. Yale Collection of American Literature Photographs, Beinecke Rare Book and Manuscript Library, Yale University.

a photographic *effect*, akin to effects produced by makeup, costumes, and lighting for characters on stage.[4] (August Strindberg, the Swedish psychological dramatist, whose work O'Neill studied, admired, and sometimes imitated, also staged depth before the camera [Figure 5], often with himself as photographer.)[5]

As I pondered the relationship between O'Neill's plays and these photographs, I found myself asking: How does the look of depth—evident in each of these photographs—mesh with the distinctively managerial look of the playwright-at-work (Figure 6)? What does their interplay imply? What does this professional "depth" tell us about how O'Neill envisioned his role as a playwright?

The metaphor "depth," resonant with psychological, pathological, therapeutic, and aesthetic associations, is in fact central to the way O'Neill and many of his reviewers, critics, and biographers have understood his work. Writing in 1926 to his dear friend Kenneth Macgowan, who shared with the playwright and with Robert Edmond Jones the Triumvirate directorship of Experimental Theatre, Inc. (1923–26), O'Neill announced that his "stuff is much deeper now."[6] At that time O'Neill was working on *Strange Interlude* (1928), which made overt use of modern depth psychology with its interior monologues. "It's the biggest ever!" he exulted. "It's a 'work.' I'm tremendous pleased with the

Figure 4. O'Neill in 1933, photographed by Carl Van Vechten. Yale Collection of American Literature Photographs, Beinecke Rare Book and Manuscript Library, Yale University.

deep scope of it."[7] O'Neill's depth drama went on to receive great acclaim as a "work." Dudley Nichols of the *World* averred that O'Neill's interior monologues in *Strange Interlude* enabled him "to dive deep in the waters of life, as a deep-sea diver who invents for himself a new kind of armored suit, and brings up the monstrous forms which inhabit there. . . . [O'Neill] has not only written a great American play but the great American novel as well . . . a psychological novel of tremendous power and depth." Robert Littell's review in the New York *Post* applauded O'Neill's nine-act psychological extravaganza as an aesthetic triumph that achieved on stage "the space and depth, the pauses and vast convolutions of a novel."[8] Recent critics still single out psychological depth as the essence of O'Neill's art and greatness.[9]

Interestingly, O'Neill repeatedly denied having been inspired by Sigmund Freud or any other contemporary depth psychologist—a denial that has failed to convince a number of critics and biographers. For O'Neill understood depth as a timeless psychological space within the self sounded by authors who knew exactly where to look for it—in the family. "Every human complication of love and hate in my trilogy is as old as literature," he wrote of *Mourning Becomes Electra*, "and the interpretations I suggest are such as might have occurred to any author in any time with a *deep* curiosity about the underlying motives that actuate

Figure 5. August Strindberg, c. 1911–12. Strindbergsmuseet, Stockholm.

human interrelationships in the family" (emphasis supplied).[10] While not discounting the influence of psychoanalysis on O'Neill's thinking (despite the playwright's disclaimers), Louis Sheaffer has sought to account for O'Neill's capacity to plumb the depths through his exhaustive two-volume portrait of the playwright's own family. O'Neill's conflicted family background, Sheaffer argues, endowed him with the "smoldering" subjectivity-in-turmoil that drove him—for therapeutic reasons—to write America's most penetrating dramas about "the depths of human nature."[11]

This therapeutic dramatization of depth brought O'Neill prestige and profit on an international scale. Not only did *Strange Interlude*, for instance, net O'Neill his third Pulitzer Prize in a span of eight years, its productions and book sales yielded a $275,000 nest egg that helped him weather the Depression wearing pinstripes and living in mansions on two continents.[12] It was precisely O'Neill's psychological and aesthetic "depth" that demonstrated the American theatre was capable of producing recognizably "literary" material and expressing distinctively "modern" themes. In recognition of this, Yale awarded O'Neill an honorary doctorate in 1926, and in 1936 he won the Nobel Prize.

Figure 6. O'Neill in the 1930s, photographed by Edward Steichen. Yale Collection of American Literature Photographs, Beinecke Rare Book and Manuscript Library, Yale University.

By the twenties, much "modern" criticism read like pop psychology. Thus Robert Edmond Jones characterized the artist as one who delves "into the stream of images which has its source in the deep unknown springs of our being."[13] Critical discourse of the nineteenth century sometimes exhibited romantic assumptions akin to those articulated by Jones. In *The Production of Personal Life* (1991), I noted that antebellum reviewers who were fascinated by Nathaniel Hawthorne's "psychological romances" introduced metaphors of surface and depth to praise his "probing of the most forbidden regions of consciousness."[14] The fictions of Hawthorne, Edgar Allan Poe, Herman Melville, and of some of their contemporaries, as well as some reviews of their work, can be taken as early signs that "the psychological" was emerging as a significant, though not yet a dominant or a particularly glamorous, middle-class cultural preoccupation. Such authors, I argued, contributed to the encoding of a psychological identity for the middle-class self and the middle-class family that, historically, makes Freud's later invention of psychoanalysis (and its enthusiastic reception in America) predictable.[15] When the subject matter and language of psychoanalysis became popular in the United States, criticism that fused premises about depth psychology and what constitutes "deep" literature (such as that of Dudley Nichols and Robert Edmond Jones) acquired a cultural capital—a *psychological capital*—that contemporary reviews of Hawthorne's romances lacked. D. H. Lawrence's modernist revival of Hawthorne, Poe, and Melville in 1923 was based on the cultural value of modern psychological capital. Lawrence made these authors "classic" in part by glamorizing them as protomodernist pop psychologists.[16] O'Neill's "classics" of the 1920s and early 1930s both partook of and enhanced the glamour of pop psychological concerns, concerns that—we will see—he at turns staged as "deep" and as intriguingly theatrical.

O'Neill's biographers and critics, notwithstanding their many insights, have seldom considered what the photographs that have so engaged me suggest—that O'Neill's well-groomed, professional "depth," rather than the unmediated expression of the playwright's poetic, conflicted, inner self, may be a calculated pose, a self-image, a conspicuous display of his "personal" wealth of psychological capital that he draws on to underwrite deep dramas. In their invaluable edition of O'Neill's letters, Travis Bogard and Jackson R. Bryer partially break from the critical tradition of accepting O'Neill's image as a deep dramatist as a given. "Before the romantic brooding figure be taken as the whole man," they prudently advise, "it may be well to remember that it is a construction of art and criticism, an image, not the man himself." The letters disclose an "ordinary man, avowing friendships, showing concern for his children [and contempt, I would add], warring with the IRS." Despite these cautionary remarks, the editors go on to reproduce the same romantic critical and biographical portrait of the deep O'Neill. O'Neill's greatness, even for them, lies in his mission as an artist of subjectivity, "the keeper of an intense flame burning out of sight of most, if not all, others."[17]

To be sure, O'Neill often recoiled from the media's crass exploitation of his "intense flame." By the late 1920s, when he was arranging his divorce from Agnes Boulton and traveling through France with his future wife, Carlotta Monterrey, O'Neill protested vociferously against "too much notoriety": "Who wants this garbage bath they are pleased to call fame? . . . I feel as pawed over by the sweaty paws of the public as a 4-bit whore—and correspondingly defiled!"[18] Even in 1919, before he had been defiled much, he could be irascibly protective about his image. "Come now, Mr. Toohey," he said bitingly to a theatre promotion photographer who wanted him to pose "pen-in-hand with the sea as a background," "that's a bit thick, isn't it? . . . There are so many others just watering at the mouth for that weapon-in-mit close-up that I won't be missed. . . . An author whose work is sincere and honest should see to it that he remains likewise. . . . His best place is—out of sight in the

Figure 7. O'Neill with
American Line sweater, c.
late 1910s, Provincetown.
Yale Collection of American Literature Photographs, Beinecke Rare
Book and Manuscript Library, Yale University.

wings."[19] Yet only a decade later, O'Neill exchanged the Jack London seascape backdrop for a Brooks Brothers pose, "weapon in mit."

By the mid-1920s O'Neill knew very well that his literary face and name were hot commodities. "How about a photo for the book?" he wrote Barrett Clark, who published his study of O'Neill in 1926. "I would like an O.K. on that as some of the photos used are very poor. Steichen took some fine ones this winter. Perhaps you could get *Vanity Fair*'s permission . . . to use one of these. If not, I strongly suggest you use Murray's enlargement of his photo taken at the 'lookout' of our house at Peaked Hill, Provincetown. This is by far best of all old ones and really represents me."[20] Notwithstanding the sarcasm he aimed at Mr. Toohey, O'Neill turned out to be quite willing to have himself framed as the romantic American author with the sea as a background (Figure 7). By 1926 O'Neill felt sure enough about the commercial potential of his plays, his image, and his name to propose to Macgowan an O'Neill Repertory Company, an entity that would replace Experimental Theatre, Inc. Three years later, sensing the market value of his scrawl, he put out feelers about selling the original manuscripts of his plays for $100,000 (he was offered $50,000 and declined).[21] Originally, he had agreed to write a foreword for his friend Hart Crane's book of poems but, in 1926, got cold feet and offered the favor of a dust jacket blurb instead, aware of Crane's publisher's wish to acquire the "notoriety-

Figure 8. O'Neill on the beach, flexing his muscles, exhibiting another side of the angst-ridden dramatist. Sheaffer-O'Neill Collection, Connecticut College Library. A stamp on the back of the photograph reads: "From the Eugene O'Neill Collection of Jere W. Hageman."

publicity value" of the O'Neill name.[22] His two-sentence blurb assured readers that Crane's poems are "deep-seeking."[23]

O'Neill was thus attuned to the cultural role of the modern artist as one who publicly symbolizes a romantic-psychological "self," and he knew well how to benefit from the equation of his image with "depth" in the popular mind.[24] In 1931, the year O'Neill was photographed in pinstripes, with his faraway interior look (here but not here), one interviewer described him as "the bronzed, handsome, graying Mr. O'Neill . . . pretty much the ideal of what a great, melancholy and brooding playwright should look like." But several years before, O'Neill had quipped, "My face is so wrinkled from the storm and stress of being a dramatist that it looks like a road map of Mars showing the canals!"[25]

O'Neill could be winningly charming and humorous as well as withdrawn and brooding, and he was at times capable of adopting an ironic view, not only of his storm and stress image (Figure 8), but of his storm and stress plays. When his legal representatives refused to allow the comedian Jack Benny to parody one of his plays on the radio, O'Neill countered by wire: "THINK BENNY VERY AMUSING GUY AND BELIEVE KID-DING MY STUFF EVERY ONCE AND A WHILE HAS A VERY HEALTHY EFFECT AND HELPS KEEP ME OUT OF DEAD SOLEMN ILLUSTRIOUS STUFFED SHIRT ACADE-MICIAN CLASS."[26] O'Neill may well have been aware of one of the most uproarious scenes in the Marx Brothers' film *Animal Crackers* (1930), adapted from their Broadway production: Groucho—eyebrows in full motion—parodies the famous "deep" interior monologues of *Strange Interlude*, at the expense of two society matrons who take his smarmy surface flattery as sincere. In 1925 the reviewer and critic George Jean Nathan was moved to compare O'Neill's "tragic" face and irreverence with Groucho's: the playwright is hardly "jocund," he admitted, but he is a "cheerful" and sometimes "even a waggish fellow, with a taste for low barroom chatter, bordello anecdotes, rough songs and other such forms of healthy obscenity."[27]

O'Neill's intense and sometimes self-mocking preoccupation with his own image is partly written into the character of Con Melody, the mid-nineteenth-century Irish immigrant tavern owner with aristocratic pretensions ("Major Cornelius Melody, one time of His Majesty's Seventh Dragoons") in *A Touch of the Poet* (1939). Like Melody, O'Neill was addicted to gazing at his image in mirrors, even in the company of others. As it happens, Con's forty-five-year-old *"ruined face"* bears some resemblance to that of the middle-aged O'Neill-in-pinstripes: *"still handsome. . . . a look of wrecked distinction about it, of brooding humiliated pride"* (3:197).* On several occasions Con is irresistibly drawn to the barroom mirror, in which *"he poses to himself, striking an attitude—a Byronic hero, noble, embittered, disdainful, defying his tragic fate, brooding over past glories"* (3:210). Each time, this highly theatrical ritual is completed with his recitation of a verse from Lord Byron's *Childe Harold*, closing with the line: "I stood / Among, but not of them" (3:215).

What is most interesting about this enactment is that Con not only looks at his "self" in the mirror, he self-consciously watches himself pose. His pose imitates the haughty individualism of Lord Byron's speaker: "I have not loved the world, nor the world me." The stagy portraits of Con suggest both that O'Neill well understood depth as an effect of a deliberate effort and, if only implicitly, that he was not averse to reflecting on his own pose in this light (the Irish American, ex-alcoholic, romantic dramatist who peered into the VOID and lived to tell about it).

Through his representation of Con's literary self-fashioning, O'Neill

*Quotations from O'Neill's dramas are from the three volumes of *Eugene O'Neill: Complete Plays, 1913–1943* (New York: Library of America, 1988); references are cited by volume number and page number.

conceptualizes "psychological" depth not as a timeless, universal vessel of desires that one expresses or involuntarily discloses through behavior and fantasy. Rather he envisions it as a highly individualized imagining of "self" brought into being both by historical pressures (Con's class and ethnic position as an Irish man in America) and by cultural narratives, vocabularies, and images that produce the notion of a particular kind of "inside" whose "essence" is defined against an "outside" (Byron's romantic subjectivity pitted against "the world"). Byron's verse offers Con a literary category of depth that he can apply to his surface, like makeup, when he poses before the mirror.

On one level Con himself knows that his semiotic act, played with a costume (uniform and sword), a particular facial expression, an aristocratic pose of the body, and a poetic script, is a staging of depth—a "con" game that sustains him in his historical moment.[28] The subjectivity he constitutes in the mirror is compensatory and therapeutic—a portrait of defiance, a gesture of autonomy, a style of class hauteur. The theatrical performances of O'Neill's "con" artist may be partly autobiographical (reminding us of O'Neill dressed in his professional "uniform" and with his "weapon in mit"); but these performances also are suggestively cultural (the acting out of poetic scripts and romantic stereotypes of "the individual"), so very cultural that they complicate the conventional assumptions one might have about autobiography as a revelation of "inner depth." *A Touch of the Poet* is focused, not on inner depth, but on staging why Con desperately yearns to see himself reflect a particular cultural image of depth.

Following O'Neill's example in this play, *Staging Depth* examines the configuration of material, cultural, and ideological forces that gave a certain concept of depth its power as a psychological and aesthetic category from the 1910s to the 1940s. The word "staging" in my title is crucial, not only for its material, structural, and theatrical meaning (scaffolding, scenery, footlights, costumes, masks, greasepaint, producers, directors, actors, designers, stage managers—stage effects), but for its associations with journeying (bringing passengers to a new stage) and with a strategic practice (staging a counteroffensive). I employ the word "discourse" in the title because we will see that O'Neill's way of making "the psychological" and the "psychological family" significant was not wholly individual but was allied to other cultural discourses that had similar agendas.

My sense of the "politics" of O'Neill's staging of depth is not narrow (as in people voting) but expansive, and it understands the internalization of conceptions of "the psychological" as having to do with the establishment of cultural power and hierarchy. Most critics from the late 1920s to the present have saluted O'Neill's "revolutionary" dismantling of nineteenth-century taboos and theatrical conventions. Mainstream critics have shown less interest in assessing the historical, social, and political implications of the modern form of subjectivity O'Neill's dramas helped fashion (and, at times, contest). The popular image of Provincetown and Greenwich Village in the 1910s and 1920s is of middle-class and upper-class intellectuals, artists, and bohemians coming to terms with their own depth. How radical was this? What kind of "inner self" did they "discover"? I propose that the "psychological self" which O'Neill's audiences discovered and applauded as deep was also a political "self," though audiences may have been unconscious of the politics of their identification with or consumption of this "self." In the interwar period the category of depth was not only elevated to great cultural, psychological, and aesthetic significance: we will find that it was occasionally used to help mystify various class, racial, ethnic, and gender identities as inherently "psychological."

O'Neill tended to stage depth more often than he dramatized it as a cultural category, an ideology, or a theatrical effect. Many reviewers, critics, and biographers of O'Neill seem to gravitate to his plays and to his image because, in combination, they appear to validate a concept of the personal—anchored by a belief in a discoverable, timeless, universal depth.[29] Hence *Staging Depth* brings numerous reviews, criticisms, and biographical accounts of O'Neill into its field of critique, for they too played a role in the literary production of the psychological self that O'Neill so richly represented—in his constructed self-image as well as his plays.

O'Neill's tendencies to produce and to demystify a modern psychological self are in fact contrary, in a state of conflict and tension. The historical and ideological crosscurrents that O'Neill channeled and that channeled him into drama are nothing if not complex. He is not an icon to be torn down but a very important cultural figure to be reevaluated historically.

Going against the grain, in Chapter 1 I take issue with scholars who have ensconced the cultural significance of O'Neill and his plays in the form of biography. Anyone who reads, studies, teaches, or enjoys seeing O'Neill's plays will find the O'Neill biographies (especially Sheaffer's) to be enlightening resources. But I will explain why it is vital to reread O'Neill's work, his family background, and some of the premises of his biographers within a history of middle-class family life. Chapter 2 argues that the history of pop psychology in the 1910s and 1920s—in conjunction with the history of late-nineteenth- and early-twentieth-century middle-class family life—offers a cultural account of why O'Neill's dramas were so consumed by the psychological. I suggest that O'Neill staged pop psychology for a professional-managerial class that was in the process of constructing and internalizing a new ideology of psychological selfhood. We will also find that O'Neill sometimes established a critical distance from the theatrical production of psychological capital for his class.

Chapter 3 discusses some of the ideological uses to which the concept of depth was put, especially in regard to the cultural making of "psychological" class and racial identities. It begins by examining O'Neill's ambivalent relationship to the radicalism of his youth (anarchism and socialism), and it recovers forgotten or ignored leftist criticisms of his plays from the 1920s to the 1940s. Critics on the Left often assailed newly emerging assumptions about psychological depth—the discourse of depth that mainstream critics frequently invoked to classify radical theatre and its representations of selfhood as shallow.[30]

My closing chapter explores how Susan Glaspell, a Provincetown Players friend and colleague of O'Neill's, challenged what was fast becoming the middle-class psychological common sense of the 1910s and 1920s with her plays *Suppressed Desires* (written with George Cram Cook), *Trifles*, *Woman's Honor*, and *The Verge*. I outline significant connections between Glaspell's work and O'Neill's. Rather than diving into a depth defined as natural or primitive by the vocabulary, narratives, and metaphors of psychoanalysis, Glaspell's feminist plays dramatize her social understanding of desire; they focus on women who struggle within oppressive cultural discourses and roles. An appreciation of Glaspell's feminism will help us see a critical side of O'Neill that has not been properly acknowledged by critics. While O'Neill was invested in staging depth, my reinterpretation of *Long Day's Journey Into Night* will contend that he, like Glaspell (whom he admired), understood that depth, desire, and gender were categories produced by culture, and further, that he grasped the subtle role played by theatre in this production.[31]

O'Neill and the

Making of the

Psychological

Family

1

In reference to *A Touch of the Poet* (1939)—O'Neill's play about an antebellum Irish immigrant family—Louis Sheaffer affirms, "Historic forces are at work here." We can in fact say the same about all of O'Neill's plays, notebooks, and letters. Biographers of O'Neill and critics of his plays have generally written within conventional notions of the scope of history (e.g., theatre history, literary history, intellectual history). But history also encompasses family life, privacy, gender, sexuality, subjectivities, and psychological discourse.[1] While biographical contributions such as Sheaffer's provide valuable insights into the family that shaped O'Neill, the history of American family life offers perspectives on the processes that shaped O'Neill's family and the discourses of "the family" that influenced O'Neill in his playwriting.[2] My aim here is to reassess several of O'Neill's plays as well as biographical approaches to the playwright by situating them in the context of a history of nineteenth- and twentieth-century family life.

When I told friends I was writing a book on Eugene O'Neill, they frequently responded: you're writing a biography? Their assumption isn't surprising. A review of publications on O'Neill—popular and scholarly—will quickly give one the idea that O'Neill's function within American literary and cultural history is to be stripped bare as the subject of biographies. Warren Beatty's film *Reds* (1984), featuring Jack Nicholson as the O'Neill-who-was-obsessed-with-Louise Bryant, both reinforces and builds on this popular impression. O'Neill himself, of course, helped set the pattern for this biographical approach in interviews he gave over the years and, most notably, by thinly veiling episodes in his own family's history in his final plays, *Long Day's Journey Into Night* (1941) and *A Moon for the Misbegotten* (1943).

O'Neill's biographers like to stress that he "was one of the most autobiographical playwrights who ever lived."[3] By implication, the literary and cultural value of O'Neill's works is enhanced *because* they disclose their author's psychological depth.[4] Biographies of O'Neill take on the character of psychological studies of the dramatist, with closing chapters almost too painful to read.

Biographers tout O'Neill's turbulent family history as a credential for his literary vocation as explorer of the self. Moss Hart's blurb on the Gelbs' biography praises their tome as having done justice to O'Neill's agony—a tell-all psychotherapy for those O'Neills still afflicting themselves in that Great Theatre in the Sky: "[The] tormented spirits of all the O'Neills must be sighing with relief and thanks to Arthur and Barbara Gelb for a memorable work." Notwithstanding O'Neill's occasional practice of slugging his wives and snubbing his children (Shane and Oona O'Neill were written out of his will), Arthur Miller's blurb frames O'Neill's "failings" and his "agony" as essential to his subjective potency and theatrical magnitude: "[The Gelbs] have brought out his failings as a writer and a person only to leave him larger than before." Theatre, Miller laments, is now "in the hands of triflers who will forever need the towering rebuke of his life and his work and his agony." Prospective book-buyers are meant to buy the idea that the playwright's gift to American drama was his own self-lacerating depth.[5] Biographical depth and drama merge—the writing of drama read subjectively as personal crucifixion.[6]

Long Day's Journey Into Night self-consciously capitalizes on the fact that its author is a member of a tortured Irish Catholic family whose men habitually hit the bottle. Irishness and drunkenness are two theatrical discourses of wounded subjectivity, stereotypes that lend added "literary" authority to O'Neill's artistic credentials as diver in the depths.[7] One perceptive reviewer of *A Moon for the Misbegotten* in 1947 drew attention to O'Neill's use of the melodramatic Irishman of myth and literature: "[His] characters . . . are actually dark, eerie, Celtic symbol-folk . . . who beat their breasts at the agony of living, battle titanically and drink like Nordic gods, but are finally seen to wear the garb of sainthood and die for love."[8] Images of the modern "dysfunctional" psychological family, tormented confessional Irishness, and stagy self-absorbed drunkenness, allied to one another, help establish the mid- and late-twentieth-century interpretive context within which O'Neill's life—like O'Neill's drama—is read as an expression of O'Neill's quintessentially individual depth.

Within this biographical enterprise, history serves as backdrop for the personal life that truly accounts for the playwright's aesthetic motivations.[9] Travis Bogard contends that O'Neill's "writing was really dedicated to exploring a private world, the life of a few people [principally the four O'Neills] shut in a dark room out of time." Although Bogard notes that *Mourning Becomes Electra* (1931) (based on the Oresteia) should be read in the context of "the twentieth-century Greek revival," his central premise is that the trilogy "emerged as the end product of private necessity."[10]

Biographical approaches to O'Neill often assume the guise not only of pop psychological case studies, but of guessing games whose object is to identify the four O'Neills who have been recast in various disguises as O'Neill's characters. O'Neill's family is represented as the allegorical key that opens the door to his conflicted psyche, his worldview, and his plays.[11] "The child is essential to the understanding of the man," asserts Sheaffer: Eugene "never really left his mother and father." Although O'Neill was a playwright, "not a do-it-yourself psychoanalyst," writes Bogard, his dramas fixated on "four people he obsessively sought to

Figure 9. Promotional flyer of James O'Neill in *The Count of Monte Cristo*.
Sheaffer-O'Neill Collection, Connecticut College Library.

understand."[12] O'Neill's biographers religiously reproduce this "obsession," as the subtitles of Sheaffer's biography show: *Son and Playwright* (vol. 1) and *Son and Artist* (vol. 2).

To be sure, Eugene O'Neill's family—like the Tyrones in *Long Day's Journey*—was torn with conflicts. James O'Neill (1846–1920), born in Kilkenny, Ireland, lived there for only a few years before the potato famine drove his family, like multitudes of other impoverished Irish families, to America. The O'Neills emigrated to Buffalo, New York, and soon after tried to establish themselves in the slums of Cincinnati, Ohio.[13] In *Long Day's Journey* James Tyrone reminisces over a childhood rocked by poverty, evictions, machine shop labor, and abandonment by his father, who retreated to Ireland and died.

But by 1866 James O'Neill found his niche in the theatre and steadily built his reputation as a promising Shakespearean actor. In 1883 he turned Charles Fechter's melodrama, *Monte Cristo*, into a moneymaker, playing Edmund Dantès escaping from Château d'If three thousand times (until his mid-sixties) (Figure 9). Three decades of *Monte Cristo* reruns made his fame and fortune (and, as Tyrone recognized, arrested

Figure 10. Photograph thought to be of Mary Ellen ("Ella") Quinlan O'Neill, "lace-curtain Irish." Yale Collection of American Literature Photographs, Beinecke Rare Book and Manuscript Library, Yale University.

the development of his talent). James O'Neill died of intestinal cancer, leaving his wife Ella an estate—mostly realty in New London, Connecticut—worth $150,000, no small sum in the early twenties.[14]

Mary Ellen ("Ella") Quinlan O'Neill (1857–1922) was born in New Haven, Connecticut. Her parents, like the O'Neills, also fled the devastating conditions in Ireland. They moved to Cleveland, where Ella's father, Thomas, thrived as the owner of a retail shop and later a liquor store. Unlike the O'Neills, they quickly climbed into the ranks of the middle class (something Ella never let her husband forget) (Figure 10). Ella spent her high school years at the exclusive St. Mary's Academy, the convent that profoundly shaped her Catholic self-image. After graduating from St. Mary's she saw James O'Neill perform, met him, and—swept off her feet—pursued and married him. A summary that Eugene wrote of his life in 1926 sketches what happened next:

M—Lonely life—spoiled before marriage (husband friend of father's —father his great admirer—drinking companions)—fashionable convent girl—religious & naive—talent for music—physical beauty—ostracism after marriage due to husband's profession—lonely life after marriage—no contact with husband's friends—husband man's man—heavy drinker—out with men until small hours every night—slept late—little time with her—stingy about money due to his childhood experience with grinding poverty.[15]

A year after her wedding, Ella gave birth to Jamie. Five years later Edmund was born and as an infant contracted measles from Jamie and died. Ella was stricken with guilt because she was on tour with her husband and had left her two boys behind. In 1888, Eugene's birth was excruciating for Ella. Her doctor prescribed morphine (Mary Tyrone called him a "quack") and turned her life-after-birth into a nightmare of addiction. There were other problems too, writes O'Neill: "She pleads for home in [New York] but [James] refuses. This was always one of her bitterest resentments against him all her life, that she never had a home."[16] They resided in hotels (even during long stays in New York City) and kept a summer house on the Thames River in New London—the setting of Long Day's Journey. Ella battled her addiction with only intermittent success—she also drank—until she returned to a convent in 1914 or 1915 and was cured.[17] After James's death in 1920, Ella grew "more self-assured"[18] and administered her husband's estate with great skill. She died of a stroke in 1922.

James O'Neill Jr. (1878–1923) was a gifted youth who seems to have plunged headlong into a downward spiral when—as Jamie Tyrone put it in Long Day's Journey—he first "caught [his mother] in the act with a hypo." His guilt over infecting Edmund with measles and his despair over his mother's addiction (Jamie Tyrone: "I'd never dreamed before that any women but whores took dope") drove him to spend his adolescence drinking and "whoring." He was expelled from Fordham for dissolute behavior in his senior year and worked off and on as an actor thereafter, though never seriously (Figure 11). After the "old man's" death, Ella's poise inspired him to sober up. But about the time of her stroke he had resumed his descent and drank himself to death a year and a half after her passing.

From early childhood Eugene (1888–1953) was close to Ella. His 1926 summary recalls: "Absolute loneliness of M at this time except for nurse & few loyal friends scattered over country—(most of whom husband resented as social superiors)—logically points to what must have been her fierce concentration of affection on the child."[19] O'Neill picks up the thread in a letter to the critic, Arthur Hobson Quinn: "After that, boarding school for six years in Catholic schools—then four years of prep. at

Figure 11. James O'Neill Jr., on right, in a promotional photograph of the play *The Traveling Salesman*. Harvard Theatre Collection, Harvard University.

The Traveling Salesman

Betts Academy, Stamford, Conn.—then Princeton University for one year (Class of 1910)—was an attempt at a 'sport' there with resulting dismissal."[20] The last straw at Princeton was when Eugene, on a drunken binge, smashed some railroad property. His adolescence, in part modeled on Jamie's, was spent boozing and "whoring." Both sons refused to fulfill their mother's middle-class aspirations for them. Eugene read widely—as Edmund's bookcase in *Long Day's Journey* suggests (3:717)—but his interest in radical books challenged conventional middle-class assumptions.

Between 1907 and 1916 he worked as a secretary of a mail order house, went prospecting for gold in Honduras, toured a bit with his father's company, gained experience as a seaman (always proud of his promotion from ordinary seaman to able seaman), married Kathleen Jenkins (1909), fled from his wife (1909), became a father in his absence (Eugene Jr. was born in 1910), divorced (1912), studied Nietzsche, Strindberg, Shaw, and Ibsen as well as anarchist and socialist theory, did a stint as a reporter in New London, and entered a sanitarium for TB, where he convalesced for six months. "After I was released," he continues, "started to write [plays] for first time. . . . In that winter, 1913–14, wrote eight one-act plays, two long plays. . . . In 1914–15 went to [Professor George Pierce] Baker's 47, Harvard. Winter 1915–16 in

Greenwich Village. Summer 1916 came to Provincetown, joined Provincetown Players."[21] The rest is literary history.

Thus Eugene grew up witnessing a constant dramatization of repression, guilt, denial, confession, compulsion, and ambivalence—as well as the intersection of class and gender tensions. While it is tempting to isolate this emotionally supercharged familial unit as the determining force in O'Neill's life and work, it must be stressed that the four "haunted" O'Neills—as intense and as "personal" as they were—enacted their dramas within history and ideology. The biographical reflex to concentrate explanation on O'Neill's private family and to detach the personal from certain dimensions of the historical process is at once reductive and revealing. Such biographical approaches reproduce, as O'Neill did himself at times, a twentieth-century psychological common sense—an ideology of the personal—that views the family-as-psychological fate.[22] We would do well to keep in mind sociologist Richard Sennett's reminder that "the alien world organizes life within the house as much as without it."[23] Literary biographers too rarely think of biography as a genre not only of literary, intellectual, and cultural history but also of the history of family life.[24]

Psychological assumptions that modern biographers often employ about family life and its determinative influence on children are themselves symptomatic of a specific moment in the formation of the family.[25] Sheaffer offers his observation that "the child is essential to the understanding of the man" as timeless truth. Yet, as historian Philippe Ariès points out, psychological common sense about childhood as the solution to the puzzle of adult personality was not always common or sensible, especially in the Middle Ages when childhood mortality rates were extremely high.

Biographical discourse, like the social arrangements of family life it both mirrors and helps reproduce, has changed remarkably over time. Sennett characterizes eighteenth-century British memoirs as envisioning childhood "as a time of innocence and modest feeling," whereas the nineteenth-century memoir (what Sennett considers to be the forerunner of psychoanalytic therapy) exhibits a search for "truth via retrospections."[26] Biographies and autobiographies in colonial America, similarly, did not ascribe special psychological significance to childhood. Joseph F. Kett, a historian of American adolescence, points out that although seventeenth- and eighteenth-century biographers and autobiographers cite unusual events that affected the subject during childhood, they put no great weight on childhood as a phase which determines adult behavior. In the early decades of the nineteenth century one finds increasing discussion of experiences that characterized the subject's youth. By the 1830s, as the cult of domesticity gained cultural momentum, biographers and autobiographers tend more frequently to portray childhood as a formative period in the development of character.[27]

Hence in the 1820s and 1830s cautionary case histories recounting the child-rearing of criminals were published by prisons and also by "mothers' magazines." Divorced parents, orphanhood, and ill-treatment of the child were cited as factors that could account for the deviant tendencies of the adult criminal. One historian's characterization of mid-nineteenth-century France holds true of America too: "Childhood became the foundation of adulthood."[28]

Childrearing practices, the encoding of childhood as a distinct psychological phase of life, and the relations of adult parents to their adult offspring, have changed in fundamental ways from colonial times to the present. Colonial Americans distributed the task of character-building "among a variety of people and institutions (parents, other kin, neighbors; churches, courts, and local government)." By the mid-nineteenth century, the cult of domesticity erected conceptual boundaries between home and world. This was radically different from the colonial idea of the household as a "little commonwealth" that was inextricably part of the community. Within the nineteenth century's increasingly privatized and sentimentalized notion of home, mothers—in place of the community at large—assumed the psychological and moral labor of building "character" in children. An intensification of emotional dependencies and a sentimentalization of expectations on the part of parents and children gave rise to what historian John Demos calls the nineteenth-century "hothouse family."[29]

Biographers generally collapse this history of the middle-class family's changing ideals, practices, and images of itself into O'Neill's "personality." Thus O'Neill's dear friend Saxe Commins, in his memoirs, interprets the playwright's obsession with privacy as a neurotic symptom of the artistic moodiness that generated deep plays: "Torn with self-reproach, tortured by fear, in perpetual nervous panic and a constantly brooding loneliness, he deliberately built barriers around himself and made himself believe that he had succeeded in shutting out a hateful world." Yet current sociologists of the family would recognize this needy, individualistic, privatized personality structure as the product of having been reared in an enclosed family.[30] This would probably not have been O'Neill's experience had he been born during the colonial period, when strong emotions were invested in church, government, and the community as well as the family.[31]

The emotional temperature of the Tyrones' New London "hothouse" was linked to the history of changing familial roles, such as the erosion of patriarchal authority. James Tyrone's compulsive "fear of the poorhouse" was endemic to fathers who had become the sole "breadwinners" for their families in the uncertain capitalist marketplace, an anxiety that was equally if not more severe in immigrant fathers striving to succeed as "stranger[s] in a strange land" (to quote Tyrone). The pressure to make good in the world beyond the home affected the father's traditional role within it. By the mid-nineteenth century, much child-rearing responsibility had shifted from the father to the mother, and by the early decades of the twentieth century the father had yielded to his spouse his "disciplinary role as 'governor' and 'moral force.' "[32]

Of Ella O'Neill and Jamie, her firstborn, Sheaffer tells us: "She so rejoiced in him, poured on him so much loving care, bound him to herself with such indissoluble ties that she was the only woman James O'Neill, Jr., could ever love."[33] The hothouse relationship Sheaffer describes has a historical basis: Ella was acting out her culturally assigned emotional role as a late-nineteenth-century middle-class "mother." The "indissoluble tie" between middle-class mothers and sons was a major factor in the historical development of an intimacy that could be psychologically tyrannical in the sentimental dependencies it nurtured.

In the Victorian middle-class family it was mother's task to impose "sweet control" on her ward by cultivating a conscience that would make her child "the emotional marionette of its parents" and would curb "rebellious expression."[34] The middle-class sentimental "angel in the house" used her "emotional skills" to implant in her child "petit bourgeois traits—honesty, industry, frugality, temperance, and, pre-eminently, self-control." Jamie's refusal to conform to this scheme of middle-class character formation (dramatized poignantly in *Long Day's Journey* and *A Moon for the Misbegotten*) is seen in his rebellion against a specifically middle-class role that would confirm his mother's identity as "mother." "I shall attain the pinnacle of success!" Jamie jokes ironically and self-deprecatingly to Edmund, about his drunken revels with the prostitute Fat Vi: "I'll be the lover of the fat woman in Barnum and Bailey's circus!" (3:817). Even his self-flagellating unruliness reveals just how effective Ella was in establishing a psychological hold over her son. Letters and diaries of modern mothers, unlike those of colonial mothers, "show them emotionally entangled with sons who were well into adulthood." A son's failure was typically blamed on the father during the colonial era, but by the time Ella reared Jamie, in the 1880s, the son's faults would more conventionally have been attributed to the character-building inadequacies or negligence of the mother.[35]

Thus it is understandable that Mary would try to transfer the blame for Jamie's misspent youth on her husband, James Tyrone, in *Long Day's Journey*: "Children should have homes to be born in, if they are to be good children, and women need homes, if they are to be good mothers" (3:166). While Jamie punishes Mary by playing his role poorly on the only stage ("home") that gives Mary a social role to play ("mother"), Mary lays the blame for this in the lap of Tyrone, whose immigrant "fear of the poorhouse" apparently prevented him from investing in a permanent stage called home: "You don't know how to act in a home!" (3:753), she charges. Mary's middle-class yearning is culturally based, a desire for the "perfect home" that had been popularly idealized as "so tranquil, so cheerful, so pure, as to constitute an almost impossible standard." The sentimental home was supposed to provide "mother" with psychological compensation for not attending to her own needs.[36] Mary Tyrone's (or Ella O'Neill's) response to the absence of home was to express retributive needs of her own that included literally and symbolically *puncturing* the middle-class stereotype of "mother."

Operating in tandem with the affectionate (and somewhat erotic)[37] yet ambivalent ties between mother and son was the nineteenth-century cult of success, which ignited competitive feelings between father and son. William Brown in *The Great God Brown* (1926), Marco Polo in *Marco Millions* (1927), and especially Simon Harford in *More Stately Mansions* (1939) all dramatize a son versus father rivalry whose edge was sharpened in the capitalist world. "I suppose," O'Neill mused in 1925, "if one accepts the song and dance complete of the psycho-analysts, it is perfectly natural that having been brought up around the old conventional theatre, and having identified it with my father, I should rebel and go in a new direction."[38] John Demos argues that the nineteenth-century cult of motherhood and cult of success, in league with one another, produced fertile ideological soil for the sprouting of a hothouse configuration of affectionate mothers, competitive fathers, and needy sons later christened by psychoanalysts the oedipal family.

Because middle-class Americans had grown up experiencing these hot-house ambivalences, Demos contends, they proved very receptive to Freud's theories, especially his idea of a "universal" oedipus complex.[39]

The hothouse family became even more tropical in the early twentieth century. This is in part because of an even greater concentration of emotional needs and expectations within the private rather than the "impersonal" public sphere. Emotional demands made by spouses on one another and by children and parents on one another, Stephanie Coontz maintains, "would have astounded previous generations."[40] Historian Elaine Tyler May concluded her study of late-nineteenth- and twentieth-century marriage and divorce in America in the same vein, calling personal life a "national obsession."[41] O'Neill's acknowledgment—"We were a very close family—too close"—described not only his own family but a modern trend.[42]

But *Long Day's Journey* suggests that historical forces had made the Irish American family, in particular, "too close." Scholars of the Irish experience in America trace this tight familial weave to the effects of England's centuries long colonial domination of Ireland. Several of O'Neill's plays, such as *A Touch of the Poet, More Stately Mansions,* and *A Moon for the Misbegotten,* as well as *Long Day's Journey,* show how an American variant of these colonial tensions was manifested in considerable friction between established Protestant Yankees and the immigrant Irish. James O'Neill spurned advice that he change his Irish name if he sought to make a name in the theatre. Eugene was proud enough of his Irish parentage to call his second son Shane Rudraighe and his daughter Oona, and he boasted that "O'Neill"—which means champion in Gaelic—was the name of Irish nobility.[43] His father had commissioned William Greer Harrison to write *The O'Neill, or the Prince of Ulster*—a play based on an O'Neill who was Earl of Tyrone and King of Ireland and who pleaded with Queen Elizabeth to grant Ireland home rule—so that it could be performed for the family.[44]

John Henry Raleigh has described the intensely private New England Irish Catholic family as "the macro-microcosm that blots out the universe."[45] The Irish colonial roots of this blotting out can be detected in Raleigh's survey of the Irish American family's typical, sometimes stereotypical characteristics—a public profile of gregariousness often privately accompanied by heavy drinking, a heightened fear of betrayal, a peculiar blend of piety and blasphemy, a severe pressure on women

to be chaste, and an attitude toward love that oscillates rapidly be-
tween sentiment and irony. The New England Yankee family of 1906 in
O'Neill's *Ah, Wilderness!* (1933), the Millers, is not without its psy-
chological undertones, but by comparison with the New England Irish
Tyrone family of 1912, in which dramatic and melodramatic perfor-
mances of confession abound, the Millers seem tame, even shallow.
There were, Raleigh claims, few "prohibitory conventions" in the Irish
American family.

Throughout the nineteenth century the Irish were popularly associated with lowly labor and, certainly in New London, were not usually
welcomed in the ranks of Protestant Yankee elites. Ruth Newcomb, a
member of New London's upper crust, reminisced that her kind "didn't
fraternize with the O'Neills and Irish stock. . . . They had no money
or prestige."[46] Ella O'Neill considered herself what was termed "lace-
curtain" Irish, having been educated in a refined Catholic convent, and
was frustrated with the relatively low social standing of her husband's
profession, by the quality of their "Monte Cristo" summer cottage,
and probably also by the marginal, no-Irish-need-apply status of the
working-class Irish. Mary Tyrone complains bitterly that their home is
not as "decent" as that of the Chatfields (3:738) and reenacts the Yankee
exclusion of the O'Neills in her condescension toward her Irish immigrant domestics—"stupid, lazy greenhorns" (3:749).

James's origins were "shanty Irish," not "lace-curtain," and, as *Long
Day's Journey* hints, he may not have been wholly desirous of being
taken up by New London's "Chatfields." An aspirant to New London
society should not wear threadbare clothes in public or clip his hedge, as
does the outwardly proud James Tyrone. The successful actor Richard
Mansfield, by contrast, bought a fine home in the wealthy Pequot dis-
trict of New London and was soon entered in the rolls of Miss Newcomb's clique.[47] James purchased a good deal of land but chose to rent it
rather than to settle on it and act the part of New England gentry.

James sent his sons to Fordham and Princeton and surely wanted
them to succeed in American society; but not if it meant effacing their
ethnic origins. When Jamie Tyrone links his father's pessimism about
Edmund's consumption to his "Irish peasant" (3:732), "bog-trotter"
(3:761) superstitions, Tyrone enjoins Jamie to keep his "dirty tongue off
Ireland" (3:732) and, later, reminds him that he wears "the map of
Ireland . . . on his face" (3:761). Yet James knew that to make it as an
actor he had to Americanize "an Irish brogue you could cut with a
knife" (3:809). Edward Shaughnessy is no doubt right in surmising that

James, Ella, and New London society sent Eugene and Jamie "mixed signals"[48] about being Irish. In a provocative reading of the O'Neills' situation as "misbegotten" Irish in New London, Virginia Floyd makes a persuasive case that Eugene's ethnic background was a foundation for his universalized feeling that—as Edmund puts it—he was "a stranger who never feels at home . . . who can never belong" (3:812).

The modern psychological family that has roots in the nineteenth century became popularly encoded as "psychological," not just sentimental, in the 1910s and 1920s. Many psychologists and sociologists in this period concurred that the word "affection" best described the social function of the modern family and sometimes viewed this as a relatively recent development.[49] Where the early nineteenth-century family produced "thread and cloth and soap and medicine and food" as well as sentiment, they noted, the products of the modern consumer family stripped of its productive functions were chiefly psychological—happiness, warmth, and, not least of all, sexual satisfaction.[50] Emotional and erotic expectations brought to domestic intimacy had escalated, they believed, especially for women for whom marriage and the family constituted the principal expressive outlet.[51] Some attributed the "sexualization of love and glorification of sex" that informed these heightened expectations not only to the increasingly popularized "Freudian gospel" and to birth control, but to movies, to confession magazines, and to a loosening of morals that was accelerated in the backseats of automobiles and in the tabooed speakeasies that flourished during prohibition.[52] Psychologists, sociologists, and social workers began to reconceive the modern family not fundamentally as a social agency—for schools, psychological experts, and welfare organizations now contributed much to the socialization of children—but as a self-absorbed, *psychological* unit, what one sociologist termed a "unity of interacting personalities."[53]

The modern psychological household was sometimes explained as the emotional flipside of the "machine age."[54] For professionals and managers who competed in the business world's "shadow of insecurity," the psychological family promised "a safe outlet for turbulent feeling."[55] For rationalized, regimented, alienated workers, domestic intimacy yielded the primary "means of satisfying human desire."[56] Expert observers noted that the psychological family which performed "rehabilitative" functions had enormous pressure placed on it to satisfy increased "craving[s] for affection."[57] This compensatory function had become more difficult to accomplish, some psychologists and sociologists suggested, because the consumer culture that grew exponentially in the twenties magnified "individual desires" within the consuming family.[58]

The ever-increasing number of family professionals—psychologists, sociologists, social workers, marriage counselors—often viewed the family as an ongoing psychological experiment in need of their management expertise. Sociologists Ernest Groves and William Ogburn proposed establishing preventive "bureaus of matrimonial" counsel that would, like travel information centers, guide couples onto smooth emotional pathways before they stumbled into the rut of family "disorganization."[59] The success of these discourses in redefining the family as a predominantly "psychological" site was partly founded upon parents' heightened anxieties that they might unknowingly sabotage an inherently fragile childhood now conceptualized as psychological fate.[60] Sheaffer's "the child is essential to the understanding of the man" had become stock psychological "insight" reiterated tirelessly by postwar psychologists and sociologists.[61] Once parents "bought" this vision of the psychological family, they could then reasonably blame their own "child within," and their own parents, for their adult vicissitudes and seek therapy from professionals—as did O'Neill in the mid-1920s. Katharine Anthony, one of America's first psychobiographers, asserted that there was no getting around it: "We are, alas, what our families make us."[62]

Popular and academic publications on the psychological family doubtless filtered into the assumptions of audiences who attended O'Neill's many family dramas in the 1920s, the early 1930s, and the 1950s, when Long Day's Journey was first produced. In Long Day's Journey Mary Tyrone accepts what she considers the irrepressible psychological truth that "past is present" (3:765), a belief explicitly stated or implicit in many of O'Neill's psychological plays,[63] and also an idea prominent in studies like Groves and Ogburn's American Marriage and Family Relationships (1928), which assured readers that "there is no past tense in the experiences of the family."[64] While psychologists made occasional references to the machine age, work, movies, and magazines as powerful cultural influences on emotional relations within families, most of them concentrated their readers' attention on the family itself as the psychological foundation of personality formation.

Notions of familial and psychological determinism were also powerful within Irish American culture. Scholars of Irish culture have outlined a relationship between Ireland's survival under longstanding colonial rule and the Irish literary and intellectual concern with heroism in the face of one's "fate."[65] This was an important theme in dramas staged by the Abbey Theatre, whose New York tour in 1911–12 inspired an O'Neill who was about ready to try his own hand at playwriting. John Millington Synge, William Butler Yeats, and Lady Augusta Gregory inaugurated an Irish Renaissance in theatre that endeavored among other things to replace the stage Irishman associated with blarney, Mother Machree sentimentalism, and top-of-the-morning-to-you cheerfulness with a new stage Irishman who possessed subjective depth and a tragic sense of fate. The stage Irishman of the Irish Renaissance represents, not the luck of the Irish, but the fate of the Irish; if he drinks, he does so not because he is superficially garrulous and likes jigs but because he is complex, feels guilty, and is fate-driven; if he cannot escape English rule, perhaps of even greater moment he cannot escape himself and his crises of faith. The colonial force that dominated Ireland for hundreds of years, and which attempted to cast darkness over the Irish sense of possibility, is in some respects reconfigured, interiorized, and ostensibly *transcended* as the Irish tragic sense of psychological fate.

O'Neill, influenced by Synge, Yeats, and Gregory (as well as by Ibsen, Strindberg, Shaw, and Hauptmann), sought to redesign the figure of the nineteenth-century American Irishman, popularized by playwrights like Dion Boucicault, John Brougham, James Pilgrim, William Macready, and Edward Harrigan (a stage Irishman undoubtedly well known to James O'Neill). It is the Irish tragic sense of determinism coupled with contemporary psychologists' pronouncements about familial determinism that partly sparks O'Neill's fascination with the "can't help it" psychological resignation of the confessional Tyrones in *Long Day's Journey*. "It was your being born that started Mama on dope," Jamie tells Edmund. "That's not your fault, but . . . I can't help hating your guts—!" (3:820). Edmund's birth accelerated the vortex of a familial fate that swallowed his brother, his mother, and his father. Jamie's discovery of his mother's unfeminine and unmotherly "fate" as an addict in turn drives him to make himself and Edmund fail: "Can't help it," he confesses. "Hate myself. Got to take revenge. On everyone else. Especially you" (3:821). These "psychoanalytic" stage Irish Americans, ensconced in their repetition-compulsion "fate," their poetic "fog" (3:795), and their emotional addictions, are encoded with what O'Neill thought of as an Irish subjectivity "deeper" than that found in the nineteenth-century melodrama of his father's theatre and perhaps "deeper" than that usually found in non-Irish Americans.[66]

O'Neill's specifically "Irish" admiration for James Joyce's infusion of tragic subjectivity into his Irish characters is manifest in a letter he wrote to James T. Farrell in 1943. Critics, he says, have overlooked the "Irish aspects of Joyce," have inadequately grasped the "Irish history, political and religious," informing his work, and are thus incapable of "feel[ing] the depth of *Irish* tragedy . . . [which] they examine as if it were . . . from Ibsen or Strindberg, illuminated by Freud." He then recommends that Farrell read Sean O'Faolain's biography of Hugh O'Neill, *The Great O'Neill*, in which the Elizabethan courtier's distinctively Irish characteristics also have a "psychoanalytic" tint (seemingly qualifying him for a role in *Long Day's Journey*): "a fascinatingly complicated character, strong, proud and noble . . . but at times so weakly neurotic he could burst openly into tears (even when sober!) and whine pitiably that no one understood him."[67] O'Neill's project in his late masterpieces (which he called his "Irish plays")[68] was to resignify the colonized, subjected Irish as aristocrats of subjectivity who had their literary, religious, fate-driven, infinitely complex, and sometimes "neurotic" subjectivity in place centuries before Ibsen, Strindberg, or Freud "discovered" theirs. *Long Day's Journey*, written in 1940 about the summer of 1912, seems to suggest that the middle-class psychological family, which increasingly drew the attention of the burgeoning American psychology industry shortly after Freud's visit in 1909, had already grown luxuriant in the dramatic, and at times melodramatic Irish American "hothouse."

At the same time, however, O'Neill associated Irishness with a histrionic quality that complicates any simple reading of Irish subjectivity as naturally "deep." In *Long Day's Journey* Tyrone tries to explain to Edmund why he "can't help being" a "stinking old miser" (3:806) by recalling the immigrant childhood that determined his present. But as he does so one gets the impression that he has recited this "can't help it" speech many times over. Its rehearsed tone is evident in the sentimental, alliterative clichés that run trippingly off his tongue to make his poverty-stricken past melodramatic. They were "stranger[s] in a strange land"; he was evicted "from the miserable hovel we called home"; his mother, a domestic servant given a Christmas bonus of a dollar (by her "Yank" employer), runs home weeping: "Glory be to God, for once in our lives we'll have enough for each of us!" (3:802–8).

His performance culminates with a meditation on how hard it is to "unlearn" the lessons of one's past, and he vows that Edmund can select any sanitorium (for his consumption) he likes, regardless of cost: "Any place you like—within reason" (3:808). Tyrone's past-is-present may have created his "depth," but, if so, an aspect of this Irish "depth" is its tendency to be melodramatic and to stage the past as its alibi so that it may continue to "act" as it does. Edmund's response is compassionate, and he tells his father—in good therapeutic fashion—that he now knows him better; yet earlier he had reminded his mother that they had "heard Papa tell that machine shop story ten thousand times" (3:787).[69]

Not only did O'Neill's work generally uphold the idea of family-as-fate, his biographers usually adopted this as their organizing premise when accounting for O'Neill's life. But I have been arguing that what we must remember when assessing the relationship of O'Neill's plays (and of biographical approaches to O'Neill) to the history of the American family is that concepts of the family as mainly "psychological," of childhood-as-fate, and of family-as-fate, are not ahistorical givens. Rather these assumptions acquired considerable cultural authority at a historical juncture when the emotional life of the family had become increasingly intense and when psychological discourses, especially the "Freudian gospel," greatly affected how people interpreted the significance of this intensity.[70] I now will elaborate some of the implications of the modern cultural making of the "psychological family" by rereading several of O'Neill's plays, some of which underplay historical forces, while others rather provocatively chart causal connections between particular historical circumstances and the production of psychological and familial "depth."

The Psychological Dyad in the
"Land of the Mother Complex"

Welded (1923), long recognized as one of O'Neill's most psychological plays, dramatizes the emotional conflicts and ambivalences of Michael Cape, a playwright, and his wife, Eleanor, an actress. There appears to be little history (or plot) in their Strindbergian struggles for psychological power over each other. "Such suffering is out of time," writes Bogard, "and the Capes are cut off from any significant outside reality." However, O'Neill's play has an autobiographical dimension. O'Neill, who met and married Agnes Boulton in 1918 (five years before he wrote *Welded*), has Eleanor mention that she and Michael have been married for five years. As Sheaffer points out, in 1924 Boulton adopted the pen name Eleanor Rand when she wrote a drama titled *The Guilty One*, based on a scenario written by Eugene. There are other biographical correspondences as well.[71]

The dialogue of *Welded* invites a psychological reading. But as my reading progresses from a consideration of psychological to historical processes, I will argue that the psychological and biographical content is itself historically revealing. The introductory stage directions highlight a psychological dyad: *"two circles of light, like auras of egoism, emphasize and intensify Eleanor and Michael throughout the play"* (2:235). Act 1 in the original production showed Michael and Eleanor sitting motionlessly on stools and delivering their lines to the audience.[72] After greeting one another, Michael inquires "(*tenderly*) Happy?" Eleanor responds impatiently, "Yes, Yes! Why do you always ask?" (2:236). Michael's dependency on such testimonies of bliss ignites feelings of confinement and ambivalence in his mate. Eleanor suggests, not long after, that the inflated psychological expectations they bring to their marriage are impossible to satisfy: "Our ideal was difficult. (*sadly*) Sometimes I think we've demanded too much" (2:239). Sheaffer notes that such exchanges dramatize Eugene's actual "straining to attain an impossible relationship with Agnes" (Figure 12).[73]

Michael and Eleanor's privatized existence also has an autobiographical basis: "It must be *he and I*, in a world of our own," wrote Boulton of her marriage to O'Neill. "As for having any children of our own, I'm sure we never thought of it. A strange attitude, perhaps, for people getting married, but then Gene was an unusual person, and so perhaps, at that time, was I." When Agnes received letters from family or friends, Eugene displayed a proprietorial "sullenness."[74] Agnes asked her parents to vacate their New Jersey farmhouse while the two of them occupied it one winter (Eugene, apparently, was unaware that her parents had been relocated for the sake of his artistic temperament). In fact, Agnes's father had to take a job in a local hardware store to pay the rent on the house to which the family moved. When Agnes's sisters paid a surprise visit on one occasion, the privatized playwright retreated stealthily to the nursery closet, fooling no one.[75]

Such singular behavior finds its way into the relationship of Michael and Eleanor, as they hear a knock on their door. Eleanor, after much tense delay, answers it, leaving Michael standing "*there fixed, disor-*

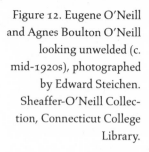

Figure 12. Eugene O'Neill and Agnes Boulton O'Neill looking unwelded (c. mid-1920s), photographed by Edward Steichen. Sheaffer-O'Neill Collection, Connecticut College Library.

ganized, trembling all over" (2:241). After John, Michael's producer and the object of his jealous suspicion, visits and leaves innocently enough, a volley of recriminations and self-recriminations ensues. Eleanor's admission that she is ashamed of her shockingly social behavior, and that she couldn't help herself, is not enough to prevent Michael from exploding, "(*intensely*) You should've been oblivious to everything! (*miserably*) I—I can't understand!" Eleanor, distressed, is driven to confess that she is a separate person: "That's you, Michael. The other is me—or a part of me—I hardly understand myself." Michael, deflated by this news, demands an explanation of her gross betrayal (i.e., opening the door): "After all we'd been to each other tonight—! . . . Nelly, why did you?" Even Eleanor's yielding—"I'm sorry. I hate myself"—cannot pacify him: "There's always some knock at the door, some reminder of the life outside which calls you away from me" (2:243).

The community outside their intimacy is perceived as a threat. The desire to taste life "outside" their union risks being taken as a sign of dissatisfaction with or a betrayal of the dyad. "I've grown inward into our life," Michael acknowledges: "But you keep trying to escape as if it were a prison. You feel the need of what is outside. I'm not enough for you." Eleanor despairs of ever "knowing" Michael and asserts a "right to herself" that signals professional frustrations: "You insist that I have no life outside you. Even my work must exist only as an echo of yours. You hate my need of easy, casual associations. You think that weakness. You hate my friends. You're jealous of everything and everybody" (2:244).

Such dialogue may seem to confirm Bogard's observation that their psychological "suffering is out of time," and that they "are cut off from any significant outside reality." On the contrary, their "suffering" and their being "cut off" are historical signs of the modern, hothouse middle-class dyad that expects all-enveloping therapeutic warmth from its self-sufficiency.[76] At the close of *Welded*, Michael asks: "(*with a dull resentment directed not at [Eleanor] but at life*) What is—it?" (2:268–69). Rather than abstracting or universalizing "it" as life, we must understand "it" as a historically specific production of emotional life.

Michael and Eleanor's "life" was not unlike the psychological puzzle of marriage written about by contemporary psychologists and sociologists who taught their readers that "plumb[ing] the depths of personality takes many years of cohabitation and eager willingness to understand."[77] Family professionals used their authority to persuade readers that encased within them were specific sorts of depths and desires which had to be plumbed. Both *Welded* and family professionals represent marriage as the therapeutic occasion for "plumbing" the interior mysteries, repressions, and obsessions of "personality." Each spouse seems to perform a "psychological" role for the other—a means to the end of diving into "the self." This process entailed risks, psychologists advised, for it could lead one to acknowledge that one's own or one's spouse's emotional and sexual needs had changed—something the Capes fear.[78]

In his effort to account for the exorbitant psychological and sexual demands brought to modern marriage and romance, the progressive popular writer Judge Ben Lindsey, of the Juvenile and Family Court of Denver, pointed to the sexual "revolt of youth" that made its presence known in his courtroom since the early years of the century. Having accepted that the "revolt" had won overwhelming grassroots support among youth, he pleaded that the concept of marriage should be modernized.[79]

Accordingly, Judge Lindsey advocated a more flexible, couple-centered bond—"already an established social fact"—that involved "legal marriage, with legalized Birth Control, and with the right to divorce by mutual consent for childless couples, usually without payment of alimony." In companionate marriage, spouses would be pals and lovers rather than unequal members of a fixed hierarchy.[80] Yet marriage experts felt that the praiseworthy companionate ideal—an emotional ideal—would make partners too dependent on one another for psychosexual satisfaction and would lead to an amplification of tensions.[81] The *uncompanionate* companionate marriage dramatized in *Welded* is a manifestation of this tension.

Statistics suggest that the companionate marriage was no surefire solution to the conventional constraints of marriage but rather a new dimension of the problem.[82] Michael and Eleanor Cape, whose ominous closing embrace is in the form of a crucifix (2:276), clashed on stage at a moment when an alarming number of American couples wanted to become *unwelded* from holy matrimony: about one-sixth of all marriages in America terminated in divorce—"the highest divorce rate in the world."[83] Eugene separated from Agnes in 1928 and divorced her the next year to marry the actress Carlotta Monterrey. He had divorced Kathleen Jenkins in 1912. In the 1920s the popular behavioral psychologist John Broadus Watson, himself recently divorced, forecast that the institution of marriage would topple within fifty years.[84]

When Michael offers enthusiastically to read his new playscript to Eleanor, calling it (in companionate style) "the finest thing we've ever done!" she objects: "I love you for saying 'we.' But the 'we' is you. I only—(*with a smile of ironical self-pity*)—act a part you've created" (2:237). Eleanor spoke for her generation of "new women." Between 1900 and the time Eleanor made her retort, there was a huge influx of women in universities. Modern women, interested in going to work,[85] and in the sexual expression authorized by pop psychology and sexology, were more frequently finding themselves disgruntled with "parts" scripted by their husbands and by a patriarchal culture.[86] Psychoanalyst Beatrice Hinkle, among others, exhorted married women to assert themselves as "individuals first, and as wives and mothers second."[87]

The fact that women and men were becoming less traditional companions put further strain on the ideal of companionate privatism. Samuel Schmalhausen, a socialist psychologist who condemned the privatized form of the family as "pathological," in 1930 portrayed modern wedlock as a "fertile breeder of malaise."[88] O'Neill's *Welded* stages the culturally rooted tensions of privatized, companionate marriage in the 1920s, but the play's immersion in the very psychological discourse that helped inflate emotional expectations that were brought to companionate marriage (making it, in Eleanor's words, "demand too much") tended to obfuscate the play's historicity in the eyes of its critics and perhaps also in the eyes of its author.

The Marxist critic Granville Hicks argued perceptively in 1933 that *Welded* and other plays O'Neill wrote in the twenties were remarkable studies of "frustration" and "disintegration." But he also claimed that while O'Neill dramatizes symptoms, he is less concerned with searching for causes or explanations. Indeed, Hicks contends that O'Neill's aesthetic makes a virtue out of portraying "futileness" and of asking "himself questions he cannot answer."[89] As such, O'Neill's plays can be frustrating symptoms of the frustration they stage. Hicks could have taken his analysis one step further by arguing that O'Neill, like contemporary family experts, had come to view marriage as the manufacturer of cumbersome psychological baggage and that the growing ideological authority of family-as-cause was probably why the playwright could not grasp the Capes's frustration with "psychological" matrimony as a historical symptom of *cultural* change.

As the psychological family became understood as the explanatory context for itself, O'Neill saw the mother figure as the psychological key within this context. Mothering was central to his understanding of the psychological role acted out by the woman in the romantic dyad, most notably in *A Moon for the Misbegotten* (1943). "Mother me," Jamie Tyrone asks of Josie Hogan sardonically, "I love it." Josie replies "(*bullyingly*) I will then. You need one to take care of you" (3:891).

O'Neill had some inkling that the emotions attached to the mother figure had a cultural grounding and in 1929 diagnosed America as "the land of the mother complex."[90] Schmalhausen saw this "mother complex" as a development of the privatized "pathological family": "Hatred can be hated. But what weapons are powerful enough against the insidious powers of love? Especially mother love?" *Long Day's Journey's* Mary Tyrone consistently uses this strong "mother love" both offensively and defensively to needle her sons and husband when they insinuate that she has returned to morphine—"It's as if in spite of loving us, she hated us" (3:801). G. V. Hamilton, a psychiatrist, and Kenneth Macgowan, O'Neill's friend and codirector of Experimental Theatre, Inc., published *What Is Wrong with Marriage*, in part to explain the potentially smothering psychological influence of mothers on their married sons, and concluded that "for the boy's future happiness in marriage it is best for him to be on friendly and affectionate terms with his mother *without over-doing it*." They recommended that a woman anticipating marriage would do best to make certain that she "resemble[s] the mother-image which this man carries about with him."[91] Neither Hamilton nor Macgowan had the historical perspective to realize that their "insight" relied on the historical emergence of a nineteenth-century cult of domesticity centered on the mother who disciplined her son—her "emotional marionette"—not by corporal punishment, but through the restraining agonies of guilt.

In *A Moon for the Misbegotten*, Jamie's anguished, confessional outpouring to Josie about his binge with a prostitute on the transcontinental train that carried his mother's coffin back East is more than a dramatization of psychological depth, and more than O'Neill's autobiographical reflections on his brother; it is an episode in the history of the romance of middle-class motherhood. Jamie admits: "It was as if I wanted revenge—because I'd been left alone—because I knew I was lost, without any hope—that all I could do would be to drink myself to death, because no one was left who could help me (*His face hardens and a look of cruel vindictiveness comes into it—with a strange horrible satisfaction in his tone.*) No, I didn't forget in that pig's arms!" He adds, compounding his guilt: "I was too drunk to go to her funeral." His transgression is ambivalent: aggression against a mother who abandoned him (as well as womanhood in general—sleeping with a woman he could designate "pig"), and a wish to lash himself with guilt so that he may reaffirm his continued need for mother's emotional sustenance. Jamie transforms a situation in which he could not "forgive her" (for dying) into one in which she would "forgive me" (3:932) (for his debauchery), thus again making "mother" requisite to his life.

This is O'Neill's insight into a historically specific mother-son relationship, an overheated bond that produces the urge to confess.[92] Jamie's mother's psychological presence impedes Josie from beginning any life of her own with her misbegotten companion, confined as she is to the role of surrogate "mother confessor": "Do what you came for, darling. . . . *She* hears. I feel her in the moonlight" (3:933).

This romantic and ambivalent mother-son power relationship is also essential to understanding charged marital relations in *The Iceman Cometh*. Although the husband-wife psychological unit was becoming what Raymond Williams terms "dominant" in the 1920s, the mother-son psychological relationship was still powerful in its "residual" status

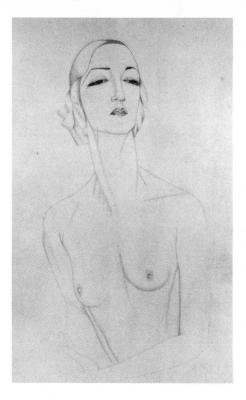

Figure 13. Drawing of Carlotta Monterrey by Eyre de Lanux, published in *The Dial*, January 1922. Sterling Memorial Library, Yale University. See the Sheaffer-O'Neill Collection, Connecticut College Library, for Louis Sheaffer's note attached to his photocopy of this drawing: "When Carlotta appeared at the New York studio of Eyre de Lanux in 1921 to pose for a sketch, the artist was surprised to find her, when she removed her coat, bare from the waist up. Why, the artist was asked years later, the scanty garb? 'I suppose,' she said, 'for dramatic effect, so that's how I drew her.' (Only the artist, now about 90, and myself know of this sketch, which appeared in a 1922 issue of *The Dial*.)"

("still active in the cultural process . . . as an effective element of the present").[93] Nineteen-twenties psychology, pop psychology, and birth control publications focused more than ever on the mother's sexuality as a need that men and women both had to acknowledge and that wives who had become mothers had to satisfy. "Keep on wooing," Margaret Sanger advised husbands, "[but] words of endearment . . . should not be used to mask neglect in [sexual] acts."[94] This growing cultural sexualization of "mother" most likely influenced O'Neill's perception of "wife" in his explicit fusion of their roles. In 1919 Eugene called Agnes "wife of all of me but mother of the best of me." This "incestuous" inflection was even more pronounced in a letter he wrote to his third wife, Carlotta Monterrey, in 1932. After labeling her his "Mistress," "Wife," "Mother" ("in your soft breasts there is a peace for me that is beyond death!"), and "Daughter," he concluded: "I cuddle you in my arms and you are blood of my blood and flesh of my flesh"[95] (Figure 13).

In *Iceman*, Hickey's long-winded confession outlines a relationship with his wife, Evelyn, that is illuminated by the pattern of maternal psychological controls which produce guilt in the son.[96] "Sometimes I couldn't forgive her for forgiving me. I even caught myself hating her for making me hate myself so much. There's a limit to the guilt you can feel and the forgiveness and the pity you can take" (3:699). The aggression Hickey channeled inward was also directed outward at Evelyn, whose forgiveness he punished by persisting in his profligacy. He finally kills Evelyn exclaiming, "You damned bitch" (3:700).

Another "damned bitch" who exercises a form of nineteenth-century maternal control is Harry Hope's long-dead wife, Bessie, who years before had tried to coerce him to conform to the success ethic. Hickey, attuned to Hope's sentimental denial of his resentment, unmasks him: "She was always on your neck," he prods, "making you have ambition and go out and do things, when all you wanted was to get drunk in peace" (3:674). Hope's bar, filled with moochers, drunks, and tarts, is the antithesis of the nineteenth-century home in which middle-class mothers sought to have their sons internalize the work ethic and moral code. In feigned anger at the hoopla made by his resident tarts, Hope exclaims hopefully, "Bejees, I'll bet Bessie's turning over in her grave!" (3:604).

It is no coincidence that Hickey's confession is interspersed with Don Parritt's. Parritt, an anarchist Judas, betrayed his mother, Rosa, to the law for her revolutionary ardor. "I loved mother, Larry!" (3:694), he protests at first. But later Parritt confesses that he betrayed her because he "hated her" (3:700). Jealous of his mother's devotion to the movement, resentful of her "free" lovers, and furious at her rejection of the sentimental norm of "mother," Parritt retaliated by symbolically killing her. Hickey and Parritt remain psychologically bound to their mother-wife figures, as does Hope, whose easy-going, boozy naughtiness is at once an expression and a repression of his resentment of his dead wife. That there is no such thing as "free love" in O'Neill's plays may be taken as a psychological or Strindbergian insight into the contest for power provoked by passion and dependency; but it is crucial to recognize this unfree love as belonging to a complex historical process that brought about a peculiarly intense mother-son/wife-husband psychological bond in what O'Neill dubbed "the land of the mother complex."

The Historicity of Ambivalence

O'Neill's *Mourning Becomes Electra* dramatizes oedipal conflicts in a hyperpsychological mid-nineteenth-century New England family, sometimes to the point of unintentional parody. O'Neill denied the influence of Freud on this Civil War trilogy, imbuing it with a timeless quality "as old as literature." But as Doris Alexander pointed out in 1953, the family in *Mourning* is locked into the psychological pattern sketched in *What Is Wrong with Marriage*: "Again and again," write Hamilton and Macgowan, "we see the misery of maturity driving men and women to teach their children exactly those things which will perpetuate the misery when the children themselves grow up." O'Neill, along with Hamilton and Macgowan, sees the "family circle" as a potential noose—a "vicious circle."[97] The trilogy stages the family as an emotional hotbed, as a site of repressed and often incestuous sexuality, as the determining psychological force in one's life, and as a closed circuit of roles (e.g., Lavinia can *only* act like her father or her mother).

In 1936 Bertolt Brecht could have had *Mourning* in mind when he charged that bourgeois plays typically offer a reductive representation of history which promotes the ideology of a timeless, unalterable human nature: "History applies to the environment, not to Man."[98] Although the action in *Mourning* is set at the close of the Civil War, this national conflict seems to stand only as a "house divided" metaphor for emotional strife among members of the Mannon family. The antebellum period was when the increasingly private hothouse family was beginning to sizzle—a historical process that, I have argued in *The Production of Personal Life*, helps explain the psychological character of gothic-domestic fictions by Hawthorne, Poe, and Melville. O'Neill's drama about this Civil War oedipal family is subject to the same criticism that sociologist Eli Zaretsky levels against psychoanalysis, a critique that can also be made of the trend in psychological and sociological treatises on the affectionate family in the 1920s: it ignores or downplays "how the family is itself socially determined" and seeks to account for the family primarily "in terms of itself."[99]

Historical explanation is supplanted in *Mourning* by a gothicized psychological discourse that recalls the gothic-domestic fictions of Hawthorne, Poe, and perhaps Melville.[100] Lavinia tells Seth "there's no rest in this house which Grandfather built as a temple of Hate and Death" (2:1046). In the final play of the trilogy, *The Haunted*, Lavinia acknowledges that she is psychologically doomed not only by the house, but by the familial ghosts who inhabit it. These domestic ghosts are O'Neill's literal expression of the fate of the psychological family as defined by numerous contemporary professionals in the field—the family has "no past tense."[101]

Although most of O'Neill's trilogy is taken up with the enactment of notions of the middle-class oedipal family, it recognized the idea that sexuality and family life differ across cultures. The South Pacific islands visited by Adam Brant, Lavinia Mannon, and her brother Orin are portrayed in pastoral terms as a lush, primitive, paradise outside both capitalism and repression. Brant tells the *"brittle"* Lavinia that the pre-lapsarian islanders "live in as near the Garden of Paradise before sin was discovered as you'll find on this earth" (2:909). When Lavinia finds herself aroused by an islander during her own sojourn there, she unwinds, realizing that "everything about love can be sweet and natural" (2:1031). The way to escape the family-as-fate, apparently, is simply to leave it and discover that the family has been invented differently elsewhere.

In the opening scene we learn that the Mannons have been "top dog around here for near on two hundred years and don't let folks fergit it" (2:895). And in O'Neill's original draft, the psychological tension between Ezra and Christine Mannon arises in part because of her independent income and the autonomy it gives her. Christine, moreover, "felt a superior disdain" for the townfolks. But this economic and class setting was largely edited out of the 1931 version of O'Neill's oedipal drama—at a time, one might note, when the social forces battering families (unemployment, bank foreclosures on mortgages, food and fuel shortages) were impossible to ignore.

In the depths of the Depression, 1935, the perspicacious leftist critic Charmion Von Wiegand compared *Mourning* to its richly historical Greek sources and took the trilogy to task for dramatizing only "purely personal motives without any profound social significance." While Sophocles and Euripides conceived of the psychological as inextricably entwined with political motivations and circumstances in their plays, O'Neill's dramatization of the Oedipus and Electra themes replaced this social complexity of motivation with a modern concept of the psychological family: "Clytemnestra's crime was not the killing of her husband but the destruction of the head of state. Electra's act was dictated by the need to obtain her portion of power and her brothers in the city state."[102]

By contrast, the first two acts of *More Stately Mansions*, which is the long, unpolished 1939 draft of a sequel to *A Touch of the Poet*, posit a dialectical relationship between capitalism and psychologically over-heated domestic arrangements. *Mourning*'s Mannons are a wealthy family who happen to be plagued by pop psychological oedipal relation-ships, while *Mansions*'s Harfords clearly are an entrepreneurial family whose capitalist possessiveness determines in part an emotional pos-sessiveness that assumes the form of oedipal tensions. The historical project of the first half of O'Neill's *Mansions* is in harmony with what Stephanie Coontz describes as the intellectual aim of the history of family life—to discern how a culture coordinates "personal reproduc-tion with social reproduction."[103] Curiously, the last two acts are fixated on the psychological relationships that had been historicized in the earlier acts.

Historians concur that the antebellum cult of domestic purity accom-modated and tempered rather than challenged the "organization of work and pursuit of wealth."[104] Thus O'Neill was on target in his effort to map connections between domestic intimacy and entrepreneurial drive in the 1830s and 1840s. In *Mansions*, Simon, son of a wealthy entrepreneur, has abandoned his distinctly anticapitalist cabin-in-the-woods—straight out of Thoreau's *Walden*—in order to achieve financial independence for his new wife, Sara, and himself. Sara, an ambitious and somewhat embittered Irish immigrant, encourages him to forego his plan to write a Thoreauvian critique of capitalism for the joys of competing in the marketplace and accumulating wealth. "If ever you saw him when he comes home to me," she tells Deborah, Simon's aristocratic mother, "so proud and happy because he beat someone on a sale, laughing and boasting to me, you wouldn't hope you could use his old dream of a book that'll change the world to dissatisfy him. . . . Simon is mine now" (3:337). Sara is perhaps too successful, for it is Simon, increasingly obsessed with competing and accumulating, who proposes that they double their $100,000 goal, tempting her with dreams of "a fine country estate and greater security for the future" (3:363). Defend-ing his transformation into a bloodthirsty entrepreneur, Simon informs his mother, "Sara's happiness . . . justifies any means!" (3:331).

Sara is just as ruthless at times, as when she insists that Simon fire striking mill hands (who are probably Irish immigrants like herself) (3:488), or when she glosses off the enslavement of "poor black nig-gers," cautioning Simon, "You are a cotton mill owner who depends on the Southern planters" (3:357). Sara, eager to accumulate wealth and aristocratic status so that no one will dare "sneer" at her Irish origins, is at times a stereotype of the quintessential capitalist wife. "She was the inspiration for my career," Simon exults. "She is the cause of the com-

pany, the spirit of its ambition" (3:409). O'Neill suggests that antebellum domesticity, in its tacit encouragement of possessive individualism and its sanctification of privatization, provided emotional fuel for
the growth of industrial capitalism.

Simon revealingly pushes this to extremes that strip the veneer off
sentimental constructs of feminine and domestic "decency."[105] When
Simon takes Sara into his business and gives her the opportunity to take
further advantage of a competitor whom he has all but squashed, he
counsels Sara not to "get life confused with sentiment as you used to"
(3:491). Contrary to domestic ideology, Sara must abandon "sentimental
lies" for the "greedy facts of life" (3:413). As Sara goes in for the kill and
Tenard, her victim, remarks in shock, "I could not believe a woman. . . ,"
she responds assertively and mechanically (like a 1939 Nazi): "I am good
because I am strong. You are evil because you are weak. These are the
facts" (3:493). Indeed, she deploys sentiment only to subdue Tenard,
who, as she suggested to him, would not dare "ruin" (3:497) his children.

O'Neill's most searing critique of feminine sentimentality is apparent in Simon's success in persuading Sara to act the role of "mistress" in
his office. Sara, already predisposed to capitalist opportunism, is over-
joyed at the prospect of "making [Simon] a slave to [her] pleasure and
beauty," but she also derides him for "buying what [he] own[s] already"
(3:412). Simon, however, is not so naive; he has set up his experiment to
show his wife how pervasively capitalist possessiveness can transform
one—"in a year she will not know herself" (3:415). Even at the outset
of this kinky arrangement, part of Sara recoils from playing her role
(3:413). At long last Sara, repelled by her own transformation, acknowledges ruefully that Simon has "made me think that life means selling
yourself" (3:490). After she sacrifices the entrepreneurial life for Simon's simple cabin-in-the-woods, Sara abjures reproducing their sons
as little capitalists (3:559).

O'Neill's dramatization of the relationship between domesticity and
nascent industrial capitalism clarifies the historicity of ambivalence
within the antebellum privatized family. Simon's experiment reveals
his ambivalence about his masculine role as ruthless entrepreneur. He is
relieved to abdicate the role of "greedy slave" (3:455) to Sara. "I was so
afraid you couldn't be proud of me," he admits to her, "unless I kept on"
(3:553). To his mother he confesses that as a capitalist he felt "spiritually degraded"—a "traitor" (3:331) to himself. At the prospect of
retreating from the capitalist maelstrom and returning to his mother's

walled-in garden of utopian fantasies, Simon reassures himself that "it will be a relief to leave this damned slave pen and talk with someone whose mind is not crucified on the insane wheel" (3:416).

Simon's resentment about having to play capitalist is directed against his mother as well as Sara. She too has "exiled" him to the "outside world" (3:532) filled with "danger and suspicion and devouring greed!" (3:534). His resentment against Sara is vented in his assertion of patriarchal authority. After informing her of his decision to take over his deceased father's ailing business, he scolds Sara, "My asking your consent has never been anything but a formality. What do you really know of business?" (3:381). Finding that his wife and his mother—normally competitors for his affection—have joined forces to ostracize him when he returns home from doing battle in the marketplace, he claims for himself patriarchal rights of ownership: "Two women—opposites—whose only relation derives from the relationship of each to me—whose lives have meaning and purpose only in so far as they live within my living—henceforth this is my home" (3:451). O'Neill portrays gender difference both as a stimulus to capitalist accumulation (Sara "inspires" Simon to be a "greedy slave") and as *productive* of psychological tension, jealousies, and resentment.

The women, too, feel resentment in their domestic positions. Sara, for example, knows that she is far too smart and ambitious to settle for the limited psychological power available to her within the home. When she does embrace domestic motherhood in league with Deborah, it is both to affirm solidarity with another woman and to antagonize Simon. "I tell you, as woman to woman," Sara advises Deborah maliciously, "I hate him so much that if I was in your place I'd give him his wish, and I'd let him go back and back into the past until he gets so lost in his dreams he'd be no more a man at all, but a timid little boy hiding from life behind my skirts!" (3:474). Deborah also resents her dependency on her son and counsels Sara to profit from her playacting as "mistress" and to grab "everything he possessed!" (3:472).

The competition between Deborah and Sara is for psychological control over Simon. O'Neill seems to be suggesting that the competition and possessiveness promoted in the marketplace is reenacted at home in multiple psychological guises. The establishment and manipulation of emotional dependencies within the home was often the only "social" position of power, authority, and prestige available to adult women. Deborah, obsessed with her fading beauty, is aware that Sara possesses a sexual influence over men that she too wielded in her youth. For Simon's wish to possess his wife as an object of desire opens up the tactical opportunity for Sara to make him emotionally dependent on her.

What Sarah Grimké in 1838 called the "bonds of womanhood" were also the emotional bonds women—in possession of sentimental power—could establish over their "breadwinners." O'Neill dramatizes the psychological competition women could engage in with one another—the unsentimental underside of what historian Carroll Smith-Rosenberg has called the nineteenth-century "female world of love and ritual."[106] That O'Neill offers us insight into the workings of ambivalence within the Harford family cannot be gainsaid; but his theoretical sophistication in this play is in the attention he pays to the historicity of the social roles and power relations that create the conditions for hothouse ambivalence.

The relationship between Deborah and Simon certainly has its incestuous or oedipal dimension. But it is Deborah's dearth of power outside of her domestic role that has much to do with this. Because the only power available to her is through desire and appearing desirable, it is no surprise that her fantasy of social power is to be an eighteenth-century courtesan in the French court, where she (as she advised Sara to do to Simon) uses her desirability to emotionally enslave the king. When Simon laughs *almost derisively* at his mother for "playing make-believe with romantic iniquity out of scandalous French memoirs" (3:329), she is devastated, for his sarcasm indicates that her power over her son as an object of his desire has waned. Michel Foucault's study of the nineteenth-century bourgeois family has led him to conclude that "where the family is the most active site of sexuality, . . . incest . . . occupies a central place; it is constantly being solicited and refused."[107] *Mansions* shows us that this hothouse antebellum capitalist family produces what Foucault calls "sexuality" (replete with incestuous feelings), a "sexuality" that twentieth-century psychologists have too often viewed as being distinct from historical forces and have abstracted as deriving from the depths of human nature.

Philippe Ariès has observed that by the nineteenth century the family came to be imagined as a "sentimental reality," not simply as a social, economic, and moral unit. The industrial revolution from which Simon Harford made his fortune was accompanied by an equally significant "emotional revolution" in the domestic sphere, characterized by what Ariès calls "obsessive love."[108] In *Mansions* O'Neill surveys the historical conditions and power struggles that were involved in this "emotional revolution." Much of O'Neill's epic-length play shows a psychological family stepping onto the stage of history; insight into this family's psychodynamics is ineluctably historical insight.[109]

The first half of O'Neill's *Mansions* does not attempt to explain the psychological family in terms of itself (as does *Mourning*). Yet the latter half of this epic is very much a symptom of the modern psychological discourse whose historical origins it seeks to uncover. As oedipal relations and psychological tensions come to dominate the last half of the play, the presence of capitalism, the cult of success, the cult of motherhood, and the cult of domesticity as forces that organize emotional tensions becomes harder to discern. O'Neill seems overwhelmed by his own fascination with dramatizing the subtleties of ambivalence and depth. Hence *Mansions* reverts to *Mourning* and becomes a case study. In the concluding Freudian act, for example, Deborah and Simon share an oedipal fantasy in which she calls him "my love," and he, in turn, refers to her—in a stereotypical Freudian slip he quickly revises—as "an old lover in my childhood" (3:538). Criticisms leveled against *Mourning*—that its characters are overconscious of their textbook Freudian drives—apply just as convincingly to the final two acts of *Mansions*.

What makes *Mansions* so suggestive ideologically, then, is that its first half relentlessly traces connections between capitalist privatization, possessive individualism, and the domestic emergence of a psychological discourse that, once unleashed, turns voraciously on O'Neill's representation of the family's social origins and gobbles up the history in the remainder of the play.[110] Oddly, the play enacts what happened when familial and psychological discourses were meshed in the twentieth century to help constitute a family that *above all* would be imagined in "psychological" terms and that would be given such supreme explanatory authority that it could account for itself and "the self." The potency of the discourse of the psychological family is such that it can disguise or at the very least overshadow its historical status as a cultural discourse by more or less conceptually detaching both the family and the self from the encompassing social conditions that produced particular forms and notions of them. The family is then understood principally as the arena of raw human nature and of psychological revelations—the privileged, multilayered, mysterious space where one's true self is located, hidden, or buried. This modern psychological common sense often relegates culture to the backdrop for the psychological actions of the familial self—actions, of course, that are seen as requiring the therapeutic intervention and management of psychological and family professionals.

O'Neill at times contributed to the cultural production of common sense about the psychological family-as-fate, as did many contemporary family experts, and as did O'Neill's biographers, who encouraged readers to interpret and to appreciate O'Neill's plays first and foremost as dramas conceived by a son and playwright. For these biographers, culture—theatre, literature, philosophy, religion—palpably influenced O'Neill's thinking and feeling, but they saw the emotional family dramatized in *Long Day's Journey* as the underlying psychological force that propelled O'Neill into artistry. Departing from this approach, I have been suggesting that O'Neill's fascination with psychological and familial determinism *as* the "deepest" subject of drama was part of a cultural trend, in a loose sense a project that should be associated with the middle- and upper-class audiences who attended O'Neill's plays (and who later bought biographies of the playwright).

No doubt contemporary psychologists and sociologists were right when they observed that American families were undergoing manifold psychological stresses owing to the changing functions of the family and to the inflated emotional expectations placed on the "rehabilitative" family in the "machine age." On one level it might be argued that O'Neill's psychological dramas are simply historical in that they "reflect" these pressures on the family. But something else of importance is at stake in grasping the historical and ideological effects of O'Neill's work: O'Neill's dramas sometimes participate in the encoding of psychological and familial determinism as the *most significant* "truth" one can explore. One might infer that many members of O'Neill's middle- and upper-class audiences *wanted* him to render what they were coming to regard as their deepest significance in the appropriate psychological and familial terms. They were not only willing but *eager* to embrace psychological and familial determinism as a mode of self-representation. O'Neill's work, in other words, tapped into a cultural agenda to *make* the family's significance preeminently "psychological."

One can assume from the enthusiastic reviews and the popularity of O'Neill's plays that many members of middle- and upper-class audiences were drawn to envisioning their significance in this way. Why and how this psychological vision of their conflicts and their significance ideologically sustained them is a complicated matter to pursue. As I noted above, *Mansions* offers a clue, for its narrative hints that psychological discourse, once let loose in the family, has the capacity to devour other more social and material ways in which the family might assign significance to itself.

Along similar lines, the "psychological" has generally dominated various readings of the meaningfulness of Long Day's Journey. The reception of Long Day's Journey in the 1950s attests to the ever-increasing cultural and aesthetic appeal of the category of the psychological family. The play won O'Neill his fourth Pulitzer Prize, three years after his death. Members of the audiences who flocked to this late masterpiece may well have seen in it a dramatization of the universal, tragic, psychological interplay of love and resentment that they thought beset all families throughout time and across cultures. The criticism and reviews of Long Day's Journey indicate that it was a hit primarily, not as a dramatic study of a privatized middle-class family racked by historically specific ethnic, gender, and class conflicts, but as a dramatic, therapeutic rendering of the universal, psychoanalytic family fraught with ambivalence, oedipal desires, and obsessional behavior.[111] However, if these 1950s audiences perceived themselves or their neighbors in the "human nature" of the "neurotic" Irish Tyrones, it is arguable that they wanted to see familial and psychological conflicts staged as universal for historical reasons.

Historians of the 1950s now underscore the ambivalence many middle-class Americans felt about privatized domestic arrangements that were less cheerful than those celebrated each week on "Ozzie and Harriet." In this "Happy Days" decade, shock treatment and tranquilizers (mostly prescribed for women) became acceptable psychiatric techniques to manage family troubles.[112] The embattled Tyrones surely struck a nerve in audiences who knew that the middle-class "affectionate" family was not always as cozy as the ones depicted on television. Long Day's Journey, for them, unmasked deeper, more radical therapeutic "truths" about families than the shallow, sanitized images of "Father Knows Best." This darker, ostensibly subversive O'Neillian "truth" may well have sustained them in part by fascinating them with their own domestic conflicts. Yet it seems only logical to point out that once the family conceptualizes its meaning, its tensions, and its depth in universal and psychological, rather than cultural, material, and historical terms, it is partly circumscribed in how it can conceive of both the foundation of its problems and the ways in which it might change itself and the circumstances that produced it.

Perhaps middle-class and upper-class families gained compensatory advantages from picturing themselves in mainly psychological terms—terms ratified and made commonsensical by family experts, therapists, playwrights, novelists, poets, critics, reviewers, and biographers. Perhaps these families derived some benefits, and not just psychological benefits, from fascinating themselves with themselves as "deep." But deep in comparison to whom? Was "depth" really meant for everyone? The popular acclaim for *Strange Interlude* in the 1920s, for *Mourning* in the 1930s, and particularly for *Long Day's Journey* in the 1950s suggests that the staging of depth can in no way be seen simply as the staging of middle-class pathology; rather, plays dramatizing familial pathology were invested with prestigious cultural value, a value that could generate considerable revenue. If pathology had become depth, and if the aesthetic representation of depth had been transformed into cultural capital, or psychological capital—the stuff that eternal dramas, great American novels, revelatory biographies, and middle-class and upper-class families are made of—what enterprises was this capital used to underwrite in modern American culture?

These are some of the complex questions that will inform my arguments in the chapters that follow. They aim to move the reader of O'Neill beyond the explanatory framework conventionally provided by psychoanalysis. For like Fredric Jameson, I am suggesting that "the Freudian raw material" (and the modern cultural *preoccupation* with this raw material)—"fixations, traumas, the Oedipal situation, the death wish"—should be read as "sign[s] or symptom[s] of some vaster historical transformation."[113] That is to say, both psychoanalysis and the cultural uses of its system of meaning require historical explanation. While an attempt to provide such an explanation is beyond the scope of this book, the discussion of O'Neill, psychoanalysis, pop psychology, and "therapeutic" theatre in Chapter 2 will help clarify what is at issue in such a project.

The questions above also undertake to move the reader's critical considerations beyond (some excellent) biographies of O'Neill and his own psychological family. When readers of O'Neill (and of the O'Neill biographies) fall into the critical mode not only of searching for particular "insights" into his characters' fixations, traumas, oedipal desires, and death wishes, but of probing for related "insights" into members of his family (masked as his characters), and leave the critical act at that, they are reading *inside* what Jameson recognizes as an allegorical framework, whose preoccupations demand to be accounted for historically. For the American "psychological" family was culturally made, made not just because historical forces such as the "machine age" intensified emotional dependencies, expectations, and stresses within more private, hothouse, families, but because a web of significance was applied to this "psychological" distension that in turn culturally remade "the family" and aesthetic value—a remaking that, we will see, had manifold cultural and political implications. "*Made* my mistakes look good. *Made* getting drunk romantic. *Made* whores fascinating vampires" (3:820) (emphasis supplied), Jamie warns Edmund. Yes, we can interpret this confession psychologically and autobiographically as an expression of Jamie's ambivalence and "sibling rivalry" (wanting Edmund to fail) in *Long Day's Journey*. But O'Neill's accent on "made" invites us to extend our analysis in a more subtle cultural and literary direction. Here O'Neill prompts us to contemplate Jamie as a compelling maker of meanings and as someone who can get an audience (Edmund) to invest in his meanings. By implication, O'Neill turns on himself, his play, and the psychological family he depicts, and he asks his audience to reconsider his authorial assignment of significance, his authorial creation of fascination, his authorial making of "depth"—the "deeper" meaning available to those who read within the system. There are startling moments like this in O'Neill's plays when he permits us not simply to work out his (apparent) meaning *within* an allegorical system (psychoanalytic, autobiographical) that guarantees a gratifying diagnostic payoff (finding the key that unlocks Jamie's "depth"), but to step outside of the system and question how (and why) it makes meaning and the brand of "depth" it seems so naturally—or psychologically—to reveal. At such moments O'Neill-the-maker moved beyond the assumptions attached to the psychological family to think through how its meaning was made and perhaps how he too played a role in making it—and sometimes in "unmaking" it—by staging it.

"DEPTH" AS A MASS-CULTURAL CATEGORY

Pop Psychology,

the Professional-

Managerial Class,

and the Aesthetic

of Depth

2

In order to understand O'Neill's investment in the early-twentieth-century cultural formation of what I have called psychological capital, we must begin by rethinking the psychological as a cultural category—often a category so taken for granted and internalized as natural that its social origins and ideological uses are unquestioned and therefore rendered invisible. The power of this category is most subtle when the "psychological" is represented as a human essence that is simply discovered rather than created as an idea and made significant in ways and forms that change over time, across cultures, and within any given era. Its power resides in its commonsensical pretense that it has nothing to do with social power, only with the clinical, literary, or artistic revelation of classifiable desires filling the contents of one's depth.[1]

My approach is akin to that of the historian Jean-Pierre Vernant, who observes that historians have conventionally regarded the psychological as a given, a universal, an established principle upon which historical explanation regarding behavior and motivation can be based. By contrast, he believes, modern historians increasingly view the psychological more open-mindedly and not as a fixed "principle of intelligibility" or as "a self-evident norm to be imposed." Instead, the psychological is now being reconceptualized and researched as a sometimes elusive piece of the historical puzzle, a dimension of cultural and political transformation, a "problem that needs to be accounted for in the same way as all the rest of the data."[2]

By viewing O'Neill's plays not just within the history of his own family but within the history of American family life—the nineteenth-century hothouse family, the Irish American family, and the early-twentieth-century formation of the psychological family—we have begun to cast historical light on the broader cultural origins of O'Neill's preoccupation with the psychological. Just as the history of the nineteenth-century American "oedipal" family helps explain the hospitable reception accorded psychoanalysis on these shores in the 1910s and 1920s, it also gives us a more cultural understanding both of O'Neill's "personal" choice of subject matter and of the popular success of many of his dramas.

Psychoanalysis, which flourished in America in various manifestations during these two decades, became a cultural force, with the power to revise how the categories of the family, parenthood, adulthood, childhood, culture, and desire are read. One commentator has christened the 1920s the "Psychoanalytic Age."[3] It could have been dubbed more precisely the "Age of Pop Psychology." Attempting to explain the literary and cultural *"mania psychologia"* that gripped the 1910s and 1920s, Houston Peterson, in 1931, cited "the disappearance of God," "the mechanization of living and working conditions," and the disenchantment with the traditional home and with romantic love; but, he concluded, "this passion for psychologizing" is mainly due to "the tremendous growth of the science of psychology" (especially psychoanalysis) and its "army of popularizers."[4] Pop psychology appeared in best-selling advice books, magazines, newspapers, professional journals, novels, and the theatre, and influenced the psychological vocabulary, assumptions, and expectations brought by couples to companionate marriage and by audiences to performances of O'Neill's dramas. I will propose that an awareness of the history of pop psychology as a mass-cultural phenomenon, in tandem with the history of the emergence of the psychological family, will further enrich our cultural perspective on why O'Neill's plays are so "psychological."

Nineteen-twenties' versions of pop psychology and psychoanalysis (in addition to O'Neill's plays) redefined the psychological in particular ideological ways. Even today an ideological foundation governs how many critics, biographers, students, and audiences think about the psychological. My approach to O'Neill's participation in the promotion of a psychological common sense moves along the theoretical trajectory sketched by recent historians who have identified the need for cultural histories of the forms, categories, codes, conventions, and narratives through which subjectivities have been organized and produced.[5] In this chapter I will make visible a number of links between O'Neill's drama, pop psychology, and psychoanalysis as a means of clarifying the forms of subjectivity (depth) O'Neill helped to put into play for his audiences. I suggested at the end of Chapter 1 that many members of O'Neill's audiences wanted to imagine their personal significance in reference to notions of the psychological family. Here I shall argue that the psychological identities O'Neill staged were ideologically crucial to the changing identity of a white-collar workforce largely made up of members of what has been termed the professional-managerial class.

O'Neill was well acquainted with several illustrious pop psychologists and psychiatrists in the 1920s and 1930s. Dr. Smith Ely Jelliffe, for example, treated O'Neill somewhat informally and irregularly from 1923 to 1925 for alcoholism as well as his discord with his second wife, Agnes Boulton. Jelliffe, an editor of *Psychoanalytic Review*, accepted many theatre people as his clients, including Robert Edmond Jones, O'Neill's innovative set designer and—with O'Neill and Kenneth Macgowan—a codirector of Experimental Theatre, Inc. Jelliffe's interest in theatre was serious enough for him to write, with Louise Brink, *Psychoanalysis and the Drama* (1922), a copy of which he inscribed for O'Neill.[6] O'Neill's neighbor in Bermuda was Dr. Louis Bisch, a psychoanalyst and pop psychologist who wrote an unpublished play called *The Complex* and popular advice books, such as *Your Inner Self* (1921), *The Conquest of Self* (1923), and *Be Glad You're Neurotic* (1936). Bisch never analyzed O'Neill, but he diagnosed the dramatist (free of charge) as "emotionally starved," as harboring "a deep antagonism toward his mother," and as having "an unconscious homosexual attraction toward his father, which he carried over to some of his friendships for men."[7]

By the mid-1920s, O'Neill's drunken sprees alarmed his closest friends. Thus in 1926 Macgowan introduced O'Neill to Dr. Gilbert V. Hamilton, a psychiatrist who was conducting psychological research on sexual behaviors that was later published in *A Research in Marriage* (1929). Both O'Neill and Macgowan became subjects in Hamilton's study, which analyzed both the sexual practices of and the parental influences on one hundred wives and one hundred husbands (not all of whom were couples). O'Neill's involvement in this research was followed up by some private consultations with Hamilton, all of which occurred over a six-week period.[8] Hamilton won the trust and respect of the thirty-eight-year-old dramatist and was able to help him with his drinking problem. O'Neill rarely resorted to the bottle for the remainder of his life.

Macgowan and Hamilton published a psychological study for popular consumption based on Hamilton's research, entitled *What Is Wrong with Marriage* (1929), several chapters from which first appeared in *Woman's Home Companion, Harper's,* and *Red Book.* Hamilton's original research showed some theoretical interest in studying "the child in the adult," but this theme was really Macgowan's thematic emphasis in his reconfiguration of Hamilton's work. As Hamilton makes plain in his preface, it was Macgowan, theatre reviewer and producer, who actually wrote the popular version. Macgowan had Hamilton's staff reevaluate the data so that the interpretive focus was on the long-lasting psychological effects of parental socialization on children (which, of course, included chapters on the Oedipus and Electra complexes). In 1927 O'Neill met with Hamilton again to seek advice on the psychological dynamics he was dramatizing in his draft of *Strange Interlude* (1928). According to Macgowan, O'Neill probably perused the magazine articles and certainly read *What Is Wrong with Marriage* before writing *Mourning Becomes Electra* (1931).[9]

Nineteen twenty-seven was also the year that Saxe Commins, another of O'Neill's best friends and also his trusted editor, ventured into the pop psychology market with *Psychology: A Simplification,* coauthored with Loyd Ring Coleman. Commins's *Obituary* (1916) was one of the first plays to be produced by the Provincetown Players in Greenwich Village. When Commins quit his dental practice in order to try his hand as an editor in the late 1920s, O'Neill helped him get established at

Boni and Liverwright, his publisher. O'Neill left Boni and Liverwright just before it went under in 1933, on Commins's advice, and made the hiring of his friend one condition of his signing with Bennett Cerf's Random House.

Floyd Dell and Max Eastman, who were active in the Provincetown Players with O'Neill in 1916–17, won fame as radical editors of *The Masses* and *The Liberator*. Yet in 1915 each of them published popularizations of psychoanalysis that not only "simplified" it, but attempted to package the Viennese import as a bourgeois commodity for the general public. Hence for O'Neill, the *"mania psychologia"* was not only "in the air," modern "discoveries" of depth were on the minds and in the writings of his friends and colleagues.[10]

The Therapeutic Playwright
and Therapeutic Theatre

Psychoanalysis had special appeal for authors in the 1910s and 1920s, as Frederick Hoffman has noted, because "it flattered the subjective importance of the artist himself" and posited the wellsprings of creativity within the artist's ever-mysterious emotional depths.[11] Influenced by psychoanalysis, O'Neill's circle valued his "neurosis" as a symptom of his subjective and artistic potency. According to Dr. Bisch, in the mid-1920s the playwright's friends "thought analysis might be good for [him] but were afraid it could harm [his creativity] as a dramatist."[12]

Pop psychology books, such as André Tridon's *Psychoanalysis and Love* (1922), portrayed the author as a psychological figure too tumultuously deep or neurotic to be peacefully married. In his chapter "Love Among the Artists," Tridon concludes: "Frequent are the divorces in the artistic world. . . . Sex in the life of an artist . . . plays an infinitely less important part than egotism." He cautions male and female artists to avoid marrying one another.[13] O'Neill reproduces this psychological profile of the artist in *Welded* (1924). Recall that Michael and Eleanor are spotlighted *"like auras of egotism . . . throughout the play"* (2:235). Their initial skirmish concerns Eleanor's uneasiness because she simply acts in the scripts that Michael creates: "You're an artist" (2:237), he must assure her.

O'Neill, who Sheaffer portrays with some admiration as an "emotional hemophiliac," viewed his writing both as a therapeutic outlet and a defense ("a suit of armor").[14] He envisioned the process of composition as what Nancy Armstrong and Leonard Tennenhouse call "writing depth."[15] Critics of the 1920s also appreciated him in this explicitly therapeutic light: "[O'Neill] builds for power," Macgowan asserted, "always getting down to the big emotional root of things."[16]

The idea of the therapeutic author was connected to the emergence of aesthetic values that are evident in Joseph Wood Krutch's paean to O'Neill-the-neurotic: "He has sought whenever he could find them the fiercest passions, less anxious to clarify their causes for the benefit of those who love peace than eager to share them, and happy if he could only be exultingly a part of their destructive fury. . . . The meaning and unity of his work lies not in any controlling intellectual idea and certainly not in any 'message,' but merely in the fact that each play is an experience of extraordinary intensity."[17] Within this value scheme, the literature that illuminates causes and conveys "messages" is aesthetically less significant than writing which expresses its author's psychological tempestuousness (as if this valuation of significance sends no "message"). This romanticizing of volcanic temperament moves toward detaching the psychological artist and his work from a consideration of social context or social responsibility. Thus when a biographer or critic who has adopted this concept of the artist and aesthetic value records that O'Neill punched one of his wives, O'Neill's "destructive fury" may be interpreted—if not quite celebrated—as a fierce expression of the depth that nourishes his "literary genius."[18]

O'Neill, in contrast to Krutch's portrait of him, was interested in psychological explanation, as his "Memoranda on Masks" (1932) attests. He experimented with masks in *The Great God Brown* (1925) and *Lazarus Laughed* (1926), he explained, to "express those profound hidden conflicts of the mind which the probings of psychology continue to disclose. . . . For what, at bottom, is the new psychological insight into human cause and effect but a study in masks, an exercise in unmasking."[19] Hence O'Neill implicitly equates literary value with the "exploration" of a masked psychological self, whose historical specificity he did not always articulate.[20]

O'Neill's thinking was in accord with theoretical assumptions adumbrated by Jelliffe and Brink in *Psychoanalysis and the Drama.* They proposed that true drama should perform a "psychotherapeutic service": "the drama releases the feeling into an intuitive freedom with itself far more profoundly effective than mere intellectual understanding of the dramatized situation." Psychological theatre is not conceptualized as entertainment, as a commercial event, or as what Bertolt Brecht called a political "theatre of learning." Jelliffe and Brink have in mind a theatre of *yearning*, a "ready avenue of release of otherwise overcharged emotions, the outlet for which is neglected or too severely restrained." This cathartic theatre will serve the ends of psychoanalysis, which are not only to unmask the unconscious but to "control" it.[21]

Jelliffe's view of the "psychotherapeutic" possibilities of theatre drew on notions that made pop psychology popular. The popular discourse of depth held that one really is a mystery even to oneself and that a knowledge of one's depths offers the possibility of control. In "Exploring the Soul and Healing the Body" (1915), published in *Everybody's Magazine*, Max Eastman represented psychoanalysis as a means of viewing what O'Neill terms the "inner drama." Everybody's depth is dramatic because depth determines the self: "The things that are in these unconscious depths—wishes, images, ideas, loves, hates, fears that we know nothing about—are often much more important than what is on the surface. They have more to do with determining our beliefs, our friendships, our health, success or failure, than any of the things that are consciously thought about."[22] The judgment that knowledge of such depths is "more important than what is on the surface" is a psychological value Jelliffe and Brink convert into an aesthetic value.

Pop psychologists sometimes remark that the discoveries of psychoanalytic therapy were made urgent by the "machine age": "At the close of a century of mechanical achievement, an age of psychological advance began," observes David Seabury in *Unmasking Our Minds* (1925); "The need was sore, for life was a riddle of which men were weary."[23] With this urgency in mind, Jelliffe and Brink prescribe a drama that provides "psychic ventilation." Jelliffe and Brink are conscious that white-collar workers attend the theatre, and that drama can offer a therapy—a talking cure—which will channel them back into the workplace feeling "released" and "unmasked." Repressed emotions, they write, are not "given sufficient outlet in useful work in our hurried and strained activities. Conversely, our work remains hurried and strained because of the partly conscious suppression and the more largely unconscious repression of all emotions. The hours at the theater should greatly relieve the strain of repression and they shall . . . awaken the sense of recognition of these inner vital factors."[24] The alienation that results from nerve-wracking activities at the workplace is thus individualized as a psychological problem. Jelliffe and Brink's focus is not on altering "hurried and strained" work, but on acknowledging "inner vital factors."[25]

The ideological benefits this "psychic ventilation" provides for an alienated, theatre-going workforce is manifest in the praise the authors lavish upon Leo Tolstoy's story, "Redemption": "It is a drama that attempts to draw no solution out of its presented features of character and action. . . . It seeks to elaborate no explanations, to point no moral. It does, however, lay human psychic life before its audience . . . [and] introduce us as it were into the reality of the psychic problems."[26] They laud its apparent ideological innocence and transparency: "no solution," "no explanation," "no moral," just "human psychic life" as it is. Thus Jelliffe and Brink's notion of therapeutic drama is tuned into the same frequency as Krutch's tribute to the volcanic O'Neill—ventilation, not explanation, is aesthetic as well as therapeutic.

The renowned producer Arthur Hopkins, who had been a patient of Jelliffe's, was a colleague of O'Neill's in the early 1920s. He produced and directed "Anna Christie" (1921) and assisted with the direction of The Hairy Ape (1921) in 1922. His monograph, How's Your Second Act? (1931), appears indebted both to Jelliffe and Brink's earlier work and to O'Neill's psychological dramas of the twenties. Hopkins aspired to make the evening-at-the-theatre the occasion of unannounced group therapy. "All the repressed desires burst forth into flames in the theatre, and for a few hours they have full sway to be silenced again until dreams have their way." The playwright's mission is to establish a private, psychological dialogue with the "public mind": "unconscious speaking to unconscious, an unconscious that easily touches the common complexes of the many."[27]

Freud not only "discovered" psychoanalysis, he helped establish "a new aesthetics" (of depth), as one critic has observed.[28] In The Theatre of Tomorrow (1921), Kenneth Macgowan predicted that the new drama "will attempt to transfer to dramatic art the illumination of those deep and vigorous and eternal processes of the human soul which the psychology of Freud and Jung has given us."[29] Sheldon Cheney had made "psychologic theatre" synonymous with the new in The New Movement in the Theatre (1914), which clearly inspired Macgowan, Hopkins, and O'Neill. For O'Neill, Macgowan, Hopkins, and other theatre people, the tenets of psychoanalysis lent cultural and scientific authority to what Cheney described as the new, noncommercial, "intimate" European drama that "grips the emotions" and is "true to the deeper motives of human character."[30] As the psychological theatre of the 1920s promoted itself as deep and honest, it categorized the nineteenth and early twentieth century's commercial theatre—its melodrama, acting techniques, staging styles—as superficial and evasive.

O'Neill-the-modernist was very much in sympathy with this classification. He made many statements about his work that resonated with the distinctly modern psychological approaches of Jelliffe and Brink, Macgowan, and Hopkins. In 1925, for instance, he regretted that his Pulitzer-winning *"Anna Christie"* "doesn't go deep enough." Modernism's promotion of depth transformed aesthetic value, so that realism and naturalism (such as one finds in *"Anna Christie"*) looked thin to some of its adherents. After the premiere of *Strange Interlude* O'Neill repudiated theatre's "so-called realism,"[31] and in doing so placed himself not only in the tradition of pioneering dramatists who experimented with psychological symbolism, like Henrik Ibsen and August Strindberg, but in the front lines of literary modernists. O'Neill, more so than T. S. Eliot in poetry and James Joyce in fiction, put the making of the psychological self at the heart of the modernist project.[32]

During an interview in 1926 O'Neill articulated the therapeutic notion of what Hopkins termed "unconscious production": "I never intended that the language of [*Desire Under the Elms*] should be a record of what the characters actually said. I wanted to express what they felt subconsciously."[33] *Mourning Becomes Electra* "drags its drama out of fresh depths," he wrote in 1931, "and in a manner less externalized than the other plays." In explaining this more "complicated" (modernist) drama to his son Eugene Jr. in 1933, O'Neill's description could easily have been lifted from Bisch, Seabury, or dozens of best-selling pop psychologists who both helped produce and tapped into a mass-cultural preoccupation with the "hidden": "As you grow older . . . you choose more complicated themes and prefer characters of more involved, modern 'civilized' psychology and less obvious, more suppressed and hidden motives."[34] Modern emotions took on a distinctly literary cast, as analysands, critics, readers of fiction, and theatre audiences came to interpret feelings as symbols, multilayered subtexts, and narrative threads.[35]

O'Neill made this new depth the basis of his understanding of drama and tragedy. One critic has written: "Before O'Neill, the U. S. had theatre; after O'Neill, it had drama."[36] O'Neill won national and international acclaim in part because his pop psychological *version* of drama was recognizable as the new, deep psychological common sense.

In *Why We Misbehave* (1928), Samuel Schmalhausen applauded the "pathological" modernist writing of O'Neill, Joyce, D. H. Lawrence, and Sherwood Anderson for having plunged into the tabooed self: "Our writers . . . have actually moved into the forbidden lands of pathology and perversion. . . . All forms of writing tend increasingly to become autobiographical and psychoanalytic."[37] The cultural authority of literature legitimated the psychological common sense promoted by pop psychology; and pop psychology, as Schmalhausen's text shows, authorized in turn this concept of literature.[38] "All normals wear a mask, a false face, and it's mighty deceptive," wrote Dr. Bisch, citing O'Neill's *The Great God Brown*, not Freud's *The Psychopathology of Everyday Life* (1901), as his authority.

In "The Sexual Revolution" (1929) Schmalhausen hailed *Strange Interlude* as a stunning example of "how saturated contemporary thinking and feeling and reading are with clinical revelations."[39] O'Neill's play, however, offers us one intriguing exchange of interior monologues that stands out because it broaches antithetical views of the discourse of depth. It is the neurologist, Ned Darrell, who unquestioningly privileges depth as a literary value and a psychological discovery. He thinks the following about Charles Marsden, a "repressed" novelist: "his novels just well-written surface . . . no depth, no digging underneath . . . why? . . . has the talent but doesn't dare . . . afraid he'll meet himself somewhere . . . one of those poor devils who spend their lives trying not to discover which sex they belong to!" (2:662). Marsden's literary superficiality is represented as a personal failing, attributable to a lack of autobiographical and psychological candor. In short, Marsden has neither confessed nor released himself through his writing. As such, his fiction is classified as a form of denial rather than a therapeutic exercise.

Darrell's diagnosis seems to fit O'Neill's characterization of Marsden, and this lends weight to his assumptions. Yet O'Neill allows us to establish a critical distance from this diagnostic pronouncement as we ponder Marsden's interior monologue, in which he sizes up not Darrell so much as the *discourse* through which he predicts Darrell will size him up: "What is his specialty? . . . neurologist, I think . . . I hope not psychoanalyst . . . a lot to account for, Herr Freud! . . . punishment to fit his crimes, be forced to listen eternally during breakfast while innumerable plain ones tell them about dreams of snakes . . . pah, what an easy cure-all! . . . sex the philosopher's stone . . . 'O Oedipus, O my king! The world is adopting you!'" (2:662). Marsden verges on thinking about depth sociologically—not as a "clinical revelation," but more critically as a mass-cultural discourse that is indeed transforming the way Marsden, Darrell, and members of their professional class imagine their selfhood, identity, and desire. A "pathological" literature that lends high cultural authority to this individualized psychological imagining of selfhood is linked with this mass-cultural discourse and often participates in its politics—which I now hope to clarify.

The Production of "Psychological" Common
Sense for the Professional-Managerial Class

Sigmund Freud's 1909 Clark University lectures gained his movement notice among American physicians. One hundred articles on psychoanalysis were published in medical journals between 1912 and 1914, and seventy appeared over the next three years. By 1915 psychoanalysis had been taken up by women's magazines such as *Good Housekeeping*. "Psychoanalysis," Nathan Hale estimates, "received three-fifths as much attention as birth control, more attention than divorce, and nearly four times more than mental hygiene between 1915 and 1918."[40] Attempting to account for the extraordinary fascination with depth psychology, Henry F. May points out that the nineteenth-century evangelical and transcendental traditions believed that "spiritual insight and exercise could tap hidden sources of energy." Moreover, the bohemian intellectuals who were already in the process of attacking nineteenth-century middle-class "puritanism" commandeered psychoanalysis as another weapon in their arsenal.[41] Hale observes that magazines in the early twentieth century had shown significant interest in "mental healing" and "cure literature."[42] Psychoanalysis retained the emphasis on healing and cure, but gave "deep" "modern" meaning to the sexual significance of "mental," thus making a range of writing on the subject more marketable as pop intellectual commodities.[43] As the commodification of psychoanalysis advanced in the twenties, the Progressive Era tendency to associate psychoanalytic self-exploration with advocacy of social reform became less fashionable.[44]

Pop psychologists were varied in their approaches and, of course, did not always subscribe to Freud. In *Psychoanalysis and Love*, for example, André Tridon drew heavily on Freud, but also criticized him for devising "far-fetched explanations for very simple phenomena in order to show the sexual nature at the bottom of them."[45] In pop psychology texts, an older style of common sense often would be integrated with or be used to argue against psychoanalytic assumptions that were vying to become the new common sense.[46] Popular accounts commonly lumped all of these approaches under the rubric "new psychology." This term was invented in the late nineteenth century to describe experimental psychology, whose experiments and discourse of "objective" empiricism gained it some broader cultural recognition.[47] By 1915 the term was associated mainly with Freud,[48] but it soon came to refer to the mental hygiene movement, to behaviorist psychology, and—as we will see—to plays staged in the twenties.

Commenting on the wildly enthusiastic reception of O'Neill's *Strange Interlude* in the late 1920s, Travis Bogard writes: "To readers of philosophers or psychoanalytic theorists, and to those who had had a chance to explore a smuggled copy of the French edition of *Ulysses, Strange Interlude* offered nothing new." Because the public was "relatively untutored" in Freud, Jung, and Joyce, "*Strange Interlude* unquestioningly appeared as a revelation—a kind of primer of new thought, couched in language and action that opened new vistas in their understanding of human drives."[49] On the contrary, the sensational box office and publishing success of the boldly experimental *Strange Interlude* can be attributed in part to the fact that pop psychology played a key role—along with the plays of Ibsen and Strindberg—in setting the stage for O'Neill's staging of modernist depth. Here my perspective is in alignment with that of Eric Bentley, who in 1962 argued that O'Neill had become the principal dramatist of middlebrow consumers to whom "psychologism" appealed, an audience that wanted their melodramas and soap operas (in my own terminology) written and staged to seem *deep*. It was the pop psychological dimension of *Strange Interlude* that made its pop modernism commercially viable.[50]

Pop psychology expanded its popularity by contributing its wisdom to the how-to-succeed genre.[51] O'Neill obliquely acknowledges this trend in his description of how Professor Leeds's study has been altered since his death. In Act 1 of *Strange Interlude*, Leeds's study is filled with classic liberal arts books on ancient Greece and Rome. By Act 4, after Leeds has died and Sam Evans, the aspiring business executive, occupies it, new books have arrived on the scene.

> *The table . . . is no longer the Professor's table. . . . The table has become neurotic. Volumes of the Encyclopedia Britannica mixed up with popular treatises on Mind Training for Success, etc., looking startlingly modern and disturbing against the background of classics in the original, are*

slapped helter-skelter on top of each other on it. The titles of these books face in all directions, no one volume is placed in any relation to the one beneath it—the effect is that they have no connected meaning. (2:692)

In a "startlingly" modern world experienced as having "no connected meaning," the imagining of a decentered self jeopardizes the standard nineteenth-century ideology of self-making. Now neurosis and the rise of a professional and managerial class are seen as complexly symbiotic. Neurotic energy, rather than the uncomplicated self-assurance of Horatio Alger, is channeled into the success game.

"Psychology," wrote Commins and Coleman, "wastes no time regretting the fact that we are in an industrial era."[52] Bisch's *Be Glad You're Neurotic,* which offers a surfeit of evidence in support of the above observation, concludes with *"five simple rules,"* the final two being, "Turn Your Handicap into Assets" and "Profit by Your Neurosis."[53] The psychological as a 1920s mass-cultural commodity—both inside and outside of O'Neill's plays—must be evaluated in the context of the growing population of university-educated white-collar workers.

White-collar progressives who bought Eastman and Dell's *Liberator* in May 1922 would have seen an advertisement for Josephine A. Jackson's *Outwitting Our Nerves,* published by Personality Press: "Psychoanalysis, the new 'miracle' science, proves that most people live only half-power lives because of repressed sexual instincts." Jackson's handy book shows "the way to Health, Happiness, and Success." Freud, superseding Frederick Taylor and Henry Ford, is embraced as the prophet of efficiency. Such advertisements imply that the drawback of nineteenth-century capitalists was that they needed to "repress" their desires in order to be successful; whereas Freud's psychoanalysis introduces the utopian possibility of capitalist accumulation without surplus repression. One can imagine Sam Evans's *Mind Training for Success,* when perused on his *"neurotic table,"* also advising "how to concentrate all your powers in the work in hand."

Freud himself was rather less optimistic about our capacity to "outwit our nerves" and to channel our depth into profit. But Freud too once attempted to take pecuniary advantage of the pop psychology market in America. In 1920 Freud's American nephew, Edward Bernays, who went on to be a prosperous founder of the public relations profession, heeded his uncle's request that he contact a popular American magazine to broach a proposition on his behalf. Freud wanted to be commissioned to write four articles, the first of which would be titled, "Don't Use

Psychoanalysis in Polemics." *Cosmopolitan* promised Freud $1,000 for his initial piece and indicated that its interest in the others would be contingent upon the article's reception. They suggested titles for the possible follow-up essays: "The Wife's Mental Place in the Home" and "The Husband's Mental Place in the Home." Freud swiftly terminated these negotiations and, according to his biographer Ernest Jones, probably felt "a little ashamed of himself at having descended from his usual standards."[54] Freud's long-standing diagnosis that American culture suffered from "Dollaria"[55] (a view shared by O'Neill) must have become somewhat complicated for Freud not only by his awareness that this condition was infectious (spreading even to Vienna), but because it was obvious that what he thought of as his "invention" had been reinvented by it. The new psychology in its sundry guises was being reconfigured in the service of the cultural and economic system for which it was expected to supply therapeutic release.

Analyzing the ideological appeal of psychoanalysis for "rebels and romantics" of the 1910s, the Marxist Joseph Freeman, editor of the *New Masses*, wrote in his memoir that the intellectuals and artists who sought "a frank and free life for the emotions" in the counterculture of Greenwich Village "could not abandon themselves to pleasure without a sense of [social] guilt"; thus, with some help from psychoanalysis, "they exaggerated the importance of pleasure, idealized it and even sanctified it."[56] To adopt the words of Michel Foucault, these romantic rebels demanded of "sex" that it reveal "the deeply buried truth of that truth about ourselves which we think we possess in our immediate unconscious."[57] O'Neill's psychological dramas of the mid- and late twenties were successful in part because professional and managerial workers—the Sam Evanses—who made up the bulk of their audiences also needed to "exaggerate the importance of pleasure" (pleasure conceptualized as removed from the cultural realm),[58] and to locate the true "truth" about themselves in their own hidden depths. Freud and O'Neill became popular icons in 1920s mass culture because both their work and their respective images spoke to needs, especially to professional and managerial workers' cultural and "psychological" needs, for highly personal imaginings of the individual.

These socially and historically based needs were sometimes alluded to and refigured by pop psychology. Bisch, for example, understands that "mass production, mass education, mass anything" threatens feelings of individuality, and thus he would have us read neurosis, not as a wholly problematic symptom, but as a sign that the neurotic "is *different* . . .

does not fit in." Hamilton and Macgowan also see the need for "spiritual strength and insight to protect us from disastrous materialism."[59] Psychology in a secular and a materialistic age attempted to fill the void left by spirituality.[60] The Marxist critic Calverton saw the need for Freudian therapy as having been produced not only by the "machine age," but by the "mad contradictions" that those who rule the machine age create and maintain.[61] More typically, however, psychological disturbances were represented, not as symptoms of maddening social pressures, but as a fundamentally personal dilemma. Max Eastman asks his readers: "*Are you worried when there is nothing to worry about? . . . It may be that your trouble is a mental cancer which can be dissected out by this new method.*" Psychoanalysis is advertised as a personal solution for a self-contained, seemingly psychobiological problem ("mental cancer").[62]

Coterminous with pop psychology in the 1920s is the mass-scale popularization of a discourse of confession. The "true" confessions in the McFadden company's *True Story Magazine* targeted a lowbrow readership and sold extremely well in the 1920s. O'Neill's interior monologues functioned as more refined "psychological" confessions in *Strange Interlude* and partly accounted for the play's great success with middlebrow and highbrow audiences. Reflecting on the contemporary fascination with confession, Commins and Coleman describe psychoanalytic confession not simply as an articulation of anxiety but as a substitutive sexual release "so delectable that the penitent actually welcomes new sins to confess."[63] Once the revelation of depth is interpreted as delectable, a literature that defines its *raison d'être* as the disclosure of depth also makes itself delectable (and sellable).

Psychoanalytic confession, to draw on Foucault, does not merely extract the truths of the self; it produces the notion that there is a definable depth whose delectable truth may be teased out and translated.[64] As Commins and Coleman note, the truth and the depth one confesses have been sexualized: "The psycho-analyst, in telling the patient to associate freely and frankly, *invites* a sexual confession. He grasps the opportunity to release the one thing which he has been trained to repress" (emphasis supplied).[65] Psychoanalytic assumptions about what confession discloses are, of course, culturally specific and rely on particular conceptualizations of personal life, sexuality, guilt, and shame.[66]

The discourse of confession contributed to the psychological redefinition of the category of the literary at the same time that, in its psychoanalytic guise, it was appropriated as a marker of middle-class and upper-class status. The cultural critic Waldo Frank caricatured the delectably expensive confessions of prosperous neurotics in "Joyful Wisdom" (1926)—"They met, in club, in salon, in bed—and 'psyched' each other. . . . Above all, they confessed."[67] And in her play *Expressing Willie* (1924), Rachel Crothers parodies upper-class psychoanalytic confession and hints wickedly that what one woman found on her analyst's couch was what men often procured elsewhere: "You *must* go to this new man. He probed the very depths of my being and *oh* the things we brought up out of my subconscious!"[68]

O'Neill's interior monologues in *Strange Interlude* often take the form of sexually titillating confessions. After Professor Leeds reveals to Marsden that Nina, his daughter, suspects him of having delayed her betrothal to Gordon in the hope that her lover might get killed in the war (which happened), confessional self-accusations burst forth from his depths: "And there you have it, Charlie—the whole absurd mess! (*Thinking with a strident accusation*) And it's true, you contemptible . . . ! (*Then miserably defending himself*) No! . . . I acted unselfishly . . . for her sake!" (2:641). Do we take his statements as truth, denial, or both—ambivalence? Does Leeds himself know? No matter which interpretation we choose, we know that O'Neill's interior monologue has given us confessional access—like tourists—to the professor's depths. Soon we learn which truth is true, as the professor confesses to Nina: "I hated him as one hates a thief one may not accuse or punish. I did my best to prevent your marriage. I was glad when he died. There. Is that what you wish me to say? . . . I wanted to live comforted by your love until the end. In short, I am a man who happens to be your father. (*He hides his face and weeps softly*)" (2:649). Pop psychology had been assuring O'Neill's audience throughout the 1920s that, reared in the psychological family, it probably repressed unconscious incestuous desires it really *needed* to confess. O'Neill deploys confession to extract the "truth" of Leeds, thereby affirming the "truth" of pop psychology and of his nine-act soap opera.

Yet Leeds's query—"Is that what you wish me to say?"—makes his confession more complex to interpret because it introduces the possibility that he reads his own love for his daughter Nina through a mass-mediated oedipal lens that now encodes paternal affection as unconsciously incestuous. Leeds's question suggests O'Neill's awareness that the professor's confessional episode with his daughter is not only personal but profoundly cultural, in that mass-cultural discourses produce psychological vocabularies, narratives, and roles that structure one's experience of the personal. O'Neill briefly brought up the cultural making of psychological identities in his "Memoranda on Masks." Although his 1932 essay took the position that the new psychology "unmasked" one's "inner drama" and one's "profound hidden conflicts," it also fleetingly interjected the heretical thought that the new psychology had in fact "only created for itself new masks."[69] The confessions in *Strange Interlude* often have a conspicuous textbookish compulsiveness. O'Neill seems to understand, on one level, that his characters wear mass-marketed pop psychological "true" confessions (psychological masks): "I've wanted to run home and 'fess up, tell how bad I've been [i.e., how many men she's slept with], and be punished!" (2:671), Nina blurts out to Marsden, knowing it will unnerve him.

The characters who feel compelled to confess in *Strange Interlude* belong to what some historians term the professional-managerial class, which emerged in the late nineteenth and early twentieth centuries.[70] University-educated, professional-managerial-class "culture" producers and managerial workers included corporate executives, advertising consultants, psychologists, social workers, corporate attorneys, engineers, architects, civil servants, publishers, editors (e.g., Saxe Commins), professors (e.g., Joseph Wood Krutch, Arthur Hobson Quinn), theatre reviewers (e.g., George Jean Nathan, Kenneth Macgowan), and playwrights (e.g., O'Neill). These "mental workers" neither work with their hands nor own the means of production. According to Barbara Ehrenreich and John Ehrenreich, the "major function [of the professional-managerial class] in the social division of labor," historically, is "the reproduction of capitalist culture and capitalist class relations."[71] In her most recent analysis of this class, Barbara Ehrenreich adds that it is plagued by "the fear, always, of falling."[72]

This model of three classes—working class, professional-managerial class, and capitalist or ruling class—revises the traditional working class versus capitalist class paradigm for a very important historical reason: the rise of monopoly or corporate capitalism from the 1890s to the 1920s. The tripartite model would not, in fact, have been outside the realm of O'Neill's own thinking: Long, the socialist seaman in *The Hairy Ape*, identifies three classes in his efforts to explain to Yank that Mildred's father, president of the Steel Trust, is the "bloody Capitalist! . . . we're [the workers] 'is slaves! And the skipper and mates and engineers, they're 'is slaves!" (2:139). Various institutions and agencies that fueled and were fueled by corporate capitalism sought on a number of fronts to contain the resistance of unionized workers and political groups (socialists, anarchists, the Industrial Workers of the World). Corporate "liberalism" accelerated, financed, and largely benefited from the formation of a university-trained class of professionals and managers who not only used their (scientific, engineering, psychological, architectural) expertise to "rationalize" the workplace, but to intervene in and monitor working-class families in the guise of school officials, psychological experts, public health administrators, and social workers.

The corporate liberalism that shepherded corporate capitalism through the Progressive Era demonstrated its flexibility in its education and support of reformers whose advocacy of "social engineering" sometimes also turned into a critique of the "inefficiency" and "waste" of corporations and the government. However, as historian James Weinstein notes, in this period "few reforms were enacted without the tacit approval, if not the guidance, of the large corporate interests."[73] In addition to corporate managers (who sometimes rose to become wealthy capitalists), and progressive reformers (who frequently worked for corporations, the government, or corporate-funded universities), this class included some university-educated socialists, who articulated a critique of capitalism and often sought to join forces, politically, with the working class.

O'Neill was neither a salaried corporate manager, nor a professional, nor a reformer who upheld ideals of efficiency and regimentation. O'Neill championed "individualism," not standardization. Nor was he stirred by socialism as a movement after his twenties. Rather he was a member of yet another more difficult to define professional-managerial-class liberal arts group that achieved cultural prominence by the mid- or late 1910s—the intellectuals and artists. Historian Martin Sklar has argued that this group emerged in response to the age of corporate "disaccumulation" in the 1910s and especially the 1920s. "Disaccumulation" is the historical point at which the industrial plant had become technologically advanced and productive enough to free up labor from the production process and to require advertising firms (hiring psychologists, artists, writers) to help create consumers who would be convinced that they "needed" certain products to fulfill their leisure. In this phase, Sklar writes, there were a growing number of university-educated intellectuals or artists who sold their intellectual and artistic wares mainly outside of academia, but who, by virtue of their connections, their credentials, and the cultural institutions that showcased their work, had a certain professional distinction. We also see in this period intellectuals and artists who had not been trained and socialized in universities.[74]

O'Neill sat astride these two groups, at least in his public image—as an Ivy league dropout, a seaman, and a patron of flophouses in his youth. If anything, he and other "romantic rebels" gained a sort of romantic, artistic, and bohemian aura among the professional-managerial class for having broken some of the rules (an acceptable cultural counterweight to the Harding-Coolidge Age of Normalcy). O'Neill and others in this group were sometimes quite adamant in their support of the "little theatre" or the "little magazine" movements and, in phases of their careers, thought of themselves as distinctly noncommercial or even anticommercial in their artistic goals. But even those who made the "little" alternative arts movements possible needed funds to do so and found that they could be limited in the kinds of criticisms they mounted.[75]

Many of the university-trained liberal arts intellectuals chose *not* to argue that the productive process had progressed technologically to the point where workers could labor for fewer hours and perform much higher quality labor (and control it themselves), or that corporate wealth and power could be radically redistributed among everyone who produced. Instead, Sklar argues, many (this would include O'Neill) pointed to "estrangement," "alienation," and spiritual "despair" as the by-products of a modernity that had to be countered with aesthetic and intellectual individualism. In *America and the Young Intellectuals* (1921), for instance, Harold Stearns pleaded, "It is through art, and art alone, that we can regain any individualism worthy of the name."[76]

In 1930 Frederick Lewis Allen observed that although the new intellectuals were relatively few in number, they were "highly vocal" and effective in shaping the taste, values, and critical vocabularies of their class. Influenced by modernism and "the devastating new psychology," they were somewhat more agitated by "cultural poverty" than poverty, and by "emotional and aesthetic starvation" than starvation.[77] O'Neill, Joyce, Freud, and some others, Allen noted, were the cultural beacons of this group.

While some members of the professional-managerial-class culture-producers—like O'Neill—may have regarded themselves as being detached not only from the rationalizing tendencies of corporate liberalism but from the conventionality of academe, their own aesthetic "liberalism" and their commitment to what they believed to be "individualism" was formed through and made possible by manifold institutional connections with the corporate world's publishing houses, magazines, newspapers, museums, concert halls, theatres, fellowship foundations, and universities. It may well have been that the campaign against aesthetic, emotional, and spiritual starvation was exactly what the more liberal professionals and managers and those who oversaw them were quite willing (often literally) to "subscribe" to as dramatic, literary, and artistic concerns. As Richard Ohmann has observed, the literary played a role in the development of this class's self-image: "Literary agents, editors, publicity people, reviewers, buyers of hardbound novels, taste-making intellectuals, critics, professors, most of the students who took literary courses, and . . . the writers . . . themselves, all had social affinities. They went to the same colleges, married one another, . . . [and] earned pretty good incomes."[78] In O'Neill's sphere, Nathan graduated from Cornell, Macgowan hailed from Harvard, Krutch received his doctorate from Columbia and became a professor there in the late thirties, Quinn was dean of the college at the University of Pennsylvania, and O'Neill attended Princeton and Harvard, and by 1926 at last attained his first university degree—an honorary doctorate from Yale.

By the mid-1920s O'Neill was extremely well connected in the "culture producing" network of the professional-managerial class, and profited in many ways from his contacts. Even in 1919 he was opening his letters to Arthur Hobson Quinn with the salutation, "My Dear Dean Quinn."[79] In a long chapter in his second volume of *A History of the American Drama* (1927), Quinn paid tribute to his correspondent. The homage included—opposite the title page—not a photograph of O'Neill, but a photograph of a bust of O'Neill, beneath which read the inscription, in the dramatist's scrawl: "With all best wishes, Sincerely Eugene O'Neill." By implication, O'Neill was not just central to the history of American drama, he was being cast in bronze as a one-man institution that would insure its splendid future.

In 1921 one somewhat hyperbolic reviewer claimed for this greatest of American dramatists a cultural power that he partly attained in the late 1920s (with promotional help from Quinn, Nathan, the Theatre Guild, three Pulitzer Prize committees, and others): "[O'Neill's] name on a manuscript is as good as 'Astor' on an I. O. U."[80] When O'Neill consented to join the editorial board of George Jean Nathan's *American Spectator* (1932–37) (along with Ernest Boyd, James Branch Cabell, and Theodore Dreiser), it was his reputation as well as Dreiser's as one of America's literary giants that lifted the literary stock of Nathan's high cultural enterprise (which, of course, had no advertising). Nathan must have known in advance that O'Neill's actual participation in the project probably would be minimal (it was) because he detested writing criticism.

O'Neill's Nobel Prize victory in 1936 was the supreme cultural triumph for the playwright as well as for a brand of pop modernist drama that suited the professional-managerial class. Not everyone welcomed the news, however. "A class," as Barbara Ehrenreich underscores, "is never of one mind."[81] Bernard De Voto, for one, dissented from the media fanfare following the Nobel announcement by contending that the upper-crust Theatre Guild manufactured the highly competent O'Neill as great because they were under cultural pressure to promote an American dramatist on their stages (which usually featured the work of European playwrights). O'Neill was in the right place at the right historical moment and was groomed to look the part.

> [The Guild's] great prestige, its power to compel the admiration of multitudes, its lavish resources for spectacular presentation and for publicity no less, and its austere authority as an arbiter of judgment combined to elevate [O'Neill] to a grandeur which neither criticism nor the public has ventured to impeach. He has had every kind of success that a playwright can have: money, fame, the best directors and designers and actors of his time, a sumptuous collected edition, a critical acclaim so reverent that the more recent treatises discuss him in language usually considered sacrilegious when applied to the merely mortal, and now the Nobel Prize.[82]

While I and many other scholars would suggest that De Voto underplayed O'Neill's playwriting abilities and contributions to theatre, he was right to emphasize the cultural authority of the commercial institution that enshrined O'Neill and helped "modernize" the cultural preoccupations of the professional-managerial class. The Theatre Guild grew out of the Washington Square Players (a prominent "little theatre" group) and began to produce plays in 1919. Three of the Guild's Board of Managers, Lawrence Langner, a patent lawyer, Maurice Wertheim, a banker, and Theresa Helburn, formerly a drama critic for *The Nation*, were in no need of income from the Guild's profits (which soared by the mid-1920s). Helburn's memoir opens with a discussion of her grandfather—a rich Manhattan real estate speculator—and goes on to describe her trips to Europe as a youth and touts what had been criticized as her Bryn Mawr "intellectualism."[83] Langner's *Magic Curtain* (1954),

Figure 14. Guild Theatre casting room. Acme photograph, 1945. Yale Collection of American Literature Photographs, Beinecke Rare Book and Manuscript Library, Yale University. The press release caption affixed to the photograph reads: "A far cry from the average casting office is this imposing room, where stage aspirants wait for interviews at Guild headquarters."

which recounts his labors on behalf of the Guild, is punctuated with alumni magazine–style bulletins about his lucrative success as a patent lawyer.[84] His career exemplifies how harmoniously the corporate liberalism and the aesthetic liberalism of the professional-managerial class could work together. One of the smartest business decisions Langner, Helburn, and their colleagues made for the Guild was to "patent" O'Neill just as his pop psychological phase peaked.

The impressive support network on which the Guild relied was both cultural and financial. When its first production failed to draw a sufficient audience, Langner kept the show running by contributing $500 each week for three weeks, and then alternated his weekly benefaction with a bi-weekly subsidy from Wertheim, the banker. After Lee Simonson, a gifted Harvard-educated set designer who was also on the Board of Managers, advised that they persuade a millionaire to help finance their venture, Langner and his colleagues visited the wealthy patron Otto Kahn in his Wall Street brokerage, a pilgrimage that resulted in their rental of Kahn's Garrick Theatre at reduced rates (only to be collected if they could afford to pay—and they always paid).[85] In 1923 Kahn was instrumental in raising over a half million dollars to build the million dollar Guild Theatre, whose Italianate design, beamed ceiling, and "expensive Gobelin tapestries" amounted to what one theatre historian terms a "damning tastefulness"[86] (Figure 14). Governor Alfred E. Smith presided over the cornerstone ceremonies in late 1924, and a few

Figure 15. Guild Theatre conference. *Left to right*: Theresa Helburn, Rouben Mamoulian, Lawrence Langner, and Richard Rodgers. Acme photograph, 1945. Yale Collection of American Literature Photographs, Beinecke Rare Book and Manuscript Library, Yale University. The press release caption affixed to the photograph describes this space as a "baronial setting."

months later President Calvin Coolidge "pressed a button in Washington that tinkled a bell in New York," a signal that raised the curtain on the Guild Theatre's first production.[87]

In his history of the Guild's first decade, Walter Prichard Eaton lists straightaway the prestigious credentials of each manager, and the managers themselves considered the Guild as a university whose mission was to instruct "intelligent" audiences in their consumption of drama (Figure 15). Eaton, an articulate spokesman for the Guild, became a professor in the Yale Drama School in 1933. The Guild's experiment in tastemaking paid off; in 1929 they had 60,000 subscribers and forecast a million dollar sale "in the near future."

While the Guild considered its cultural program to be "intellectual," to offer "the public" the "best drama of its time," critics on the Left (as did De Voto) viewed its operation as "unabashedly commercial" and its productions as beyond the means of the working poor.[88] Harold Clurman's narrative about the Group Theatre, *The Fervent Years* (1945), contains some of the most astute social observations about the Guild and its audience. (Clurman approached Theresa Helburn the second time he went to see O'Neill's *Strange Interlude* and was soon after hired as a play-reader. The Guild encouraged Clurman, Cheryl Crawford, and Lee Strasberg to organize the Group as an experimental unit in 1929.) The Board of Managers, Clurman wrote, possessed a "merchant sense" and bore a "collegiate stamp" (he himself had studied at Columbia and the Sorbonne). He portrayed the Guild as the most exclusive department store of the theatre world, "set[ting] the plays out in the shop window for as many customers as possible to buy."[89] (Lee Simonson, in fact, designed displays for posh department stores as well as sets for the Guild.)[90] Clurman characterized the Guild's subscribers as "middle class" and disparaged its productions for their "middle-class stuffiness." He felt that the Guild's productions of O'Neill's plays came across as "decorative and fake-impressive."[91]

The class cachet of the Guild was certainly one dimension of its appeal for many. The actors in *Strange Interlude*, as in many of the Guild's productions, delivered their lines with what has been called "pseudo-British stage speech."[92] Reviews of the premiere of *Strange Interlude* took on the aspect of society columns as they reported that the financier Otto Kahn and the internationally eminent theatre director Max Reinhardt had changed into evening clothes during the supper intermission.[93]

Through its sophisticated, cosmopolitan, and tasteful productions, the Guild not only challenged the traditional commercial entertainment that had prevailed on Broadway, it helped *establish* what probably was a primarily university-trained, white-collar audience that sought "adult" art and culture, not merely amusement, at the theatre. The formation of just such an audience was the trend in the 1920s. Institutions such as the Literary Guild and the Book-of-the-Month Club also tapped a "middlebrow" readership by repackaging contemporary literature for subscribers.[94]

The Guild's offerings—like its subscribers—ranged from "middlebrow" to "highbrow." Subscribers who attended O'Neill's Guild plays no doubt often brought with them tastes shaped by colleges, by magazines such as *The American Mercury*, *The Atlantic*, *Vanity Fair*, and *The Dial*, by popular yet "serious" authors like Sherwood Anderson,[95] by museums (and upscale department stores), and by learned reviewers like Brooks Atkinson, who applauded the Guild's "civilized taste." As Atkinson observed, once Al Jolson's *Jazz Singer*, the first "talkie," appeared in 1927, the theatre had to reassess how popular it could afford to be: "It charges high prices. It cultivates an exclusive attitude. . . . the superiority that comes from the impact of mind, the sting of emotion, the daintiness of artistry or even the glamour of fashion should be the modern theatre's stock in trade."[96] The establishment of the Pulitzer Prize in drama in 1917 also conferred some expectation of cultural seriousness upon the New York theatre.

The Guild's Board of Managers decided that psychological discourse was an expression of the modern appropriate for their fast-growing "public." After staying up most of the night to read O'Neill's draft of *Strange Interlude*, Langner excitedly wrote his colleagues that O'Neill's "poetry of the unconscious" and use of "the science of the new psychology" constituted "the next step forward in playwrighting." He expressed his admiration through the discourse of depth: "This play contains in it more deep knowledge of the dark corners of the human mind than anything that has ever been written before." By the mid-1920s depth psychology had attained stable value as cultural capital within O'Neill's class: "One thing we can never lose by such a course," Langner's letter guaranteed, "—our prestige and our self-respect."[97] *Strange Interlude* proved to be an exceptionally profitable investment. O'Neill's moneymaker not only allowed the Guild to consolidate its competitive position in relation to commercial theatres (the Guild simultaneously mounted four successful plays in four Broadway theatres), the play's popularity motivated the Guild to expand its operation to the road. The Guild staged depth in Chicago, Philadelphia, Quincy (O'Neill's play was banned in Boston), Baltimore, Pittsburgh, Cleveland, Washington, Detroit, Cincinnati, and St. Louis. Lynn Fontanne's acclaimed portrayal of Nina Leeds lent great sophistication and glamour to the notion of a feminine psychological self with savage impulses. Photos of the British actress in fashionable evening dress appeared not only in seemingly countless Theatre Guild press releases but in advertisements for cosmetics and other products.[98]

When *Strange Interlude* was banned by Boston's mayor, the ensuing uproar made headlines in many cities. Helburn and Langner, along with Walter Prichard Eaton, sought to mobilize Boston's 12,000 Guild subscribers into a political group on behalf of the play. They formed a "protest committee" and garnered the support of "many prominent citizens."[99] In rebuttal to Boston ministers, who charged that the play's references to abortion and incest were obscene, Eaton defended *Strange Interlude* on the basis of its modernist and therapeutic exploration of depth. "O'Neill, one of our moderns, takes the lid off the cellar of life

which we have been afraid to look into and says 'Here are certain instincts which human beings "have." ' "[100] Eaton's representation of
modernism as psychosexual candor was no doubt a factor in selling
tickets when the show went on in nearby Quincy. The battle in Boston
was a tussle between two ideologies: an older nineteenth-century bourgeois morality and a modern notion of the bourgeois psychological self.
Eaton added confidently that O'Neill's play was "striving to find a new
morality for the new world."[101] The "new world" of the Theatre Guild
was largely the world of the new professional-managerial class.

What Michel Foucault observes in the nineteenth-century middle
class is explicit in Eaton's pop modernist defense: "The task of truth was
now linked to the challenging of taboos."[102] The toppling of taboos was
again the critical thrust a year later in Helburn's New York *World*
debate with John S. Sumner, Secretary of the New York Society for the
Suppression of Vice. Helburn sees the denial of modern concepts of
depth as both unhealthy and uncultured: "Why is it that in an age
when physicians and psychologists have brought us complete evidence
and proof that taboos on sex, that shame and sex-suppression are im-
mensely injurious to spiritual and mental health, people who say they
are fighting for humanity's welfare still insist on such taboos and such
suppression?"[103] By implication, if subscribers were meant to subscribe
to the Theatre Guild's plush staging of culture and of class, they were
also meant to subscribe to its staging of depth, as exemplified by plays
like *Strange Interlude*.

O'Neill's taboo-breaking psychological drama is one cultural sign of a
shift from nineteenth-century sentimental middle-class ideologies of
selfhood that emerge from a producer culture of small entrepreneurs to
more "psychological" professional-managerial-class ideologies of selfhood that contributed to the establishment of the twentieth-century
liberal-corporate order and consumer culture. Describing the effects
this social transformation had on the personal life of early-twentieth-
century professionals, historian Jackson Lears writes that anxieties
about job specialization, about individual autonomy within the corporate order, and about mass culture shook the faith of professionals
and managers in the nineteenth-century religion of "self-made manhood."[104] Uneasy about their endangered individuality, Lears argues,
professional culture producers of the 1910s and 1920s—advertisers,
writers, critics—helped usher in a new "therapeutic" consumer culture

and psychological manhood that revived and refashioned their individuality by replacing their older confidence in self-making with a modernized faith in the new gospel of self-fulfillment, gratification, and release.[105] Nineteen-twenties' advertisements in *Vanity Fair* that made the purchase of gleaming Cadillacs seem life-enhancing, glamorous, and desirable, and plays like *Strange Interlude* that made taboo topics like incestuous impulses seem fascinating and deep, in different ways purveyed this modern "gospel" of therapeutic release.

In his recent study of several turn-of-the-century magazines that helped form the ideologies of the professional-managerial class, Richard Ohmann points out that the "therapeutic worldview" Lears finds prominent in the 1920s "is barely discernible in the mass magazines of the late 1890s" (*McClure's, Cosmopolitan, Munsey's*). These magazines promoted confidence, optimism, self-control, and the modern.[106] Yet in the same period, as Tom Lutz argues, the Protestant middle class was beginning to encode nervousness as "neurasthenia": a disorder understood as white-collar malaise (requiring rest cures) and as a sign of subjective depth (Catholics, blacks, and the working class were not deemed capable of being neurasthenic).[107] Charlotte Perkins Gilman's "The Yellow Wallpaper" (1892), a feminist tale about a neurasthenic woman, gives evidence of Lutz's thesis, but its initial reception bears out what Ohmann describes as the "daytime mood" of professional-managerial-class magazines. H. E. Scudder, the mortified *Atlantic Monthly* editor who first read Gilman's manuscript, rejected it and wrote to her: "I could not forgive myself if I made others as miserable as I have made myself!"[108] By contrast, the Theatre Guild of 1927 received O'Neill's *Strange Interlude*—which dramatized the neuroses of Nina Leeds for nine acts—as full of "deep knowledge" and of unquestionable appeal to its "public." The Guild made a shrewd economic and cultural investment by purchasing O'Neill's psychological stock: times had changed.[109]

Philip Rieff has characterized the shift from the renunciatory "moral demand system" that defined the identity of the old entrepreneurial middle class to the modern corporate ethos of consumer "release" as a transition from ascetic selfhood to psychotherapeutic selfhood.[110] Giving historical concreteness to Rieff's outline, the historian Warren Susman has examined this cultural transformation as a shift from the nineteenth century's producer culture of character (expressing morality, self-denial, self-sacrifice, the work ethic, the wish to be respected) to a consumer culture of personality (promoting release, self-realization, self-gratification, consumption, the desire to be liked). But while the popular how-to-influence-others advice literature of Bruce Barton and Dale Carnegie cited by Susman provides convincing evidence that twentieth-century white-collar workers cultivated personality (to be magnetic, attractive, masterful, creative), the plays of O'Neill and the publications of pop psychologists also suggest that the therapeutic discourse of depth arose to assist the professional-managerial class in negotiating or in adjusting itself to the contradictions, pressures, and standardization of advanced corporate capitalism.[111]

Historically, it is understandable that *two* prominent brands of pop psychology—behaviorism and depth psychology—arose to equip the professional-managerial class with its very different "tools of individuality."[112] Behaviorism, popularized by John Broadus Watson, helped usher in corporate society by teaching managers approaches to psychological engineering that would aid them in shaping the consciousness of supervisors, workers, salesmen, and consumers. This "psycho-technology"[113] stressed the control of surfaces (impression management), habits, and desires.[114] Watson, who was O'Neill's contemporary, left academia for a lucrative career as an advertising executive and a pop psychologist, and he defined individual meaningfulness as success in selling oneself, in managing others, and in remodeling one's self.[115] O'Neill's dramas of psychological, spiritual, and familial conflict, by contrast, addressed members of his social class who may have felt overly managed by "surface" meaningfulness. O'Neill's plays fortified their faith in the existence of a complex, contradictory, and dramatic psychological individuality whose depth never could be fully scripted or fathomed by corporate America.

Members of the professional-managerial class often found themselves on stage as characters in O'Neill's plays of the 1920s. Depth is precisely what Marco Polo lacks in *Marco Millions* (1927). Although his exploits take place in the thirteenth century, Marco is a composite of the nineteenth-century entrepreneur and the modern promoter of corporate bureaucracy. In his capacity as the departing mayor of Yang-Chau, he boasts to Kublai Kaan, ruler of China: "I've appointed five hundred committees to carry on my work" (2:426). Though he is successful at accumulating profits, he is a failure at writing poetry, which he declares is "all stupid anyway" (2:397). Marco again exhibits his superficiality to Kukachin, the Kaan's daughter, when she informs him that dancers and actors will perform aboard their ship: "There's nothing better than to sit down in a good seat at a good play after a good day's work in which you know you've accomplished something, and after you've had a good dinner, and just take it easy and enjoy a good wholesome thrill or a good laugh and get your mind off serious things until it's time to go to bed" (2:431). Here O'Neill satirized what one critic in 1915 termed "the Tired Business Man or Woman" who only went to plays for diversion.[116]

To clinch the point of his satire, lest the white-collar theatregoers of 1928 somehow "repress" its target, at the conclusion of the play O'Neill positioned Marco (in costume) in a front row seat so that members of the audience would see him exit *"looking a bit sleepy, a trifle puzzled, and not a little irritated as his thoughts, in spite of himself, cling for a passing moment to the play just ended."* By the time he reaches the lobby, *"his face begins to clear of all disturbing memories of what had happened on the stage."* Once outside he enters a waiting limousine, *"with a satisfied sigh at the sheer comfort of it all"* (2:467).

The representative of spiritual depth in the play is Kublai Kaan. He too is a manager—of a vast empire. It is the spiritual poverty of Marco's capitalist personality that "disgusts" the Kaan (as it did O'Neill, who revised his play at his thirty-acre Connecticut estate): "He has not even a mortal soul, he has only an acquisitive instinct" (2:420). Although Kublai Kaan recoils from Marco's crass materialism, his spiritual critique never really circles back to interrogate the authority of his own exalted position as empire manager. The problem with Marco's vacuous capitalism is not structural—who gets to be rich, who is kept poor—as much as it is spiritual and emotional. By implication, the Guild was advising the tired businessmen and businesswomen in its audience *not* to act like the shallow Marco Polo, but to act more sophisticated. The fact that Alfred Lunt, Lynn Fontanne's husband and one of Broadway's more polished actors, played Marco (an utter lout when it comes to emotional relations) and that reviewers thought he was miscast, probably underscored this point.[117] *Marco Millions* seeks to convert the Theatre Guild's materialistic professionals, not to specific social reforms, but to the gospel of depth and culture.

O'Neill's *Great God Brown*, produced by the Triumvirate in 1926, also subjects the professional-managerial class to a depth critique. As in *Marco Millions*, O'Neill pays some attention to matters of class in developing this critique. Thus the library of William Brown, professionally trained architect, bespeaks *"prosperous, bourgeois culture"* (2:506). Dion Anthony, the creative draftsman who lacks Brown's professional credentials, views his labor—as a salaried employee—as alienated:

"[Brown has] piled on layers of protective fat, but vaguely, deeply he feels at his heart the gnawing of a doubt! And I'm interested in that germ which wiggles like a question mark of insecurity in his blood, because of the creative life Brown's stolen from me!" On one level O'Neill is here articulating the aims of his own therapeutic theatre, which seeks to pierce the "protective fat" of professionals, managers, and bureaucrats, and to nourish "that germ which wriggles like a question mark of insecurity in [their] blood" (2:508). The state capitol, designed by Brown only after he has donned Dion Anthony's mask, appears on the surface "to possess a pure common-sense, a fat-bellied finality, as dignified as the suspenders of an assemblyman!" (2:524). But its irony, as Brown (having doffed the mask) announces to the bourgeois state capitol committee, communicates something else altogether: "You damn fools! Can't you see this is an insult—a terrible, blasphemous insult!—that this embittered failure Anthony is hurling in the teeth of our success—an insult to you, to me, to you, Margaret—and to Almighty God!" (2:528).

The key word in Brown's outburst is God. Here O'Neill takes his cue from Friedrich Nietzsche, who attributed modern "man's" sense of himself as "weightless" to his realization that God is dead.[118] Dion Anthony's problem is not really his exploitation by the capitalist "god" (his employer, the "Great God Brown"), it is modernity and its attendant spiritual malaise. Dion is too "deep," too disillusioned, and too plagued by self-doubt to either endure the superficiality of modernity or subscribe to conventional notions of what constitutes successful "self"-making. Underneath the young Dion's mask we see a face that is *"shrinking, shy and gentle, full of a deep sadness"* (2:479). The audiences attending performances of O'Neill's *Great God Brown* come away not having focused on the practical necessity for masks—and a split self—as a historical manifestation of the transformation of work. Rather, they are generally led to think about masks in more universal, pop psychological, and pop modernist terms—as a requisite armor that hides our need for others, as barriers to authentic intimacy, and as that which others may fall in love with or envy. "Why was I born without a skin, O God," cries Dion, "that I must wear armor in order to touch or to be touched?" (2:480).

But when Brown, the representative of the shallow professional class, puts on Dion's mask, he transforms Dion's angst into a parody of depth (resulting in a domestic softening of Dion's hard-edged cynicism that Dion's own wife and children find appealing). Perhaps this was the same effect O'Neill expected his portrayal of depth would have on the professionals and managers who consumed his plays and tried to wear his depth masks. O'Neill's critique, unlike socialist or anarchist critiques that highlight conflicting class interests, is one the more sophisticated, theatre-going members of the 1920s professional-managerial class seemed willing to entertain. O'Neill *permitted* them to acknowledge that their social roles and material aspirations were superficial—in certain terms. Brown's message for this social class at the play's climax is not conventionally radical—such as, the modern capitalist rationalization of the workplace produces a split, alienated self—but something like a parody of their anxious quest for pseudo-spiritual depth: "Sssh! This is Daddy's secret for today: Man is born broken. He lives by mending. The grace of God is glue!" (2:528). Although O'Neill may be parodying the "inspirational" "bedtime" story that the "grace of God is glue," his play still seems to posit "man's" "broken" nature as a natural or cosmic explanation for professional-managerial-class angst. The complexity of *The Great God Brown* is in its contradictory tendency to leave members of its audience both with the idea that they may not be deep enough and also with the thought that what they take to be depth is just a pompous mask—a molded surface—which in reality mocks them as "Great God" Browns.

In some respects O'Neill's *Days Without End* (1933) also seems to be about a professional-managerial-class self torn and deadened by alienating labor. John Loving is played by two actors—John, constantly wavering between Catholic faith and disbelief (like O'Neill himself, a lapsed Catholic), and Loving, the unloving, cynical advocate of atheism and distrust. Act 1, which shows John Loving surreptitiously writing a novel in his office, suggests that his office work somehow relates to his experience of himself as double: "*There is a knock on the door at rear. John immediately pretends to be writing. At the same time his features automatically assume the meaninglessly affable expression which is the American business man's welcoming poker face. Loving sits motionlessly regarding him with scornful eyes*" (3:115).

But O'Neill does not develop the alienation theme. As in the case of Dion Anthony, John Loving's malaise is mainly spiritual and derives from secular modernity. Within the framework of this ideology, the Depression is seen not chiefly as a socioeconomic contradiction or a political problem, but as a spiritual dilemma and challenge for individuals. "[America] has lost all meaning for [Americans] except as a pig-wallow," John argues. "They explain away their spiritual cowardice by whining that the time for individualism is past, when it is their courage to possess their own souls which is dead—and stinking!" (3:158). The deep explanation for the professional-managerial class's deadened self, then, hinges on spiritual self-critique and an acknowledgment of unexpressed individualism.

Paradoxically, the mass-cultural discourse of depth that offered a highly personal, therapeutic "cure" for anxieties about lost individuality, shallowness, and corporate standardization was itself predicated on the assumption of standardization. *Strange Interlude* promotes the idea that generic desire dominates us all—even professionals.[119] O'Neill's stage directions inform us that Darrell, the neurologist who falls in love with Nina, his patient, *"has come to consider himself as immune to love through his scientific understanding of its real sexual nature"* (2:661). Sam Evans assures Marsden that Darrell is "a dyed-in-the-wool doc" who would not get "close to anyone" (2:659). Yet this seasoned professional pants after Nina (Evans's wife) for the remaining six acts. "*Under the cultural veneer*, all human beings are essentially alike," affirmed one pop psychologist in 1922.[120] Psychological discourse overwhelms even the discourse of professionalism.

Taking the opposite view, Susan Glaspell and George Cram Cook's *Suppressed Desires* (1915), the first play performed by the Provincetown Players, sees the standardizing tendencies of psychoanalysis as a cultural oddity rather than a universal truth to be accepted. The play satirizes psychoanalysis as a "radical" fad among bohemian professionals in Greenwich Village. It dramatizes the social effects that vocabulary like "subconscious mind," "complex," and "inhibited" can have on one's experience of self and suggests that such terms were becoming embedded in a white-collar idiom.

By 1915 psychoanalysis already had been accepted by Greenwich Villagers as a distinctly radical discourse of liberation. Henrietta, *Suppressed Desire's* devout disciple of psychoanalysis, "wears radical clothes" (235).[121] The authors imply that psychoanalysis makes up the most stylish outfit in her radical wardrobe. They also suggest that psychoanalysis is a "radical" commodity purchased by the more "liberated" members of the professional-managerial class. Henrietta and her husband Steve, an ironical doubter of psychoanalysis, live in a flat overlooking Washington Square arch. Steve, an architect, pokes fun at how "neurotic" his worktable has become: "Psychoanalysis. My work-table groans with it. Books by Freud; the new Messiah; books by Jung, the new St. Paul; the Psychoanalytical Review—book numbers two-fifty per" (240).

Through Mabel, Henrietta's unsophisticated sister, Glaspell and Cook parody how their audience gets drawn into this imagining of the self. Mabel, who is unfamiliar with psychoanalysis, inquires: "It's something about the war, isn't it?" "Not that kind of war," Steve replies. She then asks if it is perhaps "the name of a new explosive." Steve quips: "It is" (238). Glaspell and Cook see psychoanalytic texts as prescriptive—not unlike conduct books. With the fervor of an evangelist, Henrietta attempts to install a new type of common sense in her sister based on the belief that one's hidden and forbidden desires are all-controlling: "The forbidden impulse is there full of energy which has simply got to do something. It breaks into your consciousness in disguise, masks itself in dreams, makes all sorts of trouble. In extreme cases it drives you insane" (241).[122] Repression is understood not only as that which can disturb the equilibrium of professionals, but as that which *should* do so. Only when Henrietta's psychoanalyst diagnoses Steve as in need of a divorce does Henrietta decide that, after all, psychoanalysis and the depth it confers is a form of interior decorating they can live more happily without.

Suppressed Desires is not what O'Neill in the 1920s would categorize as deep; it is neither psychological drama nor familial tragedy. Rather than dramatizing ambivalence, repression, or oedipal conflicts as revelations of the essential "human condition" underlying the taboos of culture, Glaspell and Cook focus their parody on the class and gender context in which the psychological assumptions undergirding O'Neill's notions of depth, drama, and tragedy were beginning to become stylish. The playwrights seek to distance their audience from how the professional-managerial-class couple imagines the self, its problems, its solutions, and its "radicalism."[123]

Joseph Freeman's *American Testament* (1936) testifies to the powerful cultural influence of the psychoanalytic terminology that *Suppressed Desires* satirized in 1915. Commenting on how New York intellectuals of the 1920s found themselves enmeshed in the web of a new language, a new mode of conversing about selfhood, and a new kind of self-monitoring, Freeman's own somewhat ambiguous and ambivalent stance toward psychoanalytic authority—does psychoanalysis produce or does it discover a hidden self—is evident:

We began to have alarming dreams, or perhaps, as the Freudians might say, we stopped repressing our dreams and became conscious of them. We talked psychoanalysis all day long; we analyzed each other's dreams, fantasies and slips of the tongue. . . . New fears developed. . . . we suffered from various "complexes." We concluded in turn that we were extroverts, introverts, schizophrenics, paranoiacs and victims of dementia praecox.[124]

Strange Interlude also was credited with having a compellingly disruptive power, so much so that one reviewer suggested the play's revelations would induce members of the audience to emerge from the theatre—like holy converts—"gleeful to blurt out disastrous opinions and long-guarded, brutal facts. Count that among its effects—and go armed."[125]

In the 1910s and early 1920s, articles on psychoanalysis for the "educated layman" appeared in professional-managerial-class cultural magazines like *Forum, McClure's, Century, The Dial, The Nation,* and *Vanity Fair.* Articles in these magazines suggest that the appeal psychoanalysis held for professionals was both its scientific or professional jargon and its focus on the individual as the titillating site of deep psychological mystery. Thus in "Speaking of Psycho-Analysis: The New Boon for Dinner Table Conversationalists" (1915), published in *Vanity Fair,* Floyd Dell, at his half-mocking debonair best, endorses psychoanalysis for making available "the most charmingly recondite technical vocabulary ever invented." Psychoanalysis allows us to indulge in "new extremes of frankness in regard to ourselves . . . [with] an air of heavy and pedantic importance." Such articles held out the hope that the professionals and managers of the 1910s and 1920s who experienced what Lears called "weightlessness" in their corporate routine could rediscover and revivify their individual significance by confessing the psychological self "with absolute sincerity."[126]

James Oppenheim, who had been editor of the *Seven Arts* (a distinguished "little magazine" which published O'Neill's *In the Zone* and his short story "Tomorrow" in 1917) and whose play *Night* (1917) was produced by the Provincetown Players, contributed *Behind Your Front* (1928) to the pop psychology boom. His book (a twentieth-century psychological version of the nineteenth century's phrenological advice book) celebrates both the exhilarating and "disconcerting" aspects of "making a voyage of discovery in the magical land which each of us calls

'Myself.' "[127] O'Neill makes this "behind your front" idea dramatic for Theatre Guild audiences in *Mourning Becomes Electra*. Ezra Mannon comes across as a cold, repressed entrepreneur, but his surprising confession to Christine, his disaffected wife, discloses the dominance of desires his work has not wholly sublimated. Missing Christine's affection, Ezra devoted himself to "Vinnie [Lavinia], but a daughter's not a wife. Then I made up my mind I'd do my work in the world and leave you alone in your life and not care. That's why the shipping wasn't enough—why I became a judge and a major and such vain truck, and why folks in town look on me as so able! Ha! Able for what? Not for what I wanted most in Life! Not for your love!" (2:939). The workplace self is the front or the mask behind which resides one's real depth, which is wholly personal, private, and—as psychoanalysts define it— sexual.

The Nietzschian word O'Neill (and other intellectuals) used to describe the problem with America in 1921—two years after the Red Purge of Communists, Socialists, and anarchists—was "optimism," not capitalism.[128] This critique of optimism was allied to psychoanalytic-inspired denouncements of "puritanism." Psychological radicalism depicted the nineteenth century not as the era of entrepreneurial capitalist accumulation, but as the age of puritanical repression. By relabeling nineteenth-century entrepreneurs puritans, psychological "radicals" shifted the critique of an outmoded phase of capitalism to psychosexual grounds.[129] O'Neill's portrait of Ezra Mannon, the repressed Civil War puritan whose "front" begins to crack in *Mourning*, has its basis in this concept of nineteenth-century history and is in effect a psychological diagnosis of America's business optimism. The real significance ascribed to Mannon is not his superficial quest for "mammon"—his "front"—but the hidden, desiring self that helps us reinterpret his acquisitiveness as a "neurotic" symptom: *"He keeps talking in his abrupt sentences, as if he were trying to cover up some hidden uneasiness"* (2:932).

As *Suppressed Desires* and the Theatre Guild's battle with Boston's censors suggest, the preoccupation of the professional-managerial class with psychological selfhood becomes its preferred brand of radicalism— insurrection against the cultural censorship of the "inner drama" of the "self." Part of the considerable ideological attraction psychoanalysis held for this social class in the 1910s and 1920s was that, as Frederick J.

Hoffman put it, one's "inner drama" served as "an excellent substitute for social and economic motives in explaining social behavior."[130] Psychological discourse was by no means uncritical of culture; yet it reclassified culture as prohibitions, conventions, or sometimes a vague "materialism" that inhibited the self.[131] Thus psychological discourse enabled its adherents to reinvent culture in rather narrow terms as that which imposed taboos on the desiring individual. Hence professionals and managers, like the members of all other classes, suffered psychological strain as hapless victims of culture.[132]

A romanticization of the hidden "primitive" individual was a key feature of the psychological recategorization of culture-as-repression. The adult's unconscious is forever young[133] and forever "savage." Psychological disorders "indicate a lack of coordination between the primitive and cultural components of our nature," wrote William J. Fielding in *The Caveman Within Us* (1922): "They represent a struggle between the Caveman and the Socialized Being."[134] The pop psychological notion that we are all caged "hairy apes" who never quite "belong" in culture (to use O'Neill's words) occasioned the uneasiness that, as one observer noted, "psychoanalysis proposes to strip off the veneer of civilization and reveal human beings to be fundamentally a mass of primitive impulses not so different from the rest of the untamed animal world."[135]

Yet *Strange Interlude*, interestingly, suggests that the primitive was being reencoded as a psychological sign of civilization or class. To be sophisticated, in other words, is to know you harbor a caveman or cavewoman (or both) within you. Professor Leeds, "(*thinking savagely*)," confesses to himself: "I hope Gordon is in hell!" (2:647). The more savage the thought, the deeper, truer, or more real it seems. In 1931, while preparing for the Theatre Guild's production of *Mourning Becomes Electra*, O'Neill explained to Brooks Atkinson that such assumptions were fundamental to the modernization of American drama: "What I do now [in my plays] is the struggle of the primitive to emerge in more complicated people, the drama of its thwarted, warped, revengeful, hidden emerging."[136]

This psychological drama of the "struggle of the primitive" has ideological links to bourgeois anxieties about class struggle. The Victorian ethnography Freud relied on for his anthropological speculations represented "primitives" as lower than the bourgeoisie on the evolutionary "scale of intellectual and moral development" and as "governed more by impulse." These ethnographers often pointed to local "primitives" or "savages" in Victorian society, such as working-class men and women. The language of primitivism offered ethnographers and their readers a discourse whereby threatening working-class "savages" could be recast as instinctually dangerous and in urgent need of government by the more rational and intellectual bourgeoisie.[137] Pop psychologists not only resignified the primitive as a sign of depth (following Freud's lead in *Totem and Taboo*), they also deployed the primitive to suggest that the "hairy apes" of the working class rebel for purely instinctual reasons—as William J. Fielding's chapter "The Caveman Rebels" makes plain.[138] O'Neill's *Hairy Ape* (which I will discuss at length in Chapter 3) and *Strange Interlude* exemplify the very different ideological uses to which the psychological discourse of primitivism was put in the "psychological" definition of classes.[139]

O'Neill's *Welded* dramatizes how psychological discourse and its notion of culture-as-repression could operate to obfuscate class distinctions on behalf of the professional-managerial class. Jealous of his wife Eleanor and their friend John, Michael Cape, a successful playwright, leaves home in a rage to revenge himself on his spouse by hiring a prostitute designated in the script as "Woman." Woman refuses to take Michael's psychological self-absorption seriously, accusing him of "lappin' up some bum hooch," "dopin' up on coke," and, worst of all, "talk[ing] nutty" (2:261). Finally she deduces that the playwright has positioned her as a sort of marriage counselor; but she offers him advice out of sync with what her client might have heard from accredited psychological experts: "Ferget it. It's easy to ferget—when you got to" (2:265). Woman does not have the status, leisure, or education to comprehend or appreciate the psychological idea that the "past is present." Her flagrant violation of professional-managerial-class psychological common sense is too savage for the playwright's fragile and "complicated" emotional state to endure, and he retorts: "(*very pale—stammering*) You—you make life despicable." The bemused prostitute asks why he would want to say such "rotten things" to her and demands that he take his "lousy coin and beat it" (2:265). Her refusal to confer depth on Michael's subjectivity-in-turmoil exhibits his psychological self-fascination as a class (and gender) preoccupation rather than a revelation of depth.

O'Neill, perhaps out of sympathy for his befuddled playwright, displaces the prostitute's understated class critique by enmeshing her in

Michael's psychological web of significance. When Woman accepts Michael's payment, at last, he inquires about her pimp, and whether she would be beaten upon failing to produce no "coin" in the morning. "Sure," she replies, "(*then suddenly grinning*) Maybe he'll beat me anyway—just for the fun of it?" Once she has confessed this, Michael knows he has her, but circles round his prey one more time just to make sure. "But you love him, don't you?" he probes, asking her to explain her grin. She tells him: "I was thinkin' of the whole game. It's funny, ain't it?" Michael seizes the chance to define her "it": "(*slowly*) You mean—life?" (2:266). "Sure," she admits. "You got to loin to like it!" Hence the prostitute, with her kinky, masochistic grin, has stepped into the therapeutic logic of the discourse of depth: "Yes! That's it! That's exactly it!" Michael exclaims. "That goes deeper than wisdom. To learn to love life—to accept it and be exalted—that's the one faith left to us!" (2:267).

"Life" transcends surface distinctions like class differences. Michael's encounter with Woman confirms the therapeutic common sense that comforts members of his social class: *We've all got problems.* Even a benighted working-class "whore" can be made sense of by Michael's "nutty" discourse. This is precisely the universalizing therapeutic drama that theatre producer Arthur Hopkins prescribed a few years later in *How's Your Second Act?*: "It would be a more constructive drama that showed that heartaches are heartaches in the Avenue or in the Bowery, and that love and trouble and weakness and strength are pretty much common to all kinds of people, and that no one in the world has a monopoly of anything, especially trouble."[140] The discourse of depth assures us that we're all in trouble because we all have the same (standardized) desires, and because our desires are frustrated not so much by class-specific inequalities (superficial categories), but by the prohibitions of culture and the conflicts of "life." This is the political message of *Welded.* O'Neill's play offers "psychic ventilation"; but more subtly its universalizing common sense provides ideological ventilation for a professional-managerial class in training to fret more about its tabooed, primitive depths than the "savages" it helps dominate. Insofar as this class was itself ruled by a ruling class, the discourse of depth enabled it to translate its own domination, vulnerability, or, in Barbara Ehrenreich's terms, "fear of falling," as simply *malaise.* Thus pop psychological depth was assigned considerable literary, aesthetic, and dramatic value at a moment when it did significant ideological work for the professional-managerial class.

The Psychological as a Political and Historical Category

The advertisement for Tridon's *Psychoanalysis and Love* (Truth Publishing Co.) in the September 1922 *Liberator* and O'Neill's *Desire Under the Elms,* produced three years later, have similar "truth" agendas. Indeed, the former reads almost like a description of what one can expect to find in the latter: "[Tridon] shows part of what love is, why there are many different kinds of love; just what the characteristics about certain types of people attract others and why; why love sometimes expresses itself in abnormal ways; what is behind the mask of modesty. . . . He explains why love often drives people to the most extreme acts; why it sometimes leads to sensational crimes." In the words of the Tridon advertisement, O'Neill's play is "intimate," promises to be of "intense personal interest," and unveils "deep hidden sources of love" that lead to incest and crime. Like the cartoon caveman and cavewoman featured in Tridon's ad, *Desire Under the Elms* purveys the idea of "primitive" psychological nature (Figure 16).

The principal theme of *Desire Under the Elms* is "nature owns ye." Abbie tempts Eben, her new stepson: "Hain't the sun strong an' hot? Ye kin feel it burnin' into the earth—Nature—makin' thin's grow—bigger 'n' bigger—burnin' inside ye—makin' ye want t'grow—into somethin' else—till ye've jined with it—an' it's your'n—but it owns ye, too—an' makes ye grow bigger—like a tree—like them elums—" (2:342). In case he has somehow missed her come-on, she adds: "Nature'll beat ye, Eben. Ye might's well own up t' it fust 's last" (2:342). Members of the Greenwich Village Theatre audience who felt owned by corporations or more generally dominated by the production of life under capitalism now see that they are possessed by something more elemental, a force originating in their very own depths—desire.

This sexualized notion of self-ownership competes with economic ownership as the focal point of dramatic tension. The play begins with four scenes on the theme of patriarchal economic exploitation: Ephraim Cabot, the "cussed old miser!" (2:326), ruthlessly works his three sons on the farm as cheap labor. Before Ephraim's two oldest sons, Simeon and Peter, abandon this oppression (and repression), they threaten their "primal father" as do Freud's "primal sons" in *Totem and Taboo* (1912– 13): "We're free as Injuns! Lucky we don't skulp ye! . . . An' rape yer new woman!" (2:336).[141] Their new young "Maw," Abbie, has her eye on the Cabot farm before her gaze becomes sexual and shifts to Eben,

Figure 16. Primitive love reigns supreme: an advertisement for André Tridon, *Psychoanalysis and Love*, published in *The Liberator*, September 1922. Beinecke Rare Book and Manuscript Library, Yale University.

the youngest son. "Ye hain't foolin' me a mite," Eben warns Abbie, accusing her of marrying the "cussed old miser" to get her hands on the farm (which Eben claims to have inherited from his mother). But even his accusation of gold-digging is suffused with sexual double meanings: "Ye're aimin' t' swaller up everythin' an' make it your'n. Waal, you'll find I'm a heap sight bigger hunk nor yew kin chew!" (2:342). Desire consumes them. Abbie abandons her original scheme to acquire the farm in order to own and to be owned by her new stepson. Unlike mere capitalist possessiveness, the sexual impulse to own and to be owned confers psychological significance on man and woman.

Ownership, like the discourse of primitivism, is also represented as psychological in *Strange Interlude*. The psychological ownership theme runs throughout the play, but is only labeled such in the penultimate act. In an interior monologue, prompted by Nina's jealousy of her son Gordon's fiancée, Darrell censures Nina's "ownership" (2:788) of her (and his) son. Soon after, he tells Nina directly that she must relinquish "owning people" (2:789). Thinking to himself about her long-lasting emotional ownership of him, he concludes ambivalently: "She'd like to own me again . . . I wish she wouldn't touch me . . . What is this tie of old happiness between our flesh?" (2:791). Within O'Neill's aesthetic of depth, ownership is invested with deep meaning when it is represented as a psychological relation. The pathological dialogue of *Strange Interlude* seems to cultivate a psychological—as opposed to a political, sociological, or historical—response, a perception of self that Oscar Cargill in 1941 saw as important in the shaping of class identity and taste: "If ever a play were designed to tickle the bourgeois palate, this one was."[142]

As I argued in Chapter 1, O'Neill's *More Stately Mansions*—in stark contrast to *Strange Interlude*—can be read in part as the playwright's epic effort to historicize psychological relations within the family. Although the action in *Desire Under the Elms* and *Mourning Becomes Electra* takes place in the mid-nineteenth century, both plays confine history to theatrical backdrop. This pattern corresponds to one traced by V. N. Volosinov, the Russian semiotician, in *Freudianism* (c. late 1920s). Volosinov saw psychoanalysis as fitting into the contemporary trend of bourgeois philosophies that strive "to create a world beyond the social and historical." He argued that the world these philosophers created aimed to signify the sexual as the modern essence of all meaningfulness. This meaningfulness has an ideological task. The idea of the oedipal family, for example, obscures the significance of the bourgeois family's historical and economic position (the "castle and keep of capitalism") by sexualizing it, "as if thereby, it were made newly meaningful": "The father is not the entrepreneur and the son is not his heir—the father is only the mother's lover, and his son his rival!"[143]

O'Neill, ruminating on the incestuous desires staged in *Mourning Becomes Electra*, regarded the oedipal model of the family as "the deepest inner drama."[144] Although critics and reviewers did not articulate the ideological work of this oedipal model—as posited by Volosinov—they nevertheless often took issue with O'Neill, claiming that his oedipal drama was too conscious, unsubtle, overt. Doris Alexander pointed out that O'Neill's dramatization of the oedipus complex was "non-Freudian" in the sense that it lacked "elements of . . . ambivalence and unconsciousness." Sheaffer concurred with her in his view that the incestuous Mannons were "too knowing about themselves and one another. . . . as though these Civil War–era figures had spent time on the analytic couch and could identify the impulses behind their unruly feelings." Alan Reynolds Thompson criticized the trilogy for featuring, not tragedies, but "case histories" with psychoanalytic "marionettes."[145]

None of these critics, with the partial exception of Alexander, attributed O'Neill's schematic characterizations to the cultural phenomenon of 1920s pop psychology. The ideologically "therapeutic" agenda of *Mourning Becomes Electra*, Volosinov might argue, is to extract a Civil War entrepreneurial family from social and economic history and re-signify it within pop psychology, thereby enabling its Theatre Guild audience of 1931 to mask its own class and economic significance as psychosexual.

American socialist intellectuals were developing provocative critiques of psychoanalysis—which complement the arguments of Volosinov—at the same time that pop psychological plays like *The Great God Brown*, *Strange Interlude*, and *Mourning Becomes Electra* were being staged. As early as 1915 the Marxist Louis Fraina (who later took the pen name Lewis Corey) pleaded that Marxism must turn to psychology in order to produce new political agents, and also that psychology itself must be understood as historically and socially conditioned.[146] But it was V. F. Calverton and Samuel Schmalhausen who, in their many anthologies of the late 1920s and early 1930s, and in their *Modern Quarterly* (1924–32), launched the most incisive reappropriation of the category of the psychological from professional psychologists.[147]

Three years after the first performance of *Strange Interlude*, Calverton faulted psychoanalysis for not recognizing how "connected" its historical emergence is "with the economic independence of modern woman, the bankruptcy of the old system of marriage, the decay of the bourgeoisie as a social class . . . [the] sexual revolution [grows] out of the economic background of social struggle." (*Strange Interlude* themes include the ostensibly independent "modern woman," the "bankruptcy" of marriage, and aspects of the moral "decay of the bourgeoisie," but it does not consider "the economic background of social struggle.") In various essays Calverton tried to situate psychoanalysis within a *history* of sexualities, claiming that psychoanalysis lacks "social depth" and that the "pathology of our age" has causes "far deeper" than the narrow psychoanalytic focus on individual problems suggests.[148]

Calverton realized that the individualizing discourse of psychoanalysis, by not coming to terms with its historical and sociological grounding, was engaged in the making not just of psychological but of political subjects. He projected that in the socialist or communist utopia of the future, "sex"—a concept invariably shaped by capitalist relations—

would no longer be assigned the cultural significance of a hermeneutic: "Sex will be neither maximized nor minimized, neither exalted nor degraded, neither conceded nor advertised."[149]

One contributor to the *Modern Quarterly*, Haim Kantorovitch, concentrated his critique on the category of the psychological packaged and sold by the mental health trades. Kantorovitch argued that psychological knowledge was formulated not only to help management rationalize workers and to assist advertising firms in shaping the desires of consumers, but more generally to produce highly "individualistic and subjective" Americans whose preoccupation with the self would make them less likely to imagine collective resistance against the corporate state. White-collar psychology was charged with the important ideological task of making the individualized capitalist self appear both universal and unalterable.[150]

Although Schmalhausen often wrote within the terms provided by psychoanalytic discourse in the late 1920s, he gravitated toward a radical behaviorist conceptualization of depth as a historical, social, and ideological product: "What looks like the play of deep instincts . . . [is] a mere habit formation bolstered up by customs and social pressures and institutionalised assets."[151] Calverton, Schmalhausen, and Kantorovitch all sought to use historical and cultural perspectives to defamiliarize their readers, many of whom (like O'Neill) would have been immersed in an individualizing discourse of depth widely accepted as psychological common sense.

When *Marco Millions* and *Strange Interlude* are read in the context of Calverton and Schmalhausen's efforts to rethink the psychological, it is easier to see that both plays are important historically because, taken together, they focus on the economic and the psychological ways in which the professional-managerial class sought to reproduce itself ideologically as "individuals." *Strange Interlude*, rather than being viewed as a popular masterpiece of modernist literature that explores the timeless "play of deep instincts," should be reread historically (to use Calverton's terms) as a "psychological corollary" to the "economic individualism"[152] that O'Neill overtly criticized in *Marco Millions*. Interestingly, the Guild premiered both plays in January 1928.

There is no doubt that *Strange Interlude* dramatized a modern personal life that was in crisis. Psychoanalytic theory and therapy, Joel Kovel contends, were invented to manage a crisis in which modern forms of work "crippled" the self while the compensatory psychological family "inflated" this self. These crosscurrents produce a self—labeled neurotic—that frantically seeks therapeutic insight from psychology.[153] Curiously, pop psychology, psychoanalysis, and some of O'Neill's plays contributed to the representation of the personal as mainly a subjective phenomenon[154] at the very juncture when sexuality, desire, and individuality had become conspicuously mass-mediated. This mass-cultural subjectivism helped produce Americans who—in the words of Kovel—"interpret[ed] their total alienation as a matter of neurosis."[155]

Where some psychologists and authors perceived depth in this self-in-cultural-crisis, others—like Schmalhausen—saw wreckage. To the extent that O'Neill promoted a discourse of depth rather than an alternative, socially critical discourse of wreckage, we must consider his "writing depth" as having political effects. Just as political playwrights of the 1930s sought to teach members of the working class socialist concepts of consciousness, contradiction, and conflict, O'Neill's pop psychological/pop modernist plays of the 1920s and early 1930s helped equip the workforce of the professional-managerial class to imagine its consciousness, contradictions, and conflicts in particular psychological ways. *Welded, Desire Under the Elms, The Great God Brown, Strange Interlude,* and *Mourning Becomes Electra* are in effect political plays that were (and are) staged in theatres typically attended by members of the professional-managerial class.[156] O'Neill's modernist plays not only staged depth for this class, they taught audiences to wear it as a mask—one that sometimes mocked them.[157]

Thinking about the appeal of O'Neill's plays and his audiences, Lionel Trilling concluded in 1936 that the modern "moral and psychical upheaval of the middle class" made it receptive to O'Neill's work—"it wanted certain of its taboos broken and O'Neill broke them." Trilling goes on to suggest that the "intellectual middle class" constituted O'Neill's audiences and readers of the 1910s and early 1920s, and that the "literate middle class" of the 1920s "caught up" with the intellectual-bohemian interest in O'Neill.[158] This is not to claim, however, that O'Neill's audiences were monolithic, or that the professional-managerial class was (or is) monolithic, or that his admirers' class lines were unambiguous.[159]

If the audiences of the Provincetown Playhouse in the 1910s and early 1920s and of the Greenwich Village Theatre in the mid-1920s included businessmen in pinstripes and millionaires like Otto Kahn, they also occasionally included members of the Hudson Dusters (a gang of hooligans with whom O'Neill liked to get "stinko"), radicals like Emma Goldman, and impecunious but curious college students, like Langston Hughes.[160] Observers' accounts suggest that the greater percentage of the Theatre Guild audiences that attended O'Neill's plays from the late 1920s on probably were what we now term professional-managerial class. However, this class affiliation by no means guaranteed that they would respond to O'Neill's work in only one way. The Theatre Guild's Board of Managers surely had a heightened consciousness of this during its own acrimonious in-house debates (it rejected the first few plays O'Neill sent its way), during its skirmish with Boston's censors and clergy over *Strange Interlude*, and when it reflected on irate reviews, like one from Chicago, that panned *Mourning* as "a smothering, sickening deluge of morbid psychology."[161]

Characters in *Fog* (1914), *Bread and Butter* (1914), and *Marco Millions* belonged to the professional-managerial class, but O'Neill himself—as he makes evident in all three plays—was sure these shallow men had had no interest in contemplating their own depth or anybody else's. One reviewer joked in 1920 that the New York stage can only take tragedies (such as O'Neill's) in "homeopathic doses" because the "tired businessman [must be] saved from . . . gloom in his recreation hours."[162] The next year another critic complained that in O'Neill's "effort to be grim, he approaches dangerously close to the repellent."[163] After seeing a performance of *Beyond the Horizon* (which became a big hit in 1920), James O'Neill placed his nineteenth-century concept of theatre-as-distraction in contention with his son's notion of a therapeutic theatre that riveted the audience's attention on "self": "People come to the theatre to forget their troubles, not to be reminded of them. What are you trying to do—send them home to commit suicide?"[164]

Even professional-managerial-class culture-producers such as George Jean Nathan, a master builder of O'Neill's reputation, sometimes regarded O'Neill's efforts to stage depth as wholly theatrical and superficial—unworthy of the title "drama." In 1929 Nathan wrote in a review that O'Neill's dramatization of "swollen emotion" rendered *Welded* "ineffective and occasionally even absurd," and that it "robbed *Desire Under the Elms* of the slow smoke-curling force which is drama's most vital attribute."[165] While the identifying feature of the professional-managerial class certainly was an ideology of individualism, this class had various and sometimes contradictory ways of living and expressing that ideology. O'Neill's taboo-breaking plays offered members of that class, and members of other classes who attended his plays, a depth that defied the materialistic individualism associated with the American (Marco Polo) businessman, even as O'Neill's conceptions of this depth remained very much within the ideological field of individualism. As we shall see next, O'Neill, perhaps feeling that his individualism (and "originality") as an artist was threatened, had his own bone to pick with the 1920s psychological discourse that helped make his modernist staging of depth possible, profitable, and prestigious.

O'Neill's Critique of Psychological Discourse and *Iceman*

In 1927 O'Neill wrote to Joseph Wood Krutch that he had never "thought" of his *Strange Interlude* characters "in any Freudian sense," and that he was "no great student of psycho-analysis." Although he acknowledged that his play was "full of psycho-analytic ideas," he attributed their origin, not to Freud, but to the "age-old" insight of authors:

> Any artist who was a good psychologist and had had a varied and sensitive experience with life and all sorts of people could have written *Strange Interlude* without ever having heard of Freud, Jung, Adler & Co. This doesn't apply in my case, of course. I'm simply making this statement because it seems to me that there is a tendency now to read psycho-analysis into an author's work where ordinary psychology offers a sufficient explanation—let alone imagination and intuition. All the author's pet thunder will be stolen if it keeps up![166]

What Volosinov viewed as the ideological agenda of Freudianism is discernible in O'Neill's tendency to conceptualize the psychological as outside of historical change. Also discounting the influence of psychoanalysis on *Desire Under the Elms*, he insisted: "Playwrights are either intuitively keen analytical psychologists or they aren't good playwrights. . . . Freud only means certain conjectures and explanations about truths of the emotional past of mankind that every dramatist has clearly sensed ever since real drama began. . . . I respect Freud's work tremendously—but I'm not an addict! Whatever of Freudianism is in *Desire* must have walked in 'through my unconscious.' "[167] The psychology that was well represented in the mass culture and the high culture of the twenties undoubtedly sauntered in through his conscious and unconscious mind.

O'Neill expressed some interest in the theories of behaviorism, and he also attributed his insights into psychology to his knowledge of Irish literature and culture, but his principal brief against psychoanalysis was that the dramatist—his profession—got there first.[168] His wish to distance his art from psychoanalysis was not generally directed at the latter's specific insights. Rather, O'Neill focuses on the professional *authority* psychoanalysis had culturally produced for itself, a fully credentialed "scientific" expertise that by implication makes psychological dramatists seem like unaccredited psychologists who first consult case studies and then dramatize them for the stage (which is precisely what Eric Bentley, in 1962, would suggest that O'Neill had done).[169] Krutch's reviews of *Strange Interlude* in 1928 elaborated the distinction O'Neill hoped to establish in 1927. Where O'Neill's psychological drama achieved its power by exalting emotions as "cosmically important," Freud's psychoanalysis subverts human nature by making emotions seem "petty." As if looking ahead to *Mourning*, Krutch praised O'Neill's tragic neurotics for having "assume[d] the importance of figures in Greek or Elizabethan tragedy."[170]

O'Neill's defensiveness about psychoanalysis and its capacity to steal *his* "pet thunder" also surfaces in a sketch for a play (1930) he never wrote: "Play of the psycho-therapeutist to whom a creative artist— genius or of great talent—man or woman comes in torture and half-pleads, half-challenges to have his devils cast out—the haunting ghosts of his past." The suicidal artist transfers "his horrible bitterness, his blasphemies against life, his sins of lust and cruelty" to the therapist, whom it "breaks." In the concluding scene "the artist has mercy on the doctor and kills him to free him (as he had wished to do with himself) and all his ghosts come back, the ghost of the doctor added."[171]

The therapist cannot withstand the psychological "thunder" sustained by the subjective artist who "half-challenges" him with it. The artist, through the revelation of his disturbances, proves himself even "deeper" than the therapist he destroys. Also noteworthy in this sketch is O'Neill's decision not to use psychoanalytic vocabulary (repression, projection, symptom, oedipus complex, etc.), selecting instead "age-old" terms like "bitterness," "sins," "lust," and "cruelty."[172] Three years later, with the non-"psychological" *Ah, Wilderness!* in mind, O'Neill confessed to Saxe Commins that his "unconscious had been rebelling for a long time against creation in the medium of the modern, involved, complicated, warped & self-poisoned psyche and demanded a counter-statement of simplicity and peace that tragedy troubles but does not poison."[173] In this atypical statement, O'Neill reveals that at times he comprehended his modern "medium" of depth as an aberrant depth rather than as the age-old depth in us all.

O'Neill also turned his critical eye on psychological discourse in *The Iceman Cometh* (1939). Hickey converts[174] Harry Hope's barroom pipe-dreamers into a psychological community, a transformation O'Neill goes to great lengths to dramatize as an abusive exercise of power. I do not wish to suggest that the salesman Hickey be viewed either literally or biographically as a pop psychologist; but there are, notwithstanding, intriguing correspondences between his sales rhetoric and the pronouncements of pop psychologists, like Dr. Louis Bisch, who "sold" the public on being "psychiatric-minded."

"I want neurotics to realize what they *really* are," wrote Bisch with evangelical zeal, "not what others would have them believe they are." Similarly, Hickey advised his barroom "boys and girls": "I know from my own experience it's bitter medicine, facing yourself in the mirror with the old false whiskers off" (3:629). Just as Hickey proselytized on behalf of "honesty is the best policy—honesty with yourself" (3:610), Bisch explained: "You may be puzzled over yourself because you are not thoroughly honest with yourself."[175] Bisch's *Be Glad You're Neurotic* could easily have printed a reassurance like the one Hickey offered the pipe-dreamers who grew increasingly restive with his brand of self-scrutiny: "All I want is to see you happy" (3:616). Seabury's *Unmasking Our Minds* outlines the therapeutic advantages of "look[ing] below the surface at last."[176] By the same token, Hickey represents unmasking as the therapeutic means of freeing oneself "from guilt and lying hopes" (3:680).

He who unmasks others holds power over others. Oppenheim's *Behind Your Front* touted psychological reading as an exercise of power when he predicted that his reader would want to "use this little book as a sort of x-ray on his friends."[177] Hickey's account of his own X-ray sales technique describes equally well what he does in Hope's bar: "It was like a game, sizing people up quick, spotting what their pet pipe dreams were" (3:696). Hickey's "sizing up" eschews reference to the professional psychoanalytic terminology promoted by pop psychology's best-selling salesmen. Isidor Schneider picked up on this in his 1946 review of *Iceman* for the *New Masses*, in which he attributed its "incredible impact" to "the fact that, unlike O'Neill's previous psychoanalytic plays, which were like caricatures in their literal Freudianism, what is applied in *The Iceman Cometh* is an assimilated knowledge that is used deftly and not stuck on like labels."[178] The same can be said of O'Neill's final dramas, *Long Day's Journey* and *A Moon for the Misbegotten* (1943).

Just after completing *Iceman*, O'Neill wrote Macgowan:

> You would find if I did not build up the complete picture of the group as it now is in the first part—the atmosphere of the place, the humour and friendship and human warmth and *deep inner contentment* of the bottom—you would not be so interested in these people and you would find the impact of what follows a lot less profoundly disturbing. You wouldn't feel the same sympathy and understanding for them, or be so moved by what Hickey does to them.[179]

Along the same line, O'Neill's original sketch for the play is based on the motif that "man desperately needs friendships."[180] Hickey employs the language of social cohesion (gang, governor, Old Scout), but in fact disintegrates this community of boozy pipe-dreamers by turning their gaze inward and unmasking their alibis. The unmasking of Hope's hangers-on succeeds by threatening their sense of self-legitimacy and by playing on their feelings of inadequacy. O'Neill shows that this psychological invasion secures its authority by infantalizing the pipe-dreamers. Hickey, bringing to mind psychoanalytic premises about the determinative influence of childhood on adults, repeatedly labels them "kids" or "boys and girls." He shatters community, civility, and sociability by producing (aggressive) psychological subjects.

Larry, stunned by the destructive wake of the salesman's "Reform wave" (3:652), casts forth the saving lifeline of the story: "The lie of a pipe dream is what gives life to the whole misbegotten mad lot of us, drunk or sober" (3:569–70). Even Hickey confirms this when his ruthless unmasking of the others is disclosed as a denial of his hatred for his wife, Evelyn (his "pipe dream"): "Do you suppose I give a damn about life now? Why, you bonehead, I haven't got a single damned lying hope or pipe dream left!" (3:703). Here again, O'Neill-the-dramatist is competing with a psychological discourse premised on the therapeutic and transformative benefits of unmasking. By implication, age-old drama is more humane and sympathetic in its acceptance of the compulsive pipe dreams that enable one to go on living, mad, drunk, or sober. Age-old tragedy is thus deeper than professional psychological discourse because it grasps that denial, in certain ways, can be at once life-sustaining and tragic.[181] "I don't write this as a piece of playwrighting," O'Neill wrote to Macgowan. "*They do it. They have to.* Each of them! In just that way! It is tragically, pitifully important to them to do this! They *must* tell these lies as a first step in taking up life again."[182] This statement is infused with the religious spirit of forgiveness as well as the spirit of hope that one finds in religion, such as the Catholic faith that guided O'Neill as a boy. Pipe dreams bring hope to Hope's bar. As Nietzsche, the philosopher who most influenced O'Neill, once wrote: "The erroneousness of a concept does not for me constitute an objection to it; the question is—to what extent is it advantageous to life."[183]

The binary opposition *Iceman* leaves us with is pipe dreams (the dramatist's depth) versus unmasking (the pop psychologists' depth).[184] Yet O'Neill's early draft notes focus on another theme too, as Virginia Floyd points out: the characters' opening "discourses on anarchism and the corruption of capitalism summarize O'Neill's solid statements: neither 'ism' is able to provide followers with sufficient hope for the present; *as a consequence* they retreat into a world of 'tomorrow' pipe dreams" (emphasis supplied).[185] In an interview he gave during the rehearsals of the Guild production of *Iceman* in 1946, O'Neill implicitly linked pipe dreams to what one might now label the concept of ideology (the American Pipe Dream): "This American Dream stuff gives me a pain. . . . If it exists, as we tell the whole world, why don't we make it work in one small hamlet of the United States?"[186] O'Neill refused to have *Iceman* produced at the outset of World War II because he felt its focus on pipe dreams would be inappropriate for the American war effort, perhaps meaning its propaganda campaign. But O'Neill's final version of his play mutes his disgust with the American Pipe Dream. O'Neill underplays the social reasons for why these fallen pipe-dreamers have no wish to go outside.

Arthur Miller has argued that the new social dramatist "must be an even deeper psychologist than those of the past" by recognizing "the futility of isolating the psychological life of man."[187] O'Neill isolates the psychological life of men and women in the final draft of *Iceman*. Hope's pipe-dreamers live in a psychological space built on the foundation of "swapping lies" (3:699). Within the world of Hope's bar, the "isms" are not the problem; living is, seemingly because "life" universally produces ambivalence that necessitates denial. The denial theme is, by implication, valued as deeper than the social theme of political alienation.[188] Personal pipe dreams are not only defended compassionately as therapeutic substitutes for the practice of unmasking; they also function, albeit less visibly in the play, as therapeutic replacements for a disappointing world in which systemic social change is deemed so impossible that it does not qualify as a serious dramatic issue.

Brecht had no desire to isolate the psychological life of his characters and had little use for the notion that human emotions, by their fixed nature, foreclose the possibility of structural social and political change. "Emotions, instincts, impulses are generally presented as being deeper, more eternal, less easily influenced by society than by ideas," he wrote in 1938, having fled Nazi Germany, "but this is in no way true. The emotions are neither common to all humanity nor incapable of alteration."[189] Brecht understood that the cultural categories through which psychology, the emotions, and subjectivities are organized and produced must be scrutinized as historical and political, and that if we don't recognize these categories as social in nature, we simply accept them as nature.

Of course this understanding was never foreign to O'Neill, even as he staged depth from the 1920s to the 1940s. Through Hickey, *Iceman* dramatized the subtly coercive power of psychological discourse to determine concepts of selfhood and to recast social relations. On one level *Iceman* can be read as O'Neill's self-reflexive critique of the psychological dramatist—he who *presumes* to know and to tell us who we really are, down *deep*.

But on another level *Iceman* performs an ideological maneuver quite similar to that of some of O'Neill's overtly pop psychological plays. In 1939, the year O'Neill wrote *Iceman*, Frank O'Hara's *Today in American Drama* speculated that *Strange Interlude* and *Mourning Becomes Electra* would soon be perceived, not as modern, but as "museum pieces."[190] It makes sense that O'Neill's dramatization of pop psychological depth would seem dated by the end of the thirties, a decade that saw a resurgence of realism and naturalism.[191] No doubt it occurred to O'Neill that some of the 1930s realists and naturalists who made *Strange Interlude* seem unreal had learned from his own early work. With *Iceman* and *Long Day's Journey*, he returned with consummate skill to the realism and naturalism that had seemed thin and superficial to him in his pop modernist phase, and he infused his writing with the depth he popularized in the 1920s. *Iceman* draws on some of his early experiments in naturalism: the bar in *The Long Voyage Home* (1917); the drunken reveries in *The Moon of the Caribees* (1917); the repartee in the saloon in *"Anna Christie."* The preoccupations and "insights" of *Iceman* and *Long Day's Journey* are often just as pop psychological as those of

Strange Interlude and *Mourning*, but O'Neill used his extraordinary expertise as a dramatic portraitist to make it appear that this psychology was indeed what was most human—most real—about his characters.

Yet the apparent humanity of his characters is given remarkably attenuated agency. The possibilities for action in *Iceman* and *Long Day's Journey* (as in *Strange Interlude* and *Mourning*) fall within a narrow, therapeutic register—characters are fated to contend interminably with denial, ambivalence, obsession, and their own sense of being psychologically determined.[192] Despite O'Neill's sharp critique of Hickey's ruthless psychological unmasking, the playwright's own dramatic, aesthetic, intellectual, and ideological investment is still very much in what I have termed psychological capital. Even Hickey's psychological unmasking of pipe dreams turns out to be "psychological"—a neurotic *symptom* of his own denial, a classic case of projection.

Although Isidor Schneider lauded O'Neill's ability in *Iceman* to portray characters whose Freudian complexes are "not stuck on like labels," his *New Masses* review also disarmingly stepped outside the play's ideological bubble to observe that both the play's author and its mainstream reviewers seem peculiarly oblivious to "the purposeful world outside and the undefeated people moving vigorously and freely in it, those who have the will to struggle, to forgive, to endure, who do without the paralysis and the pipe dream."[193] Schneider sensed that O'Neill deployed his naturalism and realism to make "depth" seem not only more real, more natural, and more *eternally* human than in any other of his plays, but also far more significant—as the subject of human drama—than any staging of characters as social actors whose life-saving investment is not in denial but in changing the world.[194] He found the implications of O'Neill's "therapeutic" antipolitics to be undeniably political. As we will see in Chapter 3, other articulate critics on the Left shared this view.

O'Neill and the

American Left

3

The anecdote about the Irish tenant farmer who invited his pigs to bathe in the ice pond belonging to the neighboring Standard Oil millionaire so delighted O'Neill that he recounted it in *Long Day's Journey Into Night* (1940) and later dramatized part of it in *A Moon for the Misbegotten* (1943). The earlier play has Edmund teasing his father, Tyrone, that Harker, the millionaire, "will think you're no gentleman for harboring a tenant who isn't humble in the presence of a king of America." Tyrone, scandalized by his tenant Shaughnessy's behavior, spurns him as "shanty Irish" and admonishes Edmund to cut out "the Socialist gabble." But Edmund persists in conjoining his political views to his account of Shaughnessy's audacity, observing that "our ruling plutocrats" are not "mental giants." Once more Tyrone is goaded by his son's radical idiom: "Keep your damned anarchist remarks to yourself. I won't have them in my house" (3:725). Nonetheless Tyrone, himself a successful Irish actor, is keen to hear about his countryman's performance. Shaughnessy, soused to the gills, claimed he was "a king of Ireland" and refused to be a "slave to Standard Oil" "scum" who "had stolen from the poor." Well aware that his father would prefer not to view the contest as class warfare, Edmund plays it up as the underdog's "great Irish victory" and appeals to Tyrone's middle-class sense of fair play. Yet Edmund can't resist the radical gabble for long: "He should have reminded Harker that a Standard Oil millionaire ought to welcome the flavor of hog in his icewater as an appropriate touch." Tyrone censures him, predictably, unloading both barrels: "Keep your damned Socialist anarchist sentiments out of my affairs" (3:726). This chapter will suggest that O'Neill can be read both as Edmund, who takes pleasure in the irreverence of "Socialist anarchist sentiments," and as Tyrone, who is impatient with "Socialist gabble" and "anarchist remarks."

In his late teens and early twenties, O'Neill cast his socialist gabble and anarchist sentiments in the form of poetry. His letters indicate that he savored imagining himself as radical. Pluming his feathers for Beatrice Ashe in 1914, he boasted: "Also have written much poetry—free verse—in past months and think a lot of it will eventually land in *Poetry*, *The Little Review*, *The Masses*, *Blast*, *The Flame* or some other radical publications. Used to write for the *Revolt*, the Anarchist Weekly which was suppressed by the Federal police after running for three months."[1] The young O'Neill, emulating Jack London, signed off his letters, "Yours for the Revolution," and frequently quoted Karl Marx's dictum: "From each according to his ability; to each according to his needs." Jessica Rippin, with whose family O'Neill boarded in 1914, reminisced that Eugene was full of "anarchist ideas" and was fond of reading his "radical poems" to her. Frederick Latimer, one of O'Neill's senior colleagues on the New London *Telegraph* in 1912, remembered Eugene as "the most stubborn and irreconcilable social rebel I had ever met."[2] The cub reporter, notes Louis Sheaffer, "covered Socialist events with partisan feeling." In 1912, the year in which Edmund and the other Tyrones made their long day's journey into night, O'Neill cast his vote for Eugene V. Debs, the Socialist party's presidential candidate.[3]

One of O'Neill's poems, "Upon Our Beach," written for Beatrice

Ashe in the summer of 1914, represents the poet and his beloved sun-
ning on "Our Beach," actually owned by a "food-stuffed adorer of
Mammon." Their romance is empowered with the poetic license to
redistribute private property. "There is a house on a distant hill, a cold,
lonely, ugly house, a millionaire's house. / The world would say this is
his beach; he has a stamped paper to prove it. / We know better,—and we
have our hearts to prove it. / This is Our Beach!"[4] The previous spring
O'Neill published "Fratricide," a feisty antiwar poem in the *New York
Call*, a Socialist party daily. Its themes, language, and energy resemble
agitprop workers' theatre of the 1930s. "What cause could be more
asinine / Than yours, ye slaves of bloody toil? / . . . bleed and groan—for
Guggenheim! / And give your lives for Standard Oil!" He climaxes
with the rallying cry: "All workers of the earth / Are brothers and WE
WILL NOT FIGHT!"[5] Yet two months before he voted for Debs, O'Neill's
"Laconics" column in the New London *Telegraph* featured a poem
whose speaker placed his predilection for baseball ("which is it, Sox or
Giants?") high above his concern for politics. But the speaker in "The
Long Tale" (1912), another poem O'Neill published later that season, is
"fed up with the old tale, the cold tale, thrice-told tale" of conventional
"trust"-busting politicians who had debased politics altogether.[6]

Years before, during his Betts Academy high school years, Eugene
was introduced to "anarchist sentiments" by one of America's most
famous anarchists, Benjamin R. Tucker. Tucker, the son of wealthy Massachusetts parents, was the editor of *Liberty* magazine (1881–1908) and
proprietor of Unique Bookshop, which O'Neill frequented when in New
York City. There Eugene found works by Tucker, Emma Goldman, European anarchists, and George Bernard Shaw. Tucker was a leading
proponent of philosophical or Individualist anarchism, which, in contrast to Goldman's brand of activist anarchism, advocated propaganda
only and approved of private ownership. Tucker's influence persisted for
several years: a classmate of O'Neill's at Harvard (1914–15) portrayed
the young dramatist as "intellectually . . . a philosophical anarchist;
politically, a philosophical socialist."[7]

Thus O'Neill was well prepared for the countercultural climate of
Greenwich Village in the mid-1910s. In 1916 O'Neill joined the Provincetown Players, a theatre group founded as a collective.[8] Susan Glaspell, George Cram Cook, Hutchins Hapgood, and Mary Heaton Vorse,
as well as other founding members of the Provincetown group, were
either Socialists themselves or sympathetic to socialism.[9] Max Eastman

and Floyd Dell, who edited two of the most renowned radical magazines in the 1910s, *The Masses* (1911–17) and *The Liberator* (1918–23), acted in several of the early Provincetown productions, which included four of Dell's one-act comedies. Ida Rauh, who was a Socialist, a feminist, and a supporter of workers' theatre in the 1920s (and married to East-man), acted in and directed several of O'Neill's first Provincetown plays.[10] In 1917 the fledgling Provincetown group also produced *Ivan's Homecoming,* a play by a young truck driver called Irving Granich (who later gained fame as a Communist author and columnist under the name Mike Gold).[11]

Both John Reed and Louise Bryant, two of America's most flam-boyant radical journalists, appeared in Provincetown performances of O'Neill's works. Reed had previously acquired theatrical experience in June 1913, when he was a key organizer of the Paterson silk workers' pageant in Madison Square Garden. The pageant, which involved one thousand workers, was produced to generate funds for needy strikers. It caused dissension among the participants, however, and failed to deliver financial assistance. But the event did succeed in constructing a bridge between workers and bohemian intellectuals. It was Reed, enthused by the Provincetown project, who proposed in September 1916 that the Players continue their noncommercial, experimental productions in Greenwich Village. Reed and Eastman helped draft the Provincetown Players' constitution.[12]

Hence O'Neill's exposure to the myriad types of radical discourse of the 1910s was extensive and intimate. Louise Bryant, Reed's lover, also had an affair with O'Neill. Agnes Boulton, who filled the void left by Bryant (indeed, she resembled her), married O'Neill in 1918. She orig-inally came to New York—where she met Eugene—to rouse support for Connecticut farmers waging a milk strike.[13] Not surprisingly, the first playscripts O'Neill showed his friends quickly made him one of the crowd.

Workers, Race, and
Psychological Primitives

What excited the original Provincetown group about O'Neill, besides evidence that he was swiftly learning his craft, was the subject he brought to their makeshift stages. His *Bound East for Cardiff* (1914), *In the Zone* (1917), *The Long Voyage Home* (1917), and *The Moon of the Caribees* (1917) dramatized the lives, tribulations, and accents of working-class seamen on the S. S. Glencairn—a kind of realism and naturalism unexplored on the American stage. As Eric Bentley put it, the *Glencairn* cycle departed from "the genteel tradition" and introduced New York audiences to "the rhythm of modern life—in a sense Whitman himself would have recognized."[14] Yet the young O'Neill may have been engaged more by the Jack London romance of his subject than by the opportunity it afforded him for social criticism. He saw his own experience as a seaman (1910–11) as an expression of his personal revolt against middle-class ways. "I hated a life ruled by the conventions and traditions of society," he told an interviewer in 1922. "Sailors' lives were ruled by conventions and traditions; but they were of a sort I liked and that had a meaning which appealed to me. . . . Discipline on a sailing vessel was not a thing that was imposed on the crew by superior authority. It was essentially voluntary. The motive behind it was loyalty to the ship!"[15] In one of his first published poems, "Free" (1912), O'Neill rhapsodized about being "free, on the open sea, with the trade wind in our hair."[16]

O'Neill's romanticization probably would have been qualified by Herman Melville, who wrote about the oppression as well as the pleasures that seamen often experienced on board ship (he campaigned against flogging in the 1840s). In all likelihood he would have challenged O'Neill's equally romantic "Ballad of the Seamy Side," published not long after its author voted for Debs. The gist of the poem is that the hardships endured by seamen ("bed bugs sting," "biscuits hard," "labor great," "wages small") are just "part of the game and I loved it all."[17] For O'Neill, then, "the game" of being a seaman was akin to an almost therapeutic expression of what Theodore Roosevelt termed "the strenuous life." This game offered the aspiring author access to a "real" that had been unavailable to him at Princeton: "We were not in touch with life or on the trail of real things," he opined in 1920; "my real start as a dramatist was when I got out of an academy and among men, on the sea."[18]

When literary critic Edmund Wilson, fresh out of Princeton, joined the ambulance corps as an enlisted man rather than an officer in World War I (befitting his upper-middle-class station), he too felt that he had been exposed to the "real." But the social reality he perceived was not simply the product of rubbing shoulders with working-class soldiers; it was the "real" that one discovers by learning to question power relations which had previously seemed unquestionable—assuming they had been perceived at all. Wilson's remarks, published in 1932, suggest that the Depression heightened his consciousness of this lesson:

> I know from having shifted at the time of the War out of the group with whom I should have been supposed to function, that class antagonisms, conflicts, and injustices are real, that they rarely get any publicity, that the capacities of human nature for remaining blind to the consequences of its actions where its comfort and prestige are concerned are so great that it cannot usually be induced even to notice what it is up to without a violent jolt from below, and that there is no hope for general decency and fair play except from a society where classes are abolished.

Consequently, Wilson found himself paying "more serious attention" to Marxist appeals to the working class than did most of his "bourgeois confrères."[19] O'Neill, outside of his plays, never attempted so overt a self-accounting based on his class position.

Discussing *"Anna Christie"* (1921) during an interview in 1924, O'Neill depicted the worker, not as being caught in "class antagonisms, conflicts, and injustices," but as an undercivilized real-self-we-have-lost ("we" meaning the middle class)—an ideal subject for *psychological* drama. "They are more direct. In action and utterance. Thus more dramatic. Their lives and sufferings and personalities lend themselves more readily to dramatization. They have not been steeped in the evasions and superficialities which come with social life and intercourse. Their real selves are exposed. They are crude but honest. They are not handicapped by inhibitions." He went on to explain that because they are mostly "inarticulate," he "like[s] to interpret for them" so others may know their "hardships" and thus "see and help and understand." Because he "was once one of them," O'Neill can assure his interviewer that "life on the sea is ideal. . . . Meals provided. A resting-place. No economic pressure."[20] O'Neill's association with seamen in his preliterary phase, the Gelbs suggest, "helped him achieve an identification with humanity."[21] From the vantage point of 1924, O'Neill saw himself as having brought the working class to the psychological stage in order to escort his audience into the stokehole of life to observe humanity—in its most primitive, uninhibited state—naked.

But his *Glencairn* cycle, unlike his poems "Free" and "The Ballad of the Seamy Side," did convey some of the "hardships" borne by seamen, whose occasional complaints to one another carried faint traces of socialist gabble. The seamen in *Bound East for Cardiff* are *bound* hand and foot, as one of them protests: "Plenty o' work and no food—and the owners ridin' around in carriages!" (1:90). Heartbreak in this play is literal—the outcome of laboring in a hazardous workplace. Yank has taken a fatal fall from a ladder while chipping rust and revealingly imagines his injury in metaphors of broken machinery—the pain is "a buzz-saw cuttin' into me," "my old pump's busted" (1:193). Moments before dying, he reflects unromantically on "this sailor life": "One ship after another, hard work, small pay, and bum grub; and when we get into port, just a drunk endin' up in a fight, and all your money gone, and then slip away again. Never meetin' no nice people" (1:195). His impossible dream is to break out of this vicious cycle and buy a farm with Driscoll. Thus O'Neill hints at a more subtle, only partly acknowledged heartbreak that preceded Yank's physical fall.

O'Neill's interest in the conditions of work in these early plays is eclipsed by his preoccupation with fate. His workers seem predestined to be caught in the machine of the tramp steamer. One gets the sense that Driscoll, like his dying friend, will never make it out alive. Yank's deathbunk speech is in fact the plot outline for the next play O'Neill wrote in the cycle, *The Long Voyage Home.* In this play Olson, like Yank, dreams of settling down on a farm; he too sums up his seaman's life as "work, work, work" (1:517). Shortly after Olson resigns from his position, he, Driscoll, and two of their mates go to celebrate in a saloon on the London waterfront in which "foive or six years back" Driscoll was "sthripped av [his] last shillin' whin [he] was aslape." Yet he tempts fate by returning to this corrupt "rat's hole" (1:512) with his friends. Intent on staying sober, Olson naively lets his plans and his savings be known, and, after his friends leave, is drugged, robbed, and delivered unconscious to the Amindra, which has the reputation of being a slave ship no sailor would willingly go near. Driscoll returns to this spider's-web-of-a-bar yet again, is told that Olson has disappeared with a woman, and cockily orders an *"Irish* whiskey" (1:523). O'Neill's workers seem bound to be "sthripped," by ship owners or bar owners, because of something—or something lacking—within them.

In the Zone begins to clarify what these seamen lack by comparing them to a middle-class English seaman, Smitty. When two of the men see Smitty furtively hiding a black box beneath his bunk just before midnight, his covert behavior arouses their suspicion of sabotage; for the Glencairn—carrying ammunition—has just entered the war zone and they had never been able to "figger . . . out" why the aloof Englishman was among them anyway. The difference in class between Smitty and his mates makes it that much easier for the latter to project their fears of foreign spies onto "his Lordship" (1:476). Working their anxieties up to a fever pitch, the sailors restrain Smitty so that he may observe them dismantle his secret box. "You stupid curs!" Smitty retorts, true to his class: "You cowardly dolts!" (1:484). Smitty's time bomb only contains love letters (in a rubber bag, no less) recording his break-up with his fiancée, over the issue of his intemperance. Perusing the letters, some of his frustrated accusers still want to believe that he has written in "code" (1:487). But they have simply broken open Smitty's broken heart, finding themselves "in the [war] zone" of his emotions. O'Neill portrays the seamen as psychological illiterates who retire sheepishly as the more sensitive Smitty strives to muffle his sobs (1:488).

O'Neill elaborates on the theme of middle-class subjectivity more complexly in *The Moon of the Caribees*. Through Smitty, O'Neill suggests how the white-middle-class psychological self distinguishes itself from both the working class and blacks. Here the Glencairn is anchored off an island in the West Indies where the natives croon a "melancholy chant" (1:527). "Will ye listen to them black naygurs?" Driscoll grumbles, opening the play with a touch of Irish racism: "I wonder now, do they call that keenin' a song?" (1:528). Yank imagines them eating their dead "to save fun'ral expenses," while Cocky insists that blacks are biologically different from whites because they possess "two stomachs like a bleedin' camel" (1:528).

By contrast, Smitty "sighs" (1:528). In his extended dialogue with Old Tom the "Donkeyman" (operator of a steam engine), Smitty explains that he does not like the music, not because it is "bad," but for deeper reasons—it stirs up "things you ought to forget" (1:530). Donkeyman, who in Smitty's scornful eyes personifies his work name, is unflappably anti-"psychological" in his casual outlook: "(*spitting placidly*) Queer things, mem'ries. I ain't ever been bothered much by 'em" (1:537). He offers Smitty the same unpsychological advice that Woman, the prostitute, gives Michael Cape in *Welded* (1924): when things go wrong, "ferget 'em." Unperturbed by this counsel, Smitty attempts to draw some cosmic, universal significance from his interminable angst: "We're poor little lambs who have lost our way, eh, Donk? Damned from here to eternity, what?" Yet this philosophizing evokes negligible anxiety in the Donk: "Maybe; I dunno," he says skeptically (1:538).

The Donkeyman is not the ass Smitty would like to believe he is.

Figure 17. O'Neill—the look of interiority (reminiscent of Smitty in *The Moon of the Caribees*), photographed by Nickolas Muray. Yale Collection of American Literature Photographs, Beinecke Rare Book and Manuscript Library, Yale University. O'Neill's inscription reads: "To my son, Eugene, from his Father 5/17/22."

After surmising that "there's a gel mixed up in it someplace," he spits, acknowledges that love is indeed a "queer thing," and suggests that Smitty resolve his "mem'ries" dilemma by giving "'em a whack on the ear." Smitty objects: "(*pompously*) Gentlemen don't hit women." That, rejoins the Donk, is "why they has mem'ries when they hears music" (1:538). Not only do we begin to see Smitty's preoccupation with his inner drama as "pompous," O'Neill encourages us to see it as a *pose*—a pose O'Neill himself would assume in some of his photographs: "*Smitty . . . is still sitting . . . staring off into vacancy*" (1:536) (Figure 17).

Six native women have been invited aboard, ostensibly to sell fruit, secretly to purvey rum and other pleasures. Donkeyman again offends Smitty's sensibility by advising him to take advantage of the more sensuous services the black women offer: "No mem'ries jined with that" (1:539). By implication, middle-class white women, not black women (who get paid off) or white working-class women (who get whacked), have the subjective potency to produce the inner drama that torments Smitty. Pearl, the prettiest woman, is initially drawn to Smitty's good looks and to his melancholic, gentlemanly "*vacancy*," but she finds her overtures met by his "*shudder of disgust*" (1:540). The action climaxes with drunken dancing that turns into a brawl in which the seamen vent their "primitive" natures. The "fate" of the black women is to be sent ashore, without being paid, for having brought rum on board. Smitty, who sits "*oblivious*" to this working-class pandemonium, closes the play still engrossed by the "*melancholy song of the negroes*" and utters "*a sigh that is half a sob*" (1:543).

On the one hand, O'Neill seems to represent Smitty as "deep." Smitty's scorn for Donk, registered unambiguously in the stage directions, suggests he views his own smitten subjectivity as an essence—a psychological capital—that elevates him above the donkeymen and donkeywomen who work, fight, and make love all around him. The fate of donkeymen is to be trapped in the machine of the tramp steamer that exploits them and that can literally break their hearts; whereas the higher-class psychological fate of the middle-class Englishman is to be trapped by the overwhelming meaningfulness he cannot help but ascribe to his heartbreaking "mem'ries." Donkeymen do not possess the subjectivity that would make their fate complexly tragic: the undefined determinism that leads Olson to accept a (drugged) drink and get Shanghaied on the Amindra is not nearly as grand, cosmic, or literary as the subtle, emotional fate that compels Smitty to sigh, sob, and shudder. Yank, Driscoll, and Olson are capable of being sentimental, but they lack the subjective capacity for angst that Smitty demonstrates. The Donk isn't even sentimental.

On the other hand, O'Neill's Donkeyman, who spits at just the right moments, is given the power to douse both Smitty's self-absorbed pomposity and the notion that "the psychological" is a universal core we all experience and express in the same way. If Donk's therapeutic prescriptions appear too simple, too "primitive," too patriarchal—getting drunk, sleeping guiltlessly with West Indian prostitutes, whacking women— his advocacy of "fergettin' " is given some anti-"psychological" capital in the play.

O'Neill's working class tells us less about the actual working class, perhaps, than about what O'Neill wanted this class to signify for him. What his version of this class seemed to offer him was the possibility of a crude, labor-intensive distraction from the fate-driven psychological middle-class subjectivity that defies time, space, and sleep itself in its intense and unremitting torment. O'Neill uses his rendition of the working class to establish some distance from middle-class "depth" and its vicissitudes. If the Donk is shown to be incapable of experiencing angst, O'Neill nevertheless makes it clear that he would not want to even if he could.

Sheaffer admires O'Neill's "crude, flavorsome sailor talk" in his acclaim for *Bound East for Cardiff*, but he considers the play "poetic" because it expresses "the spirit of brooding compassion, of tragic inevitability" that makes O'Neill's later work great.[22] But the brooding of these working-class seamen, like their language, is meant to be more flavorsome than deep. In this sense, as one leftist critic argued in the 1930s, O'Neill partly functioned as a tour guide for a middle and upper class fascinated by *exhibits* of "exotic" workers.[23] What mainstream reviewers found most appealing about O'Neill's dramatic tours of "rough toilers of the sea" was not that they were about the workers' struggle for survival amidst alterable hardships, but that the men he dramatized seemed to "live."[24]

O'Neill's seamen seemed not only to live but to belong where they were by virtue of their crude, flavorsome subjectivity as well as their undercivilized masculine idiom. Smitty is a self-consuming psychological tourist acting out his inner drama on the Glencairn, whereas his mates are psychological primitives ("crude but honest. . . . not handicapped by inhibitions") scripted to "live" in the machine. By making their hard lot seem flavorsome and poetic, as well as tragic but unchangeable, O'Neill could "help" audiences to feel that by applauding his daringly ungenteel choice of subject matter they were somehow doing something for workers.[25] Perhaps that is one reason why his Provincetown "interpretations" (as he put it) of workers were so well received by the "romantic rebels" who migrated to Greenwich Village's bohemia (largely populated by the immigrant working class) in the late 1910s.

O'Neill's most complex play about the relationship between middle-class subjectivity and cavemen-at-sea is *The Hairy Ape* (1921). The curtain opens to display a band of *"heavy chested"* laborers *"with long arms of tremendous power, and low, receding brows above their small, fierce, resentful eyes."* Yank, the toughest "ape" among them, inspires *"fear"* and is described in the language of evolution as *"their most highly developed individual"* (2:121). Their *"uproar"* is likened to that of *"beast[s] in a cage"* (2:121).

Despite such glaring stereotypes, O'Neill's critical perception of the workers' situation is keen. His set, for example, underscores the role of the work environment in contorting bodies so that they look "primitive." The ceiling *"crushes down upon the men's heads"* and thus *"ac-*

centuates the natural stooping posture which shoveling coal and the resultant over-development of back and shoulder muscles have given them" (2:121). One Neanderthal is blunt about what the New York–Southampton ocean liner voyage promises for those who inhabit the firemen's forecastle and the stokehole: "Six days in hell" (2:123).

Yank imagines his Neanderthal masculinity in metaphors of a workplace he has clearly internalized and made the source of his strength: he is, he says, "steam and oil for de engines" (1:128) and "steel-steel-steel" (2:129). Because he considers his workplace his "woild," Yank imagines himself and his labor as independent of "whoever owns dis [ship]" (2:126) or "dem slobs in de first cabin"—they're "just baggage" (2:125). His masculine bravado, however, is undermined early on by O'Neill's staging of the men as the bell summons them to work: they *"jump up mechanically"* and *"file through the door"* marching in *"a prisoner's lockstep"* (2:129). Yank's self-image as a caveman of steel is challenged by the old Irishman, Paddy, who draws on memories of his years in sailing ships to contend that their manhood has been debased by industrial conditions of labor. He speaks dreamily of a more organic work process in which men were skilled, had "straight backs and full chests" (2:126), and truly "belonged" (2:127), not only to the ship, but to "the sea as if 'twas the mother that bore them" (2:126). Their stokehole, by contrast, is a floating "zoo" in which they are "bloody apes" "caged in by steel" (2:127). Yank dismisses Paddy's history lesson as mere nostalgia, as a sign of unmasculine weakness. But shortly after, Yank's practical advice to the disgruntled Paddy sounds more like the recommendation of a low level supervisor than that of the autonomous worker he believes himself to be: "Act like yuh liked it, yuh better" (2:129).

While Paddy argues that times have changed for the worse, Long's socialist emphasis is on who made them change for their own betterment: "the damned Capitalist clarss!" Wearing his masculinity like an armor, Yank is as uninterested in thinking of himself politically as he is in viewing himself historically: he derides Long's "Socialist bull" as feminine "Salvation Army" (2:125) sentiment—"Votes [are] for women!" (2:147). Nonetheless, through Yank's ongoing antagonism with the unseen engineer who keeps blowing his whistle and (in Yank's words) "crackin' de whip" (2:135), O'Neill suggests that Long's stubborn focus on power relations makes sense.

It is Mildred Douglas, the "Steel Trust" heiress, not Paddy or Long, who smashes Yank's defenses by reinterpreting his masculinity, not as powerful and enviable, but as subhuman and loathsome. Mildred, we learn, has in the past "posed" as a social-service worker to "discover how the other half lives." Her slumming functions therapeutically for her as a "nerve tonic" (2:131). Thus Mildred uses her father's influence to coerce one of the engineers to take her on a tour of the stokehole, where she finds Yank cursing fast and furiously at the unseen "yellow" engineers. Here she "discovers," not someone who will genuflect to her class superiority and play the needy victim, but an *"unknown, abysmal, brutality . . . a gorilla face."* Yank is confused and enraged by her revulsion, as she gasps, "The filthy beast!" (2:137), then faints and is whisked away. Paddy half-jokes that she acted as if she had "seen a great hairy ape escaped from the zoo" (2:141), and Long blames the "bloody engineers" who are now "exhibitin' us 's if we was bleedin' monkeys in a menagerie" (2:139). By implication, O'Neill suggests that he himself aims to play a role other than that of a literary "engineer" who *exhibits* "hairy apes" of the "other half" to his higher-class audiences. O'Neill also seems to self-consciously distinguish his motives from those underlying Mildred's poses among the poor.

Long's socialist goal is to convince Yank that he occupies the position of a "proletarian" and that his encounter with Mildred was not "personal" (2:146) but representative of class conflict. Yank begins to learn this political lesson on Fifth Avenue in New York City, when he and Long run into the wealthy as they are leaving church. O'Neill has them dressed as *"gaudy marionettes"* whose masks and mechanical, *"affected politeness"* (2:149) operate as screens that make workers like Yank and Long invisible. Wholly ignored by this group, the incensed seaman tries to rip up the curb and a lamppost to break through their barriers but in doing so is knocked over by a gentleman running to catch a bus. Yank eagerly pommels him, but the gentleman is impervious to his force. O'Neill shows his audience and Yank that the "hairy ape's" physical resistance to institutional and ideological ruling class power is futile. The controlling engineer's whistle of the corporate-industrial state is now replaced by the disciplinary whistle of the police, and Yank is summarily tossed in jail.

Yank does achieve a limited political "awakening" as the play progresses. He moves from a metonymic individual-centered fantasy— "Steel was me, and I owned de woild"—to an awareness of himself as socially and economically produced—"Now I ain't steel, and de woild owns me" (2:159). In jail on Blackwell's Island he begins to "tink" about how corporate power maintains its power. Thinking of Mildred's father, president of the Steel Trust, he rails, "He made dis—dis cage! . . . holdin' me down wit him at de top!" (2:154). Later Yank offers his services to the Industrial Workers of the World, not to assassinate Douglas, but to blow up his factories. Yet his motivation is still fundamentally individual and personal, for he proposes to do this mainly so that he could then boast of his crime to Mildred to "square tings" (2:158) with her.

Leftist playwrights in the 1920s and especially in the 1930s looked to *The Hairy Ape* as a model, albeit sometimes a problematic one, of a play that was innovative in its staging of political concerns. The chorus of drunken Neanderthals in the firemen's forecastle and the chorus of masked, wealthy churchgoers are deindividualized as "Voices" in the text. Whenever Yank says he is trying to "tink," his mates respond "Think!" in unison, sounding like mechanical *"phonograph horns"* (2:124). O'Neill departed from naturalism—with the play's stage sets, masks, and metallic voices—to experiment with ways of representing social groups, not just individuals. Mike Gold's *Strike!* (1926) had a similar goal. Gold's short play is a "mass recitation" (based partly on those he observed in Russia) in which actors chanted, played allegorical roles (Wealth, Poverty, Young Leader, Young Worker), and attempted to eliminate "any outcropping of individualism"[26] to better dramatize the clash of social groups and ideological positions. But Gold and other playwrights who explored these possibilities knew well that the first mainstream American play to have attempted this sort of abstraction was *The Hairy Ape*. Some of O'Neill's satirical touches resurfaced in important political plays of the thirties. "Dear Doctor Caiaphas," the Fifth Avenue minister whose sermons are "about the radicals . . . and the false doctrines that are being preached" (2:147), turns up seventeen years later in Marc Blitzstein's *Cradle Will Rock* (1938) as Reverend Salvation, who (in Steeltown) preaches whatever the steel interests want him to preach. O'Neill's Senator Queen, whose speech branding the Industrial Workers of the World as a red "menace" (2:152) is read aloud to Yank from the newspapers in jail, made appearances in various guises in the "Living Newspaper" plays produced by the Federal Theatre Project in the late 1930s. And Clifford Odets's explosive agitprop play, *Waiting for Lefty* (1935), borrowed from O'Neill's subjective drama, his dramatic abstraction of class forces, and his satire (while also improving his working-class accents).[27]

Despite O'Neill's illumination of class ideologies, and notwithstanding *The Hairy Ape*'s impact on political theatre in the 1920s and 1930s, O'Neill's main interest seems to be other than politics. Paddy and Long offer cogent speeches advocating a political conception of the self and of work, but they remain subsidiary spokesmen dwarfed by Yank's dramatic presence. Paddy is tired, resigned, and easily placated with a drink, while Long's soap-box socialism has a wind-up, sloganeering quality. Both flutter around Yank like mosquitoes, in danger of being swatted if they get too pesky or bite too hard. Rather than functioning as compelling explanatory forces in the play, these "characters" seem more often to provide flavorsome, local color. Their relative weakness can be contrasted with the linguistic and physical vitality of the "young leader" character whose rousing oratory is meant to rally audiences to "change the world" in political plays like *Strike!*, *The Cradle Will Rock*, and *Waiting for Lefty*.

O'Neill's deep interest seems to be in creating a working-class seaman who has been converted to professional-managerial-class angst. Yank finally sees his problem as being deeper than being exploited by the Steel Trust. "Cut out an hour offen de job a day and make me happy! Gimme a dollar more a day and make me happy! . . . dat don't touch it." No, Yank's liberal arts alienation is spiritual, psychological, and philosophical; it goes "way down—at de bottom" (2:159). The point of Paddy and Long's speeches, and of Yank's ineffective assault on the wealthy Fifth Avenue marionettes, is that Yank has been shaped by material and ideological relations. But his grasp of this is ideologically transmuted into a universal malaise that supervenes matters of class, history, and production: "I ain't on oith and I ain't in heaven, get me? I'm in de middle tryin' to separate 'em, takin' all de woist punches from bot' of 'em" (2:162). This is simply another version of Smitty's "we're poor little lambs who have lost our way" speech, the kind that only prompts the Donk to spit. Yank's affinity with Smitty's "damned from here to eternity" lament may also be suggested by his real name, Robert Smith.

In the final scene, Yank, smitten by malaise, goes to the zoo, converses with an ape (about his not belonging), frees the ape, and is hugged to death and thrown in the cage, with the closing stage directions philosophizing: "*And, perhaps, the Hairy Ape at last belongs*" (2:163). Many critics on the Left in the 1930s suspected that these universalized plaints about "not belonging" and middleness were, "at de bottom," those of a "middle-class intellectual"[28] only costumed as a worker. (Interestingly, the man who achieved fame in the role of Yank, Louis Wolheim, held a bachelor's degree from the City University of New York and a master's from Cornell, was fluent in three languages, had worked as an engineer, and had taught mathematics at Cornell University Prep School before acting on stage and screen. He had broken his nose three times playing football for Cornell and looked tough.)[29] By making the animal body versus heavenly spirit quandary of "humanity" the ultimate, overriding concern of a worker who has spent so many years in a stokehole that he has persuaded himself he *is* steel, the play promotes what one recent reader has astutely termed a "class ideology of classlessness."[30]

In 1922 O'Neill explained that he did not want *The Hairy Ape* to "fit into any of the 'isms' although there is a bit of all of them in it."[31] Almost twenty years later he asserted that the play's message probes deeper than politics: "Not superficially about labor conditions . . . but about Man, the state we are all in of frustrated bewilderment."[32] This was precisely why the eminent producer Arthur Hopkins esteemed *The Hairy Ape* as O'Neill's "most important work": Hopkins wanted to believe that we're all "desperate Yanks" who don't "belong" because of our corporeal and spiritual nature.[33] By invoking the "language and imagery of class struggle"[34] only to transcend it with a more "significant" psychological and spiritual "bewilderment"—"not belonging" and middleness—the play could appeal on a therapeutic plane to professional-managerial-class Yanks who would be refreshed by the thought that their own angst-filled "depth" ("de bottom") even existed in workers whose evolutionary development made them capable of feeling like "individuals" (2:121). As such, *The Hairy Ape* may have served as an ideological "nerve tonic" (2:131) of sorts. In the process of identifying with Yank, some auditors may have obfuscated their awareness that they play a role in the exploitation of "hairy apes" as professionals and managers (and that they too are exploitable "hairy apes").

On another allegorical level, it would perhaps make sense that professional-managerial-class audiences of the early twenties would indeed identify with someone who thinks of himself as pinned "in de middle" between the "oith" (working class) and "heaven" (corporate capitalist class), anxious about "takin' punches" from "bot' of 'em." And on yet another level, O'Neill's *Hairy Ape* seems caught "in de middle" between its author's youthful "Yours for the Revolution" predilection for socialism and his growing interest in pop psychoanalytic notions of the "primitive" self. The final, bizarre, philosophical zoo scene by no means effaces O'Neill's dramatic concerns with the hardships of the working-class "hairy apes" who are "crushed" at sea. Nevertheless, his play does seem to go out of its way to make these "labor"[35] issues the scenery for the one he wants to stage as more significant and more dramatic—deeper—for his own class.

O'Neill's pioneering dramatizations of blacks in *The Dreamy Kid* (1918), *The Emperor Jones* (1920), and *All God's Chillun Got Wings* (1923), like his staging of "flavorsome" hairy apes, is not without its contradictions and complexities. *The Dreamy Kid* was the first American drama to offer roles to an all-black cast, and the parts of Dreamy, Brutus Jones, and Jim Harris are all powerful. O'Neill's efforts won approval from the likes of W. E. B. Du Bois and Langston Hughes.[36] In his essay on theatre in Alain Locke's important collection, *The New Negro* (1925), Montgomery Gregory hailed O'Neill as a "genius" and praised him for having "dignified" black drama and made it "serious."[37]

Other more critical reviewers, however, harbored doubts about whether the word "serious" accurately described the cultural effects of O'Neill's dramatizations of blacks.[38] Black intellectuals of the 1920s and 1930s were often tactful in their criticisms of O'Neill because they recognized that he had offered black actors such as Charles Gilpin and Paul Robeson a chance to demonstrate their skills in the spotlight of what James Weldon Johnson—with understated irony—called "the legitimate stage."[39] Furthermore, as Jessie Fauset pointed out, O'Neill enabled black actors to appear in tragic roles, not blackface caricatures performed by minstrel comedians, singers, or dancers. On some level, Fauset hoped, this would demonstrate to white audiences the reality that blacks "possessed . . . wells of feelings" and experienced a range of complex human emotions.[40] O'Neill's black critics acknowledged this as a significant advance because, as Locke noted, American theatre, literature, and the arts had been instrumental in misrepresenting the black American as "a formula [rather] than a human being."[41] Both *The Crisis* and *Opportunity*, two of the most distinguished black publications, recruited O'Neill to lend his cultural prestige to the work of aspiring black dramatists in his capacity as judge of playwriting contests in the mid-1920s.[42] "Be yourselves," O'Neill advised; "Don't reach out for our stuff which we call good!"[43]

From the outset of his career, O'Neill viewed himself and his writing as progressive on matters of race. Although he did not like to act, and appeared in brief roles in only three of his earliest one-act plays, the longest role he took on was one in which he put on blackface as the

Figure 18. O'Neill (in blackface), George Cram Cook, and Louise Bryant in the 1916 Provincetown Players production of *Thirst* at the Wharf Theatre in Provincetown. Yale Collection of American Literature Photographs, Beinecke Rare Book and Manuscript Library, Yale University.

taciturn mulatto sailor in *Thirst* (1913), produced by the newly formed Provincetown Players at the Wharf Theatre in Provincetown in 1916 (Figure 18). This drama is about three survivors of a shipwreck, the sailor, a white female dancer, and a white gentleman, all of whom are dying of thirst aboard a "white" raft (1:31) in shark-filled waters. The play exposes racist fears of the whites, who suspect that the sailor has stolen their small supply of water. When the dancer attempts to bribe and then seduce the sailor into sharing his water, and he insists that he is not hiding any (on the raft), she castigates herself for having "abased myself" to a "black animal," a "dirty slave" (1:48). While the extremity of their predicament at times modifies the social pretensions of the two whites, their deeply ingrained racial roles remain in force.[44] *Thirst's* climax is a race war in which the dancer goes crazy and dies, the mulatto proposes eating her, and the gentleman objects and attacks the mulatto. The latter defends himself ably by stabbing his assailant, but the white man succeeds in pulling him overboard. When "*the Sailor's black head*" bobs to the surface before sinking and leaving behind a "*black stain*," his features are grotesquely described in the stage directions as being "*distorted with terror, his lips torn with a howl of despair*" (1:51). Despite the playwright's vague association of the mulatto with superstition and cannibalism, and notwithstanding his oddly horrific picture of the sailor's "black" bloody demise, O'Neill portrays this man as strong and self-possessed. The whites, on the other hand, become increasingly and annoyingly hysterical. One might infer that years of experience made the mulatto more accustomed to and collected about surviving against all odds, including lack of nourishment, in a confined white space in a shark-filled ocean.

O'Neill's moral commitment to staging controversial racial issues seems unambiguous in his refusal to call off the production of *All God's Chillun Got Wings*, his play about an interracial marriage poisoned by internalized racism. The playwright and his stars, Paul Robeson and Mary Blair, received hate mail and death threats as the premiere approached in 1924. When O'Neill perused a letter from the Grand Kleagle of the Georgia Ku Klux Klan that threatened the life of his infant son Shane, he immediately scrawled on the note (in atypically large handwriting): "Go fuck yourself!"—and remailed it to Georgia.[45] Yet O'Neill's own interpretation of his most explosive drama about racism curiously erased the dimension of race and universalized the relationship of Jim and Ella as he did the predicament of Yank in *The Hairy Ape*: "The racial factor is incidental," he claimed. "The play is a study of two human beings."[46] (Of course, this humanist disclaimer was issued to the press in an atmosphere boiling over with racial tensions.)

When *The Iceman Cometh* (1940) was scheduled to be performed in the 1940s at the National Theatre in Washington, D.C., a theatre that refused to seat blacks, O'Neill unequivocally assured a group which protested this policy that he always has "been opposed to racial discrimination of any kind" and "will insert a nondiscriminatory clause in all future contracts." He urged them to publicize his pledge.[47] Nonetheless, a few years earlier he had prevented a black troupe affiliated with the Federal Theatre Project from producing *Mourning Becomes Electra* (1931), arguing that they should perform nothing but "my negro plays."[48] His trilogy's "timeless" psychological truths, by implication, were timeless for whiteface subjectivities only.[49]

O'Neill's stance against "discrimination of any kind" was probably rooted in some historical awareness that the Irish and the blacks were both victims of similar cultural stereotypes disseminated since the mid-nineteenth century (frequently by the American theatre). Nineteenth-century blackface minstrel shows often lampooned the Irish as shiftless, ignorant drinkers and featured actors in blackface dancing Irish jigs.[50] The term "Irish nigger" originated in the antebellum South, where the Irish were employed as cheap, expendable laborers on jobs too dangerous to be undertaken by black "property."[51] Well aware of this association, blacks often made the "greenhorn" immigrant group—with whom they competed for jobs—the butt of their jokes and tall tales, for the Irish were one of the few white groups they could caricature, usually as ludicrous bumblers.[52]

By the 1850s, when James O'Neill emigrated to America, the Irish were widely represented as a "race" marked by physical features, such as low brows and simian facial structure.[53] In 1876 Thomas Nast, the celebrated political cartoonist for *Harper's Weekly*, published a cartoon entitled "The Ignorant Vote," which depicted a large scale, resembling a playground swing: on one side sat a southern Sambo caricature wearing a straw hat, grinning complacently; on the other a northern Paddy caricature almost growling, with simian features (Figure 19).[54] Strangely, O'Neill himself reproduced this stereotype in *The Hairy Ape*: Paddy is described as a *"wizened Irishman"* whose *"face is extremely monkey-like, with all the sad, patient pathos of that animal in his small eyes"* (2:123). Eight years after O'Neill put on blackface as the mulatto sailor in *Thirst*, Congress heard "scientific" testimony that Irish immigration should be restricted because the Irish were the most "degenerate" and "defective" of all immigrant groups.[55]

O'Neill certainly knew from his father that the newly arrived Irish withstood jarring discrimination from northern Yankees, and this may have made him alert to the hard times experienced by the droves of southern blacks who migrated North to fill openings in factories and to take jobs in cities, especially during World War I. In *The Dreamy Kid*, Dreamy's "mammy" reminisces that he was given his nickname while still a babe in the South because of his dreamy look—read as symbolic of the dreams they hoped would come true for them in the North. But years in the North have hardened this dreamy boy into a defiant urban gang leader who, we find, has just "croaked . . . a white man. . . . [who was] lookin' for trouble" (1:680). Torn between his anxiety about his dying mammy, who threatens ever so sweetly to put a curse on him if he leaves her deathbed, and his fear of the police, who are hot on his trail, the doomed Dreamy is O'Neill's embodiment of the black dream of freedom in the North turned into a nightmare.

The militancy that the audiences of 1918 saw driving Dreamy, and that the audiences of 1916 detected in the mulatto sailor, was what whites feared in the black soldiers who would return from action in World War I. Within weeks of the East St. Louis race riot of 1917, in which 200 blacks were killed, the black soldiers of the Twenty-fourth

Figure 19. Thomas Nast, "The Ignorant Vote— Honors Are Easy," *Harper's Weekly*, December 9, 1876. Sterling Memorial Library, Yale University.

Infantry Battalion rebelled against the discrimination they endured in the army and in town, killing seventeen whites in Houston.[56] Amidst some controversy, Du Bois supported black participation in the war because he believed that the soldiers, having demonstrated their valor and self-worth in the field, would return intolerant of intolerance, prepared to keep on "fighting."[57] In February 1919, the fighting men of New York's much-publicized black Fifteenth Regiment, who were awarded some of France's highest honors for their victories, marched in combat gear from downtown up to Harlem and symbolized to thousands of onlookers the dream that things would change.[58]

O'Neill wrote *The Emperor Jones* in the period of the bloody race riots in East St. Louis, Houston, Chicago, and many other cities, and within this context it is significant that he costumed his defiant black American "emperor" in a uniform (Figure 20).[59] The resourceful Brutus Jones, probably in flight from the law, has jumped ship in the Caribbean and has managed to make himself emperor of an island. But the action begins just as his highness is due for a fall. The play shows this emperor only in retreat from the island's seemingly primitive "woods niggers,"

Figure 20. Charles Gilpin as the Emperor Jones in uniform, smiling defiantly, from a 1920 production. Yale Collection of American Literature Photographs, Beinecke Rare Book and Manuscript Library, Yale University.

whose ominous drums drive Jones out of his palace and into the forest. As the emperor loses his bearings in the woods, he shreds and sheds his uniform in a physical and psychological striptease that prepares him for the silver bullets of those he has oppressed. In O'Neill's narrative, the uniformed black militant/gunslinger is hunted and executed by vigilantes who are members of his own race.

Brutus Jones bears some resemblance to what in the late 1910s was called the "new negro." *The Messenger*, a black socialist monthly, published two cartoons in September 1919 illustrating opposing visions of the "negro." Complacent "Old Crowd Negroes" are garbed in respectable business suits and counsel "turn[ing] the other cheek" as the key to race improvement. By contrast, the militant "New Crowd Negro"— reminiscent of O'Neill's gun-toting Dreamy—rides in a car whose protruding, somewhat phallic guns make it look more like a tank; its banner lists cities shaken by race riots. Frightened crowds scatter before it (Figure 21). Henry Louis Gates has observed that the Harlem Renaissance,

Figure 21. Cartoons, "Old Crowd Negro" versus "New Crowd Negro," *The Messenger*, September 1919. Sterling Memorial Library, Yale University.

Figure 22. Charles Gilpin as the Emperor Jones, now submissive before a masked, "primitive" Congo witch doctor, from a 1920 production. Yale Collection of American Literature Photographs, Beinecke Rare Book and Manuscript Library, Yale University.

led by intellectuals like Alain Locke, transformed the militant socialist concept of the "new negro" of the late 1910s into the mid-1920s aesthetic "new negro," who was both artistic and primitive.[60] Curiously, *The Emperor Jones* anticipates this shift in the signification of the "new negro" by casting the aggressive Brutus Jones as a victim of his own racial primitivism (Figure 22).

The militant "new negro" of the late 1910s had ideological agendas quite different from those of the American Emperor Jones, whose militancy is channeled into the exploitation of West Indian blacks. W. A. Domingo, a militant Socialist columnist for *The Messenger*, consistently made a case for the overthrow of capitalism and colonialism and for the liberation of black workers everywhere.[61] William Bridges, editor of *The Challenger*, another black radical newspaper, exhorted his readers to oppose the oppression of both American and West Indies blacks.[62] O'Neill was not unaware of imperialism in the Caribbean. His sharply ironic prefatory description imagines the action taking "place on an island in the West Indies as not yet self-determined by White Marines" (1:1030).

But the play itself sidesteps any consideration of white colonialism in order to spotlight a conflict between a power-hungry black American and the island's natives.

The most publicized black "emperor" in uniform in 1920 was a Jamaican, Marcus Garvey. Garvey settled in New York in 1916 and used his dynamic oratory to win support for a movement to resettle blacks in Africa. Although in the mid-1920s he would be convicted of defrauding investors in his Black Star steamship line, in the early years of the decade he was enormously popular as a racial spokesman and drew fire from eminent members of the black intellectual community. Something of a showman, Garvey had himself made "Provisional King of Africa" and convened "a court of nobles" with dukes and knights, all in uniform. Like some of his associates, James Weldon Johnson was critical of Garvey but recognized his substantial contributions to the cultivation of black cultural pride and solidarity. Comparing "King" Garvey to the Emperor Jones, he averred that the former had played an "imperial role such as Eugene O'Neill had never imagined" for his own uniformed creation.[63] Garvey himself detested the 1933 film version of *The Emperor Jones* as racist and feuded with Paul Robeson (in print) for consenting to star in it.[64]

According to the historian Nathan Huggins, "travesty" describes one of the most important ideological elements of the nineteenth- and early-twentieth-century blackface minstrel shows. By bearing names and wearing costumes that signify exaggerated grandeur, blacks are travestied. Slaveowners, for example, sometimes mocked the abject condition of their slaves by naming them after leaders of the Roman empire: Caesar, Pompey, Cato (the name of a black coachman in *A Touch of the Poet*), or Brutus (as in Brutus Jones). Marcus Garvey's own middle name may have been Aurelius. Antebellum politicians like Daniel Webster were often caricatured by blackface minstrels, whose bombastic oratory in stage "negro" dialect functioned to make fun of the ungrammatical blacks even more than of the politicians.[65] As emperor, Jones models himself after crooked politicians and businessmen—"de white quality"—he overheard for years as a porter on Pullman cars: "For de little stealin' dey gets you in jail. . . . For de big stealin dey makes you Emperor." But O'Neill shows us that "de" black emperor cannot quite pull off what he himself calls his "big circus" (1:1035).

In this way Jones resembles the black gamblers who were travestied in "coon songs" from the 1890s to the 1920s. The "coontown billionaire" or the "lucky coon" not only attempted to behave like whites, he wanted a white chauffeur. But "coon songs" reassure listeners that the "coon" really poses no threat to the established racial order after all, for his fate is to be either completely laughable—like a child dressed up in adult's clothing—or to fall on his face.[66] An element of travesty in O'Neill's play may also be seen in its evocation of Shakespeare's classics: Othello's militancy and pride bound to fall, the stripping of Lear's kingly habiliments and his sense of majesty on the heath, and Macbeth's encounter with the ghost of Banquo. By contrast, "de" emperor who addresses himself as "nigger" (1:1047), who importunes his feet to "do yo' duty!" (1:1039), who prays frantically to the "Lawd" for protection from "dem ha'nts" (1:1049), and who is "meltin' wid heat" (1:1049), seems framed more as ridiculous than tragic.

To a degree O'Neill's play seems to suggest that Jones is psychologically fated to be only a travesty because, like the "black trash" (1:1043) and the "black" woods (1:1044) that "ha'nt" him, he is inescapably primitive and *black*. The "black" psychojungle Jones gets lost in was, in fact, a cultural discourse of black primitivism that both whites and blacks popularized in the 1920s. Albert Barnes, a wealthy white contributor to *The New Negro*, associated the black's "psychological complexion" and "tremendous emotional endowment" with his or her "primitive nature," but regarded this as a distinct asset for literary and artistic labor. J. A. Rogers, a black contributor, characterized black jazz as "the revolt of the emotions against repression."[67] The white preoccupation with "primitive" Harlem and its arts and nightclubs in the twenties constituted what Huggins has termed a therapeutic "soft rebellion" for whites who saw themselves in need of emotional release from the "Babbittry and sterility" of mainstream American culture.[68] The striptease that actors Charles Gilpin and Paul Robeson performed when playing Jones identified them with a sexuality that white audiences could both fascinate themselves with as an embodiment of their own psychological primitivism, yet at the same time spurn as "nothing more than a prancing darky on a stage."[69]

Jones himself is driven (by O'Neill) to wonder: "Is you civilized, or is you like dese ign'nent black niggers heah?" (1:1049). Many reviewers felt sure that deep down Mr. Jones was indeed one of the "bush niggers," despite his veneer of Yankee imperialist ingenuity, and that O'Neill's play confirmed an American "race psychology" predicated on the belief that blacks everywhere would be tripped up by their "primitive minds."[70] The term that crops up in reviews is "negro psychology" (a "weird play of negro psychology"). *The Emperor Jones* is about a "des-

Figure 23. O'Neill in a photograph published in *Town and Country* in October 1946. The caption explains that he began his mask collection after writing *The Emperor Jones*. To be "deep," by implication, one must be willing to explore a "primitive" that is in some displaced way linked to ideologies of imperialism and racism. The photograph positions O'Neill as a Great White Hunter of the "self." Yale Collection of American Literature Photographs, Beinecke Rare Book and Manuscript Library, Yale University.

pot," wrote one Philadelphia reviewer in 1921, "who fell when he found his psychological powers were exhausted. . . . The intent of the author is to show an American negro's devolution to the lowest depths of the congo forest."[71] Such reviewers saw O'Neill's emperor partly as a dramatic figure, but more as an exhibit of a psychological primitive (Figure 23).[72] This placed black intellectuals of the 1920s in a quandary: they hoped that the new psychology's concepts of repression could be deployed to resignify the primitivism long associated with blacks as an emotional depth that all humans needed to acknowledge and as a creative energy that could enliven and reinvent the arts; but their endorsement of primitivism risked underwriting a discourse that frequently represented blacks as possessing a distinct racial psychological self unsuited for intellectual and social accomplishment.[73]

Where white reviewers perceived "negro psychology" in *The Emperor Jones*, at least one black audience saw only absurd stereotypes of psychological primitives. Langston Hughes tells the story of how Jules Bledsoe attempted to bring " 'Art' to Harlem" with his revival of O'Neill's play at the Lafayette Theatre in the 1930s. When Bledsoe's Jones found himself set upon by what he takes to be "ha'nts" in the forest, members of the audience yelled with derision and mirth: "Them ain't no ghosts, fool! . . . Why don't you come on out o' that jungle—back to Harlem where you belong?" Bledsoe finally interrupted his performance to lecture his audience on art and decorum, but many continued to howl and laugh. "And that," concludes Hughes, hinting at his own reading of the play, "was the end of *The Emperor Jones* on 135th Street."[74]

Had these auditors perused the stage directions, no doubt they would have been provoked to voice disapproval of a number of stereotypes. Jones's features are sketched as *"typically negroid, yet there is something decidedly distinctive about his face—an underlying strength of will."* Another pivotal "yet" follows the description of his brightly colored uniform: *"Yet there is something not altogether ridiculous about his grandeur"* (1:1033). After Jones confronts the "ha'nt" of Jeff, a man he killed over a gambling dispute, his eyes—in stereotypical minstrel or coon song fashion—*"roll wildly"* (1:1048). The leader of the "woods niggers," Lem, whose "black" magic intimidates, manipulates, and finally executes Jones, is imagined as an *"ape-faced old savage of the extreme African type"* (1:1060). Lem sounds very much like a stage "Indian": "I cook um money, make um silver bullet" (1:1061). His language fits James Weldon Johnson's description of the stage accent Gilpin had to mimic when he played the role of the black preacher, William Custis, who visits the President in John Drinkwater's *Abraham Lincoln* (1919): "[It was] a dialect . . . such as no American Negro would ever use. . . . a slightly darkened pidgin-English or the form of speech a big Indian chief would employ in talking with the Great White Father at Washington."[75]

The American history of racist iconography reveals other stereotypes in the text that inhabited the cultural swamp of O'Neill's literary imagination. In the penultimate scene Jones finds himself in a part of the woods he recalls somehow having known before, a space by a river in which he must contend with the apparition of a "Congo witch-doctor" (1:1057), whose incantations summon a crocodile god with an appetite for would-be black emperors. Jones has presumably stumbled into the depths of his racial unconscious formed in darkest Africa. Yet when the crocodile god emerges from the river to consume his holy sacrifice, and Jones shoots this "ha'nt" with his last bullet (thereby leaving himself truly defenseless against his island pursuers), it would have been clear to at least some black and white auditors that they had seen such images elsewhere—imprinted on cigar boxes and post cards, and molded in the shape of useful domestic objects like letter openers. One cigar box, titled

Figure 24. "Little African: A Dainty Morsel" (c. 1910), image on a cigar box. This object is, as Jan Faulkner has pointed out, part of the "alligator-bait" genre. Collection of Jan Faulkner, as photographed and published in *Ethnic Notions*, ed. Robbin Henderson et al. (Berkeley: Berkeley Art Center, 1982).

"Little African: A Dainty Morsel" (c. 1910), shows a naked black infant crawling away from a sharp-toothed alligator climbing over a river bank in a jungle setting (Figure 24). Even when the gator's victims are adults, as in the postcard "A Darkey's Prayer" (c. 1940), they are really children at heart, for such images promote the idea that blacks are inept, jungle primitives who—even when costumed as white-collar workers—are incapable of growing up (Figure 25). The black intellectual George Schuyler, writing in 1929 about white literary stereotypes of blacks, perhaps with O'Neill's crocodile god in mind, criticized the image of the "civilized" black who is secretly ever ready to "strip off his Hart Schaffner & Marx suit, grab a spear and ride off wild-eyed on the back of a crocodile."[76]

Charles Gilpin, who dazzled audiences with his performance of the emperor in the original production, found himself haunted by racism both off and on stage. When the New York Drama League conducted its annual poll in 1920–21 to determine who the theatre community regarded as the season's greatest contributors, Gilpin's name, along with O'Neill's, made the list. The League initially refused to seat Gilpin at its annual awards dinner. O'Neill helped lead the charge against this racism, and Gilpin was seated (gaining much publicity for himself, O'Neill,

Figure 25. "A Darkey's Prayer" (c. 1940), postcard. Collection of Jan Faulkner, as photographed and published in *Ethnic Notions*, ed. Robbin Henderson et al. (Berkeley: Berkeley Art Center, 1982).

and the play in the process).[77] But when Gilpin began excising some of the racist language in O'Neill's script (e.g., "nigger") during his riveting performances (as did Paul Robeson by the late 1930s), the playwright warned the "black bastard" that he would "beat [him] up" unless he stopped.[78]

O'Neill dumped Gilpin for Robeson after the American run: "[Gilpin] played Emperor with author, play & everyone concerned," he grouched to a friend. "I've corralled another Negro to do it over there [London]." In 1933 he told Eugene Jr. that it was merely a "superstition to think [that] only a coon can play [the role of Jones]."[79] Claude McKay,[80] the astute black Caribbean novelist who wrote for *The Liberator* in the early 1920s, held a higher opinion of Gilpin than of his venue: "[Gilpin] made the play. . . . [He] saves [it] from becoming a mere comic grotesque."[81]

O'Neill's *Emperor* was also hit hard by 1930s critics on the Left. In 1935 Robert Stebbins bemoaned that Robeson, who starred in the 1933 film version, was "forced into caricatures of his people," including the "swamps and jungle" metaphor of the black "primitive mind."[82] Charmion Von Wiegand noted that although the play seems to allude to the dictator of Haiti, it does not concern itself with the "*history* of the struggle of Negroes on the islands." What we get, rather, is "merely a jungle backdrop"—a theatrical stereotype.[83] Perhaps in his own eyes, the O'Neill who once wrote radical poems and who made himself at home in Greenwich Village flophouses frequented by immigrants and blacks never had any intention of (as he put it) "discriminating," but critics like McKay, Johnson, Stebbins, Von Wiegand, and others suggested that the black people whom O'Neill thought of himself as uplifting through drama were, at times, white theatrical, psychological, and commercial stereotypes of black people. This was, for some, the real tragedy of *The Emperor Jones.*

But O'Neill's play is not without its complexity and critical edge. The forest or jungle that Jones traverses exposes him to historical scenes of Africans cramped in the hull of a ship making its passage to America and of a nightmarish slave auction in which he is a living commodity. A history of enslavement is thus linked to the eerie "formless fears" that bedevil Jones. This history undergirds Jones's own willingness to dominate blacks. Sadly, the emperor's words show that he has internalized the very language of domination that, historically, has subjugated blacks in both America and the West Indies. When he is awakened by the sound of Smithers's whistle, his threatening response sounds like that of a plantation overseer: "I'll get de hide frayled off some o' you niggers sho'!" (1:1033). Jones's values are those of the crudest capitalist individualist—"I'se after de coin" (1:1042). Thus O'Neill sees his emperor in no one-dimensional way as a timeless psychological primitive but as a man whose subjectivity has been structured by the history and partly colonized by the ideologies of American racism.

O'Neill also made it patent that the black Jim Harris and the white Ella Downey have internalized racist ideologies and stereotypes that sabotage their "psychology" in *All God's Chillun Got Wings.* Jim's first romantic stirrings for Ella drive him to drink "chalk 'n' water tree times a day" (2:281) in the hopes of turning white, while Ella (only as a young girl) wishes she were black. But both Jim and Ella value white as a symbol of goodness, purity, and superiority. "All love is white" (2:293), says Jim. Ella employs "white" to signify Jim's love for and loyalty to her, but she also uses it to signify social and intellectual achievement. The issue that serves as a lightning rod for racial tensions between them is Jim's strenuous effort to "pass" the bar examination, to prove that intellectually, as well as emotionally, he is (in Ella's words) "the whitest of the white" (2:304). The possibility that Jim might "pass" intellectually, and thus, by implication, surpass his own white wife, is what makes Ella hysterical.

Notwithstanding O'Neill's endeavor to establish a social context for his audience's reading of emotions, his opening stage directions disclose that he too can be complicit in Ella's racist assumption that blacks behave in certain ways because "it's in the blood" (2:304) (perhaps what one sees in *Thirst* as the mulatto sailor's "*black*" blood). The black children playing in the street are defined as unfettered emotional "*participants in the spirit of Spring,*" whereas the white kids laugh "*constrainedly in natural emotion.*" Natural versus constrained emotions exemplify "*their difference in race*" (2:279). Here O'Neill reproduces contemporary assumptions about black primitive emotions as that which "repressed" whites can envy. O'Neill would probably disagree with Jim that "natural laws" (2:313) finally prevent him from "passing" (the "bar"), but his stage directions show that he also could slip into this ideology of racial psychology, giving evidence of what Stebbins termed (racist) "automatic writing."[84]

O'Neill's emphasis on psychological determinism in both *The Emperor Jones* and *All God's Chillun* often stands in contradiction to his insights into the internalization of racist language and images. The defiant Jones becomes increasingly hysterical as he realizes that he is a psychological victim of his "primitive" African past and of the American history of enslavement. The past that asserts itself as present makes his escape impossible and his failure unavoidable. Jim too is compelled to conclude that his racial past wholly determines his present: "We're never free—except to do what we have to do" (2:292). We see both Jones and Harris succumb to a racial psychological fate that overshadows other themes in these plays which suggest that social forces, not an atavistic black psychological self, crush the efforts of blacks to succeed.

It was precisely Jim's astonishing oversusceptibility to the internalization of white racism that some black critics found implausible, vexing, and damaging to the image of blacks.[85] Joe Mott, the black gambler in *The Iceman Cometh*, also suffers from an overdose of the desire to be called "white" (3:590). But Joe, unlike Jim Harris, for a time reveals this "pipe dream" to be a racist nightmare from which he is desperate to awaken.

As *Emperor* and *All God's Chillun* stand, neither the corrupt version of the militant "new negro" nor the insecure version of the professional "new negro" is able to keep his head above water, away from the sharks. Notwithstanding O'Neill's nondiscriminatory intentions, to some extent his race plays performed similar services to those provided by the nineteenth century's minstrel shows: "a racial structure," writes Eric Lott, that is ideologically and psychologically unstable requires "its boundaries to be staged."[86] In his late "Irish plays," O'Neill endowed his Irish with a fate-driven "psychology" that made them seem deep and complex, even in—perhaps because of—their domestic turbulence. Some of the fate-driven working-class primitives he dramatized in his *Glencairn* cycle were given subjectivity enough to be sentimental, if not quite to experience middle-class angst, as does Yank in the concluding scene of *The Hairy Ape*. By contrast, O'Neill's 1920s infusion of "psychology" into stage blacks often exhibited them as fate-driven primitives, sunk by the "depth" within.

The postwar years, during which O'Neill's plays about workers and racial tension helped establish his reputation, were tumultuous ones, literally exploding with various kinds of social protest accompanied by the state and institutional repression of radicalism. The union movement had gained considerable strength and confidence during and just after the war, when O'Neill wrote and staged his *Glencairn* cycle. By 1919, five million workers had joined unions and four million participated in strikes and lockouts.[87] The U.S. Steel strike (365,000 workers), the United Mine Workers' strike (400,000), the Boston police strike, and the Seattle general strike (supported by the Industrial Workers of the World) convinced many commentators that America was primed for its own postwar "red" revolution.[88]

Hysteria about impending revolution was intensified on May 1, 1919, when a New York postal clerk discovered eight mail bombs addressed to top government officials (thirty-six bombs were finally located). One bomb exploded in the yard of Attorney General Mitchell A. Palmer, who retaliated by arresting anarchists, Socialists, Communists, and members of the Industrial Workers of the World in the late autumn of 1919, on January 2, 1920 (the big raid), and also throughout the spring and summer of 1920. Thousands of radicals were deported on the Buford, the "Soviet Ark," as Palmer implemented his "ship or shoot" policy.[89] The "blaze of revolution," Palmer warned, "was eating its way into the homes of the American workman, . . . licking the altars of churches, leaping into the belfrey of the school bell, crawling into the sacred corners of American homes, seeking to replace marriage vows with libertine laws." He pledged that he would sweep "the nation of . . . alien filth."[90] O'Neill, who was certainly attuned to these developments,[91] probably was satirizing Palmer (or one of his congressional supporters) in *The Hairy Ape*, when the prisoners read Yank passages from the newspaper's report of Senator Queen's speech. The senator fulminates against the Industrial Workers of the World as "the Industrial *Wreckers* of the World" (2:152) and swears to safeguard an America where "Truth, Honor, Liberty, Justice, and the Brotherhood of Man are a religion absorbed with one's mother's milk, taught at our father's knee" (2:153).

It became risky to be "red." The New York State assembly expelled five Socialist members in 1918; teachers were forced to take a patriotic oath of allegiance; college alumni and students demanded the dismissal of radical professors; immigration laws were devised to restrict the influx of politically "alien" immigrants. Although the purge subsided by fall of 1920, the "fear of being thought radical persisted,"[92] and the decade of the "Tired Radical" had begun.[93] By 1925, Frederick Lewis Allen inferred, the college socialist of 1915 "cared not at all" about the exploitation of steel workers: "Fashions had changed."[94] A 1926 *Survey Graphic* symposium on "Where Are the Pre-War Radicals?" asked pre-war reformers to account for the ostensible political fatigue. Several maintained that a number of radicals had grown too prosperous; Charlotte Perkins Gilman suggested that some had substituted activism with "wallow[ing] in Freudian Psycho-analysis"; and Norman Thomas proposed that intellectuals entranced by the *American Mercury*, edited by H. L. Mencken and George Jean Nathan, were more agitated by cultural shallowness than by economic deprivation.[95]

O'Neill began his decade by winning two Pulitzer Prizes for *Beyond the Horizon* (1921), about emotionally frustrated impoverished farmers, and for *"Anna Christie,"* about a former prostitute who finds true love. In an interview he gave in 1922, the thirty-four-year-old O'Neill recanted the socialist and anarchist sentiments of his teens and early twenties, sounding very much like a bored radical: "Time was, when I was an active Socialist, and, after that, a philosophical anarchist. But today I can't feel that anything like that matters."[96]

O'Neill made a swift transition from sleeping on lumpy mattresses in the Hell Hole in 1915 to being tired in style, in mansions far more stately than those most playwrights owned in the 1920s and 1930s: Brook Farm, his country house in Ridgefield, Connecticut (1922–26), Spithead in Bermuda (1926–27), Château Le Plessis in France (1929–30), Casa Genotta in the wealthy community of Sea Island, Georgia (1932–36), and Tao House in Marin County, California (1937–44). In the mid-1940s, when an acquaintance described herself to the playwright as "philosophically . . . an anarchist but in practical matters a capitalist," he hailed her as "the wisest woman he had met in a thousand years."[97] During rehearsals for *The Iceman Cometh* (1940) in 1946, O'Neill's third wife, Carlotta Monterrey, reproached a reporter for inquiring about her husband's political beliefs: "A writer who talks about politics is a fool. He should never talk about politics because politics change, art doesn't." The O'Neill who had been photographed "weapon in mit" in Madison Avenue–style pinstripes appears to have subscribed in part to his wife's observation.[98]

Yet during these same rehearsals, O'Neill mounted a spirited verbal assault on the American Pipe Dream, insisting that if a true American history were ever written and taught, the portraits of "our great national heroes" would have to be "taken out and burned." Croswell Bowen, the interviewer, diagnosed these unpatriotic pyrotechnics as an expression of O'Neill's "Black Irishness," a symptom of his loss of Catholic faith. Bowen partly defused O'Neill's radicalism by reading it as a captivating ethnic performance "in the tradition of all the great half-drunken Irishmen who sound off in bars all over the world. . . . extravagant, rambling, full of madness and violence, but studded with enough essential truth and insight to force you to listen with troubled fascination."[99]

Socialist and anarchist "gabble" left its enduring and sometimes ambiguous echoes in O'Neill's work and, as we will see, contributed much to the historical complexity of his staging of "depth." O'Neill's plays are, ideologically, sometimes far more multifaceted and contradictory than his own directives about how to read them suggest. In the sections that follow I will help clarify the historical context of both his plays and the discourse through which he wished us to value and interpret them by continuing to engage the Left's contemporary responses to O'Neill, which have been largely forgotten by many mainstream O'Neill scholars whose work is more current.[100]

O'Neill and the Anarchist-Feminist Critique of Personal Life

A substantive history of radical critiques of personal life in America from the antebellum period to the present has yet to be written.[101] This context, like the history of American family life and the cultural history of pop psychology discussed in previous chapters, sheds crucial historical light on the ideological tensions informing O'Neill's representation of the personal in his drama. American Fourierists, anarchists, and socialists in the mid-nineteenth century—such as Arthur Brisbane, Stephen Pearl Andrews, Marx Lazarus, and Robert Owens—inaugurated a holistic critique of society that encompassed marriage, sexual behaviors, and gender construction.[102] But in the early twentieth century mainstream Socialists far outnumbered other Socialists who sought to make women's emancipation, sexual liberation, and birth control central components of a Socialist program for cultural transformation.[103] Historian Mari Jo Buhle argues that at this key phase the failure of Socialism to develop and promote a revolutionary critique of the personal doomed it to "the backwash of history."[104] The birth control movement in the 1910s, led by Margaret Sanger, threatened to open up the Socialist concept of revolution so that it would address problems of gender, sexuality, and the family, as well as economic and political exploitation. But conventional Socialists—men and women who subscribed to the ideology of separate spheres—sought to maintain (or even to establish) the "respectability" of their party by holding this new morality at bay.[105]

By the 1910s socialist intellectuals and bohemians such as Max Eastman and Floyd Dell sought energetically to fuse socialism with feminist arguments, birth control agitation, and the campaign for freedom of sexual behavior. The July 1915 issue of *The Masses*, for example, not only represented traditional socialist concerns, it introduced a new category of books in its advertisement section: "Sex" (listing thirteen "sex" books). Yet historians have noted that this ostensibly progressive critique sometimes elided fundamental economic, political, and class matters.[106]

After the period of the Red Purge, there emerged a split between the traditions of personal liberation and social transformation. In the twenties, Eli Zaretsky writes, "movements such as progressive education, psychoanalysis, and sexual freedom reflected the illusion that personal life could be transformed without a transformation of the mode of production."[107] During this decade, proponents of pop psychology and psychoanalysis generally detached the category of the psychological and their notion of therapy from mass radical politics.[108] "You could get only a handful of Village radicals to demand the liberation of Eugene Debs, Tom Mooney or Sacco and Vanzetti," Joseph Freeman recalled about the late 1910s and 1920s, "but you could organize a one hundred per cent united front in protest against the suppression of Arthur Schnitzler's novelette about Casanova. . . . [who] symbolized the dream that everything is permitted."[109] Another factor in this split was the burgeoning postwar advertising industry, which mass-produced individualizing ideologies of the personal that sought both to narrow the social interests of consumers and to structure and profit from their anxieties.[110]

As the breach between personal and political liberation took shape, O'Neill was securing his reputation as America's greatest playwright. O'Neill's psychological plays, *Welded* (1924), *Desire Under the Elms* (1924), *Strange Interlude* (1928), and *Mourning Becomes Electra* (1931), and his spiritual-psychological crisis plays, *The Great God Brown* (1926), *Lazarus Laughed* (1927), and *Days Without End* (1933), offer dramatic evidence of how O'Neill had come to look to "life outside production for [his] sense of personal meaning."[111] O'Neill's angst-filled "hairy ape," Yank, acted out aspects of this ideological rift in 1921, as he moved from a belief in himself as steel and in his workplace as "de woild" (where he "belonged") to fevered anxieties about being "born" (2:160), about spiritual rootlessness (not belonging), and about being trapped "in de middle" between heaven and "oith." What could easily have been a dramatic treatment of the industrial class struggle—"fratricide"—bleeding America in the late 1910s and early 1920s was intended, in O'Neill's words, to be (therapeutic) "propaganda . . . [about] man, who has lost his old harmony with nature, the harmony which he used to have as an animal and has not yet acquired in a spiritual way."[112]

The strikes of 1919, the government repression of radical groups, and factional disputes within the Socialist party combined to heighten the authority and heroic stature of revolutionary Russia in the eyes of American Communists and of many intellectuals on the Left.[113] As the Communist Left became dominated by the Soviet Union in the 1920s, revolution came to signify solely the transformation of the state and the economy. Some evidence of this shift can be seen in the difference between *The Masses* of the 1910s and the *New Masses* of the 1930s. Probably out of nostalgia for *The Masses*, edited by Eastman and Dell, O'Neill supported the founding of the *New Masses* in 1925–26 as a contributing editor. His endorsement was used in the new magazine's promotional campaign: "I believe *The New Masses* will bear the same relationship to the commercial press as the experimental theatre does to Broadway. My blessing and lustiest cheers."[114] At this point the *New Masses* ranged from liberal to Left in its editorial policies and contributions; but by the late 1920s it adhered more sternly to Soviet guidelines. Only a few years after O'Neill gave the new magazine his "lustiest cheers," contributors to *New Masses* and other leftist magazines castigated his plays as reactionary. By the outset of the Depression, Dell, a committed Socialist, felt that the increasingly sectarian *New Masses*, spearheaded by Mike Gold, promoted (in the words of Daniel Aaron) "a too narrow and rigid construction of the revolution."[115]

Gold, for example, in his "Defense of Agitprop" (1934), published in the Communist party's *Daily Worker*, assured his readers that "subtle realism and psychology have little place in the workers' theatre. Subtlety and psychology are the fruits of leisure."[116] Gold censured bourgeois psychological dramas, such as O'Neill's, on these grounds. As "currents of personal radicalism" vital to leftist critique in the 1910s were increasingly deprecated by Communists as "petty bourgeois" or romantic, the "various ideologies of personal life" reciprocated by rejecting socialism as "irrelevant" to their therapeutic goals.[117] O'Neill's plays at turns contributed to and contested this momentous modern ideological trend—the dichotomization of the categories of the personal and the political.[118]

This break would have seemed alien to the O'Neill who had studied anarchism and who wrote his first full-length play, *The Personal Equation* (1915), about an anarchist-feminist.[119] Early-twentieth-century American anarchists had a singularly expansive notion of revolution and thus developed shrewd critiques of bourgeois ideologies of personal life. O'Neill was as familiar with these critiques as he was with some of the anarchists who wrote them. Winifred Frazer has argued persuasively that O'Neill met Emma Goldman, America's most well-known anarchist-feminist, in either Provincetown or Greenwich Village in the late 1910s, although there is no known written evidence to confirm this. Goldman's *Social Significance of Modern Drama* (1914) had its basis in stenographic notes made by an admirer of her lectures at New York's Berkeley Theatre in 1914. O'Neill spent 1915–16 in lower Manhattan and certainly would have been interested in her readings of Ibsen, Strindberg, Shaw, and Hauptmann as social iconoclasts. Her view of American theatre in 1914 was identical to O'Neill's criticism of what he in the 1930s called the "amusement-racket": Americans, she lamented, "have so far looked upon the theater as a place of amusement only, exclusive of ideas and inspiration."[120]

The anarchist magazine *Mother Earth* (1906–17), founded by Goldman, often featured articles on the politics of modern drama. Goldman knew O'Neill's work. When residing in London in 1925, she tried to arrange protests against the banning of the Boston production of *Desire Under the Elms*. That year she lectured on O'Neill in Manchester.[121] Saxe Commins, O'Neill's dear friend and editor, was Goldman's beloved nephew. Both Commins and his sister, Stella Commins Ballantine, participated in the Provincetown Players' productions. In June 1937, O'Neill wrote Commins to request publications by "Emma," probably in reference to anarchist themes in plays he was planning to write.[122]

O'Neill had close ties to several anarchists who were on intimate terms with Goldman. Terry Carlin, for instance, spent much time with O'Neill both in Greenwich Village and Provincetown in the mid-1910s. It was Carlin who told Susan Glaspell, of the newly formed Provincetown Players, about O'Neill. He was an occasional guest of the O'Neills at Peaked Hill Bar in the early 1920s. Carlin, whom O'Neill helped support financially years later, was the model for Larry Slade, the disillusioned philosophical anarchist in *Iceman*.[123] Carlin actually lived with the infamous Donald Vose in 1915. Vose, the model for Donald Parritt in *Iceman*, betrayed his anarchist colleague Matthew Schmidt to the authorities. Hippolyte Havel, a friend of many in the Provincetown crowd including O'Neill and Carlin, frequently contributed his essays on anarchism to *Mother Earth* and edited the short-lived *Revolt* (1916), to which O'Neill claimed (to Beatrice Ashe) he had contributed some of his poetry. He too was the original for an anarchist character in *Iceman*. O'Neill was fond of the anarchist editor M. Eleanor Fitzgerald (Fitzi), whom he knew as the indefatigable business manager of the Provincetown Playhouse on Macdougal Street. When Fitzgerald suffered financial hardships in the late 1940s, O'Neill assisted her. She was first brought to the Provincetown Playhouse by Goldman, to see Jig Cook's *Athenian Women* (1918).[124] Fitzgerald worked with Goldman on *Mother Earth* and later married Goldman's ex-lover Alexander Berkman. Fitzgerald and Berkman founded *Blast* (1916–17), a magazine that reported and analyzed labor's struggle with capital and the state.

O'Neill's respect and admiration for Berkman's integrity as an anarchist activist is manifest in his correspondence with him in 1927. (Berkman had attempted to assassinate Henry Clay Frick, the steel magnate, in 1892, and was imprisoned for fourteen years.) O'Neill wrote Berkman about the possibility of commissioning him to translate his plays into Russian: "I had had a very deep admiration for you for years, and that [first] meeting [in Greenwich Village] was sort of an unexpected fulfillment. As for my fame, (God help us!) and your infame, I would be willing to exchange a good deal of mine for a bit of yours. It is not so hard to write what one feels as truth. It is damned hard to live it!"[125]

O'Neill's preferred brand of anarchism, however, was the Individualist anarchism espoused by Benjamin Tucker. Tucker targeted personal relations as a crucial object of critique. In 1888, he argued that anarchism advocates open-ended ("varied") sexual relations predicated on economic independence. Anarchists "look forward to a time when every individual, whether man or woman, shall be self-supporting . . . when the love relations between these independent individuals shall be as varied as are individual inclinations and attractions; and when the children born of these relations shall belong exclusively to the mothers until old enough to belong to themselves."[126] Tucker, nonetheless, as his statement about mothers suggests, did not allow his advocacy of free love to disturb his conventional notions of gender difference, convinced as he was of "the general inferiority of woman as worker."[127]

The most sophisticated anarchist critiques of the personal came from Emma Goldman and contributors to *Mother Earth*. Goldman and her colleagues linked their attack on the institution of private property to their critique of the "ownership" of women in marriage. Thus John R. Coryell's "Value of Chastity" (1913), in its criticism of the double standard, defined female chastity as a woman's "physical fidelity to her owner"; whereas "in man [chastity] has never meant more than abstention from injuring the property of other men."[128] In an earlier piece Coryell characterized "love" within this ownership scheme as producing "victims of a morbid and unhealthy sexuality."[129] Goldman, who always kept in mind the range of victims of sexual ideology, argued that prostitutes are subjected to a hypocritical moral censure because they sell their bodies "out of wedlock."[130]

The anarchist-feminist critique of the capitalist romance-as-ownership attitude resonates with themes in many of O'Neill's plays. The romance of Evelyn and Jack, the elite university couple in *Abortion* (1914), is based on principles of ownership (and, unbeknownst to Evelyn, the double standard). As Evelyn watches Jack excel on the baseball diamond, she reacts to other female spectators as if they are ocular trespassers: "I felt like standing in my seat," she tells her fiancé, "and shouting to all of them: 'What right have you to think of him? He is *mine, mine!*' . . . Or will be in three months" (1:208). Christine Mannon's bold defense of her marital infidelity to her daughter in *Mourning*

Becomes Electra resounds with the logic of *Mother Earth*: "I'm talking to you as a woman now, not as mother to daughter! . . . I want you to know that's what I've felt about myself for over twenty years, giving my body to a man I—" (2:916). Soon after, she accuses her husband of treating her as his "property" (2:944).

While early-twentieth-century conventional feminists typically focused their critique on legal and political matters rather than on sexual and domestic problems, anarchist-feminists launched both economic and psychological critiques of wedded and familial "bliss."[131] Anarchist-feminists saw privatized marriage based on emotional ownership as psychologically volatile. Of the young couple who enter the privatized bonds of matrimony, Voltarine de Cleyre wrote: "[They] are thrown too much and too constantly in contact, and speedily exhaust the delight of each other's presence." This intensity makes divorce psychologically devastating.[132]

Goldman understood jealousy, not as a core of possessive desire emerging naturally from within one's darkest depths, but as an emotion squeezed into being by assumptions about ownership. Goldman tied jealousy to the historical institution of monogamy, and monogamy to economic history, to support her proposition that jealousy is "the artificial result of an artificial cause." Actual ownership of women, she argues, sets the historical stage for psychological ownership. Jealousy in women, Goldman concludes, usually originates from "economic fear for herself and her children."[133] This social analysis is not "deep" in a 1920s pop psychological sense (unmasking a "hidden" self); rather, its theoretical scrutiny is on a socially pressured and positioned feminine "self" forced to cultivate psychological survival strategies.[134]

Goldman repeatedly criticized the fiction (and friction) of "the dualism of the sexes."[135] In *The Social Significance of Modern Drama*, she praised Strindberg's *The Father* (1887) for recognizing that the false division of the sexes helps create the conditions for ambivalence and psychological domination. Strindberg's play, she argued, understood that the sentimental mother imposes on her young a "bondage harder to bear and more difficult to escape than the brutal fist of the father." But Goldman held that the emotional enslaving of another is "by no means a [political] step toward advancement."[136]

By the late 1910s and early 1920s, O'Neill was at a significant theoretical and cultural crossroads. He had available to him both the anarchist-feminist social critique of the personal and the increasingly popular psychoanalytic imagining of the personal that posited assumptions about psychological depth.[137] He favored the latter. While pop psychoanalysis often promoted sexual expression as the means of self-realization, anarchist-feminists envisioned sexual liberation more expansively as only one dimension of revolutionary change.[138] O'Neill's *The Personal Equation*, written in 1915 while he was studying playwriting under George Pierce Baker at Harvard, exhibits both his impressive grasp of and his ambivalent relationship to the exhaustive anarchist-feminist critique of personal life.

Olga Tarnoff, the fiery advocate of anarchist-feminism in *The Personal Equation*, is perhaps the most politically articulate character in all of O'Neill's oeuvre. She sounds much like Emma Goldman. Her opening volley is a striking, "masculine"-sounding diatribe against the Socialist faith in the ballot. "How I loathe their eternal platitudes, their milk-and-water radicalism, their cut-and-dried sermons for humble voters! As if to vote were not also to acquiesce in the present order of things, to become a cog in the machine which grinds the voter himself to bits!" (1:311). Personal life, as she understands it, does not exist outside the political: "What are we beside the ideal we fight for?" she asks Tom, her lover. "We cannot change conditions in our lives, perhaps, but we can make our lives a living protest against those conditions" (1:315).

O'Neill is sensitive to the predicament of radical women who must unceasingly contend with deep-rooted sexism both inside as well as outside the movement. The newspaper, for instance, offers a blatantly sexist account of Olga's antiwar speech in Union Square: "Over-strung lady anarchists of the Olga type are a constant and dangerous menace to society and should be confined to some asylum for the criminal-insane." Male anarchists, of course, would not typically be psychologically branded as hysterical—"over-strung." Tom sympathizes by wrapping his arm around Olga. She rebuffs her lover's *protective attitude* (the stage directions inform us) and continues to frame a political response to the newspaper's account. "It seems I'm a dangerous anarchist inciting to murder because I call upon men not to shoot their brother men for a fetish of red, white and blue, a mockery called patriotism." Tom, locked into his role as protector, condemns the article on chivalrous grounds, indicting the reporter's "manhood" for slinging "his muddy ink at a woman." Olga recoils from being classified primarily within the category "woman" and again tries to instruct Tom, realizing that the personal may be even more difficult to transform than conventionally political relations: "What an old-fashioned idea! Aren't we equals when we fight for liberty—regardless of sex?" (1:313). She would surely have agreed with Goldman who, in her book on modern drama, wrote: "The radicals, no less than the feminists, must realize that a mere external change in their economic and political status, cannot alter the inherent or acquired prejudices and superstitions which underlie their slavery and dependence, and which are the main causes of antagonism between the sexes."[139]

O'Neill shows how notions of social change can be grievously reductive when they ignore questions of sexism. The anarchist Enwright, in reference to the utopia to come, has the audacity to tell Olga and another male comrade: "The civilized woman has long been living beyond her mental means. She will be only too glad to find a good excuse to throw aside her pretence of equality with man to return to polygamy" (1:321). And Cocky, a sexist seaman who lives up to his name, reacts violently to Olga's speech urging the seaman to strike: "Let 'er be 'ome a-nursin' of 'er babies, I says. Men is men and—" (1:351). Olga knows what she's up against. When Tom proposes that they marry to avert the stigma of living in sin, Olga protests disappointedly: "There's no feeling of enforced servitude on my part. There can be no complacent sense of ownership on yours. (*with smiling irony*) Perhaps that's what you regret?" (1:315).

Here, then, was an opening for O'Neill to dramatize the impulse to own others, not just psychologically (as he would later do in *Strange Interlude*), but as a sociological manifestation. Through Olga, O'Neill began to scrutinize how socially constituted roles, attitudes, and expectations generate ambivalence. Curiously, O'Neill's letters to Beatrice Ashe, composed just before and while he wrote *The Personal Equation* in the winter of 1915, show him consumed by his dependency on her and by his desire to own her. In November, he nominated himself her "much-abused slave"; in December, he compared himself to a watch running down, "My Own, My own . . . when you are taken away—I stop!"; in February, he addressed Beatrice apprehensively as "My Own (?)."[140] But if O'Neill can be read self-reflexively as Tom, the wavering anarchist, he is also part Olga. The playwright's fierce antiwar sentiments ("Fratricide" appeared in the Socialist *Call* in May 1914) and his own prominent "large spirited black eyes" (1:311) associate him with his redoubtable heroine. What the anarchist leader Hartman recognizes about patriotic workers—that ideology grips the emotions—is surely what Olga realizes about Tom, and possibly even what O'Neill understood about himself in this period of emotional crisis with Beatrice Ashe: "At the first blare of a band, the first call to fatherland and motherland or some such sentimental phantoms, they will all our teachings forget. Now they are in his brain only. The emotional crisis blots them out" (1:320).

Although O'Neill grasped the political significance of emotional conditioning, *The Personal Equation* exhibits his ambivalence about—perhaps even his resentment against—the anarchist-feminist critiques of the personal voiced so vigorously and incisively by Olga. The call of both the "fatherland" and the "motherland" signal the victory of the "personal equation" over the political. As Hartman predicted, patriotism as a proof of manhood takes precedence over anarchist antiwar arguments, even among activists like Whitely. Reading about German atrocities in an English newspaper, Whitely responds manfully to the clarion of the "fatherland": "By God, if they keep on doing things like this—(*slapping the newspaper*) I will enlist! And so will every other red-blooded man" (1:385). And Olga answers the call of the "motherland." The ideological plot machinery of O'Neill's appropriately titled play enacts the sexist jeer of Cocky: "Let 'er be 'ome a-nursin' of 'er babies." Once Olga becomes pregnant, she is feminized. When Tom undertakes a precarious mission of sabotage (violent anarchist activity was, historically, a rare occurrence),[141] Olga attempts to dissuade him, having—in her own words—"grown so weak and tender toward him" (1:383). She is conscripted by the "motherland" in a double sense; in addition to being the mother of a child, Olga becomes Tom's caretaker-for-life after he suffers brain damage (the result of his abortive attempt at sabotage).

Notwithstanding this "motherland" feminization, Olga rallies in her final speech to argue that the war is a capitalist ploy to deflect the workers' attention from conflict between the classes (O'Neill's argument in "Fratricide"—"workers . . . are brothers"). She subordinates her personal misfortune to the cause: "What is my small happiness within the light of so great a struggle? . . . It is enough for us to know we are doing our small part, and that our little lives and little deaths count after all. . . . I am proud that I can still call from the depths of my soul. It is well done! Long live the Revolution!"

Her battle cry is undercut by the unexpected interjection of her brain-damaged lover, Tom: "(*with a low, chuckling laugh—mimicking Olga*) Long—live—the Revolution. (*His vacant eyes turn from one to the other of them. A stupid smile plays about his loose lips. Whitely turns* away with a shudder. *Olga stares at the figure in the bed with fascinated horror—then covers her face with her hands*)" (1:386–87). The audience also is expected to "*turn away with a shudder.*" The radicalism of Olga's concluding oration is sabotaged by the power of the personal equation. Words like "revolution," "struggle," and "working class" are rendered superficial as mere impersonal, propagandistic anarchist slogans, parroted by those whose brains have been scrambled.[142]

O'Neill wrote *Now I Ask You* (1916) not long after he arrived in Provincetown and joined the new theatre group. It shows ample evidence of the witty, satiric influence of Glaspell and Cook. Young Lucy Ashleigh, the "lady anarchist" (1:416), professes interest in the birth control movement, free love, psychoanalysis, and Ibsen's *Hedda Gabler*. The sharpness of the anarchist-feminist critique of the personal that one perceives in so many of Olga's speeches is here blunted. Lucy's Grammercy Park bohemianism is merely an expression of her wish to appear unconventional—to pose depth. The stage directions are evident: "*Lucy is an intelligent, healthy, American girl suffering from an overdose of undigested reading, and has mistaken herself for the heroine of a Russian novel.*" Lucy poses depth much as O'Neill often seemed to do before the camera: "There is so much turmoil in my soul. (*appealing to [her family] with a sad smile*) Strindberg's daughter Indra discovered the truth. Life is horrible, is it not?" (1:414). "Life" is justification for her tragic pose. Lucy's stagy anarchist-feminism is pure theatre and is, in effect, a parody of Goldman's tenet: "Anarchism does not involve a choice between Kropotkin and Ibsen; it embraces both."[143]

Lucy's anarchism is safely categorized by the psychology of adolescence as merely the "wild spirit of youth." Mrs. Ashleigh teaches Tom, Lucy's businessman suitor, how to manage the young anarchist's growing pains through psychology (anticipating the deployment of psychology by personnel departments in the 1920s).[144] She instructs him not to exercise the "kindly tolerance" of a patriarch or a brother, but to display his "sympathetic understanding" (1:411–12) in order to tame Lucy.

As in the conclusion of *The Personal Equation* and in some (though not all) of Long's soap-box orations in *The Hairy Ape*, radical critique is neutralized as sloganeering. Lucy refers to the "mob" of people who would attend her wedding as "Stupid bourgeois!" (1:417). Leonora also strikes a bohemian pose when hurling the insult "Bourgeois rhymster!"

(1:431) at Gabriel. When would-be bohemian rebels use the word "bourgeois" in this parodic context, its designation of class appears only as pure surface, as crude propaganda, as mere cant.

The genuine radicalism of *Now I Ask You* is that it demonstrates how the bourgeoisie can take the bite out of potentially radical critique: they simply classify radical discourse as the psychological (adolescent) impulse to be unconventional and to express depth.[145] But *Now I Ask You* never goes on to examine why would-be bohemians struck the pose of "radicalism" at this historical juncture. The ideological tendency of O'Neill's satire is to drain the content of radicalism altogether, by representing it as consisting of only trendy slogans or adolescent rantings. Yet his play also enables one to see that if the bourgeoisie succeed in discarding "bourgeois" as a social category, then they have prevailed by mystifying their own interests and position as a dominant class.

In *The Iceman Cometh*, depth is no longer exhibited as an adolescent pose. Here depth is used to expose the hopeless naiveté of anarchism. Larry Slade is too "deep" for political movements, which he classifies as superficial. Disputing Rocky's portrayal of him as "de old anarchist wise guy, dat knows all de answers," Larry remonstrates: "Forget the anarchist part of it. I'm through with the Movement long since. I saw men didn't want to be saved from themselves, for that would mean they'd have to give up greed, and they'll never pay that price for liberty. . . . I took a seat in the grandstand of philosophical detachment to fall asleep observing the cannibals do their death dance" (3:570). In a letter written just after he had completed *Iceman*, O'Neill explained that human nature is what makes radical political change a pipe dream: "What have you left when you turn over a manure pile—but manure?"[146] Larry too abandons the movement due to "the breed of swine called men" (3:580). His two-sided depth is explicitly antiradical.

> I was born condemned to be one of those who has to see all sides of a question. When you're damned like that, the questions multiply for you until in the end it's all question and no answer. As history proves, to be a worldly success at anything, especially revolution, you have to wear blinders like a horse and see only straight in front of you. . . . The material the ideal free society is constructed from is men themselves and you can't build a marble temple out of mud and manure. (3:580–81)

O'Neill's Individualist anarchism was so individualist that it seemed to recoil from political change entirely: assuming "any social structure will be evil," writes Doris Alexander, "[O'Neill's social philosophy] sees salvation in purely destructive terms."[147]

As in *The Personal Equation, Now I Ask You*, and (to some extent) *The Hairy Ape*, political vocabulary is neutralized as the repetition of hollow slogans. Hugo Kalmar, the perpetually soused anarchist, repeats like a broken record the term first used by Lucy Ashleigh: "Stupid Bourgeois!" As Hugo closes the final act singing the French "Carmagnole," anarchism is staged as nothing more than a barroom joke. The boozy community of pipe-dreamers has turned into a privatized substitute for an anarchist utopia:

> (*They all turn on him and howl him down with amused derision. He stops singing to denounce them in his most fiery style.*) "Capitalist swine! Stupid bourgeois monkeys!" (*He declaims*) "The days grow hot, O Babylon!" (*They all take it up and shout in enthusiastic jeering choruses*) "'Tis cool beneath thy willow trees!" (*They pound their glasses on the table, roaring with laughter, and Hugo giggles with them. In his chair by the window, Larry stares in front of him, oblivious to their racket.*) (3:711)

O'Neill's stage directions are explicit: the audience too is meant to respond to this carnival with laughter, giggles, and amused derision. Again, the social category "bourgeois" is rendered into a drunken, meaningless, harmless joke. Hugo can also be read as a personification of a 1930s political theatre or workers' theatre whose purpose is, in the words of Mike Gold, to "change the world." But the slogans declaimed on such political stages are, through Hugo, "exposed" as crude, clownish, self-deceptive. Sounding like Hitler in one Freudian slip after another, Hugo "proves" that every revolutionary disguises an autocrat: "Gottamned liar, Hickey!" Hugo expostulates. "Does that prove I vant to be aristocrat? I love only the proletariat! I vill lead them! I vill be like a Gott to them! They vill be my slaves! (*He stops in bewildered self-amazement—to Larry appealingly*) I am very trunk, no, Larry?" (3:659). But his "truth" slipped out of his depths. Larry is right, apparently: revolution, like all else, is just a racket.

Doris Alexander was the first critic to establish significant biographical connections between Hugo Kalmar and Hippolyte Havel. The original name for Hugo in O'Neill's notebooks, unavailable to Alexander in 1953, is "Hip" or "Hipp." But Alexander overstated her case when she claimed that O'Neill "reproduced" Havel "accurately" as the fictional Hugo Kalmar.

Havel's many contributions to *Mother Earth*, as well as to other magazines he edited, distinguish him as a politically committed and clearheaded intellectual who was interested in the transformative potential of literature. In his *Mother Earth* piece, "Literature: Its Influence upon Social Life" (1908), the role he envisioned for the "creative artist" was "prophet of the future social order."[148] He writes in a coherent, persuasive, self-assured, political voice not heard in *Iceman*. Because Havel advocates a sophisticated aesthetic, he is impatient with uncrafted, "politically correct" commodities. Thus he lambasted Upton Sinclair's muckraking novel *Moneychangers* (1908), an indictment of Wall Street, on aesthetic grounds. Havel could have been describing O'Neill's Hugo Kalmar: Sinclair's characters are "stilted figures without life or psychological definiteness."[149]

The idea of depth was important to Havel in his essay "The Brothers Karamazov" (1913). Havel's ire is aroused by hack translations of Dostoyevsky's "psychological masterpieces" that reduce them to "dime novels." Inspired by Dostoyevsky, Havel's measure of a "great book" is that "it disturbs one's soul to the utmost depth." O'Neill, who regarded Dostoyevsky as one of his masters, had much in common, intellectually, with "Hip."[150]

In 1912, the temporal setting of *Iceman*, Havel published a moving piece, "The Faith and Record of Anarchists," in which he argued that writers and reporters continually misrepresent anarchists as crude. Sadly, Havel could have been gazing into a crystal ball, viewing O'Neill's rendering of Hugo Kalmar, yet another caricature of an anarchist: "The Anarchists welcome the honest critic. . . . But they resent it strongly if a writer, under the mask of impartiality, offers to the public a work on Anarchy which is tainted with dishonesty. Such a writer is far more dangerous than the ignorant penny-a-liner who fills up his columns with misinformation and false statements."[151] O'Neill's profile of the drunken Kalmar in his introductory stage directions suggests at the outset that he is self-consciously not assuming the role of what Havel called the "honest critic" of anarchists: *There is a foreign atmosphere about him, the stamp of an alien radical, a strong resemblance to the type of Anarchist as portrayed, bomb in hand, in newspaper cartoons* (3:566).

Havel, like Olga Tarnoff, was politically articulate. In no way did he retreat from what O'Neill called "life": he engaged it and tried to change it through his writing. While we must not forget that Kalmar is the playwright's fictional creation, O'Neill's decision to make this cartoon-like anarchist resemble Havel invites us to ponder the implications of the comparison. Mike Gold was in a position to accept this implicit invitation. In an offhand response to the Theatre Guild production of *Iceman* (which he did not go to see, but had heard described), he reminisced in the *Daily Worker* about the nights he spent with Havel and O'Neill in the Hell Hole in Greenwich Village during his Provincetown Players days. "Hippolyte, as a person, was unforgettable in his picturesqueness—he knew a dozen languages, was the offspring of a Czech father and Gypsy mother; had spent his youth in jails and saloons and anarchist enclaves of France, Italy, Bohemia, Poland. The trouble with bourgeois authors like Eugene O'Neill was that the picturesque always impressed him more than the essential."[152]

O'Neill's ambivalence about the anarchist-feminist critique of the personal also is evident in his representation in *Iceman* of Donald Parritt's relationship to his mother Rosa, another anarchist who, like Olga Tarnoff, bears some resemblance to Emma Goldman. Their tense mother/son relationship again demonstrates O'Neill's awareness that anarchism was one of the most difficult revolutionary approaches to put into practice precisely because its political critique included the "personal." Parritt's antagonism toward his mother is directed more at her refusal to conform to feminine stereotypes of motherhood than the substance of her critique of the state and the political economy. Critiques of jealousy and conventional sex roles in *Mother Earth* come to mind when reading Parritt's complaints to Larry, one of his mother's former "free lovers": "I remember her putting on her high-and-mighty free-woman stuff, saying you were still a slave to bourgeois morality and jealousy and you thought a woman you loved was a piece of property you owned. I remember that you got mad and told her 'I don't like living with a whore, if that's what you mean!' " Larry, flustered, denies this exchange. Parritt's raging jealousy (she turned their house into a "whorehouse") prompts him to extol the "bourgeois, property-owning family" (3:635) and "our government" (3:636). What remains intriguingly ambiguous in O'Neill's portrayal of Parritt's jealousy and Larry's possible jealousy is whether he imagines such jealousy as emerging naturally from the psychological depths of the self, or, quite differently, whether he views it as socially produced by stereotypes of womanhood and motherhood and the tight-laced expectations engendered by these roles.

Winifred Frazer, in her provocative interpretation of Rosa Parritt as a figure for Emma Goldman, concludes that O'Neill "necessarily de-stroyed [Emma Goldman] as Rosa, for the vision of the anarchist is as impossible of realization as the tomorrow dreams of becoming a lawyer or newspaperman or politician in the bourgeois world."[153] This read-ing subscribes to Larry's political resignation. By incarcerating Rosa Parritt–Emma Goldman offstage, O'Neill, in 1940, may have been making a veiled statement about politically conscious theatre, for Gold-man, like Havel, championed the transformative possibilities of theatre. Just as Parritt's relationship to Rosa had a supercharged oedipal charac-ter, perhaps, as Frazer hints, O'Neill's political-intellectual relationship to Goldman's anarchist-feminism also was ambivalent, thereby dictat-ing her removal from his stage. But if so, echoes of O'Neill's anarchist sentiments reverberate in his tendency to "parrot" Goldman's critique of a "bourgeois morality and jealousy" that erroneously equated "love" with the ownership of property.

The Propaganda of "Life"

Winifred Frazer has argued that O'Neill's "betrayal" of Rosa Parritt–Emma Goldman conforms to "his general lack of belief in anything." [154] But O'Neill often expressed an ardent belief in what he called "life"—a term related to and just as important to him as "depth." In *Iceman*, for example, O'Neill's category of life displaces the social vision of anar-chism. "Life is too much for me!" (3:710), exclaims Larry Slade, the ex-anarchist—slain by "life." Life breeds resignation: "All I know is I'm sick of life" (3:636). O'Neill regarded this resignation as both "tragic" and "deep." On the eve of World War II, he wrote: "There are moments in [*Iceman*] that suddenly strip the secret soul of man stark naked, not in cruelty or moral superiority, but with an understanding compassion which sees him as a victim of the ironies of life and of himself. These moments are the depths of a tragedy with nothing more that can possi-bly be said."[155] Some of Larry's speeches as well as O'Neill's letter are basically more philosophical-sounding versions of Smitty's angst-rid-den "we're poor little lambs who have lost our way" (1:538) lamenta-tions in *The Moon of the Caribees*.

The political assumptions lodged in O'Neill's concept of "life" are worth clarifying. In 1940 O'Neill reassured George Jean Nathan that *Iceman* "is not 'timely' and has no social significance, as such signifi-cance is defined nowadays."[156] The "nowadays" in O'Neill's statement is crucial. Recall that Goldman's book published in 1914 was titled *The So-*

cial Significance of Modern Drama. Goldman embraced O'Neill's heroes, Shaw, Ibsen, and Strindberg, as "socially significant." Some members of the 1930s Left revised the concept of "socially significant" theatre and occasionally criticized many of the "masters" of modern drama—as well as O'Neill—as bourgeois. Even so, several years before this "sectarian" redefinition of political theatre held sway, O'Neill voiced a somewhat ambivalent and sometimes ambiguous aversion to "socially significant" theatre.

Malcolm Mollan, one of O'Neill's former colleagues on the New London *Telegraph,* interviewed the playwright in 1921. He remembered the twenty-four year old as a crusader and enthusiastically cast the Pulitzer-winning O'Neill in that role: "His work is a continual outcry against poverty, ignorance, human degradation and the vices and miseries that grow out of them. Propounding no theories of reform, with native strategic genius he has sensed the need that first of all the more intellectual and consequently more powerful minority be pricked and stabbed and slashed into acute consciousness of the state of the majority."[157] The increasingly successful dramatist remonstrated that "just life," not politics, is the true subject of drama:

> You perhaps lay too much stress on the sociological bias in back of my work. I'm not a propagandist—not consciously, at any rate—in any sense of the word. I'm a dramatist through and through, that's the answer. What I see everywhere in life is drama. It's what I instinctively seek—human beings in conflict with other human beings, with themselves, with fate. . . . it is just life that interests me as a thing in itself.[158]

"Sociological bias" is reductive; whereas those who dramatize what O'Neill terms life are, by implication, unbiased. This was the source of Mary Mullett's acclamation of O'Neill in an interview he gave shortly after the one with Mollan: "courage and sincerity" is exemplified by his unwillingness "to preach a hidebound creed. He does not tell us what we 'ought' to do."[159] "In special pleading I do not believe," O'Neill told another interviewer in 1924. "Gorki's *A Night's Lodging,* the great proletarian revolutionary play, is really more wonderful propaganda for the submerged than any other play ever written, simply because it contains no propaganda, but simply shows humanity as it is—truth in terms of life. As soon as an author slips propaganda into a play every one feels it and the play becomes simply an argument."[160] But who is the "we" Mary Mullett had in mind when she hailed O'Neill for avoiding didacticism; and who is the "every one" O'Neill refers to who shrinks from "propaganda"? What kind of "hairy apes"—"desperate Yanks"—shrank from "propaganda" in New York's theatres in the twenties?[161]

As much as O'Neill liked to interpret his plays as being about "humanity" and "life," as opposed to "propaganda for the submerged" or anyone else, the plays themselves complicate these abstractions, as in the case of *Welded*. Recall that Woman, the prostitute, considers Michael Cape's self-absorbed psychological hang-ups as "nutty," the result of "bum hooch" or too much "coke." When Michael discerns that she likes giving her "coin" to a pimp who beats her, he can then incorporate her into his universalizing discourse of life. "You got to loin to like it," she confesses, referring to "life." The message, as in O'Neill's statements about *The Hairy Ape*, is that we've all got problems, we're all bewildered, we all "don't belong," we've all "got to loin to like it." This universal "it," however, does not wholly obscure the fact that Michael's "it" is the life of a successful playwright; whereas Woman's "it" is the life of a hooker who hustles rather differently to get her "coin," and who lacks the leisure and the education to learn how to "talk nutty." By the same token, Yank's "not belonging," in or out of the stokehole, is not precisely analogous to O'Neill's experience of "not belonging" in Brook Farm (Ridgefield), Spithead, the château at Le Plessis, Casa Genotta, or Tao House.[162] As preoccupied with "life" as O'Neill was in statements about his dramas, his plays in the 1920s and thereafter wrestle with theoretical concerns shaped by his early intellectual engagement with anarchism and socialism.

O'Neill's poet in *Fog* (1914), unlike the 1920s playwright dramatized in *Welded*, specifies that an inequitable social structure produces different social forms of life. Having survived the sinking of their ocean liner, the poet and a businessman debate the meaning of life in a lifeboat, adrift in an icy fog. The demise of an infant from steerage provokes the poet to challenge the businessman: "What glowing opportunities did life hold out that death should not be regarded as a blessing for him? . . . Surely his prospects of ever becoming anything but a beast of burden were not bright, were they?" (1:99).

The poet's observation does not develop into a systemic critique of child labor, capitalism, or inequalities between social classes as it might have in a 1930s "propaganda" play. Rather, the poet appeals to the businessman's middle-class sense of fair play: "Do you think you would be as successful and satisfied with life if you had started with handicaps, like those which that poor child would have to contend if he had lived?" (1:100). In response to the businessman's dismissal of his "impractical" "Socialistic ideas," the poet, perhaps much like O'Neill at this stage of his life, counters: "I'm not a Socialist—especially—just a humanist" (1:102). When they are rescued, the sensitive humanist elects to remain on the lifeboat, now his deathboat. The poet's depth, we may infer, is the result of his having been wounded by life. In 1914 with *Fog*, O'Neill offers us a businessman who finds the idea of such a wound incomprehensible. But by the 1920s the rupture between poet and businessman had begun to mend ideologically, as plays, novels, and poems published by members of the professional-managerial class for the professional-managerial class suggest that "we" take the "woist punches" from life and are injured, regardless of trifling distinctions like class.

Once the overarching problem is framed as life, one equally ideological solution is an elegiac romance with its opposite—death. "As it is," Edmund muses in *Long Day's Journey*, "I will always be a stranger who never feels at home, who must always be a little in love with death" (3:812). Edmund's tendency to universalize his alienation as life is proof of his depth. In *A Moon for the Misbegotten*, Jamie Tyrone is portrayed as having been injured by life, while Josie is used to make death seem poetic. By morning, with Jamie's head on her breast, she muses maternally: "I hate to bring you back to life, Jim, darling. If you could have died in your sleep, that's what you would have liked, isn't it?" (3:939). The closing line of *Moon* affirms this romance with death: "(*her face sad, tender and pitying—gently*) May you have your wish and die in your sleep soon, Jim, darling. May you rest forever in forgiveness and peace" (3:946). The final line of O'Neill's original draft, by contrast, recalled Phil Hogan's (Shaughnessy in *Long Day's Journey*) socialistic trouncing of the millionaire neighbor who disliked the flavor of hog in his ice-water: "To hell with England, down with bloody tyrants, and God damn Standard Oil!" Josie responds: "Amen!"[163]

In *Long Day's Journey*, "life" sometimes operates as an explanatory substitute for history and for anarchist-feminist issues of concern like gender construction. Mary Tyrone, whom Jamie suspects of having again injected morphine, invokes life as an explanation for her son's sneering incredulity: "But I suppose life has made him like that, and he can't help it. None of us can help the things life has done to us. They're done before you realize it, and once they make you do other things until at last everything comes between you and what you'd like to be, and you've lost your true self forever" (3:749). As in *Iceman*, "life" forces one into a posture of resignation and malaise: things get done to you. On the one hand, O'Neill seems to "preach" an ideology that would have us take Mary at her word that she and Jamie have been hurt by what she names life. On the other hand, he offers us some understanding of Mary's specific background, thereby suggesting that she has been damaged by a particular social and cultural arrangement of life.

Louis Sheaffer gives us an example of what this rhetoric of life can occlude in one of his comments on *Long Day's Journey*: "The family's tragic history appears to have developed less from James Tyrone's strain of penuriousness and other flaws than from Mary Tyrone's abiding immaturity, her inability to face the realities of life and fulfill her obligations as wife and mother."[164] Here Sheaffer does not emphasize that the "realities of life" which position Mary "as wife and mother" are historically and ideologically produced and therefore require critical scrutiny. Mary is judged simplistically as being psychologically immature: she can't face life as "we" know it. But *Long Day's Journey*, as Sheaffer well knows, dramatizes a woman's "life" that is thoroughly influenced by ideologies of the middle class, of femininity, and of Irish Catholicism.

Significant strains in O'Neill's use of the category of "life" surface in *A Touch of the Poet* (1939) and its sequel, *More Stately Mansions*. In *Touch*, Simon's Thoreauvian utopian vision, in his wife Sara's words, conceptualizes life in distinctly social terms: "[a] world [that] can be changed so people won't be greedy to own money and land and get the best of each other but will be content with little and live in peace and freedom together" (3:195). This notion of life, as Simon elaborates it in *Mansions*, is based on the Rousseauian premise that "human nature" is benign and has been corrupted by "civilization." O'Neill complicates our view of this idealism in a number of ways. Through Deborah, Simon's mother, O'Neill suggests that Simon's "emancipation" is partly a liberal arts fantasy (3:223, 226) made possible by his family's entrepreneurial success and his experience at Harvard. The radicalism of *Mansions* is in its dramatization of capitalism's seemingly irresistible power to redefine Simon's concept of life. We witness the transformation of Simon from a Harvard utopian who quotes Rousseau into a cutthroat entrepreneur. When Simon joins the competitive fray to support his family, he "loin[s] to like it." Training Sara in his tactics, he characterizes his business as "a battlefield of reality" (3:491).

Capitalism's hegemony induces Simon to imagine a degraded marketplace human nature as universal—"one-tenth spirit," he concludes, ousting Rousseau, "to nine-tenths hog" (3:360). O'Neill sees ante-bellum capitalist values as so effective in their capacity to reproduce possessive individuals that Americans come to regard capitalist competition as natural (an expression of selfhood). Abstractions, such as life and man in *Mansions*, persuade Simon that there are no viable alternatives to capitalism's social, economic, political, and cultural organization. This is the kernel of the critique of capitalism in *Mansions* that O'Neill did not fully develop.[165]

Floyd Dell's *Intellectual Vagabondage* (1926) recognized the propaganda of life as a postwar phenomenon. Dell saw that this ostensibly apolitical ideology produced both a political aesthetic and political subjects. It represents life as static, not as a social formation that can be criticized and changed. This reification is elevated as a literary value: "We are happy, then, pathetically happy, to find in this new literature of ours some apparently valid excuses for our inaction, in the form of revelations of the wildness and unharmoniousness of life itself and the ridiculousness and futility of seeking a meaning in it."[166] His kind of writing, he protests, has been relegated to a lower echelon of the literary. "It is evident that we, at this moment in history, do *not* want life to seem capable of being interpreted and understood, for that would be a reproach to us for our own failure to undertake the task of reconstituting our social, political and economic theories, and in general, and in consonance with these, our ideals of the good life."[167]

For O'Neill, however, to write of "life" constituted a rebellious refusal to conform to the conventions of nineteenth-century theatre and early-twentieth-century commercial theatre—"the Showshop Racket."[168] "I don't get any of the characters as characters," O'Neill wrote to a friend in 1915, criticizing his conventional melodrama. "They're simply types—types I've met before in the theater."[169] "Tragedy" requires "characters." In the vocabulary O'Neill employed most often in the twenties, his friend's characters lacked depth and his play avoided life.

This was also the aesthetic taste of many of the Broadway reviewers who heralded tragedies like *Beyond the Horizon* and *Desire Under the Elms* as startlingly new. Brooks Atkinson felt that *Beyond the Horizon* transformed the best efforts of popular playwrights like Augustus Thomas, Edward Sheldon, and Eugene Walter into "hokum dramas."[170] O'Neill's dramatization of pop psychological depth convinced many critics that he had gone beyond theatrical realism to stage *life*: "He fishes out of the void not a life, but life itself," wrote Dudley Nichols in his rave review of *Strange Interlude*.[171] As I have noted, Walter Prichard Eaton unabashedly informed Boston's reporters that *Strange Interlude* had been censored because it had lifted "the lid off the cellar of life." Since everyone possessed the depth plumbed by the new psychology, it seemed commonsensical to assume that O'Neill was dramatizing "life itself"—a subject far more grand and universal in its significance than concrete social issues.

If the subject of life was not commercial when *Beyond the Horizon* arrived on Broadway in 1920, it quickly became so. The more frequently O'Neill's tragedies migrated "uptown," the more O'Neill understood that his subject was "life." *Beyond the Horizon* premiered uptown, while *The Emperor Jones, The Hairy Ape,* and *Desire Under the Elms* soon moved there.[172] The modest, though sometimes impressive, productions of the Provincetown Players could no longer succeed in staging life once O'Neill's standards became more "professional" and his ambitions more commercial.[173]

As O'Neill's productions became more commercial, they also became increasingly preoccupied with the theme of spirituality—a concern that O'Neill came to view as much deeper than the radical gabble of his youth. Writing to Lawrence Langner about one reader's misreading of *Days Without End*, O'Neill objected that the reader favored "sociological solutions" over "mystic undertones."[174] In *Days Without End*, socialist and anarchist beliefs are understood as substitutes for one's lost religious faith, as mere symptoms of a deeper spiritual crisis. Father Baird maps this fall from faith in the career of his nephew, John Loving: "First it was Atheism unadorned. Then it was Atheism wedded to Socialism. But Socialism proved too weak-kneed a mate, and the next I heard Atheism was living in free love with Anarchism, with a curse by Nietzsche to bless the union. And then came the Bolshevik dawn, and he greeted that with unholy howls of glee and wrote me he'd found a congenial home at last in the bosom of Karl Marx" (3:122). He then adds, with a note of triumph: "I knew Communism wouldn't hold him long— and it didn't. Soon his letters became full of pessimism, and disgust, with all sociological nostrums" (3:122). In its beginning and ending, this flow chart accords fairly closely with O'Neill's own early development.

O'Neill's spiritual-malaise plays of the 1920s and 1930s tackled what he termed the "Big Theme."[175] Materialism is the word O'Neill substitutes for capitalism when contextualizing this "Big Theme." He wrote Nathan: "[*Dynamo*] is really the first play of a trilogy that will dig at the roots of the sickness of today as I feel it—the death of the old God and the failure of Science and Materialism to give any satisfying new one for the surviving primitive religious instinct to find a meaning for life in, and to comfort its fears of death with." For O'Neill, the artist who fails to probe the "big [spiritual] subject behind all the little subjects" is merely "scribbling around on the surface."[176] Within this scheme of significance, economic, class, racial, and gender systems are the epiphenomena of something deeper (and more amorphous and difficult to alter)—a godless modernity that breeds (classless) malaise.

O'Neill's statement distinguishes him as a product and a producer of a 1920s literary critical common sense (still in force today). Its Big Themes aim either to minimize the significance of "sociological nostrums" or to supplant them altogether. This universalizing criticism is often based on the premise that, as George Jean Nathan averred, "human nature never changes."[177] A depth psychology that reveals the "human condition," therefore, is valued as bigger and deeper than sociological issues. Bogard, with *The Personal Equation* and George Pierce Baker's teaching in mind, complains that in O'Neill's early plays there is no "psychological space," just "sociological realism." The young O'Neill attempts to deliver a "practical message" instead of dramatizing "man's inner life."[178] C. W. E. Bigsby, like Bogard and others, tends to prize O'Neill's "gothic imagination" and his proclivity to "dramatise the underside of the mind" over his interest in "the ephemeral problems of manners and the simple drama of social relationship." O'Neill's depth is found in his explorations of "the abyss" and his delineation of "entropic reality in aesthetic form." Granted, O'Neill dramatizes "social realities, but, more disturbingly, [he stages] metaphysical truths."[179]

Convention and conformity, along with materialism, constitute the social criticism vocabulary of this literary critical ideology of life and depth. O'Neill's comments on *The Hairy Ape* carefully redeploy what his interviewers might have taken as his unambiguous critique of the capitalist exploitation of the working class as, more appropriately, his scathing indictment of convention and conformity.

In the scene where the bell rings for the stokers to go on duty, you remember that they all stand up, come to attention, then go out in a lockstep file. Some people think even that is an actual custom aboard ship! But it is only symbolic of the regimentation of men who are the slaves of machinery. In a larger sense, it applies to all of us, because we all are more or less the slaves of convention, or of discipline, or of a rigid formula of some sort.[180]

After all, the wealthy Fifth Avenue churchgoers (who wear masks and speak in "toneless" voices) are also represented as automata.[181]

Convention is "larger" than class as a category. The more universal the critique ("of some sort"), the bigger and deeper it is.[182] To engage Big Themes, as defined by this critical ideology, one must do approximately as follows: write about fate, materialism, and standardization (in a general sense), not dwell on the particulars of an economic system; dramatize man, not just workers; stage the constraints of convention and conformity, not ideology; muse on the ironies of life, not exploitation.[183]

O'Neill associates guiding terms like life, spirit, fate, and man with his efforts to stage depth. But while such terms enabled him to describe what he thought he was writing in his plays (Big Themes), the plays themselves are often more mixed in what they exhibit, and they owe a debt to his earlier concerns with capitalism, workers, ideology, and alienation—"propaganda" concerns that never ceased to influence his work. What we find in O'Neill's plays, then, is neither a univalent propaganda of life nor a propaganda of socialism or anarchism, but rather a complex staging or playing out of contradictory and multivalent ideological tensions rooted in O'Neill's social world (as opposed to his hidden "depths"). Samuel Sillen, who partly addressed this issue in the *Daily Worker* in 1946, long before the advent of postmodern theories of authorship, argued that "the artist's distortions of reality . . . are not exclusively located in his own psyche but in the contradictory pressures of reality itself."[184]

O'Neill, the Left, and Social Depth

Joseph Freeman reminisced that the modern category of the literary performed a prominent role in his own 1910s and 1920s training as an Ivy League cultural "rebel." "Who were our literary heroes?" he asks in his autobiography, responding with "Ibsen and Dreiser and O'Neill— the 'men against the mob.'" Yet, he goes on, these "so-called pioneers and rebels" really "preach[ed] bourgeois ideals": "They wanted to reform middle-class conduct in the light of middle-class utopias. . . . What the enlightened Babbitt hated was proletarian art."[185] It would have been no surprise to Freeman that O'Neill's distaste for propaganda led to his dismissal of political theatre. The category of deep implies a category of surface, and O'Neill, like many other authors and critics of his day, pigeonholed political theatre as fitting snugly in the latter category.

In 1926 O'Neill gave Mike Gold his opinion of *Hoboken Blues*, an expressionistic, experimental political play whose wretched dialogue unintentionally caricatures the black community Gold meant to celebrate. After (over)praising the first act, O'Neill tactfully panned the "familiar propaganda" of the last part: "Don't get me wrong. My quarrel with propaganda in the theatre is that it's such damned unconvincing propaganda—whereas, if you will restrain the propaganda purpose to the selection of the life to be portrayed and then let that life live itself without comment, it does your trick. . . . If you want my most candid dope, I think you ought to keep the artist, Mike Gold, and the equally O.K. human being, the Radical editor, rigidly segregated during their respective working hours. I advise this in the name of flesh & blood propaganda."[186]

I have no wish to defend Gold's mishmash of a play; but one should bear in mind, nonetheless, that when O'Neill describes Gold's propaganda as "unconvincing," he is writing from a position that, by 1926, associates "flesh & blood" with the adoption of a particular pop psychological notion of depth.[187] Around the time he wrote to Gold, O'Neill had done extensive work on *Strange Interlude*, which can be read as a pop psychological and pop modernist propaganda of "flesh & blood." O'Neill clearly takes the political position that art and politics should be "rigidly segregated" (as if such a thing were a matter of choice). Two years later O'Neill, who admired Gold's *Fiesta* (produced in 1929), agreed to recommend the radical playwright and founder of the New Playwrights for a Guggenheim fellowship. He wrote Gold: "I've made it as strong as—well, as strong as I feel you deserve."[188]

Critics on the Left were often sympathetic to criticisms such as the (magnanimous) one O'Neill made of *Hoboken Blues*. In "Workers' Theatre: A Criticism" (1934), Conrad Seiler emphasized that "slipshod" craftsmanship is in no way made up for by "correct ideological content." Yet he also recognized that the prevailing ideas about aesthetic craftsmanship were culturally shaped in particular ways: "non-revolutionary audiences—the kind we must attract—are used to the smoothness of the bourgeois theatre and the films, and consequently the lumbering, painfully trying performances given by so many workers' groups will excite nothing but amused tolerance or derision."[189]

O'Neill's name was often synonymous with playwriting craftsmanship for 1930s leftist critics who sought to reform workers' theatre. Herbert Kline, editor of *New Theatre* magazine, suggested: "It would be a fine thing to see workers' theatre plays with a bit of poetry in them. . . . not big speeches but the kind Sean O'Casey gave his Irish rebels in the days when he wrote *The Plow and the Stars,* the kind that O'Neill wrote in his fine short plays of the sea."[190] O'Neill's *Glencairn* cycle as well as *The Hairy Ape* helped enable political playwrights of the 1930s to write their "propaganda."

O'Neill's letter to Gold was written graciously to make it seem as if he might welcome a better-crafted propaganda, but in fact by the 1920s he was already venting some hostile sentiments about radical theatre. In 1939, after a decade of the Depression, the birth and death of the Federal Theatre Project (which provided a significant forum for overtly political plays—as well as for some of O'Neill's works), and the ascendancy of Clifford Odets, O'Neill found himself both irritated and disappointed that the talented Sean O'Casey, his Irish compatriot, had gone "red" with his new play, *The Stars Turn Red.* He fulminated to Nathan that many playwrights who "get caught in the sociological propaganda mill . . . have nothing much to lose, and the sociological attack helps them by giving a lot of shallow stuff a phoney partisan importance. But O'Casey is an artist and the soapbox is no place for his great talent. The hell of it seems to be, when an artist starts saving the world, he starts losing himself. . . . the interesting thing about people is the obvious fact that they don't really want to be saved—the tragic idiotic ambition for self-destruction in them."[191]

This is political theory masked as tragic philosophy or psychology (i.e., radical social change is futile because of a human drive for self-destruction), and is close to Freud's own "tragic" vision in *Civilization and Its Discontents* (1930). Because the death drive, as defined by the "science" of psychoanalysis, is so powerful, Freud sees Communist change as merely a Marxist pipe dream (in O'Neill's terms).[192] The psychological depth model that features assumptions about innate self-destructiveness is what authorizes O'Neill to portray political theatre as "shallow stuff" of "phoney partisan importance."[193]

It is possible that O'Neill's irascible stance toward the "propaganda mill" was provoked by some awareness that his work had been relentlessly bombarded by leftist critics and dramatists in the thirties.[194]

O'Neill would have been well within his rights to dismiss some leftist criticisms as misreadings. From the 1920s through the 1950s, for example, a number of such critics rather simplistically cast the early O'Neill as the radical who betrayed the cause. When O'Neill won the Nobel Prize in 1936, Edwin Seaver of the *Daily Worker* portrayed the young Irish maverick as a proletarian: "Sometime sailor, gold prospector, cub reporter, mail order house clerk, and worker in a wool-packing house, an electrical company, and a sewing machine firm." But the Nobel Prize, Seaver adds, was not awarded to him "for being a revolutionary writer, the chronicler of workers, dreamers and rebels, of hairy apes and underdogs." O'Neill's betrayal of his proletarian credentials, his change of subject, and his wealth have made him "increasingly safe and conservative."[195] John Howard Lawson, in his 1950s reappraisal, hailed O'Neill's 1910s *Glencairn* cycle as being composed of "mature and powerful" plays that "reflected the feeling of anger and betrayal, the increasing social consciousness, the search for new values that stirred American intellectuals in the time of the Versailles conference and the Palmer raids." O'Neill's dramatization of seamen was often taken by the Left as a self-evident sign of radical sympathies. Thus, leftist romanticizing of O'Neill sometimes supplants a more judicious unpacking of what the playwright actually wrote.[196]

O'Neill was irritated by such misrepresentations of himself and his work. In reference to reviews of *The Hairy Ape* in 1922, he complained to a friend: "Both the *Tribune* and *Solidarity*—the I. W. W. organ—praise me editorially—both for something I didn't mean." R. Robbins, the reviewer for *Industrial Solidarity*, lauded O'Neill's play for absolving the Industrial Workers of the World "of advocating excessive means to accomplish their ends"—which it does, to its credit, in passing. Although Robbins pointed out that "Mr. O'Neill proclaims no tendency," he celebrated *The Hairy Ape* as a "masterpiece . . . of Propaganda in Art." Yet what Robbins sees as the critical center of the play—Yank's obdurate ideological resistance to a political understanding of his condition— diverges from O'Neill's own reading of it as a tragedy of universal man.[197]

The assumption that the dramatization of a particular subject— working-class life—is more "real" (and thus politically "deeper") than other subjects is a recurring problem in leftist criticism of O'Neill. McAlister Coleman of the *Call* suggested that O'Neill was awarded the Nobel Prize because the subjects of his plays were divorced from "the world we live in." In 1954 Lawson saw O'Neill's tragedy as that of an "artist who loses contact with the living forces of his time."[198] Plays like *The Great God Brown, Strange Interlude, Mourning Becomes Electra,* and *Days Without End,* however, had a good deal to do with the ideological world O'Neill inhabited and are invaluable to the cultural and literary historian because they reveal much about how the professional-managerial class reproduced its identity through new psychological models of selfhood. By categorizing such plays as unreal, leftist critics risked shrinking the concept of the political, so that only "radical" theatre would be seen as performing political work.

Much leftist criticism of O'Neill from the 1920s to the 1950s was subtle, suggestive, and employed a value scheme strikingly different from the one found in that of contemporaneous mainstream critics who reserved their acclaim for dramatizations of depth, life, fate, man, and the abyss. Samuel Sillen of the *Daily Worker* interpreted the political premise of *Iceman* (that the world cannot be changed because man is manure), not as depth, but as a spurious presupposition that makes sense of O'Neill's incapacity to imagine his characters as social beings "with a positive purpose." What Mary Mullett cited as an aesthetic virtue in O'Neill— "he does not tell us what we 'ought' to do"—Sillen sees as a problem, one he does not find in Anton Chekhov, whose plays make you "feel, besides life as it is, the life which ought to be, and that captivates you."[199] Rather than subscribing to the belief that O'Neill's dramas had unmasked the essential individual, Virgil Geddes's *The Melodramadness of Eugene O'Neill* (1934) concluded: "O'Neill is individualism out of control."[200] And Charmion Von Wiegand, one of the most provocative critical voices on the Left in the 1930s (along with her husband, Joseph Freeman),[201] read O'Neill's confrontation with "blind fate" and a "hostile cosmos," not as a sign of his literary intrepidity, but as a bourgeois theme that functions to obscure the "social causes or relationships" which illuminate behavior.[202] Several contributors to the radical magazine *New Theatre* endeavored to situate O'Neill in a particular historical conjuncture, not only a biographical or literary background, that would explain his choice of literary themes.[203]

A number of critics on the Left relabeled O'Neill's use of the psychological model of depth. Where O'Neill dramatized depth, they often perceived decay. Michael Blankfort, for instance, saw in *Strange Interlude,* not a dramatization of depth, but rather "the portrayal of upper-class, psychological conflicts. . . . neuroses which emerge from decay."[204]

Lawson described the "reactionary theatre" of 1934 as one of "decay"; it justifies "the vagaries of capitalism in terms of art and psychology."[205] Another word used by the Left in place of depth is "sick": O'Neill is the playwright of a "sick middle class," wrote Seaver.[206] O'Neill's psychological concerns were characterized as a mass-mediated "Sunday-supplement-use of Freud . . . exactly what the doctor ordered for aristocrats bored with excessive stock market prices."[207]

In *The Awakening of American Theatre* (1935), Ben Blake focused his criticism on how exactly the middle-class psychological imagining of "self" operated to distort the middle-class perception of the working class. Writing about Broadway in the 1920s, he observed (bringing to mind *Welded, The Great God Brown, Dynamo,* and *Strange Interlude*): "Humanity was becoming neurotic, developing split personalities, becoming either philistine or pathological." Psychological categories, he thought, operated as filters for more than middle-class self-reflection; they filtered out the category of class, so that when working-class "hairy apes" were viewed onstage and offstage, they were seen mainly in "Freudian terms of greed, lusts, appetites." This way of seeing "hairy apes" conveniently dissolves the significance one might attach to "the basic forces, political, economic, or cultural, at work in the contemporary world."[208]

Calverton took the next step on this critical path in 1932, when he suggested that overtly political plays which do dramatize these basic forces—rather than taking O'Neill's detour into contemporary ideas about the unconscious—are what really make American theatre culturally vital.[209] Eleanor Flexner, an editor of *New Theatre,* continued along this trajectory in 1938, when she argued that "so-called propaganda dramatists" had already succeeded in moving beyond predecessors like O'Neill because they dramatize "life and character as the product of social forces and social relationships in perpetual conflict and dynamic evolution." Political playwrights such as Lawson, George Sklar, Albert Maltz, and Paul Peters shift their "emphasis from the depiction of tragedy as such to a concern with its causes . . . [and this] leads to struggle based not only on heroism but on an understanding of those principles."[210] Flexner's concept of tragedy, unlike O'Neill's, concentrates on the relationship between social causality and motive, and leads not to resignation or mere amusement in auditors, but, more purposively, to cultural critique and political action. "Tragedy is the tragedy of forces," Geddes insisted, "not of weaknesses."[211] In sum, Von Wiegand, Geddes, Calverton, and Flexner indicted O'Neill's plays for lacking "social depth" (and read his work shrewdly and also sometimes misread it in making their case).

Ah, Wilderness! and the Reproduction of the Middle Class

The Left berated *Ah, Wilderness!* more caustically than any other of O'Neill's plays. It was first staged in 1933–34, the same theatre season hailed by one leftist critic as "tremendously significant"—"it has seen the first flowing of revolutionary plays dramatizing the class struggle directly."[212] This radical aesthetic ferment made leftist critics particularly vitriolic when evaluating O'Neill's offerings. "In *Ah! Wilderness* [O'Neill] dropped into a meaningless, air-pocket condition which only in derision could be called comedy," Geddes snapped in "The End of O'Neill" (1934).[213] That same year Blankfort, who marveled at the play's apparent weightlessness, dubbed it "an ocean of whipped cream."[214] Also in 1934 Lawson censured it as "a new-fascist glorification of the American home and American idealism" and mocked mainstream critics for finding "wisdom in [its] *Saturday Evening Post* conventionality."[215] A year later Von Wiegand, perhaps with some of O'Neill's pinstriped photographs in mind, offered a perceptive critique: "Only a decade before, he had slammed the back door of respectable middle class society, and like Ibsen's Nora had gone forth to see the world. Now he has returned, contrite prodigal in the well-pressed clothes of success to be admitted to the front parlor, there to repent at leisure his associations with outcasts, sailors, workers, prostitutes, Negroes, free women, artists."[216] And Doris Alexander, in her impressive 1952 critique of O'Neill's politics, upbraided *Ah, Wilderness!* as "a lyric acceptance of the status quo": "Love and bourgeois conventions live happily ever after."[217]

Two years before the prestigious Theatre Guild served O'Neill's "whipped cream," Harold Clurman, Cheryl Crawford, and Lee Strasberg quit that organization, in protest against its bourgeois offerings, to establish the Group Theatre's autonomy. Clurman's view of the Board of Managers is in perfect harmony with Von Wiegand's and Alexander's reading of O'Neill: "They were symbolic of a Greenwich Village grown prosperous. . . . destined to become an institution."[218]

These leftist appraisals have merit: *Ah, Wilderness!* is on one level a sentimental celebration of the turn of the century middle-class family. But I shall argue also that O'Neill's play offers a subtle critique of how a producer-culture middle-class family reproduces its subjectivity, and further that the play suggests how this mode of reproduction is, by 1906, beginning to change. Moreover, *Ah, Wilderness!* casts a critical eye on new ways in which a middle class–in-transition sanctions a *permissible* "rebelliousness." In sum, I suggest that O'Neill's "whipped cream" is a revealingly contradictory play that should have been given more weight by leftist critics, and that it has—because of its contradictory ideological crosscurrents—considerable "social depth."

To argue this is to contest O'Neill's own description of the play, sent to Eugene Jr. in 1933: "It *is* a comedy—and not in a satiric vein like *Marco M*—and not deliberately spoofing at the period." The word that stands out is "deliberately," as if, even in the writing of it, O'Neill already anticipates readings divergent from the one he has prescribed for his son. "Spoofing at the period" sounds innocent enough. O'Neill also advertises his play as a much needed "mood of emotion" (or perhaps mode of emotion) for 1933. "No, it is purely a play of nostalgia for youth, a sentimental, if you like, evocation of the mood of emotion of a past time which, whatever may be said against it, possessed a lot which we badly need today to steady us." This is O'Neill's response to the depths of the Depression, not in a political sense, but in a therapeutic vein, as if to say: Let's recall the middle class of bygone times and learn again to laugh at our problems. But there remains an undertone here that is unelaborated—"whatever may be said against" this "past time."

What could possibly be said against a play of nostalgia for youth? O'Neill goes on to explain that he has attempted to capture the apple-pie wholesomeness of the middle-class family's producer ethos, one aspect of what Warren Susman terms the nineteenth-century culture of "character": "The good idea of the simple old family life as lived by the typical middle class hard working American of the average large-small town which is America in miniature—the coming of the new radical literature of that day to youth (Shaw, Ibsen, Wilde, Omar Khayyam, etc.)—that's what I tried to do in the play. A play about people, simple people of another day but real American people."[219] Perhaps here we find, in 1933, O'Neill's nostalgia for an older, more personal lifestyle radicalism.

A few days before, O'Neill had written a letter to Saxe Commins that framed his new script as a "rebellion" against his own plays whose characters had "modern, involved, complicated, warped & self-poisoned psyche[s]." But he added provocatively, "this simple, sentimental comedy . . . [comes with] undertones, oh yes, with undertones."[220] That it does. Here I wish to build on Thomas Van Laan's insight that *Ah,*

Wilderness! both endorses and criticizes middle-class family life.[221] Perhaps the play's "darkest" political undertone can be found in its tendency to show how the middle-class family contains political critique from within its ranks, and, moreover, how this containment relates to a new ideology of selfhood that will be represented as depth.

The opening scene echoes an earlier O'Neill play. Mr. Miller, master of middle-class common sense, revives Mrs. Ashleigh's tactics in *Now I Ask You* to manage his son's socialist gabble and anarchist sentiments: he interprets Richard's radical tendencies as adolescent rebelliousness. Miller's favorite epithet, "darn," sprinkled throughout the play, consistently makes any domestic explosions—actual fireworks or political ones—unthreatening ("Darned youngster!"). Prior to Richard's political critique of Independence Day, we are warned by Miller that his son's "red meat nowadays . . . [is] love poetry and socialism, too, I suspect, from some dire declarations he's made" (3:11). Socialism and love poetry are both seen as romantic fads. Richard, like Lucy Ashleigh in *Now I Ask You*, is suffering adolescent growing pains which must be treated with a dose of sympathy.

Both Miller and the stage directions are clear on this. Thus Miller tries to explain Richard's adolescent symptoms to Mr. McComber, Muriel's father, who is aghast because Richard has sent scandalous love poems to his daughter: "Can't you see Richard's only a fool kid who's just at the stage when he's out to rebel against all authority, and so he grabs at everything radical to read and wants to pass it on to his elders and his girl and boy friends to show off what a young hellion he is!" (3:20). The stage directions also implicitly invoke this psychology of adolescence, just after Richard is rebuffed by Muriel (at McComber's insistence): *"Richard stands, a prey to feelings of bitterest humiliation and seething revolt against everyone and everything"* (3:34). Even before this emotional crisis occurs, the stage directions have us interpret Richard's radicalism, like Lucy Ashleigh's, as an adolescent posing of depth. *"In a manner he is alternately a plain simple boy and a posey actor solemnly playing a role"* (3:12). The category of revolution is subsumed by the category of adolescence.[222]

O'Neill gives Richard's socialist criticism a certain edge, even though he cushions its impact (*"dire* declarations"). Richard's polemic against the "fourth" is reminiscent of O'Neill's antiwar poem, "Fratricide." "I don't believe in this silly celebrating the Fourth of July," he declaims.

Miller tolerates this with a "Hmmm" and a *"Twinkle in his eye."* Richard, *"getting warmed up,"* views the holiday as more of a sham than his adjective "silly" conveyed: "The land of the free and the home of the brave! Home of the slave is what they ought to call it—the wage slave ground under the heel of the capitalist class, crying for bread for his children, and all he gets is a stone! The Fourth of July is a stupid farce!" Miller inflates the radicalness of Richard's speech as a means of deflating it: "You'd better not repeat such sentiments outside the bosom of the family or they'll have you in jail." But Richard becomes more hyperbolic: "I'll celebrate the day the people bring out the guillotine again and I see Pierpont Morgan being driven by in a tumbril! (*His father and Sid are greatly amused; Lily is shocked but, taking her cue from them, smiles* .)" His father teases him: "(*solemnly*) Son, if I didn't know it was you talking, I'd think we had Emma Goldman with us" (3:13).

The O'Neill of 1933 is rereading his own "Fratricide" radicalism of 1914 (when he was twenty-six) as adolescent. Just as Miller claims that his son—in his Emma Goldman mode—is not quite himself, so O'Neill may be hinting that the younger O'Neill who shocked his "elders" with socialist views was not himself. The reference to Goldman is suggestive and multivalent, because she championed a "socially significant" theatre that members of the 1930s Left had redefined and accused O'Neill of having betrayed.

Workers' theatre troupes across the country produced politically "significant" plays while the Theatre Guild featured *Ah, Wilderness!* They dramatized what Richard described as the "wage slave ground under the heel of the capitalist class." In 1932 the League of Workers Theatres was founded, and the magazine *Workers Theatre* (renamed *New Theatre* in 1933) became its "official organ."[223] By 1934, 400 workers' theatre groups were established.[224] John Gassner, having left the "new theatre" movement far behind him by 1940, categorized many of the political playwrights of the 1930s as "immature" and as "sociologists rather than artists"—"they were prone to blame every intestinal disturbance on the big bad wolf 'Capitalism' or on the 'System.' "[225] So when O'Neill deploys the middle-class 1906 "normalcy" of Miller to undercut Richard's "dire declarations," he may also have had other "adolescent" theatrical rebels from the early 1930s in mind.

Closer to home, O'Neill may very well have been aware of the Group's dramatic declaration of independence from the Guild in 1931. Indeed, he helped provide financial support for the Group's first production, Paul Green's *The House of Connelly* (1931)—a hit.[226] Helburn, like

Langner, interpreted the Group's political challenge as simply the re-bellion of youth: "[Their] attitude was that of the child toward its parent." When Clurman was summoned before the Board and asked if he "would have anything to tell Eugene O'Neill?" he horrified the managers by answering, "Certainly." Helburn, much like O'Neill's Mr. Miller, counseled her colleagues: "But they are young . . . [and] should be helped."[227]

Miller's paternal humor has a political purpose: our laughter is intended to defuse Richard's remarks about "starving wage slaves" as mere cant. Miller continues, "(*with a comic air of resignation*) Well, Richard, I've always found I've had to listen to at least one stump speech every Fourth. I only hope getting your extra strong one right after breakfast will let me off for the rest of the day. (*They all laugh now, taking this as a cue*)" (3:14). This is the audience's cue too: laughter lets it off for the rest of the evening.

Richard discharges more hyperbole, but hyperbole that Depression era audiences would have recognized. Richard could be the younger O'Neill railing at his Theatre Guild audience of 1933–34: "(*somberly*) That's right, laugh! After you, the deluge, you think! But look out! Supposing it comes before? Why shouldn't the workers of the world unite and rise? They have nothing to lose but their chains! (*He recites threateningly*) 'The days grow hot, O Babylon! 'Tis cool beneath thy willow trees!' " No doubt, members of O'Neill's Guilded crowds must have been wondering if all the gabble about workers of the world uniting and rising was going to amount to something in 1933. Although the action takes place in 1906, Richard is allowed to leap ahead in time, for the "O Babylon" quote comes from the concluding line of Ferdinand Freiligrath's "Revolution," published in the March 1910 issue of *Mother Earth*, a journal which, in its fifth year of publication, bristled with the writings of Goldman and Havel. Hugo Kalmar also sings this tune—while babbling on—in *Iceman*, but only to demonstrate that he and his revolution have been farcically reduced to vacuous slogans.

Miller's management tactics are elastic, as he greets "O Babylon" with another "Hmmm" and praises Richard for having been inspired by Carlyle's *French Revolution* (not Marx): "Glad you're reading it, Richard. It's a darn fine book." His son is taken aback that his father knows the book. "Well you see," he explains, "even a newspaper owner can't get out of reading a book every now and again" (3:14). Miller's strategic "darn" was probably more potent for Guild audiences than his son's "workers of the world unite." While the son, speaking of "chains," may have seemed narrowly propagandistic, the "liberal" father—perhaps like the older O'Neill—says, yes, we should be aware of such sentiments and particularly the classics they come from. Miller sidesteps the (1933) logic of Richard's slogan with his reference to Carlyle. Perhaps O'Neill saw this as the responsibility of "the theatre" in 1933—not to engage the logic of propaganda, but to sidestep such adolescent enthusiasms with laughter. But if this was the covert function of his own play, why expose it?

O'Neill's undertones expose much else. Through references to Yale, which Eugene Jr., a brilliant classicist, entered in 1927 (he later did graduate work and taught at Yale), O'Neill exposed the ideological role played by liberal arts. After Richard's outburst, his older brother, Arthur, jumps in: "Never mind, Pa. Wait till we get him down to Yale. We'll take that out of him!" Richard is unintimidated: "(with high scorn) Oh Yale! You think there's nothing in the world besides Yale. After all, what is Yale?" His brother retorts, ominously: "You'll find out what!" (3:14). When Richard shows up tipsy late that night, Arthur responds hypocritically (he was to have gone to the bar in his brother's place): "We'll take that out of you when we get you down to Yale!" (3:73).

O'Neill himself, expelled from Princeton at the end of his freshman year (1907), was less than awed by Princeton's intellectual and disciplinary regime. The fishnet that hung from his dormitory wall was ornamented with stockings, brassieres, and used condoms, trophies of his excursions beyond Princeton's gates.[228] Princeton's snobbishness and dullness drove him to Benjamin Tucker's New York bookstore, where he explored anarchism, socialism, Wilde, Shaw, Conrad, and Nietzsche.[229] In 1943 he wrote Saxe Commins about the possibility that he might be approached to receive an honorary doctorate from Princeton: "You know what I think of honorary degrees. Crap cum laude."[230]

But O'Neill had agreed to accept such an award seventeen years earlier—from Yale. George Pierce Baker, who taught O'Neill playwriting at Harvard in 1914–15, and who was wooed to Yale in the mid-1920s to build its drama department (which became the drama school), was partly responsible for Yale's decision to tap O'Neill. When O'Neill was invited to attend Yale's 1926 commencement to receive his honorary doctorate, Baker wrote to him and politely *instructed* his illustrious but rather aloof and occasionally irreverent student how to respond.

Baker represented the honor about to be bestowed on the playwright as evidence that a new Yale had begun to acknowledge the artistic potential of American drama. "Even men who, by their training, might have been expected to question somewhat publicly stamping with approval writing as independent and as unconservative as yours, have shown that they feel your honesty of purpose and the significance of the accomplishment." Baker stressed that O'Neill "ought to feel profoundly gratified" and that he should "let nothing stand in the way of being here to receive the degree." His presence would not only help elevate the stature of American theatre in the academy, it would encourage academics to show greater respect for free-thinking playwrights and the seriousness of their work. "Coming from Yale," O'Neill replied with no little irony, "I appreciate that this is a *true* honor." "*But*," he added, still courteous but clearly anxious about being hemmed in, he could not absolutely guarantee his attendance because his public appearances usually brought on "a most appalling attack of stage fright." Thus he had Baker promise to insulate him from additional academic social functions during his day and a half in New Haven, and to secure tickets to the Yale baseball game the evening before the commencement.

Baker's next official "invitation" was less successful. The year before he created the Richard Miller who would scoff defiantly, "What is Yale?," O'Neill declined to attend a Yale production of *Bound East for Cardiff* and *The Emperor Jones*, at which Baker was to be presented with Edmond Quinn's bust of O'Neill (an event made much of by the Yale University News service). The Baker-O'Neill correspondence from the mid-1920s to the early 1930s suggests that O'Neill knew that Baker—with some cooperation from Yale—was consciously enlisting O'Neill to enhance the academic prestige of American drama, his department, and Yale itself. Yet it must be said that O'Neill was not above trying to use Baker, Yale, and their cultural capital to further his own more elaborate, risky, and costly projects of the mid-1920s, as his negotiations with Baker about possible world premieres of *Marco Millions* and *Lazarus Laughed* at Yale make plain.[231]

O'Neill was aware that the university operates not simply as a center for the production of knowledge, but specifically for the production of class knowledge, taste, and manners—an education that outfitted one for what Thorstein Veblen termed "conspicuous leisure."[232] As Richard Ohmann has observed, the new universities founded all over America at the turn of the century were joining forces with the older ones as the primary "institution[s] for training and promoting a new professional-managerial class."[233] When he was writing *Marco Millions* in 1922,

O'Neill also sketched an idea for a play entitled "Homo Sapiens," which represents the university as a corporate bureaucracy. He drafted a summary of one encounter between Prof. Zoroaster Brown and the president of Yarvard. The president, with "the face and manner of Warren Harding or a movie banker," has summoned Brown to fire him, but he is absorbed in "the game" between Yarvard and Hanton being broadcast on his radiophone. "The President begins to state the case against Brown in stilted blank verse. His manner is that of a businessman reproving a subordinate for inefficiency. He is constantly interrupting himself with comments on the progress of the game in the excited slang of a fan." O'Neill's sympathies are with Zoroaster Brown, whose intellectual transgression is, one may infer, political, religious, or both: "Behind [Brown's] mask an unleashed, bewildered spirit is writhing in freedom, and his eyes glare boldly and resentfully through the glasses."[234]

T. Stedman Harder, the Standard Oil millionaire in *A Moon for the Misbegotten*, is profiled in lengthy stage directions as a ruling class product of the university. The same year that he derided an honorary degree as "crap cum laude," O'Neill singled out college as the foundation of Harder's ruling class outlook: *"No matter how long he lives, his four undergraduate years will always be for him the most significant in his life, and the moment of his highest achievement the time he was tapped for an exclusive Senior Society at the Ivy university to which his father had given millions."* This social and ideological network confirmed in him *"the self-confident attitude of acknowledged superiority"* (3:884). Harder was based in part on the actual Standard Oil millionaire, Edward S. Harkness, a Yale graduate whose family gave millions to the university in the 1910s and 1920s and who aimed to remodel the campus architecturally on the design of Oxford and Cambridge. It was Harkness who owned the "cold, lonely, ugly house, a millionaire's house" in O'Neill's "Upon Our Beach." It was also Harkness—as O'Neill probably knew—who funded Baker's department of drama at Yale in the mid-1920s.[235]

The social self-confidence that justifies the professional class to itself—through its speech, manners, taste, and allusions—is understood as a university product in *Abortion*, which O'Neill wrote while he was studying playwriting at Harvard in 1914. From the first scene we see how this confidence is constituted by class banter. One of Jack Townsend's cohorts ejects Murray, a mechanic, from Jack's dorm room with aplomb, remarking to his classmates: "Pleasant little man!" (1:205).

Jack, a baseball star, possesses the *"easy confident air of one who has . . . become a figure of note in college circles and is accustomed to the deference of those around him"* (1:206). Extracurricular experience teaches one not only about class boundaries, but how to cross them with discretion. Jack, who has impregnated Murray's sister, Nellie, requires more careful instruction in this particular sport. His father reproves him for his lapse of "good taste" (1:213).

O'Neill probes how class identity, authority, and alibis can be supported by liberal arts allusions. Feeling guilty about having cheated on Evelyn, his university fiancée, Jack asks his dad, "Do you suppose it was the same man who loves Evelyn who did this thing? No, a thousand times no, such an idea is abhorrent. It was the male beast who ran gibbering through the forest after its female thousands of years ago" (1:212). Mr. Townsend, a defender of the middle-class code of fair play, is disappointed by his son's analogy. Thus he parries Jack's Anthro 101 rationalization with his own English 101 analogy of the split self (which O'Neill would stage in *The Great God Brown* and *Days Without End*): "Come, Jack, this is pure evasion. You are responsible for the Mr. Hyde in you as well as for Dr. Jekyll" (1:213–14). When Joe Murray, the mechanic, finally corners Jack to inform him that Nellie, whom Jack cut off, died as the result of an abortion, the college star panics: "This would kill my mother if she knew." Murray retorts crisply: "You killed my sister" (1:218). If members of the working class are "nobodies" for professionals-in-training, their deaths don't matter. But Nellie's demise makes Jack ashamed, lest someone should discover his ignominious role in it. Consequently he shoots himself as his classmates outside sing: "For he's a jolly good fellow, which nobody can deny" (1:220).

By making an utter fool out of Arthur, *Ah, Wilderness!* undercuts the class authority legitimized by the use of literary or cultural allusions. Arthur stupidly enters a family debate about Oscar Wilde to explain the reason for the author's arrest: "(*suddenly solemnly authoritative*) He committed bigamy. (*then as Sid smothers a burst of ribald laughter*) What are you laughing at? I guess I ought to know. A fellow at college told me. His father was in England when this Wilde was pinched—and he said he remembered once his mother asked his father about it and he told her he'd committed bigamy" (3:15). The paradox here, of course, is that O'Neill relies on his university-educated audience to recognize straightaway that Arthur got it wrong (thereby confirming what he just ostensibly undermined—class identity constituted through the exchange of literary allusions). By 1933 O'Neill's own plays were assigned in universities and provided the literary allusions (and illusions) that the professional-managerial class used to consolidate its identity. O'Neill's "crap cum laude" irreverence as well as his consciousness that universities had become marketplaces for his wares are both present in a letter he wrote to Commins in 1945, in which he blasted academics who had requested permission to reprint his plays gratis: "I wonder how professors in our university English Departments think authors and publishers live? In fact I wonder why the hell professors in our English Departments live?"[236]

Arthur's anecdote about Wilde, narrated in Act 1, signals a key shift from socialist or anarchist politics to sexual transgression as the central adolescent problem that preoccupies the Miller family. Anxiety about sexual behavior centers on women. O'Neill, perhaps with some of the anarchist critiques from *Mother Earth* in mind, stresses that female chastity is crucial to the ideological maintenance of middle-class identity. When Miller argues with McComber about the moral effects of Richard's poems on Muriel, he assures him that his daughter is "a darn nice girl" who "knows a lot more about life than you give her credit for" (3:20). But when he actually peruses the Swinburne poems sent secretly by Richard to Muriel, he is alarmed and his "darn" turns to "damn": "It's no joking matter. That stuff *is* warm—too damned warm, if you ask me! I don't like this a damned bit, Sid. That's no kind of thing to be sending a decent girl" (3:23). Radical politics calls for suppressed chuckles from the adults on stage, while the exposure of a "decent" middle-class girl to racy poetry is taken as serious business. Proposing that "workers of the world [should] unite" to cast off their "chains" is one thing, but tampering with middle-class femininity is quite another matter!

When Miller learns that Richard had spent the evening with a "tart," the crisis deepens. Richard's continuing reverence for Muriel's femininity, however, ensures his participation in middle-class norms. He redeems himself to himself in his unsparing denunciation of Belle, the tart: "She was just a whore," Richard ponders; "she was everything dirty" (3:87). Shortly after, he reassures Muriel, "Fall in love with that kind of girl! What do you take me for?" (3:95). Richard, unlike Jack Townsend in *Abortion*, vigorously asserts his ability to discriminate between "decent" and "indecent" femininity.

Yet O'Neill complicates our perception of middle-class femininity with more undertones. Richard's mother, for example, constantly insults their Irish maid, Norah, in harsh language: "that stupid girl" (3:38); "She'll be the death of me! She's that thick" (3:28). Mrs. Miller's femininity seems to thrive on classifying Norah's femininity as inferior. The stage directions describe Norah as "clumsy," "long-jawed," and "beamingly good-natured" (3:27), but not in Mrs. Miller's nasty tone.

O'Neill also unveils the underside of Miller's view of middle-class female chastity. After spending much time fretting about Richard's relations with Muriel and Belle, Miller tiptoes around *recommending* that his son engage tarts with discretion. Tarts provide middle-class males with a useful sex education usually unavailable from the women they marry.

> Well, you're a fully developed man, in a way, and it's only natural for you to have certain desires of the flesh . . . certain natural feelings and temptations—that'll want to be gratified—and you'll want to gratify them. Hmmm—well, human society being organized, as it is, there's only one outlet for—unless you're a scoundrel and go around ruining decent girls—which you're not, of course. Well, there are a certain class of women—always have been and always will be as long as human nature is what it is—It's wrong, maybe, but *what* can you do about it? . . . lots of 'em are pretty, and it's human nature if you—But that doesn't mean to ever get mixed up with them seriously! You just have what you want and pay 'em and forget it. . . . don't think I'm encouraging you to—If you can stay away from 'em, all the better—but if—why—hmmm—

Middle-class women, he concludes, are "apt to be whited sepulchres," and "darn it, you've got to know how to—" (3:104).

Historians have noted that in the early twentieth century, "many middle-class men bought sex at some time. . . . [and] college students explored vice districts together." But some of Miller's remarks also suggest that "the sexual values of the middle class were on the verge of a decisive transformation."[237] In a middle-class, common-sense idiom Miller installs the "desires of the flesh" as the depth of "human nature" and moves away from the "moral demand system" of the producer-culture ethos toward a consumer ethos of gratification and release. Miller advocates what Arthur has learned at Yale: do it, but don't get caught. This sexualized common sense also inscribes class differences as natural, for it is unchangeable "human nature"—not socioeconomics and gender ideologies (as Emma Goldman would argue)—that accounts for "a certain class of women—always have been and always will be." In certain ways Miller, caught up in the double standard, lags far behind Judge Ben Lindsey's 1920s modern common sense, which accepts that "decent" girls do it and like it. But in other respects, Miller's "desires of the flesh" speech inches toward Lindsey's stance: "Sex is simply a biological fact," wrote Lindsey. "It is as much so as the appetite for food. Like the appetite for food it is neither legal nor illegal, moral nor immoral."[238]

Thus we see in Miller's man-to-man common sense the glimmerings of a new middle-class ideology of selfhood that draws closer to the psychological depth model which, when dramatized on stage, brought O'Neill fame and fortune. This modern middle class, to again use the words of Foucault, defines the "task of truth" as "the challenging of taboos."[239] The Theatre Guild's "refined subscription audience"[240] of 1933 is meant to congratulate itself on being "liberated" compared to the taboo-ridden Muriel: "[Belle] was low and bad," she tells Richard (never having laid eyes on Belle), "that's what she was or she couldn't be a chorus girl and her smoking cigarettes proves it" (3:93). Muriel, unlike the Guild audience, has not yet come to terms with her "deeper" self.

The middle class of 1906 does not entertain seriously the challenge posed by Socialism because it has begun to make the preoccupations of love poetry its preeminent concern. The ideological shift to desire as the essence of the self, the problem of the self, and the liberation of the self redirects attention from social reality to "life" and to convention. Richard sends love poetry (the mode of his anticonventionality) to Muriel (the object of his anticonventionality) because he "wanted her to face *life* as it is" (3:25) (emphasis supplied). He confesses to her: "But I'm not sorry I tried it [Belle] once—curing the soul by means of the senses, as Oscar Wilde says" (3:82).

Although Richard's depth presented problems for Mr. and Mrs. Miller at the outset of the play—a depth produced by what O'Neill termed "the new radical literature of that day to youth (Shaw, Ibsen, Wilde, Omar Khayyam, etc.)"—by the play's conclusion this troublesome depth has undergone a dramatic reassessment in middle-class values. Mrs. Miller points to depth as Richard's intellectual qualification for Yale. When her husband proposes to punish Richard by not letting him attend Yale, Mrs. Miller is up in arms at first for conventional middle-class reasons: "Every man of your means in town is sending his boys to college! What would folks think of you!" But she doesn't stop there, much to Miller's amazement: "He's proved it [his "exceptional brain"] by the way he likes to read all those *deep* plays and books and poetry. . . . that boy's going to turn out to be a great lawyer, or a great doctor, or a great writer" (3:99) (emphasis supplied). O'Neill inserts "writer" into this cluster of university-trained professionals. Depth, as O'Neill's own career demonstrated, is eminently commodifiable in the form of "deep plays" for professional-managerial-class audiences. The depth playwright—or depth propagandist—will be charged with the subtle ideological task of training his social class to read fate and life as deeper causal forces than capitalism's social and economic relations, desire as a more worthy focus of concern than politics, and subjectivity as a psychological essence that is detached from production.

Although Richard's "adolescent" agitation for revolution never survives Act 1, O'Neill's play, read historically, is about the revolution that actually did transform the middle class. As Frederick Lewis Allen put it in 1931, the "foreign propaganda" that did bring about revolution in America came "not from Moscow, but from Vienna," and was disseminated "not in obscure radical publications or in soap-box speeches, but right across the family breakfast table into horrified ears of conservative fathers and mothers."[241] *Ah, Wilderness!* is about the ideological plasticity of the middle class—how it incorporated the "sexual revolution" as a way of displacing or diverting attention from the need for political and socioeconomic revolution.[242] This rebellion against the suppression of desires did not threaten or destabilize the power of the middle class, as Goldman, Dell, and Eastman hoped it would; rather, it enabled the middle class to redefine itself and to imagine itself, in the words of Walter Prichard Eaton's defense of *Strange Interlude*, as lifting "the lid off the cellar of life." The narrative structure of O'Neill's comedy, which deposits socialist and anarchist revolution in the first act only to ignore it in subsequent acts concerned with Richard's romantic life, enacts the 1920s split between leftist critiques of personal life and psychotherapeutic discourses of "personal emancipation."

Guild audiences of 1933 who viewed O'Neill's play would understandably revel in the knowledge of their plasticity—their newly "liberated" therapeutic standards of sexual behavior, especially for women (no longer what Miller termed "whited sepulchres"). The cultural forces behind this "liberation" and what Judge Ben Lindsey called the "revolt of youth" were not in the main Goldman, Eastman, and Dell; they were Havelock Ellis, Sigmund Freud, the legions of Sunday-supplement pop psychologists in the 1920s, and even more so, perhaps, the new glossy lifestyle magazines and Hollywood movies.[243] O'Neill, too, was a cultural leader in the revolution that reorganized the middle class. *Ah, Wilderness!* locates nostalgically the adolescent stirrings of this revolution within the middle class and mutes its other Red Emma radical origins.

It is not surprising that leftist critics, fired-up by plays like Paul and Claire Sifton's *1931—* (1931), would label *Ah, Wilderness!* so much "whipped cream." Compared to *1931—*, which brought the unnerving wilderness of the unemployed onto the stage of the bourgeois theatre (Clurman, Crawford, and Strasberg's last hurrah with the Guild), *Ah, Wilderness!* must have seemed shallow. And yet just as psychoanalysis and pop psychology in the 1920s succeeded to a great extent in cornering the market on the category of the psychological, the Communist Left of the 1930s endeavored to colonize the categories of the radical and the social (reclassifying Ibsen, Shaw, and O'Neill—the "men against the mob"—as promoters of "bourgeois ideals").

Ah, Wilderness! is not a "revolutionary" play, as was *1931—*, and it seems at times to coat "bourgeois ideals" in the sickly sweet syrup of nostalgia. The agitprop Left, however, did not recognize the O'Neill who—like the Edmund that teased Tyrone about Shaughnessy and his pigs—would not drop entirely an older style of "Socialist gabble" and "anarchist sentiment." It was this more complex and conflicted O'Neill who *exposed* how the middle class—with its common sense, its literary allusions, its universities, its taste, and its incorporation of depth— sought by cultural means to contain agitation for the "adolescent," workers-of-the-world-unite revolution that Paul and Claire Sifton, Joseph Freeman, Mike Gold, and others hoped would still erupt. And it was this liberal O'Neill who recoiled from a particular ideological *version* of the category of "the Left," which may have found its most theatrical expression in what historian Paul Buhle has called the "megalomaniac sectarianism" and "proletarian posturing"[244] of Mike Gold in his role as commissar of the *New Masses*.

Nineteen thirty-one overtook O'Neill in 1934. His 1934 plan for a sequel to *Ah, Wilderness!* used World War I to blow apart the safe and secure Miller family. O'Neill did not allow the middle-class Millers and their quaint "bourgeois conventions" to "live happily ever after" (in contrast to Doris Alexander's prediction). Richard goes to Yale, to his father's newspaper, and to war, but is left "maimed, embittered, idealism murdered." Miller, that self-possessed master of middle-class common sense, is "prostrated by death of wife—lost, bewildered in changed times—waiting for death—same about everything."[245] The playwright moved the domestic devastation of the Depression back in time to World War I (which, recall, the younger O'Neill saw as a "fratricide" engineered by "Guggenheim and Standard Oil"). It is in this brief 1934 sketch that O'Neill exhibits the savage side of his ambivalence about the Sunday-dinner, middle-class "mood of emotion" that the Guild audiences of 1933–34 required—like a stiff drink—to "steady" (as O'Neill put it) their nerves.

Possessors, Self-dispossessed

One can only wonder what Von Wiegand, Lawson, Flexner, and Geddes would have said about O'Neill's cycle, *A Tale of Possessors, Self-dispossessed* (1935–), had it been completed in the 1940s. In 1946 O'Neill, echoing Walt Whitman's *Democratic Vistas* (1871), explained that his epic eleven-play project was predicated on "the theory that the United States, instead of being the most successful country in the world, is the greatest failure. It's the greatest failure because it was given everything, more than any other country. . . . Its main idea is that everlasting game of trying to possess your own soul by the possession of something outside of it."[246] The eleven plays were to focus on American families from 1775 to 1930. O'Neill's handling of the psychological was resolutely historical: to demonstrate "the development of psychological characterization in relation to changing times—what the railroads, what the panics did to change people's lives."[247]

O'Neill destroyed part of the cycle in 1944 and tore up and burned the rest just before his death in 1953, save *A Touch of the Poet*, which he revised in 1942. Although *More Stately Mansions* was burned in manuscript, a typescript survived apparently by accident with instructions affixed to it: "Unfinished Work. This script to be destroyed in case of my death! Eugene O'Neill."[248] O'Neill's worsening neurological tremor made it next to impossible for him even to hold a pencil for sustained periods after 1943, and he feared that his unfinished manuscripts would be completed and botched by others. The two survivors, *A Touch of the Poet* and its sequel, *More Stately Mansions*, are searing critiques of the effects of capitalism on the family. Although newspapers in 1946 reported that O'Neill intended to allow the Guild to produce *A Touch of the Poet* in 1947, the play had its American premiere in 1957, four years after O'Neill's death. O'Neill's drama was not produced by the Guild (well past its prime), but it was directed by Harold Clurman.[249]

What O'Neill offers in the highly polished *Touch of the Poet* is more theoretically complex than what Eleanor Flexner demanded (the dramatization of "character as the product of social forces") or what Virgil Geddes prescribed ("the tragedy of forces, not weaknesses"). The historian Jean-Pierre Vernant, in outlining new historical approaches to conceptualizing the psychological, could easily be describing what O'Neill accomplished in this late play: "psychological history . . . does not unfold alongside and, so to speak, parallel to a history that is technical, economic, social, religious, and so on; it is worked out in them and through them."[250]

A Touch of the Poet dramatizes the hidden and not-so-hidden injuries that the categories of class, gender, and ethnicity inflicted on Irish immigrants in mid-nineteenth-century capitalist America.[251] Con Melody, the Irish immigrant tavern owner with aristocratic daydreams, poses as a Byronic hero in his barroom mirror as a means of shoring up a class, gender, and ethnic identity that has been ravaged by the society he scorns through his recital of *Childe Harold*: "Among them, but not of them." His pose is not mere egotism, arrogance, or obsession; it is a defense against his position in a New World that does look down on an Irishman whose father (as his wife Nora confesses) was not an aristocrat but rather a "thievin'" tavern owner "who kept a dirty shebeen" (3:256). The mirror reassures Con that by controlling how he sees himself, he may have some measure of control over how others perceive him.

Because Nora knows the truth about his past and because she can hide neither her own Irish peasant origins nor her brogue, she must ceaselessly be insulted by Major Cornelius Melody, one time of His Majesty's Seventh Dragoons (the embittered Irishman in the mirror). As I noted in Chapter 1, O'Neill's own father soon learned that he had to suppress his brogue in order to succeed as an actor (he eventually prospered by playing noblemen).[252] Con, who can switch on his own brogue at will, habitually projects the shame he feels about his "shebeen" origins onto his wife. But it is American culture that makes him ashamed. Thus Nora lovingly and self-consciously functions both as his audience (a human mirror) and his whipping "girl." She knows that without an auditor who will support his performance and without a human being he can put down, his beleaguered masculinity cannot be "kept up": "*At first, he poses to himself, striking an attitude—a Byronic hero, noble, em-bittered, disdainful, defying his tragic fate, brooding over past glories. But he has no audience and he cannot keep it up. His shoulders sag at the table top, hopelessness and defeat bring a trace of real tragedy to his ruined, handsome face."*

Con's daughter Sara is the outspoken feminist-capitalist in the play who thoroughly deplores her mother's romantic subservience and vo-ciferously objects to "slaving as a waitress and chambermaid so my fa-ther can get drunk every night like a gentleman" (3:197). Yet the un-educated Nora comprehends and sympathizes with Con's class-based, gender-based, and ethnic-based psychology far better than her daughter does. When Con leaves to seek out Mr. Harford, the rich Yankee, to challenge him to a duel as a means of avenging Sara's—really his own—"honor" (Harford's lawyer tried to pay off Con to terminate Sara's engagement to Harford's son, Simon), Sara muses: "All I hope is that whatever happened wakes him from the truth of himself in that mirror" (3:263). Nora knows that such an awakening would crush him.

Con does awaken from his pipe dream and the Major is crushed. When he arrives at Harford's estate, the Major and Corporal Creegan encounter not Harford, but rather his servants. They get pommeled and are arrested in the bargain. Con's humiliation is compounded ten times over because Harford's wife, the aristocratic Deborah whom he had tried vainly to romance earlier in his tavern, witnessed the brawl from her window. Her class, her refined femininity, and her old Yankee stock combine ideologically and psychologically to shatter Con by making his "con"—the Byronic Major-in-the-mirror—into an obvious farce.

I have sketched the lines of conflict in *Touch* to suggest that O'Neill here—in 1942—sees the social, the ideological, and the psychological not as distinct categories but as categories complexly intertwined. O'Neill's historical and political thinking about the psychological is far more sophisticated than what John Howard Lawson derogated as the drama-tist's "Sunday-supplement-use of Freud." O'Neill does not choose be-tween what Virgil Geddes called a "tragedy of forces" and a "tragedy of weaknesses"; rather he shows how the two are historically and psycho-logically inseparable. *Touch* exemplifies what O'Neill recommended that Michael Gold try writing in 1926: "flesh & blood propaganda."

Leftist critics indicted O'Neill for not being a Socialist, but they them-selves were not always progressive enough when assessing what he put in place of a Socialist critique that could be limited by its own conventions and narratives. Nor was O'Neill always the best judge of this, especially in the 1920s. His unfinished cycle, which set out overtly to demystify the American Pipe Dream, showed signs that he had progressed into Big Themes and Big Questions inflected by the sort of social contradictions and social criticism that preoccupied the Left. What *Touch* does not do so clearly on its own, but what it might have done in the context of a completed eleven-play cycle about the "possessed" and "self-dispossessed" from 1775 to 1930, is to evince what Samuel Sillen called "positive purpose"—to suggest (as did Chekhov, for Sillen) "the life which ought to be."

Other plays in the 1930s turned to history in order to accomplish this. Arthur Arent's "Living Newspaper," *One-Third of a Nation* (1938), which criticizes capitalist possessive individualism as expressed through the New York City real estate business from colonial times to the 1930s, is motivated by "positive purpose." This Federal Theatre Project Living Newspaper is a sterling example of what Brecht termed a "theatre of learning" (and unlearning). "The learning-play," Brecht wrote in 1935, "is essentially dynamic; its task is to show the world as it changes (and also how it may be changed)."[253] *One-Third of a Nation* relentlessly and dramatically stages the exploitation of tenants in slums from the mid-nineteenth century to the Depression (opening with a contemporary tenement-in-flames) and argues explicitly that housing laws must be changed. It dramatizes what is from one point of view a tragedy, but a tragedy that is effectively unmasked as an outcome of an organization of social, economic, and political power, a "fate" that can be altered by members of the audience. *A Touch of the Poet, More Stately Mansions,* and *One-Third of a Nation* in various ways all achieve what some leftist critics thought of as "social depth," but only the latter play—a civic play not generally acclaimed by mainstream literary critics as Big, Deep, Timeless, or Great—sought to persuade its audiences to take an active role in transforming the culture it had staged as a problem.[254]

THE TRAPPINGS OF
THEATRE, GENDER,
AND DESIRE

Glaspell and O'Neill

4

In the preceding chapters I have argued that critics must be attentive not only to the nineteenth-century taboos that O'Neill helped
break down, but also to the political form of subjectivity and understanding of the psychological that he participated in setting up. I also
have occasionally offered evidence of a less conspicuous side of O'Neill
that would have been very much attuned to this book's approach to his
work: the side represented in Charlie Marsden's detachment from the
mass-cultural popularization of psychoanalytic depth in *Strange Interlude* (1928)—"a lot to account for, Herr Freud. . . . Sex the philosopher's

stone . . . 'O Oedipus, O my king! The world is adopting you!' " (2:662). It is to this other intriguing side of O'Neill that we shall now turn.

Marsden's point was made at length by Stephen Brewster over a decade earlier in Susan Glaspell and Jig Cook's *Suppressed Desires* (1915), the Provincetown Players' extremely popular[1] play that parodied the psychoanalytic discourse of depth as a commodity. In this chapter I will sketch thematic connections between O'Neill's dramas and Glaspell's feminist plays, which, like *Suppressed Desires*, concentrated their critique on the cultural making of forms of selfhood.[2] We will see that O'Neill, like Glaspell, his Provincetown friend and colleague, was indeed conscious that gender stereotypes are built into the depth that one experiences as personal or instinctual. As my reinterpretation of *Long Day's Journey Into Night* (1941) will show, it was especially when O'Neill represented theatre as a cultural force producing gendered forms of subjectivity that he attained a critical distance from the discourses of depth and desire which he dramatized as essence in much of his work.[3]

Before examining thematic links between Glaspell's and O'Neill's critical perspectives on desire as a cultural construction, my discussion of changing attitudes toward desire in Chapter 3 needs elaboration. The cultural meanings of desire had shifted considerably between the late nineteenth century and the 1920s. The notion of what has been labeled the "spermatic economy" of desire was first popularized in the mid-nineteenth century. Sperm was imagined as a fixed supply of energy like money in the bank. Women were represented as both sexual and economic threats in their roles as "sperm absorbers" and consumers—spenders of money men had earned.[4] The idea of the "spermatic economy" was one aspect of a comprehensive middle-class effort to control the body—particularly what left and entered it (manifested as vegetarianism, temperance, phrenology, the water cure, and taboos against masturbation). Some historians have viewed these programs of bodily control as compensatory emotional responses to socioeconomic changes that were experienced as out of control.[5] It was the middle-class woman's cultural and familial responsibility to help man control himself.[6] Emma Crosby, O'Neill's taboo-ridden heroine in *Diff'rent* (1920), conceives of desire within this nineteenth-century model: she rejects Captain Caleb Williams's proposal of marriage after being told that he had sex with a "brown, heathen woman" (2:13) during a voyage. (Mr. Miller, in *Ah, Wilderness!* (1933), would no doubt have classified this excessively "decent girl" as a "whited sepulchre.") Emma thought that Caleb and their relationship were "diff'rent."

This concept of desire began to alter within what Tom Lutz calls the turn-of-the-century "discourse of neurasthenia." American industrial capitalism, as I have noted, was then undergoing a shift from a producer culture to a consumer culture. One aspect of this shift was in the reinterpretation of the expenditure of desire "as energizing rather than depleting."[7] It was now salutary to spend. "The new morality does not consist in saving, but in expanding consumption," economist Simon Patten preached in *The New Basis of Civilization* (1907): "Vice is energy aborted by . . . the imprisonment of desires."[8] Nina Leeds in *Strange Interlude*, unlike Emma Crosby in Act 1 of *Diff'rent*, does not subscribe to the "imprisonment of desires" sexual economy or to what Philip Rieff termed the "moral demand" system. After learning of her fiancé's death in the war, her notion of nursing her soldier-patients back to health includes having sex with them. The thoroughly "modern" Nina goes on to have a child, not with her husband, Sam Evans, but with her physician, Ned Darrell.[9]

If one significant emotional response to the uncertainty of the nineteenth-century marketplace was to control the body and its desires, one mass-mediated emotional response to the alienation, standardization, and opportunities of corporate America in the 1920s was a "disaccumulation" of desires. O'Neill's Emma Crosby spurned Captain Caleb Williams in 1890 for yielding to temptation on one occasion, but by the spring of 1920 Emma, a frustrated and bitter spinster for three decades, seeks to recapture her unspent youth by releasing her desires with all the gusto of the mourning Nina Leeds. The changing pattern of her behavior followed the resignification of sexuality in America's modern "therapeutic" culture of consumption sketched by Lears, Susman, and Rieff.[10]

In their popular book, *The Revolt of Youth* (1925), Judge Ben Lindsey and Wainwright Evans could have had O'Neill's Emma Crosby in mind when they wrote that "primitive desires attain undue authority over individuals in any civilization whose methods of education fail to produce a culture capable of placing a right valuation on such desires."[11] This "hydraulic" formulation is essentially a popularization of Freud's 1908 thesis that, although "civilization" relies on the "suppression" of instincts (the older spermatic economy model), "civilized" sexual morality was much too repressive and, for therapeutic reasons, had to be relaxed.[12] In their defense of instincts, Lindsey and Evans, like Freud, categorize "suppressed" "primitive desires" as outside of or beneath "civilization."[13]

Once desire is extracted conceptually from the very culture that determines its meaning, it can be represented commonsensically as the inner psychological self. In the words of Richard Sennett, sexuality can then be imagined as a "state of being," a "revelation of self," and an "expressive state, rather than an expressive act."[14] This is precisely what happened in the shift from the discourse of neurasthenia to that of psychoanalysis: the latter, observes Tom Lutz, placed an individualizing stress "on the intrapsychic"—rather than the environmentally rooted— "nature of conflict."[15] Yet, as historians have noted, the pop psychology industry, advertising industry, romance novels, true confession magazines, and films of the twenties contributed to the mass production of desire through images of desire and assumptions about desire more than ever before.[16] In the 1920s, desire was not "beneath" mass "civilization": the idea that desire was being suppressed had become one of this civilization's best-selling commodities.

As I suggested in Chapters 2 and 3, scholarly and popular versions of psychoanalysis retreated from the 1910s classification of desire and gender as political-psychological categories and redefined them more narrowly as psychosexual categories. Historian Mary Ryan offers one example to illustrate how the "sexual" effects of this were inimical both to feminism and to sexual expression: "By 1920 the *Ladies Home Journal* had a new rationale for ushering women into homes and nurseries: not only the dictates of biology and 'divine purpose' but 'sex psychology' as well. When in the same year an anonymous woman was interrogated about her sex life, she had already mastered the new jargon, rhapsodizing about the 'deep psychological effect of intercourse, making possible complete mental sympathy.'" The woman interviewed, Ryan argues, does not disclose her deepest, desirous "self"; rather she recites a discourse that has defined her "self" as being psychological, sexual, and feminine in particular terms. The excerpt from the interview reveals how mass culture's psychological standards of masculinity and femininity produced what were taken to be the "remotest recesses" of the self.[17] I shall argue that Glaspell's plays of the 1910s and early 1920s grasped the political significance of this mass-cultural production of gendered "depth"—and that O'Neill was paying attention.

Glaspell and the Cultural Fashioning
of Gender and Desire

In 1916 Louise Bryant, no "whited sepulchre," sent her lover John Reed an alluring photograph of herself in the nude (Figure 26). She was sitting on a deserted Provincetown beach—her head tilted back, her tousled hair touching the sand—with twin grassy-tipped dunes behind her and one grassy mound in front of her. Her inscription on the back of the photograph says: "This is to remind you of 'the Dunes' and all the nice months after the convention."[18] Bryant's representation of her sexuality was artful, befitting the Provincetown artists' colony: her carefully situated pose suggests that "the dunes" (placed in quotes) she invites Reed to recall, wistfully, are not simply those made of sand and grass. Culturally, the Provincetown photograph can be taken as a sign of how freely (or eagerly) the middle-class or upper-class white New Woman of modern times expressed her desires. Biographically, the photograph gives us some sense of the sexual daring that drew both Reed and O'Neill, and perhaps Jig Cook, to Bryant's dunes—at the same time.

But as I indicated above, cultural historians are now questioning how liberating this liberation of "desire" actually was for New Women. After reviewing Mabel Dodge's grief caused by John Reed's infidelities, and Neith Boyce's anguish over Hutchins Hapgood's many extramarital affairs, Ellen Kay Trimberger concludes that "gender inequity" was a component of sexual radicalism and that the Provincetowners' "sexual culture" was very much "defined by the hegemony of male experience."[19] Hapgood, for instance, encouraged Boyce to seek out lovers; but even when she developed close (nonsexual) friendships with other men, he broke into a jealous rage. Boyce's literary response to this sexual tension was to write *Constancy* (1916) for the new Provincetown theatre group, a satire of so-called free love. The "liberation" of sexuality was by no means tantamount to emancipation from gender constraints, especially, notes Lois Rudnick, "when women's sexuality became the defining factor of her modernity."[20] Louise Bryant's own Provincetown play, *The Game* (1916), cast "The Girl" in the traditional, unliberated role of emotional-crutch-for-the-male.[21]

Susan Glaspell (c.1876–1948) had a conventional middle-class upbringing in Davenport, Iowa. After finishing high school in Davenport she contributed a column, "The New Girl," to a society magazine and

Figure 26. Louise Bryant on Provincetown Beach. Houghton Library, Harvard University. Her inscription on the back of the photograph, meant for John Reed, reads: "This is to remind you of 'the Dunes' and all the nice months after the convention. Please, Honey, take good care of yourself out there—."

worked as a legislative reporter. She attended Drake University in Des Moines, Iowa, and later spent a year studying at the University of Chicago. After 1901 she increasingly concentrated her efforts on writing fiction, publishing the first two of her nine novels, *The Glory of the Conquered* (1909) and *The Visioning* (1911), as well as a collection of short stories, *The Lifted Mask* (1912). She wed George Cram Cook in 1913 and soon moved to Greenwich Village.[22]

Agnes Boulton wrote that O'Neill and other men noticed that Susan Glaspell "was very attractive" (Figure 27), but also that her gregarious husband Jig Cook "gave her considerable to think about."[23] Provincetown observers have speculated that Cook may have had romantic involvements with Bryant, Ida Rauh, Edna St. Vincent Millay, and Eunice Tietjens.[24] Robert Sarlós has written that Cook, who had taught Greek at Iowa State and Stanford, consciously took a Dionysian approach to the organization of the Players—integrating "intoxication, sexual rites, and theatre"—and that Glaspell, the Apollonian, "accepted" his "philandering."[25] We shall find that several of her plays written during this

Figure 27. Susan Glaspell at work, c. 1910s. Henry W. and Albert A. Berg Collection, New York Public Library, Astor, Lenox and Tilden Foundations.

period suggest that Glaspell's critical response to the Dionysian bohemianism of the 1910s was not so much Apollonian as it was feminist.

Even before he met and grew to admire Glaspell, O'Neill was aware that the political women of the 1910s sometimes found it challenging to contend with the "new sexuality." In *Servitude* (1914), O'Neill's Mrs. Frazer demonstrates her integrity in the face of this challenge. Frazer's life changes radically when she sees a feminist play written by a man named Roylston. When she travels late at night to the playwright's home to seek his advice about her own oppressive domestic predicament, she discovers that he takes her more seriously as an object of desire than an intellectual and political agent: "(*intensely*) Do you realize how beautiful you are?" (1:254), Roylston asks. Frazer parries his advances and finally, perhaps learning more from her discouraging encounter with him than from his plays, lets him have it: "(*mockingly*) I was truthful enough to tell you I did not love you. That was horrible of me. How could you endure hearing a woman say she did not love you? And how bored you must be when you hear them say they do love you!" (1:276). Yet O'Neill reduces Frazer to feminine "servitude" before the curtain falls—disenchanted with Roylston, she idealizes his irredeemably self-sacrificial, submissive wife as her new role model.[26]

Notwithstanding *Servitude*'s weird blend of feminist and antifeminist sentiments, a few years later O'Neill unambiguously employed feminist irony as a gesture of his respect and affection for Glaspell. In 1920 he reported to Agnes Boulton a conversation he had had with George C. Tyler, a producer much in need of consciousness raising. Glaspell was the subject:

> He said "that *girl* has a real touch of genius"—(he evidently thinks Susan is about as old as Helen Hayes), and he added with a questioning misgiving: "If the damned Greenwich Village faddists didn't get her into the radical magazine publications class." I didn't disillusion him about Susan being 19 and at the mercy of the faddist world—it was too funny—but I did say she was married to a very sensible man. Upon which Tyler heaved a sigh of relief and ceased to "view with alarm."[27]

O'Neill clearly relished parodying Tyler's patriarchal prejudices.

Glaspell was an active member of the Heterodoxy club, a feminist association based in Greenwich Village. This group was founded by twenty-five women in 1912 as what might have later been called a "consciousness-raising group." Many of the middle-class and upper-class Heterodites were actively political in their concerns, particularly women's suffrage, and they were also "inward-looking," "individualistic," and stressed "self-development." Membership peaked in the 1910s and 1920s, waned in the 1930s, and finally dissolved in the early 1940s. Provincetown Players who belonged to the Heterodoxy club also included Mary Heaton Vorse, Mabel Dodge, Ida Rauh, Stella Commins Ballantine, Crystal Eastman, and Edna Kenton.[28] Thus O'Neill knew not only some of the leading psychoanalysts, pop psychologists, anarchists, and Socialists of his day, he was on good terms with formidable feminists.[29]

So far as anyone knows, O'Neill did not attend Heterodoxy mass meetings to support feminism (as did Max Eastman and Floyd Dell). But he probably learned from Glaspell's feminism in two ways. The influence that Glaspell had on O'Neill's *Now I Ask You* (1916) is obvious. Glaspell was interested not simply in "fads" (as Tyler assumed) but more complexly in the cultural discourses that shape one's conception of selfhood and desire. I think it likely that her plays taught O'Neill something about the pervasive effects of discourse on subjectivity.[30] It is of course impossible to know what O'Neill and Glaspell discussed when he stayed overlong at her house in the process of borrowing the paper (a habit that agitated his wife, Agnes), or during Cook's Dionysian communal drinking revels in Provincetown and Greenwich Village; however, we shall see that there are themes in O'Neill's plays from the 1920s to the 1940s that are very much on the same wavelength as Glaspell's powerful feminist works for the Players.

Although Glaspell—as an established novelist—was lauded in early reviews of her work for the Provincetown Players (O'Neill the newcomer a close second), she did not adopt the emerging depth model in her plays and, ultimately, was not canonized.[31] The critical trend of the 1920s was apparent in Arthur Hobson Quinn's *History of the American Drama* (1927), which devoted four pages to Glaspell and forty-one to O'Neill. In defiance of this trend, one critic claimed in 1927 that Glaspell had been unjustifiably obscured by the cultural shadow of O'Neill. In his review of Barrett Clark's study of O'Neill, Walter Long pointed out that, while Glaspell was credited along with O'Neill for having brought fame and distinction to the Provincetown Players, Clark nonetheless failed to discuss Glaspell's contributions: "There is not a single short play of O'Neill's which can compete with Miss Glaspell's *Trifles*. Mr. O'Neill's *Ile* and *Bound East for Cardiff* are undoubtedly superior to Miss Glaspell's play in emotional intensity, but they lack the nice constructive method and subtlety of approach so evident in Miss Glaspell's work." Long attributes the expurgation of Glaspell to "the strong myth-making tendencies of nearly all American critics and friends of Mr. O'Neill."[32]

Because *Suppressed Desires* placed its spotlights not only on taboos that were being questioned but on the ideological production of a psychological selfhood that understood "liberation" in narrowly individual terms as opposition to these taboos, the play is of enduring historical importance. *Suppressed Desires* is also historically significant because it suggests that women, in particular, were drawn to psychoanalysis. Henrietta Brewster derives enormous power and satisfaction from "psyching" her friends. In the 1910s psychoanalysis brought into public discourse personal issues that were of pressing concern to women whose pain and powerlessness was experienced by them as fundamentally personal and familial in scope.

Alice Gerstenberg's *Overtones* (1913), produced by the Washington Square Players (which rejected *Suppressed Desires*) in 1915, also suggests that women in the 1910s sought to explain their discontent through the psychoanalytic repression model. *Overtones* dramatizes the divided self we later see in O'Neill's *The Great God Brown* (1926), *Strange Interlude* (1928), and *Days Without End* (1933). In *Overtones* Harriet, the public, domestic self, is constantly accompanied by Hetty, her hidden, desirous, discontented self: "*Harriet never sees Hetty, never talks to her but rather thinks aloud looking into space.*" The other character, Margaret, "*a cultured woman,*" is joined on stage by Maggie, "*her primitive self.*" Hetty explains: "I am the rushing river; you are the ice over the current." Harriet responds: "I am your subtle overtones."[33] The divided self device allows Gerstenberg to stage the ambivalence Harriet must "repress" about her spouse (the Hetty within her really loves John Caldwell, Margaret's husband). *Overtones*, as a very early example of staged pop psychology, offers historical indications that women who attempted to account for their discontent in the terms provided by psychoanalysis were participating in their ideological positioning as sexualized and privatized subjects for whom the personal was everything.

Glaspell's feminist plays, by contrast, steadfastly focused on gender rather than pop psychological or pop modernist depth when attempting to understand the politics of women's suppression and women's desires. *Trifles* (1916) dramatizes the aftermath of Mrs. Wright's murder of Mr. Wright. The sheriffs, having searched the Wright home, are at a loss to determine if and why Mrs. Wright killed her spouse—who was found hanged. From her jail cell, Mrs. Wright has made the seemingly trivial request that her preserves be looked after. The sheriffs consider such domestic concerns to be mere female "trifles" (9), as does the patronizing county attorney.[34] The latter's remarks to the two women who have been asked to tend to the preserves begin to reveal what Mrs. Wright felt was wrong:

> [*with the gallantry of a young politician*] And yet, for all their worries, what would we do without the ladies? [*the women do not unbend. He goes to the sink, takes a dipperful of water from the pail and pouring it into a basin, washes his hands. Starts to wipe them on the roller-towel, turns it for a cleaner place.*] Dirty towels! [*Kicks his foot against the pans under the sink.*] Not much of a housekeeper, would you say, ladies? (9).

The two "ladies" who have come to honor Mrs. Wright's request perceive more than "trifles" at the scene of the crime. They begin to identify clues that the sheriffs and the county attorney are unable to read. An empty birdcage speaks volumes to them. So does the missing bird, whose neck has been broken. They discover it carefully laid to rest in a "fancy box." Glaspell's play, then, is about the long-term suppressed violence in caged women that finally explodes. Only women who have experienced such a suppression in their own lives possess the empathy to recognize such "trifles" as damning evidence of a husband's longstanding domestic crimes—evidence they agree to suppress on behalf of Mrs. Wright.

In *What Is Wrong with Marriage* (1929), G. V. Hamilton and Kenneth Macgowan noted that the wives interviewed tended to "say *everything* is wrong [with marriage]. They see far more difficulties. . . . Though the women are more disturbed about sex than the men, their peculiarly complex and delicate consciousnesses seek a substitute for the purely physical in the matter of affection which the women alone complained about" (emphasis supplied).[35] Neither Hamilton and Macgowan in their analysis nor the sheriffs in their investigation quite see what Glaspell wants us to recognize in *Trifles*. While O'Neill's *Desire Under the Elms* (1924) installs sexualized desire as the driving force in the self, Glaspell's Mrs. Wright is driven to violence by the whole production of her life.

Her predicament, never narrowed by being named, is not the centrality of a desire (reductively) defined as sexual, but rather the oppressiveness of the positions women occupy in the culture. Mrs. Wright's dilemma extends beyond Mr. Wright to culture, and specifically to the social organization of sexual difference that produced her husband. Mrs. Hale tells Mrs. Peters: "I know how things can be for women. . . . We live close together and we live far apart" (27). As their analysis of Mrs. Wright's "trifles" circles back to self-examination, both women begin to establish a social grasp of how and why "*everything* is wrong." Some critics got the message. One New York reviewer heralded *Trifles* as "the most noteworthy achievement of an American dramatist within the last five years. . . . we merely put the five years in as a sort of check because we realize our tendency to unbridled enthusiasm."[36]

In *Woman's Honor* (1917), Glaspell again portrays women engaged in unlearning their subject positions. Unlearning of this kind is, of course, not classified as one of O'Neill's "Big Themes" (like life and fate). Glaspell's story is simple but clever. A man on trial for murder is in need of a woman he spent the night with to come forward so that he can establish his alibi. Once the woman appears in court, however, some people, particularly the prisoner, will view her "honor" as stained. The defense attorney, confident of his reticent client's innocence, publishes the details of the case in the newspaper in hopes of inspiring the woman involved to step forward voluntarily. To the prisoner's and to the attorney's amazement, several women, unruffled about their so-called honor, present themselves as eager to testify for him. Once in jail these women attempt to reeducate the prisoner on the issue of woman's honor, and ultimately fail—he opts to be executed.

Shielded One protests the interpretation of female honor as chastity, asking her fellow volunteers: "Aren't we something more than things to be noble about?" Motherly One recognizes that masculinity is a form of deep-seated emotional conditioning. Men are socialized to be femininity addicts: "If we could only get them to be noble about something else. I should really hate to take it from them entirely. It's like giving up smoking or drinking. You have to do it gradually, and there should be something to put in its place" (145).

Scornful One resents honor because it positions women as hypersexual subjects: "Did it ever strike you as funny that woman's honor is only about one thing, and that man's honor is about everything but that thing?" (134). *Suppressed Desires, Trifles,* and *Woman's Honor* are about dismantling cultural constructions of emotional life. The point of *Woman's Honor* is not to delve into "womanly depth," but rather to demystify the ideological invention of it. Glaspell's play acknowledges sexuality as an important part of a woman's humanity (as does her later drama, *The Verge*) without inflating it into the very essence of her humanity. Female sexuality is not blown up into a hermeneutic—the key to a woman's mysterious self.

Glaspell's *The Verge* (1921) formulates a socially complex understanding of psychological tension and depression in women-on-the-verge. Claire Archer, who refuses to play the conventional part of wife and mother, spends most of her time inventing hybrid plants in her greenhouse: "We need not be held in forms molded for us," she tries to explain. "There is outness—and otherness" (19). Her experimental greenhouse draws the heat from the main house, leaving the occupants frigid. Claire's "queer" commitment to "making things that never grew before" baffles and unsettles her husband, Harry. Her horticultural battle is symbolic of her conflict with the inventions of common sense and domestic life that produce her womanhood in specific ways. Through Claire, Glaspell prods us to think about reification—how ideological patterns come to seem natural, invisible, taken-for-granted: "Back here— the old pattern, done again, again and again. So long done it doesn't even know itself for a pattern—an immensity" (52).

Glaspell's critical project is much like that of her fellow Heterodite, Charlotte Perkins Gilman, who, in "The Yellow Wallpaper" (1892), envisioned domestic women as under house arrest, incarcerated within patterned wallpaper. Gilman's narrator's subversive aim is to resignify the meaning of the grotesquely sentimental pattern and to peel off the paper from the wall (and, by implication, from herself). Claire Archer's challenge, like that of the narrator of Gilman's story, is to "get past what we've done. Our own dead things—block the way" (54).[37] Glaspell's critique is materialist: discourses of gender and domesticity ("dead things") represent feminized depth as natural.

Susan Glaspell and Claire Archer are creating a new feminist aesthetic. To do so they must supplant the very forms of the production of life itself—and specifically they must uproot common sense about gender.[38] The feminist edge of Claire's creative project is keen. Adelaide, Claire's sister, censures Claire's unfeminine pattern-breaking: "A mother who does not love her own child! You are an unnatural woman." Claire retorts: "Well, at least it saves me from being a natural one" (72). When Claire is complimented as being "beautiful," she declines the "honor" of being framed as an aesthetic object: "I'd rather be the steam rising from the manure than be a thing called beautiful!" (112).

In "A Valediction Forbidding Mourning" (1970), Adrienne Rich writes about "the failure of criticism to locate the pain."[39] Glaspell's play is about a powerful, frustrated woman who knows that she lacks the critical vocabulary to name the pain. The Verge is no simple drama dramatizing a depth already known (publicized by pop psychology and aestheticized by modernism); it intentionally puzzles our common sense.[40]

By the early 1920s, psychoanalysis, the discourse Glaspell parodied in 1915, had begun to colonize the way psychological breakdown was explained on a mass-cultural scale. As Richard Ohmann put it, this cultural invention of the psychological as a category could mystify "the way social roles and power relations translate into personal illness."[41] Claire is disturbed; but how do we read her predicament? W. David Sievers's psychoanalytic diagnosis exemplifies the psychological common sense that Claire—and Glaspell—were up against. Sievers's misreading of Claire's depression enacts a displacement of the social and political issues that Claire's feminist aesthetic broaches. His diagnosis strains to appropriate this complex play by "Cook's wife" for psychoanalysis.

The author draws a terrifyingly real portrait of maniac-depressive psychosis. The heroine, Claire, has brilliant flashes of rationality, but in Act I is obsessed with a desire to cross-breed plants in a hot house. She is strangely troubled with the compulsion to break out of molds—to be something that has never been before. This compulsion begins symbolically as an expression of rebellion . . . against her monotonous pattern of marriage. . . . But it grows perilously close to psychosis as she believes she has grown a new species of perverted plant which has found "otherness."

What Sievers terms "rationality" is in Glaspell's play nothing less than capitulation to common sense arrangements of social forms and roles. Sievers's psychoanalytic diagnosis consistently individualizes Claire's predicament; whereas Claire herself keeps referring to forms, patterns, and molds as the difficulty. He praises Cook's wife's "real portrait of maniac-depressive psychosis." But Claire herself disrupts the production of the "real" and the "natural" by recognizing them as socially made forms. Again Sievers invokes the "real" in his diagnosis of Claire in Act 3: "Gently singing 'Nearer My God to Thee,' Claire has completely lost touch with reality as the curtain falls on this haunting experience within the mind of a psychotic individual, whose oversensitivity—and possibly her unconsciously homosexual wish to be 'other' than woman—drove her past the verge of insanity."[42] Sievers never realizes that Claire may have been on the verge of discovery. His psychoanalytic approach constantly sexualizes Claire as a way of explaining her, thus thrusting her into the very subject position she rejects. Sievers's diagnosis of Claire (like Sievers's reading of Tennessee Williams's Blanche DuBois—whom he diagnosed as a "schizophrenic") deploys a psychological discourse that occludes our vision of the sociality of desire.[43]

Sievers, writing in the 1950s, was plodding in the august footsteps of Arthur Hobson Quinn who, in 1927, both praised The Verge as an "extraordinary play" and did his damnedest to trivialize it as "a study of a neurotic woman who is going insane." Nineteen-twenties psychoanalytic discourse enabled Quinn to recast Claire as a kind of crazed Ophelia-gone-berserk. Referring to Margaret Wycherly's strong performance as Claire, he argued: "She showed the gradual increase in violence of the symptoms of a woman in that condition, but the question remains, is the whole thing worth while?" Quinn's answer is no: the solitary "coherent idea" in the play, he says, is that one can grow only through "violence and wreckage," and this is a false notion.[44] Psychobabble insulates Quinn and Sievers from recognizing the feminist concerns that fueled Claire's anger. Even the bohemian Hutchins Hapgood, who (thought he) knew Glaspell well, considered her play to be "half mad feminism."[45] Yet he also observed that the Heterodites who saw a performance of *The Verge* in 1921 were awestruck, as if they were "in church."[46]

There is no record that O'Neill saw the Provincetown Players' production of *The Verge* in 1921. It may have been the manuscript of *The Verge*, however, that he discussed with the producer George Tyler on Glaspell's behalf.[47] Themes in several of O'Neill's plays resonate with Glaspell's feminist critique of roles, forms, and patterns. Deborah Harford, for instance, while waiting to meet her son Simon at his cabin after their long estrangement in *More Stately Mansions* (1939), expresses resentment about her fading beauty and, thus, her waning power: "(*looks around clearing bitterly*) And I hoped [Simon] would be here, eagerly awaiting me! (*She forces a self-mocking smile.*) What can you expect, Deborah? At your age, a woman must become resigned to wait upon every man's pleasure, even her son's" (3:315). Soon after, she again reproaches herself: "I am disgusted with watching my body decay" (3:316). When Simon does arrive and asks what role she now plays, she responds brittlely: "I? What nonsense, Dear. You forget I have no audience now" (3:326).

Glaspell's Claire Archer refuses to observe herself within this pattern. In preferring to "be the steam rising from the manure" rather "than be a thing called beautiful" (a notion that Quinn and Sievers would certify as cuckoo), Claire recoils from both the power and the entrapment of what cultural critic John Berger terms feminine aura or presence. Feminine presence, he writes, is "a kind of heat or aura" achieved "at the cost of a woman's self being split into two." The "feminine" woman constantly scrutinizes and gauges the way men value her "aura," much in the manner that Deborah Harford sees her emotional hold on her son as contingent on how he surveys her body.[48]

In O'Neill's *The Personal Equation* (1915), the anarchist-feminist Olga Tarnoff—like Claire Archer—is aware that her sexuality and body give her power, but also that this power, once she exercises it or encourages others to regard it as such, situates her in a position of inequality. Olga, unlike Deborah Harford, perceives the "protective masculine atti-

tude" (1:315), not as reassuring, but as dangerous. She understands, as
does Claire, that if a woman permits herself to be surveyed as "beautiful," her assent categorizes her as an object to be acquired: "Do you
want a signed certificate proving I am yours—like a house and lot?"
(1:315), she asks her lover, Tom.[49]

O'Neill's middle-aged Christine Mannon, uncertain about her control over Adam Brant's desire to possess her in *Mourning Becomes
Electra* (1931), surveys herself as she assumes men do: "I'm old and ugly
and haunted by death! (*then, as if to herself—in a low desperate tone*) I
can't let myself get ugly! I can't!" (2:997). Having internalized her role
as the surveyed, she views her body with self-recrimination and desper-
ation. In *A Moon for the Misbegotten* (1943), Josie Hogan, fearing the
loss of the farm, fantasizes about trapping Jamie Tyrone, her landlord,
to retain it. Her plan is to invite a photographer to surprise them in bed
and then threaten to circulate the photo to the papers. But her scheme,
based on her position as the surveyed, is actually an exercise in self-
flagellation. "It's the disgrace to his vanity—being caught with the likes
of me—(*falteringly, but forcing herself to go on*) My mug beside his in
all the newspapers—the New York papers, too—he'll see the whole of
Broadway splitting their sides laughing at him" (3:905). Josie pictures
Broadway laughing at her.

In such passages O'Neill, like Glaspell in *The Verge*, illuminates the
ideological roots of women's depression. Deborah Harford, Christine
Mannon, and Josie Hogan are all caught in the self-pathologizing forms,
patterns, and roles that Olga Tarnoff rejects and that Claire attempts to
break away from, if only symbolically, in her hothouse experiments in
"otherness." Feminine "beauty," Olga and Claire understand, is really a
subtle form of social "pathology."

O'Neill's poem "Sentimental Stuff" demonstrates that he had a critical awareness of this social pathology as early as 1912. After composing
a sonnet, a ballad, a "soulful" villanelle, a rondeau, and an ode flattering
the eyes, hair, mouth, nose, and "symmetry" of the young woman he is
surveying and pursuing—without success—he finally scribbles "a feeble
triolette" praising "the keenness of her wit. . . . [and] She fell for it."
Rejecting her literary positioning as sentimentalized tenderloin, this
independent "bunch of femininity" enlightens him: "I'll love you if
you'll can / That horrid sentimental stuff— / I've had enough."[50]

O'Neill was undoubtedly sensitive to the woman-as-the-surveyed
because an exaggerated version of it was ever present in his own family
when he was growing up. In *Long Day's Journey*, Jamie voices doubts to

Edmund about their mother's will power: "I can't help being suspicious. Anymore than you can. (*bitterly*) That's the hell of it. And it makes it hell for Mama! She watches us watching her" (3:734). When Jamie accuses Mary of once again being addicted to morphine, and she denies it, he retorts aggressively: "No? Take a look at your eyes in the mirror!" (3:750). Mary is not only "haunted" (as O'Neill's epigraph indicates), she is hunted: O'Neill dramatizes the visual stalking of female game.

Mary Tyrone, along with the other surveyed women depicted by O'Neill, is trapped psychologically in a culturally produced body. Claire could very well be referring to the cultural encoding of female bodies when she insists, "We need not be held in forms molded for us. There is outness—and otherness" (19).[51] Desire and depth take on particular configurations for women because they are squeezed, patterned, molded, and formed by the social pathology of constructs like beauty, aura, and presence.[52]

The Cultural Web in O'Neill's *Journey*

Glaspell may have been more attentive than O'Neill to the function that cultural discourse plays in producing forms of desire, depth, and bodies. But when O'Neill did turn his gaze in this direction, he often thought provocatively about the subtle effects theatre and fiction have on the making of subjectivity. In 1921, for instance, he made some intriguing comments to George Jean Nathan about the mass-mediated form of Anna Christie's "psychology" and "emotions": "From the middle of that third act I feel the play ought to be dominated by the woman's psychology. And I have a conviction that with dumb people of her sort, unable to voice strong feelings, the emotions can find outlet only through the language and gestures of the heroics in the novels and movies they are familiar with—that is, that in moments of stress life copies melodrama." Defending his happy ending in *"Anna Christie"* (1920), which reviewers had singled out for criticism, he continues: "Anna forced herself on me, middle of third act, at her most theatric. In real life I felt she would unconsciously be compelled, through sheer inarticulateness, to the usual 'big scene,' and wait hopefully for her happy ending. . . . Of course, this sincerity of life pent up in the *trappings of theatre*, is impossible to project clearly, I guess" (emphasis supplied).[53] O'Neill sees the "trappings of theatre" as capable of producing "life."

O'Neill recognized that the "trappings of theatre" and fiction structure the depths of persons in all classes, not just "dumb people of [Anna Christie's] sort." In *Now I Ask You*, Lucy Ashleigh—from New York City's fashionable Grammercy Park—strongly identifies with Ibsen's Hedda Gabler (in the Prologue she enacts shooting herself) and Strindberg's "daughter of Indra": she *"is an intelligent, healthy American girl suffering from an overdose of undigested reading, and has mistaken herself for the heroine of a Russian novel"* (1:414). The middle-class Richard Miller of *Ah, Wilderness!* (1933) is *"alternately plain simple boy and a posey actor solemnly playing a role"* (3:12) based on his reading of Swinburne, Wilde, Shaw, and Ibsen. Con Melody's compulsive pose as the romantic, aristocratic individualist in *A Touch of the Poet* (1939) is made possible in part by Lord Byron's *Childe Harold*. But Lucy, Richard, and Con, unlike Anna Christie, somewhat consciously pose literary or theatrical depth.

In *Ile* (1917), as in his letter to Nathan, O'Neill is interested in a woman who is less conscious of the cultural and literary basis of her depth and desire. When Captain Keeney asks his wife, Annie, why she wished to sacrifice her "woman's comforts" in order to bear the hardships of a man's whaling voyage to icy northern waters, she offers the very reason she had for wanting to marry him: "I guess I was dreaming about the Vikings in the story books and I thought you were one of them" (1:500). Annie's mass-mediated femininity associated whaling with a romantic storybook masculinity. O'Neill views dreams and daydreams as products of a mass culture that circulates gender narratives and gender expectations.

In *Servitude*, O'Neill reflects on the role that theatre plays in shaping desire, womanhood, and particular modes of female rebellion. "I had been to see your play 'Sacrifice' the night before for the tenth time," Mrs. Frazer explains to Roylston. "It seemed to breathe a message for me over the footlights. You remember when Mrs. Harding in the play leaves her husband with the words: 'I have awakened!' . . . When I heard her say those words. . . . I felt that I, too, had awakened; that the time had come to assert me—" (1:246). In another passage, the "awakened" Frazer goes further and represents herself to the playwright as his cultural product: "Mentally, I am your creation. That you had no knowledge of my existence when you wrote does not lessen your responsibility in my eyes. I demand that you restore my peace of mind by justifying me to myself" (1:249). For Benton, Roylston's butler, Frazer's response is unexceptional. The "trapping of theatre" is something of a racket for his employer. Roylston's dramas of female liberation have touched the chords of many female fans: "He likes to have them crazy about him," Benton reveals, "but when they get too mushy—he doesn't like complications—they interfere with his work" (1:257).

The "trappings of theatre" is how O'Neill begins, historically, to comprehend Mary Tyrone in *Long Day's Journey*, and perhaps also his mother, Ella. Mary's femininity is constituted partly by theatre and fiction. This is evident in her account to her servant Cathleen of the first time she saw her future husband, James Tyrone, "made-up" on stage: "He was handsomer than my wildest dream, in his make-up and his nobleman's costume that was so becoming to him" (3:778). Her "wildest dreams" have their foundation in mass-mediated narratives and in theatre troupes passing through town. Mary is able to point to her husband's immigrant family history in order to explain and to forgive his obsessive fear of the poorhouse; but she cannot quite grasp the social "make-up" of her own feminine "personal" needs and expectations. "We've loved each other! We always will!" she exclaims wearily to her husband. "Let's remember only that, and not try to understand what we cannot understand . . . the things that life has done to us we cannot explain" (3:764).

Yet "life" takes on specific cultural lineaments as Mary grows more conscious of the patterns, roles, and forms that Claire sees as destructive in *The Verge*. In her woman-to-woman talk with Cathleen, Mary is on the verge of attaining a clearer understanding of what she regards earlier as perplexing. After reminiscing to Cathleen about Tyrone's theatrical "make-up," she reproaches herself: "(*bitterly*) You're a sentimental fool. What is so wonderful about that first meeting between a silly romantic schoolgirl and a matinee idol?" (3:779).

There may be yet another autobiographical level to O'Neill's representation of Mary-the-fan and James-the-star. Agnes Boulton's account of her courtship and early married life with O'Neill, *Part of a Long Story* (1958), at times reads like a sentimental "true confessions" narrative written by a "romantic schoolgirl" about the man who successfully established himself as her "matinee idol." Drinking in the Hell Hole saloon with her new acquaintances, O'Neill and Dorothy Day, Boulton positively rejoices in her status as the surveyed. "I saw it in his eyes, that I looked beautiful; and that I was silent, and that I loved him. . . . and that he wasn't looking at Dorothy now, but at *me*." During their courtship in Greenwich Village, O'Neill, she writes, disclosed his own romantic fantasy about taking over a tall building and leading five other revolutionaries with machine guns in "the revolution." Not only was he "deeply moved," so she thought, his dramatic scenario "deeply moved" her. Boulton's adulation is expressed in the language and tone of magazine romances: "What great manner of man is this, the dark poet and understander of everything?" During their marriage, Eugene referred to Agnes as his "little wife."[54]

Boulton's feminine socialization is precisely what Claire attempts to make visible and to discard in *The Verge*. Interestingly, Boulton confesses that she *"was* jealous" of Glaspell when they lived nearby one another in Provincetown—jealous not only because O'Neill liked Glaspell so much but because of why O'Neill and others admired her: "She seemed to me an ethereal being, detached and yet passionate. She was so far beyond me in her knowledge and understanding of everything that was going on in the world—economics, the rights of mankind, the theater, writing, people—and she was able to talk of them when necessary with charm and interest, while I, it seemed to me, only managed to stutter mentally when I tried to put anything into words."[55] Despite her occasional criticisms of O'Neill, Boulton, still the romantic schoolgirl in the late 1950s, seems overwhelmed by nostalgia for her "matinee idol."

One suspects that O'Neill—like Glaspell—had thought more rigorously about gender socialization (or standardization) than had Agnes Boulton. In the stage directions that describe Margaret Anthony's mask of femininity in *The Great God Brown*, for example, O'Neill makes explicit what Mary Tyrone comes close to gleaning about her own feminine "mask." When Margaret appears on stage for the first time as a graduating high school senior, *"her face is masked with an exact, almost transparent reproduction of her own features, but giving her the abstract quality of a Girl instead of the individual, Margaret"* (2:477). Gender stereotyping can be "almost transparent," but it remains a cultural mask. A few years later Margaret uses her feminine mask to charm Billy Brown into giving her husband Dion (Brown's former rival for her affections) a job: *"Her face is concealed behind the mask of the pretty young matron, still hardly a woman who cultivates a naively innocent and bravely hopeful attitude toward things and acknowledges no wound to the world"* (2:488–89). Yet it is this very mask—more like a second skin—that she finds impossible to remove when Dion momentarily takes off his own. Her intimacy with Dion remains determined by the roles and masks they have been issued by their culture. Mary Tyrone, too, is confined behind a "romantic schoolgirl" mask that she can try to subvert, or use to her advantage, but which she cannot completely cast off.

The theatrical plot of *Long Day's Journey* thickens when we keep in mind that Mary-the-romantic-schoolgirl herself aspired to go on the public stage as a performer. She must inject morphine, she informs Cathleen, because of hands no longer able to perform:

> I have to take it because there is no other that can stop the pain—*all* the pain—I mean, in my hands. . . . they were once one of my good points, along with my hair and eyes, and I had a fine figure, too. (*Her tone has become more and more far-off and dreamy.*) They were a musician's hands. . . . I had two dreams. To be a nun, that was the more beautiful one. To become a concert pianist, that was the other. . . . I haven't touched a piano in so many years. I couldn't play with such crippled fingers, even if I wanted to. For a time after my marriage I tried to keep up my music. But it was hopeless. (3:776–77)

In the margins of the proofs of Barrett Clark's early study of his plays, O'Neill wrote, explaining his love for music: "My mother was a fine pianist—exceptionally fine, I believe."[56] Mary, like Ella O'Neill, may have felt positioned within the nineteenth-century pattern of socialization described by historian Josephine Withers: middle-class women were encouraged to be artistic, but not to become artists.[57] "They don't know that not one in a million who shows promise ever rises to concert playing," James Tyrone rationalizes. "Not that your mother didn't play well for a schoolgirl, but that's no reason to take it for granted she could have—" (3:801). Mary goes on to describe her nonperforming hands with the same self-deprecation we find in Deborah Harford, Christine Mannon, and Josie Hogan: "See, Cathleen, how ugly they are! So maimed and crippled! You would think they'd been through some horrible accident! (*She gives a strange little laugh.*) So they have, come to think of it" (3:777).

For all the psychological stress it places on inescapable ambivalence, guilt, denial, and oedipal tensions in the Tyrone family, *Long Day's Journey* was not entirely written within the depth model O'Neill helped popularize through *Strange Interlude* and *Mourning Becomes Electra*. In *Long Day's Journey*, especially in the final act, O'Neill repeatedly turns to theatre as a theme and thus moves toward a socially expansive conception of gender and desire. As the play nears its climax, Jamie and Tyrone engage one another in a debate about theatre—Jamie satirizing nineteenth-century acting styles as well as his father's idol: "(*jeeringly*) I claim Edwin Booth never saw the day when he could give as good a performance as a trained seal. Seals are intelligent and honest. They don't put up with any bluffs about the Art of Acting. They admit they're just hams earning their daily fish" (3:822–23). Jamie's theatrical "trained seals" speech works like a cue for Mary. A few lines later she makes her sudden theatrical entrance, startling her male audience: "*Suddenly all five bulbs of the chandeliers in the front parlor are turned on from a wall switch, and a moment later someone starts playing the piano in there—the opening of one of Chopin's simpler waltzes, done with a forgetful, stiff-fingered groping, as if an awkward schoolgirl were practicing it for the first time.*" Her face is that of an aging actress who, miscast in the role of a younger woman, relives her theatrical past: "*Experience seemed ironed out of it. It is a marble mask of girlish innocence, the mouth caught in a shy smile.*" Her prop is a dress she carries over one arm, "*trailing on the floor . . . an old-fashioned white satin wedding gown, trimmed with duchesse lace*" (3:823–24). This is the same gown about which Mary said earlier, laughing, "[it] was nearly the death of me and the dressmaker, too" (3:784). In Sidney Lumet's compelling film of *Long Day's Journey* (1962), Mary (played by Katharine Hepburn) descends the stairs dragging what from a distance eerily resembles a loose, eviscerated, dead body, or a doll whose back has been broken.

O'Neill suggests that the nineteenth-century theatre Jamie has just mocked has played an important role in producing how men survey Mary and how Mary surveys herself (in her marble mask of girlish innocence). Jamie next casts his mother as a melodramatic character who appeared often on the nineteenth-century stage in hyperfeminine forms: "(*breaks the cracking silence—bitterly, self-defensively sardonic*) The Mad Scene. Enter Ophelia! (*His father and brother both turn on him fiercely. Edmund is quicker. He slaps Jamie across the mouth with the back of his hand.*)" The language of Tyrone's rebuke to his son is melodramatic and theatrical, and—in its modern psychoanalytic resonances—carries sexual associations: "The dirty blackguard! His own mother!" (3:824). The figure of Ophelia was invested with autobiographical significance for O'Neill: Ella, his mother, once ran screaming to the Thames, the river in back of their New London summer home, apparently intending to drown herself.

The nineteenth century's Ophelia surfaced not only on stage, but in pre-Raphaelite paintings and psychiatry texts. In her history of representations of Ophelia, Elaine Showalter indicates that the romantics portrayed Ophelia as "a girl . . . who drowns in feeling." Romantic critics often depicted Ophelia's problem as an insanity rooted in female biology. Alexandre Dumas, author of *The Count of Monte Cristo* (1844–45) (James O'Neill's moneymaker, when adapted for the stage), said of Harriet Smithson's emotional performance as Ophelia in 1827: "It was the first time I saw in the theatre real passions."[58] But in the 1870s the celebrated actress Ellen Terry, notes Showalter, broke from this hypersubjective, feminine Ophelia to offer her audiences "a consistent psychological study in sexual intimidation, a girl terrified of her father, of her lover, and of life itself."[59]

Offstage Ophelias also appeared in nineteenth-century British asylums. The Ophelia role had become a way for physicians to stereotype their female patients and, even more insidiously, Showalter observes, a way for agitated women to express "conflicts in the feminine role itself."[60] Sometimes physicians dressed up their female wards as Ophelias before photographing their feminine "madness," while in other cases women cast themselves in this part. When Ellen Terry visited an asylum to study "real" life Ophelias, she encountered patients who were "too *theatrical*"—too scripted.[61]

Mary Tyrone "plays" up the Ophelia-as-madwoman theatrical stereotype. The stagy quality of her grand entrance, and her eagerness to make a spectacle out of her pain, are Mary's strategy—and O'Neill's—to prompt us to think about the theatrical and cultural origins of her so-called madness. Autobiographically, O'Neill implicitly acknowledges that he, his father, and his brother participated in theatrical and cultural traditions that produced "mad Ophelias" onstage and offstage. Through Mary's "mad scene," O'Neill identifies a link between the "trappings of theatre" and the trappings of gender. There is method in Mary's "mad scene"—she is no "trained seal." Mary both enacts and explores the trappings of gender that return her to the scene of her marriage, and before that, to the institution that gave her middle-class feminization Catholic sanction—the convent.

Hamlet would not have had to tell Mary Tyrone, "Get thee to a nunnery." Mary's damaged hands conjure her convent days in her imagination, as she acts out her regression before her male spectators. "I play so badly now. . . . something horrible has happened to my hands. The fingers have gotten so stiff—(*she lifts her hands to examine them with a frightened puzzlement.*) The knuckles are all swollen. They're so ugly. I'll have to go to the Infirmary and show Sister Martha . . . she has things in her medicine chest that'll cure anything" (3:824). Her swollen hands resemble those that have been in a fight: indeed, she has both defended herself against and attacked the men in her family psychologically throughout their journey into night. There are neither men nor fights in the nunnery. When Edmund, panicking, grabs her arm and reveals that the doctor has diagnosed his illness as consumption, Mary retreats like a shy schoolgirl: "No! . . . you must not try to touch me. You must not try to hold me. It isn't right when I am hoping to be a nun" (3:826). Tyrone believes that, like Ophelia, she has gone under. Yet Mary's theatrics sink them as well: "It's the damned poison. But I've never known her to drown herself in it as deep as this," exclaims Tyrone. "(*gruffly*) Pass me that bottle, Jamie" (3:827).

Mary's performance idealizes her memories of the convent and thus insulates her from the men who surround her. But there is a disturbing rub in Mary's account. Her narrative suggests that she moved from one coquettish schoolgirl romance to another: from that with the all-loving, seemingly sexless Mother Elizabeth who praises her piano playing, to that with James Tyrone, the immigrant matinee idol made-up as a nobleman. Thus she feels jilted when Mother Elizabeth, upon hearing of her decision to be a nun, recommends instead that she leave the convent for a period to "prove [that her holy vision] wasn't simply [her] imagination" (3:827). Tyrone, Mary's Hamlet-in-the-wings, catches Ophelia on the rebound. "I fell in love with James Tyrone and was so happy for a time" (3:828).

The play concludes with "Ophelia" high on morphine, victimized by what she categorizes as "life" or "fate." By contrast, the real Ella returned to the all-female Catholic community of the "nunnery" in the 1910s and regained her health, strength, and resolve. When James O'Neill died in 1920, Ella took over his sizable estate with aplomb and deftly untangled his extremely knotty real estate affairs. Jamie, inspired by his mother's miraculous recovery, followed her example and abstained from drink until just before her death in 1922.

Prior to *Long Day's Journey*, O'Neill's only portrait of Ophelia was in *Ile*. O'Neill deviated significantly from Provincetown gossip about the woman who was the model for the character of Annie Keeney (Ophelia) in *Ile* in order to close his play with an Ophelia-victim. Viola Cook, the feisty Provincetown original on whom Annie Keeney was based, had sailed on one of her husband's whaling expeditions, but not without ill effect: "[She] had been broken not so much by the isolation and bleak surroundings of the voyage as by her husband's cruelty to his men; it was said in fact that he had shot and killed one of the mutineers. . . . And there was a story that she had taken to honing her kitchen knives as sharp as whaling knives, while her husband never went to sleep without shoving heavy furniture against the door."[62] Cook, repulsed by her husband's domineering ways, lived out her days symbolically wielding her own harpoon.

The conclusion of *Ile* does not lead us to imagine that Annie is capable of assuming anything remotely like a strong role in the Keeney home. Annie—like the stiff-fingered Mary Tyrone at her piano—plays the crazed victim (with curiously sexual resonances): "Her whole attention seems centered on the organ. She sits with half-closed eyes, her body swaying a little from side to side to the rhythm of the hymn. Her fingers move faster and faster and she is playing wildly and discordantly" (1:508).

But Mary Tyrone is not simply a victim; she is (like Viola Cook) willing and able to needle the male Tyrones with her "harpoon." Her capacity to needle is especially obvious in O'Neill's preliminary draft of the final act. Edmund taunts: "You ought to read Heine's poem on morphine, Mother." Rising eagerly to the challenge, Mary pipes up: "Morphine! I have enough now to last for a while—when that's gone, pawn another piece of jewelry—Doctor said I was taking enough drugs to kill [a] herd of elephants. (*She smiles with a precocious childish pride—they shudder*)." This draft version shows us not only that Mary needs the morphine, she desires it.[63] An addiction to morphine is usually not excessively difficult to break.[64] Mary Tyrone, particularly in this early draft, is a defiant Ophelia who is cognizant not only of what morphine does to her but what it does for her.

Even in O'Neill's final version of the play, Mary's ostensible victimization has a boldly aggressive and transgressive side to it. At the beginning of Act 4, as Tyrone and Edmund play cards and philosophize about "life," the latter concludes: "Who wants to see life as it is, if they can help it? It's the three Gorgons in one. You look in their faces and turn to stone" (3:796). Life is figured as a petrifying woman. For the Tyrones, Mary acts the role of Medusa as well as that of Ophelia. As the men hear her attempting to play her piano, stiff-fingered, "*they listen frozenly*" (3:823). When Mary begins to speak, "*they freeze into silence again, staring at her*" (3:824). Mary self-consciously petrifies the men in her family: the surveyed female turns her male surveyors to stone.

Mary's power resides in her willingness literally as well as figuratively to pierce the stereotype of mother. She does so each time she reenacts her original transgression against her maternal role—as in an episode narrated by Jamie to Edmund: "Never forget the first time I got wise. Caught her in the act with a hypo. Christ, I'd never dreamed before that any women but whores took dope!" (3:818). During Mary's "journey" in the summer of 1912, Margaret Sanger's controversial birth control column, "What Every Mother Should Know" (1911–13), appeared in the Socialist *Call*, and argued that mothers have sexual desires. In this same period, narratives of prostitution recounted how procurers and madames would addict young women to alcohol and drugs as a way of making their return to "society" impossible.[65] Mary's addiction radically destabilizes the fixed cultural meanings and norms attached to both "mother" and "whore."

In addition to the sexual associations of injecting herself with morphine (getting "caught in the act"), we should recall that Mary—like "whores"—injected herself in hotels while accompanying Tyrone's theatre troupe on the road. The O'Neills, moreover, lived in a Times Square hotel during their extensive stays in New York City. In Act 1, the men are distrustful of Mary because she chose to sleep alone in the spare room the previous night. After breakfast, she retired to her bedroom for a nap. They know she is, in effect, cheating on them with her hypo. Like Annie Keeney, playing her organ, her body swaying from side to side (an image based perhaps on Eugene's recollections of Ella at her piano), Mary uses her hypo to attain a symbolic sexual independence from the men who survey her. Having been (for some years) "caught" in an "act" that her men identify with the role of "whore," Mary plays on the fear that, as Anita Levy observes, all middle-class women harbor *inside* them the desires of the "other" woman—"the savage, the prostitute, or the madwoman"—and thus potentially endanger the integrity, meaning, and stability of civilization.[66]

Along these lines, O'Neill associates Mary with Fat Vi, the unprofitable prostitute visited by Jamie.[67] At the outset of Act 1, Tyrone compliments his wife as "a fine armful now." When Mary says she "ought to reduce," he assures her she is "just right. We'll have no talk of reducing" (3:719). Jamie, too, must reassure Fat Vi that she is "just right." Mamie Burns, Fat Vi's madame, unloads her troubles on Jamie, who recounts them later that night to Edmund:

> Beefed how rotten business was, and she was going to give Fat Violet the gate. Customers didn't fall for Vi. Only reason she'd kept her was

she could play the piano. Lately Vi's gone on drunks and been too boiled to play, and was eating her out of house and home, and although Vi was a goodhearted dumbell, and she felt sorry for her because she didn't know how the hell she'd make a living, still business was business, and she couldn't afford to run a home for fat tarts. (3:816)

Elizabethan audiences knew very well that when Hamlet told Ophelia to get herself "to a nunnery," that "nunnery" was a euphemism for a house of prostitution. O'Neill takes advantage of the different meanings of "nunnery" to shatter middle-class stereotypes of motherhood. Mamie Burns is an infernal inversion of the celestial Mother Elizabeth (mommy burns). Mamie Burns contemplates giving Fat Violet "the gate," while Mother Elizabeth actually gave Mary "the gate." In neither case is the piano playing of the young woman in question sufficient to retain her in the "nunnery." When Jamie casts the drugged-up Mary as Ophelia, his defense mechanism is literary. Likewise, Jamie dons a distinctively literary armor upstairs with Fat Vi, drunkenly reciting Kipling, Swinburne, and Dowson: "She . . . got the idea I took her upstairs for a joke. . . . Said she was better than a drunken bum who recited poetry. Then she began to cry. So I had to say I loved her because she was fat" (3:816).

Although Michael Cape does not mention motherhood in *Welded* (1924), his view of Woman, the prostitute, is the antithesis of the stereotype of the redeeming mother: "You're all the tortures man inflicts on woman—and you're the revenge of woman! You're love revenging itself upon itself!" (2:263). Mary knows that the men in her family read her sexually resonant addiction as "the revenge of woman! . . . love revenging itself upon itself!" Fat Vi pressures Jamie into saying that he "loved her because she was fat." Similarly, Mary needs the men in her home to say they love her because she is addicted and because she needs their love. But she takes her revenge on something more than them, something perhaps only Claire in *The Verge* could begin to articulate. By playing the "whore" who eagerly injects dope, she undermines the cultural, religious, and theatrical production of herself as "mother," "wife," and "woman." At the same time, part of her remains wedded to these cultural categories. After her descent on the staircase, Mary hands over her wedding gown to Tyrone, at his "gentle" insistence, lest she "get it dirty dragging it on the floor. Then you'd be sorry afterwards" (3:825) (Figure 28).

Figure 28. James Tyrone (Fredric March) holding Mary Tyrone's (Florence Eldridge) wedding dress—like a dead body—as Jamie (Jason Robards, right) and Edmund (Bradford Dillman) look on in José Quintero's 1956 New York production of *Long Day's Journey Into Night*. Yale Collection of American Literature Photographs, Beinecke Rare Book and Manuscript Library, Yale University.

O'Neill's first play, *The Web* (1913), offers a sympathetic portrait of a prostitute who struggles unavailingly against all odds—ruthless pimp, poverty—to be a mother to her newborn babe. Writing in the anarchist and socialist traditions, O'Neill indicted the socioeconomic positioning of women that accounted for much prostitution. Rose explains to Tim the gangster (who has just rescued her from being beaten by her pimp):

> Yuh don't know what I'm up against. (*bitterly*) I've tried that job thing. I've looked for decent work and I've starved at it. A year after I first hit town I quit and tried to be on the level. I got a job at house-work—workin' twelve hours a day for twenty-five dollars a month. And I worked like a dog, too, and never left the house I was so scared of seein' someone who knew me. . . . What job c'n I git? What am I fit fur? Housework is the only thing I know about and I don't know much about that. . . . That's the trouble with all us girls. Most all of us ud like to come back but we jest can't and that's all there's to it. (1:21–22)

Mary too is caught in a web—a cultural web that seems invisible because it is woven into the fabric of middle-class daily life. Like Rose, she could say to the men she loves—who bear a share of the responsibility for spinning this web—"You don't know what I'm up against," and "I'd like to come back but I can't and that's all there is to it." Glaspell's Claire Archer, who has a clearer inkling of the roles, patterns, and forms she is "up against" in *The Verge*, does not wish to "come back" to the production of life, depth, and desire she left behind—"that's all there is to it." Travis Bogard writes about the opening scene of Act 1: "[Mary] emerges in the few moments of normalcy as the source of life for them, the quiet hub around which they move, happy in her presence."[68] Both Mary and Claire, with different degrees of critical awareness, refuse to enact the role of "quiet hub" and angrily tear the discursive web of middle-class feminine "normalcy"—even as their webs continue to enmesh them.

Not content to dramatize depth or desire as essence in *Long Day's Journey*, O'Neill sharpens his perception of the kind of cultural life and depth he saw as constituting Anna Christie—a life in which "life copies melodrama," and a depth "pent up in the trappings of theatre." The social depth O'Neill achieves in his *Journey*, like the social depth Glaspell dramatized in her feminist plays, brings us closer to a cultural understanding of why the wives interviewed in Hamilton and Macgowan's study tended to say "*everything* is wrong." A sign of this "everything" can be detected, perhaps, on O'Neill's parents' gravestone, which reads: for James, "actor"; for Ella, "his wife." In his focus on the "trappings of theatre" that ensnared Mary Tyrone, O'Neill also self-reflexively confronted his *own* theatrical complicity in staging the trappings of sexual difference as normal.

The radical center of *Long Day's Journey*, I would contend, is not so much O'Neill's brilliant, moving, and often compassionate dramatizations of guilt, denial, and compulsion, or his poignant portrayals of ambivalence and confession, but rather his occasional perception that cultural discourses which produce forms of subjectivity materially construct what we imagine, experience, and perform as depth. *Long Day's Journey* shows that O'Neill, like Glaspell, was aware that depth, desire, and gender are subtle constructions that can make unequal arrangements—in which one's father acts and "his wife" appears, then disappears—seem natural. O'Neill wept as he wrote *Long Day's Journey*, for all four of the "haunted" Tyrones.

AFTERWORD

As the twentieth century draws to a close, most critics still regard O'Neill as the "greatest" American dramatist. His contributions to American theatre and drama are legion. An unflinching believer in his innovative vision, he pushed set designers to invent the illusion of great spaces on small stages, actors to expand their skills to embody his sketches of characters, and directors to stage plays that ran for four or five hours for long runs to sold-out houses.[1] O'Neill was an indefatigable risk-taker, ever on the move, even when he stumbled: "He has worked," wrote John Mason Brown in 1946, "as a naturalist, an expressionist, a Freudian, a mystic, a symbolist, or as a poet whose poetry was deader than the feeblest prose even when his prose as spoken burned with the fires of poetry."[2] He was startlingly creative: his notebooks contain ample evidence that, had O'Neill completed his cycle as well as the other plays he made notes for in his last years, he would have been even more difficult to classify.

From his early Provincetown days, O'Neill was singled out as America's torchbearer in the field of drama. He did much to help swing Broadway into the orbit of international theatre and literary modernism. When Gerhart Hauptmann toured the United States in 1932, he emerged from *Mourning Becomes Electra* with accolades for the American theatre's "progress toward esthetic and intellectual maturity," and was convinced that O'Neill was "far and away the greatest dramatic genius America has yet produced."[3] O'Neill no doubt appreciated this approbation from one of the elder statesmen of modern European drama he most admired; yet only one year before, on his return from Europe, newspapers ran the story, "O'Neill Says Europe Will Seek Theatrical Guidance Here Soon."[4] In 1922 George Jean Nathan regretted that only "critical charity" would enable one to label American theatre "theatre."[5] O'Neill did more than any other American playwright to change that. Sinclair Lewis's Nobel Prize speech of 1930 paid homage to O'Neill for having brought American drama "in ten or twelve years from a false world of neat and competent trickery into a world of splendor, fear and greatness."[6]

When O'Neill's plays were constantly breaking new ground in theme and production in the late 1920s, Barrett Clark stated the obvious: "He still refuses to stay put, and defies anything like a final analysis." Almost forty years later, when O'Neill's career had long since ended and scholars had had time to ponder his accomplishments, John Henry Raleigh concluded the same: "The ideas keep changing from play to play, and there is not . . . a consistent ideological pattern."[7] And nearly three decades after Raleigh arrived at this judgment, I couldn't agree more. What makes O'Neill provocative, in part, is his often complex and contradictory movements between ideological positions not simply from play to play but within individual plays.

Above I have surveyed some of the long-standing reasons why scholars have rightly viewed O'Neill's contribution to the modernization of American theatre as historically important. This book suggests, however, that we are now at a juncture where we can grasp the historical significance of O'Neill's work in new ways and, thus, wish to read his plays and see them performed for new reasons. Especially when teaching O'Neill, it is sometimes tempting for me simply to affirm Brooks Atkinson's evaluation that O'Neill turned Broadway into a "Theatre for Adults"[8] and to add my voice to the hallelujah chorus of reviewers and critics who have hailed O'Neill's defiant taboo-breaking dramatizations of "self" and "desire." But in an era some have called postmodern, many scholars, myself among them, have come to realize that commonsensical words like "adult," "self," "desire," and "depth" constitute what is tantamount to jargon, an ideological jargon that contributes to the cultural fabrication of a particular kind of individualized self.[9] What O'Neill's critics and biographers tend to leave unexamined is O'Neill's historical and political role—as well as their own role—in making the psychological "individual" seem natural and self-evident.

Here I am thinking about individualization[10] as a cultural and political process. What we need to bring to O'Neill is not only histories of the family and of psychological discourse, but some sense of the history of individualization. In a valuable essay on this history, Peter Stallybrass reverses Louis Althusser's much quoted formulation: "Ideology interpellates individuals as subjects." On the most basic level, Althusser means that ideology *subjects* (subordinates, dominates) the "individual," whom he imagines as the "center of free consciousness and independent judgment." Instead, Stallybrass proposes that "within a capitalist mode of production, ideology interpellated, not the individual as a subject, but the *subject* as an *individual*." In his discussion of the seventeenth century and the English Civil War, Stallybrass traces the emergence of a radical language of "the individual" that was used by dissenters to criticize, not only King Charles (who demanded the submission of his "subjects"), but Oliver Cromwell. "The individual," then, was invented to oppose hierarchical relations legitimated by the concept of "subject."[11]

Alan Sinfield, writing about the eighteenth century, also points out that the development of "the idea of the individual" can be seen as an advance for the bourgeois contestation of aristocratic authority. But in the nineteenth and twentieth centuries, in both Britain and America, this "individual" came to be thought of "as the opposite of the social and the political, as a state of essential human values to which those 'public' discourses could contribute little and from which they might well detract."[12] The modern bourgeoisie often represents this ostensibly autonomous, private "individual" as what O'Neill called "Man."

A history of individualization would make it clear that Anglo-American culture since the seventeenth century has produced *individualisms* of different though related sorts. There is the possessive individual of the marketplace[13] satirized by *Marco Millions* (1927), and also the domestic individualisms[14] represented by *Ah, Wilderness!* (1933) and *Long Day's Journey* (1941). These individualisms, economic and domestic, could cooperate with one another and at other moments be in friction with one another (as I suggested in Chapter 1). In addition there are the sundry anarchist individualisms propounded by Benjamin Tucker and Emma Goldman in the late nineteenth and early twentieth centuries. In connection with these individualisms, we see the emergence of sentimental and "psychological" individuals in the nineteenth century,[15] whose social origins O'Neill sought to trace in his cycle, *A Tale of Possessors, Self-dispossessed*, particularly in *More Stately Mansions* (1939). Although O'Neill sometimes universalized the bourgeois individual as Man in his work, he also, most patently in his cycle, had a sense that "the individual" is not born, but is fashioned by historically specific political, economic, cultural, sentimental, and psychological discourses.[16]

In some respects leftist critics erred when they read the preoccupation of bourgeois authors and playwrights with neurosis and the psychopathological family as a sign of class "decay" or "sickness." When O'Neill helped transform a nineteenth-century theatre of "character" and melodrama into a theatre of the modern bourgeois psychological self, he *rejuvenated* bourgeois individualism with a new "depth." The psychological discourse O'Neill staged had the remarkable ideological capability of making the alienated "individual" seem, not historically or socially produced, but born from within. As I have argued, this discourse authorized members of the professional-managerial class to conceive of themselves in psychological and universal terms (alienated hairy apes in pinstripes) that permitted them to deflect their vision from the oppressive class structure they had a hand in producing ("we've *all* got problems") and to encode their own fear of falling within this treacherous socioeconomic system as malaise (indicative of individual "depth"). This modern therapeutic individualism *eagerly* decentered an older bourgeois model of the individual self in order to create itself anew (as the Theatre Guild's battle with Boston's censors makes evident).[17] O'Neill's dramas are a signpost that cultural discourses of interiority had become as crucial as political and economic discourses in the reproduction of individuals within the professional-managerial class.

This is certainly one important political dimension of O'Neill's contributions to the dramatizing of "individual" depth.

Yet, to echo Clark, O'Neill's work "refuses to stay put." There are other radically different dimensions of the politics of psychological discourse in the drama of O'Neill that must not be overlooked. O'Neill's plays often make "the individual" into a container of a psychological and spiritual time bomb that keeps exploding with devastating effects. Since O'Neill did not count on revolution to "change the world," he constructed—sabotaged—the psychological individual so that the possessor would necessarily dispossess himself or herself, as the title of his unfinished cycle suggests: *Possessors, Self-dispossessed*. From what one can glean from *More Stately Mansions*, O'Neill's Cycle seemed to be moving toward a psychological critique of possessive individualism. *Mansions* suggests that O'Neill's motives for staging Man with a self-destructive depth had an uncompromisingly radical side.

Arthur Miller recognized this psychological undermining of the possessor as an objective of *The Iceman Cometh* (1940). It led him to surmise that O'Neill was far more hostile to "bourgeois civilization" than was Odets: "Odets, after all, would have reformed capitalism with a degree of socialism; O'Neill saw no hope in it whatsoever."[18] The eminent Marxist theoretician Georg Lukàcs also admired the critical social awareness that gave O'Neill's "tragicomic defiance" its cutting edge (a defiance he regarded as indebted to Ibsen and Chekhov).

At the same time, Lukàcs (as did some American Left critics of O'Neill in the 1930s and 1940s) understood that modernist angst made doubts about "the scope and possibilities of human action" dangerously stylish (and "deep") in intellectual, academic, and literary circles.[19] The limitation of O'Neill's retributive theatrical invention of the self-dispossessed possessor is that he or she is by nature psychologically and spiritually untrustworthy in the matter of organizing to resist oppression and to bring about significant social change. Thus we are left with a down-and-out nihilist like Larry Slade who, convinced that "man *is* manure," sits out the struggle in the grandstand (or is it quicksand) of philosophical detachment—"stinko" in Hope's bar.[20] On the brink of World War II (seeing the "icemen" about to "cometh" in hordes), O'Neill dramatized his radical pessimism[21] about "the individual" as the deeper significance that replaced (and dismissed) radical politics—a pessimism he couldn't bear to make public until the war's end.

A third political dimension of the staging of depth is that O'Neill occasionally perceived depth as a cultural category. If Brutus Jones loses his way in the "primitive" jungle of the unconscious (posited by a racist "negro psychology" in the early 1920s), O'Neill also comprehends Jones's unconscious as manifestly political and historical and haunted by American racism. If *Strange Interlude* played a role in helping the professional-managerial class dramatize itself as "neurotic" by suggesting—like pop psychology—that this class *should* be plagued by "suppressed desires," O'Neill's sensationally popular play also understood depth as a mass-cultural discourse that sold depth of a peculiar stamp ("O Oedipus, O my king! The world is adopting you!"). And if Mary Tyrone welcomes the morphine and the fog as a partial release from a home "life" constituted by ambivalence, obsession, and denial, *Long Day's Journey* reveals at various points that her "hothouse" family has been set aflame by historical and ideological forces.

It is crucial to take a critical step back from O'Neill-the-"greatest"-American-dramatist (made so very *individual* by his biographers) so that one can perceive the historically complicated nature of the corpus of plays known as "O'Neill."[22] Raymond Williams argues that cultural historians should pay heed to the hegemonic forms, conventions, and figures that materially constitute "structures of feeling."[23] The work termed "O'Neill" offers a rich cultural record of how the trope of depth helped organize an emerging "structure of feeling" that was internalized by, used by, and resisted in a number of ways by a changing professional-managerial class. Ideology, observes Terry Eagleton, "is less a question of ideas than of feelings, images, gut reactions."[24] To appreciate the historical significance of O'Neill's gut-wrenching dramas and the feelings they dramatized and made real, we must grasp not only that O'Neill staged ideology but also that ideology staged "O'Neill." Culture makes up O'Neill's "depth."

In arguing that the psychological discourse which O'Neill both promoted and at times contested should be reconsidered as a historical, political, and cultural discourse, I have sought to reopen the scholarly appraisal of O'Neill's legacy. His work calls for a new kind of reader and auditor who would be aware that O'Neill is not only staging depth, but that he is staging—sometimes self-consciously, sometimes not—the ideological and cultural power of the emerging *category* of the psychological. Historically, what O'Neill's dramas display is not just "the individual" but a modern form of individualization. An awareness of this in no way diminishes the literary value of O'Neill's dramas but instead stimulates a more "self"-questioning critical engagement with the aesthetic, historical, and political complexity and subtlety of his work. As the forms of professional-managerial-class subjectivities, and the codes, metaphors, and narratives used to represent these subjectivities, shift and multiply, audiences will continue to find O'Neill's plays provocative: not because they unmask the workings of some natural or timeless self, but because they dramatize how modern ideologies of the self that sought to universalize our vision of the "psychological" "individual" took root in us.

NOTES

At the Beinecke Rare Book and Manuscript Library, Yale University, there
are five volumes of scrapbooks of reviews of O'Neill's plays and publications from
1915 to 1922. Apparently these were compiled by O'Neill's second wife, Agnes
Boulton. Sometimes the information about the sources of the clipping is incom-
plete. Consequently I indicate the information that is available as well as the volume
in which the clipping is contained. In addition, I have consulted many volumes of
the Theatre Guild Press Books housed at Beinecke. Here, also, publication information on articles about O'Neill and on reviews of his plays is sometimes missing. Articles and reviews cited in the O'Neill scrapbooks (abbreviated OS in the
notes) and the Theatre Guild Press Books (abbreviated TGPB) are not listed in the
bibliography.

Introduction

1. I have had the pleasure of examining the many photographs of O'Neill at
Beinecke Rare Book and Manuscript Library, Yale University, at the Sheaffer-
O'Neill Collection, Connecticut College Library, and at the Harvard Theatre Collection and Houghton Library, Harvard University, as well as photographs published
in books about O'Neill.

2. See the photographs of a well-tailored O'Neill chosen to adorn the three
volumes of the Library of America edition of his plays.

3. Khachig Tölölyan astutely observed this resemblance.

4. Also see the extreme close-up of O'Neill on the cover of Arthur Gelb and
Barbara Gelb's *O'Neill*. The photographer (unacknowledged in the text, but very
likely Van Vechten) uses shadows to heighten the dramatist's subjective intensity.

5. See O'Neill's program notes for the 1924 Experimental Theatre production of
Strindberg's *The Spook Sonata*: "Strindberg and Our Theatre." Also see O'Neill's
acknowledgment of his indebtedness to Strindberg in his "Nobel Prize Acceptance
Letter" (1936). Both documents are reprinted in O'Neill, *Unknown O'Neill*, pp.
387–88 and pp. 427–28, respectively. I am grateful to Alfred Turco for pointing out
to me Strindberg's proclivity to "pose depth." On Strindberg's photography and
self-portraits, see Michael Meyer, *Strindberg*, pp. 452, 250. Meyer reprints the
photograph of Strindberg (c. 1911–12) pen-in-hand that bears an uncanny resemblance to the 1939 photograph of O'Neill ostensibly writing *Iceman*. The photograph of Strindberg, like the one of O'Neill, offers us a portrait of a playwright with
demonized intensity. Strindberg's hair is combed up, as if ablaze. Also see Meyer's
reprint of Strindberg's self-portrait of 1906.

6. O'Neill, *"Theatre We Worked For,"* p. 122.

7. Ibid., p. 152. O'Neill was less "tremendous pleased" with *Strange Interlude*'s
depth in 1932, after having written *Mourning Becomes Electra*: "As for *Strange
Interlude*, that is an attempt at the new masked psychological drama . . . without
masks—a successful attempt, perhaps, in so far as it concerns only surfaces and their

immediate subsurfaces, but not where, occasionally, it tries to probe deeper" (quoted in Gelb and Gelb, *O'Neill*, p. 662).

8. Sheaffer, *Son and Artist*, p. 288. O'Neill was eulogized for his exploration of "depth" throughout his career. In 1946 George Jean Nathan praised O'Neill's *Iceman Cometh* for having an X-ray vision that "pictures vividly the innards of even the least of his variegated characters" (see TGPB, 217: Nathan, "Iceman Cometh, Seeth, Conquereth," *New York Journal American*, Oct. 14, 1946). For a provocative discussion of O'Neill's novelistic tendencies (his "novelizing" of melodrama into modern drama), see Kurt Eisen's *Inner Strength of Opposites*.

9. Bigsby, *Critical Introduction*, 1:68.

10. Sheaffer, *Son and Artist*, p. 332.

11. Ibid., pp. 245–46.

12. In 1932 Ed Sullivan mused in his column that the indefatigable O'Neill was both the "artiest" and the most "prolific moneymaker" of American dramatists (*Strange Interlude* "ran up the staggering gross of $4,000,000"). See TGPB, 124: Sullivan, "Sees Broadway," *New York Evening Graphic*, Jan. 15, 1932. When *Strange Interlude* was banned in Boston, the Theatre Guild was able to move it to Quincy. Busloads of Bostonians as well as those who lived in Quincy flocked to the show. The four-and-a-half-hour play had a long dinner intermission. One restaurant, on the verge of bankruptcy, profited from these intermissions and, as a result, transformed itself into a national chain that is still thriving: Howard Johnson (see Langner, *Magic Curtain*, p. 237).

13. Jones, *Dramatic Imagination*, pp. 15–16. Jones discusses O'Neill in this same context in his 1952 Harvard lectures, *Towards a New Theatre*, pp. 29–34.

14. Pfister, *Production of Personal Life*, p. 27. Henry T. Tuckerman wrote, in reference to Hawthorne, "What the scientific use of lenses—the telescope and the microscope—does for us in relation to the external universe, the psychological writer achieves in regard to our nature" (p. 27).

15. Ibid., pp. 49–58.

16. Lawrence, for example, celebrates Hawthorne's "inner diabolism" beneath the surface, his "blood-knowledge," and his "dirty understanding" (*Studies in Classic American Literature*, pp. 83, 84, 85). On Lawrence's role in elevating Hawthorne's reputation, see Brodhead, *School of Hawthorne*, p. 209. In relating Hawthorne and O'Neill to one another, I have no intention of effacing the half-century of cultural, intellectual, and literary history that separates the final writings of the former and the early experiments of the latter. Hawthorne did not use "depth" as a key trope to define his aesthetic aims, and if he had employed it more often, in all likelihood he would have invested it with somewhat different—more sentimental, not modern pop psychological—associations (e.g., the deep, hidden "mysteries" of the divided "heart"—not the deep, unconscious workings of "ambivalent" "primitive" instincts). Nonetheless, in some senses O'Neill can be viewed as having inherited a later version of Hawthorne's ideological project. At different phases in American history, both Hawthorne and O'Neill participated in psychologizing the "individualization" of the middle class (for a discussion of this process see the Afterword), and both writers sometimes were critical of their participation in this ideological identity formation. We can see, for example, the modern understanding of culture-

as-repression and the (somewhat reductive) notion of "liberation" as instinctual rebellion against the "taboos" or prohibitions of culture—evident in O'Neill's dramas (see Chapter 2)—taking shape in some of Hawthorne's fictions, such as "The Maypole of Merrymount" (1836), "Main-Street" (1849), *The Scarlet Letter* (1850), and *The Marble Faun* (1860) (see my comments on these fictions in *The Production of Personal Life*). In O'Neill's dramas and Hawthorne's fictions, some characters—often artist figures—exhibit a "deep," conflicted subjectivity that seems to confer on them a psychological capital that, at least in their own vision, elevates them above other "shallow" characters (see Chapter 3, especially my discussion of *The Moon of the Caribees* [1916], and see Hawthorne's "The Birth-mark" [1843], "Egotism; Or, the Bosom Serpent" [1843], "The Artist of the Beautiful" [1844], and *The Blithedale Romance* [1852]). But O'Neill and Hawthorne at times parodied such pretentious, self-consumed figures. Both writers could be keenly attentive to the historical forces, ideological narratives, and cultural roles that structure particular impressions of what it means to be "deep." Hawthorne and O'Neill offer some startling opportunities for one to distance oneself from the very ideologies of subjectivity their writings can seem to make inherently "psychological."

17. O'Neill, *Selected Letters*, pp. 1, 2.

18. Sheaffer, *Son and Artist*, p. 362; O'Neill, *Selected Letters*, p. 341.

19. O'Neill, *Selected Letters*, p. 92.

20. Ibid., p. 203. Although Barrett Clark cites O'Neill's opinion that a book about him might be "premature" (1927), he also quotes O'Neill's acceptance of this seeming inevitability: "On the other hand, if it's got to be done" (*Eugene O'Neill*, p. 7).

21. Gelb and Gelb, *O'Neill*, p. 704. In 1927 O'Neill enthusiastically, and somewhat ironically, consented to be an "advertisement medium" for the Bermuda Trade Development Board, which, as recompense for using photographs of the playwright, arranged for "obliging and reasonable . . . rates" between Bermuda—O'Neill's new home—and New York (O'Neill, *Selected Letters*, p. 236).

22. O'Neill, *Selected Letters*, p. 212.

23. Sheaffer, *Son and Artist*, p. 208.

24. "Since the rise of romanticism," writes Eli Zaretsky, "the artist has symbolized the free individual who brought to society not the performance of an assigned function but his or her own self" (*Capitalism, the Family, and Personal Life*, p. 92).

25. O'Neill, *Conversations with Eugene O'Neill*, p. 115; Gelb and Gelb, *O'Neill*, p. 612.

26. O'Neill, *Selected Letters*, p. 443. His wire was sent on January 29, 1935.

27. O'Neill, *Conversations*, p. 140.

28. Here O'Neill conceptualizes subjectivity much like the critic Stuart Hall, who describes the "I," not as "the seat of consciousness and the foundation of ideological discourses" but as "a contradictory discursive category constituted by ideological discourse itself" ("Cultural Studies and the Centre," p. 33). Hall is discussing Louis Althusser's Marxist structuralist contribution to cultural studies. Terry Eagleton points out that Althusser theorizes ideology as "an indispensable medium for the production of human subjects. Among the various modes of production in any society, there is one whose task is the production of forms of subjectivity them-

selves; and this is quite as material and historically variable as the production of chocolate bars or automobiles" (*Ideology*, p. 148). Hall's work on subjectivity also draws on the writings of Antonio Gramsci. See Gramsci's *Prison Notebooks*, in which he argues that "'human nature' is the 'complex of social relations' . . . because it includes the idea of becoming (man 'becomes,' he changes continuously with the changing of social relations) and because it denies 'man in general.' . . . One could also say that the nature of man is 'history'" (p. 355). For a discussion of British cultural studies' and American Studies' contributions to the historical study of forms of subjectivity see Pfister, "Americanization of Cultural Studies," pp. 218–22.

29. John Henry Raleigh's *Plays of Eugene O'Neill* (1965) offers some of the most astute cultural readings of O'Neill's works. But even Raleigh tends to exempt O'Neill's preoccupation with emotions and depth from history and ideology, arguing that his plays "contain an overall quality . . . that is not ideological at all. Profound, obscure, dark, fortuitous, and powerful emotions are brooded over" (p. 243). Michael Manheim's preoccupation with O'Neill is informed by the modern therapeutic culture that O'Neill helped produce for his social class: "The real impact of O'Neill is only beginning to be felt, in the process meeting the resistance that work which probes terrifying areas of man's nature inevitably meets. . . . [O'Neill fascinates] audiences coming to grips with the mysteries of human emotion" (*Eugene O'Neill's New Language of Kinship*, p. 1).

30. Here my thinking has been influenced by Christopher Herbert, who notes that "depth" is a "trope endowed with . . . much coercive rhetorical power" (*Culture and Anomie*, p. 256).

31. Contributors to *American Quarterly* have justifiably charged that American Studies has paid too little notice to American drama. See Smith, "Generic Hegemony"; Flynn, "Complex Causality of Neglect"; and Bigsby, "View from East Anglia." *Staging Depth* aims to help redress this shortcoming.

Chapter 1

1. The first comprehensive contribution to this field was Arthur Calhoun's three volume *A Social History of the American Family* (1917–19). Calhoun, a Socialist academician, was a contributor to Victor Francis Calverton and Samuel D. Schmalhausen's *Modern Quarterly*. For an illuminating discussion of the history of the history of family life, see John Demos's recent overview, "Family History's Past Achievements and Future Prospects." Historians put the history of family life on the map in the 1970s. The impulse to do so, for some of these historians, began in the political upheavals of the 1960s and early 1970s. Writing about the 1960s New Left and its gradual recognition of the personal as political, Linda Nicholson observes: "Differentiating the new and old left was a concern on the part of the former with the psychological, viewed not as a substitute for but as a component of the sociological. . . . While attention to the psychological components of social oppression followed from New Left politics, an examination of the family and personal life did not. A component of our modern domestic/nondomestic separation has been the pervading belief that both family and personal life exist outside the domain of politics" (*Gender and History*, pp. 64–65). An early version of Zaretsky's New Left–

inspired *Capitalism, the Family, and Personal Life* (1978) first appeared as a series of articles in *Socialist Revolution* 13–15, Jan.-June 1973.

2. I am not the first scholar to suggest this general approach. In 1978 Tom Scanlan argued, "O'Neill's vision of family life is a symbol not only of personal psychological experience, but of a social history larger than his own." Dramatists of the family, such as O'Neill, Tennessee Williams, and Arthur Miller, he concluded, are not "projecting only their private neuroses, anxieties, and psychic histories" into their plays; they are preoccupied by the American psychological family for historical reasons (*Family, Drama, and American Dreams*, pp. 84, 214). However, the history of the family and gender that would have enabled Scanlan to build a substantive historical argument to support and elaborate his thesis was just becoming available. Although Scanlan's readings of O'Neill's plays contain useful insights, they are largely unhistorical.

3. Sheaffer, *Son and Artist*, p. vii. "In the thirty years of his creative life," writes Travis Bogard, "[O'Neill] completed drafts of sixty-two plays. Eleven were destroyed, and of those remaining, over half contain discernible autobiographical elements. No play written after 1922, except for his figurative adaptation of Coleridge's *Rime of the Ancient Mariner*, was free of them" (*Contour in Time*, p. xii). Virginia Floyd, referring to O'Neill's notebooks and early drafts of plays, singles out their "pervasive autobiographical nature: the repeated depiction of the four O'Neills in various guises" (*Eugene O'Neill at Work*, p. 383).

4. After praising *Long Day's Journey* as "perhaps the finest play (and tragedy) ever written on this continent," John Henry Raleigh goes on to suggest that the play achieved magnificence because O'Neill—after writing about race, neurotics-with-masks, dynamos, etc.—at last became unreservedly personal: "He finally returned home to New London, Connecticut, to his family, and to himself" ("O'Neill's *Long Day's Journey*," pp. 124–25). Floyd attests that the study of O'Neill's work "allow[s] insight into his complex personality" (*Eugene O'Neill at Work*, p. 383). In his introduction of Arthur Gelb and Barbara Gelb's biography of O'Neill, Brooks Atkinson lauds the playwright as "a highly personal writer who proceeded through a succession of obsessions from the wistfully romantic sea plays to the ruthlessness of *Long Day's Journey Into Night*" (*O'Neill*, p. xix).

5. In his extravagantly melodramatic tribute, Tennessee Williams opined, "O'Neill gave birth to the American theatre and died for it" (Gelb and Gelb, *O'Neill*, p. 877).

6. See Michel Foucault's classic essay, "What Is an Author?" in which he broaches important historical questions about how and when the author became culturally "individualized" (see esp. pp. 101, 118). Pierre Bourdieu also underscores the importance of moving beyond the biographers' "ideology of creation, which makes the author the first and last source of the value of his work." Rather, Bourdieu is interested in the "field of production" (the literary and cultural institutions, constructions of literary value) that "authorize the author" (*Field of Production*, p. 76).

7. Andrew M. Greeley contests the stereotype of the Irish drunk (perpetuated in *Long Day's Journey*): "Their distinctive drinking patterns are part of the burden of a long history of [British] oppression and caricature that they must carry with them" (*Irish Americans*, p. 182). O'Neill helped convert the nineteenth-century stereotype

of the Harry Hope easy-going Irish drunk into one of the Irish artist whose expertise is subjectivity. Drunkenness often loosened the tongue of the ordinarily taciturn and slow-of-speech O'Neill. Yet he never deluded himself that he could write while either soused or hung over. Part of the reason why he quit drinking in 1926—under the treatment of psychiatrist G. V. Hamilton—was that playwriting was more important to him than drinking. If anything, O'Neill was more prolific (and his plays longer) after he stopped drinking. See Dr. Donald W. Goodwin's chapter on O'Neill in *Alcohol and the Writer*, pp. 123–37, and Tom Dardis's chapter on O'Neill in *Thirsty Muse*, pp. 211–56. See also Edmund Wilson's somewhat fussy account of a protracted evening he and his wife, Mary Blair, spent with an O'Neill-who-got-"stinko": "His talk was an unbroken monologue. And he drank up everything we had in the house: when a bottle was set before him, he simply poured drinks for himself, not suggesting that we might care for any. If we said we ought to go to bed, he paid no attention to this" (*Twenties*, pp. 111–12). Could O'Neill have been partly putting him on (playing the "Irish"—getting Wilson's upper-middle-class goat)? On the theme of alcoholism in *Long Day's Journey* see Steven F. Bloom's "Empty Bottles, Empty Dreams."

8. The reviewer, Russell McLaughlin of the *Detroit News*, is quoted in Raleigh's excellent short essay, "The Irish Atavism of *A Moon for the Misbegotten*," p. 229. O'Neill, in fact, once attempted to study Gaelic (Alexander, *Tempering of Eugene O'Neill*, p. 62).

9. Floyd writes: "O'Neill functioned as national archivist, social critic, and moral guide. He held a mirror up to American society in a period bracketed by World War I and World War II and became its conscience. Yet the dramatist transcends the barriers of time and place. As the poet of the human heart, O'Neill bears a message for all men of every era" (*Plays of Eugene O'Neill*, p. xvi).

10. Bogard, *Contour in Time*, p. 355.

11. I should add that when autobiographical dramas like *Long Day's Journey* do deviate from known biographical details, the careful attention paid to such facts by Sheaffer, the Gelbs, Bogard, Alexander, and others is valuable. Raleigh summarizes the pattern of discrepancies that distinguish O'Neill's *Journey* from his family history: "[O'Neill] telescoped events, suppressed some facts, distorted others, invented some more, and transferred some others" (*Plays of Eugene O'Neill*, p. 95). Raleigh's point, however, is that biographers are sometimes tempted to forget that O'Neill's plays are *plays*. The most sophisticated biographical-critical study of O'Neill's plays is surely Alexander's 1992 book, *Eugene O'Neill's Creative Struggle*.

12. Sheaffer, *Son and Artist*, pp. viii, vii; Bogard, *Contour in Time*, p. 449. Atkinson, in the same vein, commends the Gelbs for having recognized that O'Neill's philosophical orientation "developed out of [the] experiences and temperaments of his mother and father" (see Gelb and Gelb, *O'Neill*, p. xix).

13. See Sheaffer, *Son and Playwright*, p. 27.

14. Sheaffer, *Son and Artist*, p. 39.

15. Sheaffer reprints the summary in ibid., p. 510.

16. Ibid., p. 511.

17. Sheaffer, *Son and Playwright*, p. 280.

18. This is Sheaffer's description of her in *Son and Artist*, p. 39.

19. Ibid., p. 512.

20. O'Neill, *Selected Letters*, p. 170.

21. Ibid.

22. While Raleigh, in 1959, moved in the direction of a cultural history of O'Neill's preoccupation with the personal, by arguing that the psychological "turbulence" in *Long Day's Journey* must be read in the context of Irish American "family-culture," he also subscribed to commonsensical ideological divisions between public and private, self and society: "Save for the reference to the Standard Oil Company and a trip to the drugstore," he wrote, "modern American society plays no role in the play" ("O'Neill's *Long Day's Journey*," p. 137). Raleigh also argued: "Social forces, as such, do not exist [in the play] and, as in Greek tragedy, we are face to face with guilty-innocent humanity *on the purely personal level*" (pp. 125–26; emphasis supplied). To say this is to overlook that American culture *produces* ideologies of the personal, gender, sexuality, and the family. The family-as-fate logic employed by O'Neill's biographers rose to prominence by the 1920s. See Reed Whittemore's rather general discussion of twentieth-century American biographies, which concludes with a monitory note about the influence of psychoanalysis on modern biographers (*Whole Lives*, p. 164).

23. Sennett, "Destructive Gemeinschaft," p. 109.

24. See Jean-Paul Sartre's complex theoretical remarks on the relationship between the literary work, the author's biography, and history in what is still the best introduction to cultural studies and dialectical thinking: *Search for a Method*. Especially see Sartre's brilliant outline of what is at stake in reading *Madame Bovary*, which leads us to Gustave Flaubert's biography, which then leads us to an analysis of the class position of Flaubert's family. "It is History itself which we must question" (p. 144). On Flaubert as an object of cultural and historical study, see pp. 140–50. Sartre was drawn to psychoanalysis because it "allows us to discover the whole man in the adult" (p. 60), which is also Sheaffer's premise. "Today's Marxists," Sartre writes, "are concerned only with adults. . . . They have forgotten their own childhoods." Yet Sartre, writing in 1960, seems to exempt childhood from history: "The family in fact is constituted by and in the general movement of History, but is experienced, on the other hand, as an absolute in the depth and opaqueness of childhood" (p. 62). That same year Ariès published his pioneering study of the history of family life from the medieval family to the modern family, *Centuries of Childhood*. Ariès demonstrated that childhood is in fact historically variable. A synthesis of the history of family life and biography is now possible, as can be seen in Steven Mintz's pioneering *Prison of Expectations* (1983), which studies the families of six Victorian authors. In discussing patterns of ambivalence between middle-class fathers and sons, Mintz asserts, "No understanding of the pattern of emotional relationships within a Victorian home can be complete without a recognition of the way family experiences embodied larger cultural concerns involving such basic concepts as authority, duty, legitimacy, and personal responsibility" (p. 59). T. Walter Herbert's cultural biography of Nathaniel and Sophia Hawthorne's family, *Dearest Beloved* (1993), also moves in this theoretical direction.

25. My critique is based on the history of family life, but it also could be made on the basis of cross-cultural scholarship on family life, gender, sexual practices, and

beliefs about psychology. As Stephanie Coontz demonstrates, "Cross-culturally, families vary so greatly in their gender, marital, and child-rearing arrangements that it is not possible to argue that they are based on universal psychological or biological relations" (*Social Origins*, p. 8). She then discusses cultures in which mother-child relations are not "critical to the family" and cultures in which the nuclear family is not the "central reference point" (p. 8). Nicholson observes: "there [are] types of families outside the modern family and types of societies where the concept of the family is not helpful either" (*Gender and History*, p. 107). Also see Gadlin, "Private Lives and Public Order"; Sirjanaki, *American Family*; Ronald L. Howard, *Social History of an American Family Sociology*; and, more generally, Anderson, *History of the Western Family*; Rosenberg, *Family in History*; Shorter, *Making of the Modern Family*; and David Levine et al., *Essays on the Family and Historical Change*. Another resource is *Journal of Marriage and the Family*.

26. Ariès, *Centuries of Childhood*, p. 39; Sennett, *Fall of Public Man*, p. 168.

27. Kett, "Adolescence and Youth in Nineteenth-Century America," p. 98. Also see Shea, *Spiritual Autobiography*; Delany, *British Autobiography*; and Altick, *Lives and Letters*.

28. Perrot, *From the Fires of Revolution to the Great War*, p. 213. Studying over a hundred of his own diaries, Henry Clark Wright, a mid-nineteenth-century reformer and evangelist, sifted through his childhood inscriptions in search of clues to his adult character. His biographer makes the intriguing historical observation that Wright "sounds like one of Freud's patients, preoccupied with some bit of information about himself but unable to decide its meaning" (Perry, *Childhood, Marriage, and Reform*, pp. 63, 95). Also see Scott Caspar's fascinating "Constructing American Lives." In Chapters 2 and 3 Caspar reviews debates about whether biography should expose the private, "inner man" or focus on the subject's civic deeds as the principal evidence of selfhood. As one might expect, as the nineteenth century progresses (under the sway of the cult of domesticity) biographers tend both to imagine the "real" subject as the private, "inner man" and to reconceptualize their project as fundamentally literary (akin to writing novels), not just didactic (inscribing profiles of "great men" to be imitated). On case studies made by prisons in the 1820s and 1830s, see Rothman, *Discovery of the Asylum*, pp. 178, 65–76. For information on childhood histories in magazines for mothers, see Wishy, *The Child and the Republic*, p. 28.

29. Demos, "Oedipus and America," pp. 28–29.

30. Commins, *O'Neill-Commins Correspondence*, p. 2. O'Neill lived with his parents on Broadway, on tour, and in New London during the summer in his early years. At age seven he was sent to St. Aloysius boarding school in Riverdale, New York, and remained in boarding schools until 1906, when he entered Princeton. His early years as well as his summertime reunions with and separations from his parents seem to have amplified the needs and expectations he brought to intimate relations. Sociologists Michelle Barrett and Mary McIntosh write: "The typical personality of the normal successfully-reared child may have its undesirable features: a need to form intimate one-to-one ties to the exclusion of a more diffused bond to a wider group, a tendency to go it alone as an individual and a lack of concern for group support and approval or group ties." Bruno Bettelheim's 1969

study of the Israeli kibbutz (whose communal childrearing practices are closer to that of colonial than to nineteenth- or twentieth-century America) makes available a cross-cultural perspective that helps us recognize that what middle-class Americans consider to be common sense assumptions about individuality, depth, and neurosis are in fact rooted in culturally specific constructs of family life. Although Bettelheim saw group-oriented "children of the dream" as less "individual" and "subjective" than middle-class American adolescents, he reserved praise for their "intense group ties," especially when he pondered their political implications: such ties do not "breed human isolation, asocial behavior or other forms of disorganizations that plague modern man in competitive society" (quoted in Barrett and McIntosh, *The Anti-Social Family*, p. 52).

31. Coontz, *Social Origins*, p. 88. Demos also discusses fatherhood and motherhood as "cultural inventions" in *Past, Present, and Personal*. Even when kibbutz parents have strong emotional ties to one another and to their offspring, "the child will respond first to his awareness that the parents' deepest allegiance is to the kibbutz and only secondly to his sense of belonging to each other and their child" (Bettelheim, *Children of the Dream*, p. 255).

32. On the erosion of patriarchal authority see Demos, *Past, Present, and Personal*, pp. 53, 58, 117. Also see Mintz (from whom I quote), *Prison of Expectations*, p. 117, and Griffen, "Reconstructing Masculinity." Stuart Ewen discusses the relationship between the erosion of the patriarchal family and the emergence of a culture of consumption in *Captains of Consciousness*, pp. 113–29, 151–57. On nineteenth- and twentieth-century Irish emigration to America and the difficulties of this cultural passage, see Kerby A. Miller, *Emigrants and Exiles*. For a more general overview of the Irish American family, see Greeley, *That Most Distressful Nation*, pp. 95–116.

33. Sheaffer, *Son and Playwright*, p. 16.

34. See Ryan, *Empire of the Mother*, p. 52 (also see p. 57). In addition see Ryan, *Cradle of the Middle Class*, pp. 232 and 238, and Brodhead, "Sparing the Rod." Demos describes this as a "disciplinary regime" based on the psychological power of the mother to make her child feel guilty. Mother's construction of her psychological power over her son is exemplified by the cliché, "All that I am, I owe to my angel mother" ("Oedipus and America," pp. 32, 31).

35. Consult Ryan (*Cradle of the Middle Class*, p. 161) on the internalization of petit bourgeois traits. Demos discusses shifts in motherhood and fatherhood in *Past, Present, and Personal*, p. 57.

36. Demos, *Past, Present, and Personal*, p. 33.

37. Together, the cult of motherhood and the cult of domesticity formed the silken strands of a sentimental discourse that nourished ambivalent bonds between mothers and sons—bonds with pronounced erotic undertones. On this subject Ryan notes that the intense and even erotic mother-child bonding celebrated by antebellum "mother's magazines," advice books, and sentimental fiction "suggest[s] that domestic writers had not anticipated Freud's notion of the Oedipal crisis. Indeed, [the writers] were largely oblivious to the dangers of excessive attachments—both social and sexual—between mothers and sons" (*Empire of the Mother*, pp. 57–58). My own work on mid-nineteenth-century middle-class fiction has turned up

some anxieties about privatized childhood and too close a mother-son bond (*Production of Personal Life*, pp. 52–54).

38. See Demos, "Oedipus and America," p. 34. O'Neill is quoted in Sheaffer, *Son and Artist*, p. 181. Yet he added that *Monte Cristo*, the play his father made famous (intoning his famous line: "The world is mine!"), was the best of the nineteenth-century melodramas (Fechter, *Monte Cristo (James O'Neill's Version)*, p. 96). By 1925, O'Neill could afford to be generous, capable as he was of proclaiming: "American drama is mine!" "How better," notes Eric Bentley, "can a man outdo an actor than by becoming a playwright? The actor is the playwright's mouthpiece and victim. . . . [O'Neill's] father's theatre . . . was an actor's theatre. The modern theatre would be a playwright's theatre, and Eugene O'Neill was one of the principal playwrights who made it so" ("The Life and Hates of Eugene O'Neill," p. 32). Note that Barrett Clark, in reprinting Charles Fechter's version of *Monte Cristo* in *Favorite Plays of the Nineteenth Century* (1943), made explicit mention of the senior O'Neill: *Monte Cristo (James O'Neill's Version)*.

39. Demos, "Oedipus and America."

40. Coontz, *Social Origins*, pp. 354, 356.

41. Elaine Tyler May, *Great Expectations*, p. 163.

42. Quoted in Gelb and Gelb, *O'Neill*, p. 239.

43. O'Neill said in 1946: "The critics have missed the most important thing about me and my work, the fact that I am Irish" (Shannon, *American Irish*, pp. 278, 279).

44. See Alexander, *Tempering of Eugene O'Neill*, p. 62.

45. Raleigh, "O'Neill's *Long Day's Journey*," p. 138. Harry Cronin's *Eugene O'Neill* builds on Raleigh's efforts to situate and reread O'Neill's plays in an Irish Catholic cultural and intellectual context.

46. Floyd, *Eugene O'Neill*, p. 190.

47. Sheaffer, *Son and Playwright*, p. 45.

48. Shaughnessy, *Eugene O'Neill in Ireland*, p. 15.

49. Groves and Ogburn, *American Marriage and Family Relationships*, p. 16.

50. Ibid., p. 97.

51. Fass, *Damned and the Beautiful*, p. 82.

52. Ibid., p. 75; Allen, *Only Yesterday*, p. 103.

53. Quoted in Fass, *Damned and the Beautiful*, p. 109. Ronald L. Howard describes how the sociology of the family in the 1920s became increasingly influenced by psychoanalysis and psychology so that domestic "interactions" were understood to be meetings of "personalities," not just family members (*A Social History of American Family Sociology*, pp. 63–94). Also see Habermas, *Structural Transformation of the Public Sphere*, pp. 152, 155–56.

54. O'Neill offers a bizarre melding of these flipsides in *Dynamo* (1929), in which Reuben Light incestuously embraces a dynamo he thinks is his mother and is electrocuted.

55. Groves and Ogburn, *American Marriage and Family Relationships*, pp. 19, 79.

56. Fass, *Damned and the Beautiful*, p. 117; Groves and Ogburn, *American Marriage and Family Relationships*, p. 29.

57. Mowrer, *Family*, p. 278; Groves and Ogburn, *American Marriage and Family Relationships*, p. 23.

58. Groves and Ogburn, *American Marriage and Family Relationships*, p. 23.

59. Ibid., p. 114.

60. "Application of 'psychology,' " wrote Ernest Mowrer, "takes the place of older controls" (*Family*, p. 275).

61. "Modern psychology and psychiatry are agreed," Phyllis Blanchard and Carlyn Manasses reported in 1930: "attitudes formed in childhood are those which tend to persist throughout the life of the individual" (*New Girls for Old*, p. 15). Also see Blanchard, *Child and Society*, p. 36.

62. Anthony, "Family," p. 335.

63. Simon first uttered this phrase verbatim in *Mansions* (3:430). Sara, whose thoughts sometimes dwell on her own charged relationship with her father, Con Melody, also views her past as a psychological web in which "the dead [are] mixed up with the living" (3:457).

64. Groves and Ogburn, *American Marriage and Family Relationships*, p. 80.

65. See Raleigh, "Communal, Familial, and Personal Memories," p. 66.

66. See Edward Shaughnessy's description of the "depth" (familial conflicts, concerns with fate, emotional crises) O'Neill would have seen staged by the Abbey Theatre's troupe on their 1911–12 tour. O'Neill saw, for example, John Millington Synge's *Riders to the Sea* and T. C. Murray's *Birthright* (*Eugene O'Neill in Ireland*, pp. 34–36). John Brougham's *O'Flannigan and the Faeries* (1856), a sentimental temperance comedy, dramatizes heavy drinking and familial discord in an Irish family; but O'Flannigan lacks the ambivalence and the tragic self-deluding characteristics of a Con Melody or a Jamie Tyrone. O'Flannigan drinks because it is fun; Con Melody and Jamie Tyrone drink because life has wounded them, fate has struck them, and their drunken performances sustain them.

67. O'Neill, *Selected Letters*, p. 545.

68. See O'Neill's letter to Sean O'Casey (ibid., p. 546).

69. Tyrone's speech is that of a nineteenth-century stage Irishman who is confident that he can upstage his son; just as he puts aside his cards, he begins his oration (as if challenging the playwright himself): "Whose play is it?" (3:806). Later Jamie disparages this as "the old sob act" (3:814). The nineteenth-century historian Thomas Macaulay wrote, "The Irish . . . were an ardent and impetuous race, easily moved to tears or laughter, to fury or to love." But as Nathan Glazer and Daniel Patrick Moynihan note, Macaulay's "words evoke the stage Irishman, battered hat in hand, loquacious and sly, proclaiming 'Faith, yer Honor, if I'd of known it was Hogan's goat' " (*Beyond the Melting Pot*, p. 238).

70. As psychological discourse grew popular in the early twentieth century, families tended to express their conflicts and feelings in "psychological" terms and to explain them according to "psychological" models. This psychological modeling of the family drew comment and criticism. Psychologist Samuel D. Schmalhausen argued that the hothouse or oedipal family is "in reality [a] great anti-social agency" and suggested that it be replaced by "more impersonal groupings, in which parents will no longer occupy omnipotent posts of divinely prerogatived policemen, but will be the tenderly, impersonal companions and tutors of young lives they have had the honor, thoughtfully and deliciously, to bring into this incredible world" ("Family Life," p. 294). See Demos on the inscription of the early-twentieth-

century family within psychological discourse, *Past, Present, and Personal*, p. 61. Sociologist Ruth Reed's *Modern Family* (1929) includes a chapter on "The Hypertrophy of Family Bonds," which argues that the privatized, middle-class family produces "affectional bonds of a particularly deep and absorbing nature between parents and children.... [that] if sufficiently intense, may inhibit normal development to maturity and produce in adults desiccated and impoverished personalities" (pp. 103–4). Reed also quotes from Edward Carpenter's popular *Love's Coming of Age*, in which Carpenter suggests that the privatized couple degenerates into "a mere egoism *a deux*" (p. 105).

71. Bogard, *Contour in Time*, p. 188; Sheaffer, *Son and Artist*, p. 147.

72. See Wainscott, *Staging O'Neill*, p. 131.

73. Sheaffer, *Son and Artist*, p. 75.

74. Boulton, *Part of a Long Story*, pp. 171–72, 170.

75. Ibid., pp. 254, 286. When Brooklyn Boy, the O'Neills' dog, was found dead with his throat slit, Agnes surmised that it was an expression of their neighbors' resentment toward her and Eugene (p. 282).

76. "In one sense what happens between women and men in love is beyond history," writes cultural critic John Berger; "in an embrace very little changes. Yet the construction put on passion alters. Not necessarily because emotions are different but because what surrounds the emotions—social attitudes, legal systems, moralities, eschatologies—these change" (*And Our Faces, My Heart, Brief as Photos*, pp. 66–67). I have grave doubts that "emotions," "love," or "sexuality" are in *any* sense "beyond history," but I very much agree with what Berger argues about the historical, social, and cultural situatedness of love and passion. On the history of twentieth-century attitudes toward jealousy, see Stearns, *Jealousy*, pp. 66–87, 114–51.

77. Blanchard and Manasses, *New Girls for Old*, p. 189.

78. Ibid., pp. 233–34.

79. Expressing his views in the language of middle-class common sense, Lindsey exhorted his readers in 1925 to accept the reality that "modern youth"—"beneath the surface"—engage uninhibitedly in sexual practices, and that, like it or not, "they are changing our social codes" (Lindsey and Evans, *Revolt of Youth*, p. 53; also see pp. 54, 62, 140). For some brilliant sociological perspectives on the shift that Lindsey describes, see Robert S. Lynd and Helen Merrell Lynd's classic 1929 study of daily life in a mid-American urban community, *Middletown*, especially Part 4, "Using Leisure," pp. 225–312.

80. Lindsey and Evans, *Companionate Marriage*, p. v. Sociologist Ruth Reed added in 1929 that the companionate wife is often "economically independent of the husband," and that this arrangement is advantageous to professional couples that do not yet want children (*Modern Family*, pp. 170, 171). "The term 'companionate' to describe this new form of marriage," she notes, "was first used by M. M. Knight in an article which appeared in *The Journal of Social Hygiene* in May 1924" (p. 170). Marxist critic V. F. Calverton cheerfully characterized this shift as a significant transition from "procreational" to "recreational" sex (*Bankruptcy of Marriage*, p. 121). Also see Sidney Ditzion's discussion of companionate marriage in *Marriage Morals and Sex in America*, pp. 381–83.

81. Historians Steven Mintz and Susan Kellogg generalize: "The goal of marriage was no longer financial security or a nice home but emotional and sexual fulfillment and compatibility." Once marriage was rendered as psychological in this way, marriage experts determined that "contrary to older Victorian ideals of romantic love, conflict and tension were normal parts of married life" (*Domestic Revolutions*, p. 113; also see pp. 115, 116, 128).

82. See Elaine Tyler May, "Myths and Realities of the American Family," pp. 554–55.

83. See Mintz and Kellogg, *Domestic Revolutions*, p. 109. J. P. Lichtenberger's *Divorce: A Social Interpretation* (1931) estimated that "by 1916, in San Francisco, one out of every four marriages ended in divorce; in Los Angeles, one out of every five; in Chicago, one out of every seven" (quoted in Mintz and Kellogg, *Domestic Revolutions*, p. 108). As proof of the unstoppable sexual "revolt of youth" and the inadequacy of contemporary marriage laws and conventions, Judge Lindsey cited the crisis in his own hometown: "For every marriage in Denver during the year 1922 there was a separation. For every two marriage licenses issued there was a divorce suit filed" (Lindsey and Evans, *Revolt of Youth*, p. 211).

84. Watson is quoted in Mintz and Kellogg, *Domestic Revolutions*, p. 108.

85. Oscar Cargill observes that the 120,000 women clerical workers in 1890 increased to 2,000,000 by 1930 (*Intellectual America*, p. 627).

86. Ruth Reed, who taught at Mount Holyoke College, observed in the 1920s that while marriage was on the rise, the rate of women college graduates who married was in decline as job opportunities for white-collar women opened up—adding wryly: "The attitudes and customs which govern the marriage relationships were evolved and developed with regard to the needs and personality of a group of women who had not undergone any considerable degree of personal development, but who remained immature and pliable individuals in the family circle. . . . Male ideals of love are still largely associated with notions of dominance and superiority" (*Modern Family*, pp. 65–66).

87. Hinkle, "Chaos of Modern Marriage," p. 9.

88. Schmalhausen, "Family Life," p. 291.

89. Hicks, *Great Tradition*, pp. 253, 255.

90. O'Neill, *Selected Letters*, p. 326. "Mother's day," Coontz reminds us, "is a twentieth-century invention" (*Social Origins*, p. 351). Mothers also became the object of anthropological and sociological study in the 1920s. See Robert Briffault's massive three-volume *Mothers*. Alfred B. Kuttner, who contributed his essay "Nerves" to Harold Stearns's *Civilization in the United States*, suggests that this cultural preoccupation with the mother produces much repression. The American who boasts about loving his mother "grows violent when the incest-complex is mentioned" (p. 438). O'Neill, by contrast, was positively delighted to discuss and dramatize it. Sidney Howard's *Silver Cord*, produced by the Theatre Guild in 1926, staged the psychological tyranny of mother love before O'Neill's *Strange Interlude*, *Dynamo*, and *Mourning Becomes Electra* contributed to the genre.

91. Schmalhausen, "Family Life," p. 281; Hamilton and Macgowan, *What Is Wrong with Marriage*, p. 154. Harvey O'Higgins's chapter, "Love and Marriage," also represents the memory of the mother as a determinative force in the husband's

relationship to his wife. See O'Higgins's pop psychology text, *Secret Springs*, pp. 15–47.

92. Such a confession would have been unlikely to surface in the kibbutz communities studied by Bettelheim in 1969, where "multiple mothering" was instituted to preempt "a disturbance marked by the child's utter dependence on his mother, which prevents him from having any life of his own" (*Children of the Dream*, p. 306).

93. Raymond Williams, *Marxism and Literature*, p. 122.

94. Sanger, *Happiness in Marriage*, pp. 221–23.

95. O'Neill, *Selected Letters*, pp. 97, 399. See also Barlow, "O'Neill's Many Mothers."

96. In 1962 Bentley observed that "the perfect marriage which Evelyn offered was the union of mother and child" ("Life and Hates of Eugene O'Neill," p. 56).

97. O'Neill, *Selected Letters*, p. 386. See Alexander, "Psychological Fate," and Hamilton and Macgowan, *What Is Wrong with Marriage*, pp. 307–8.

98. Brecht, *Brecht on Theatre*, p. 97.

99. Zaretsky, *Capitalism, the Family, and Personal Life*, p. 99. Also see Joel Kovel's contention that bourgeois psychology "has been constructed to help reproduce a family structure that appears free standing, separate from history, and sufficient unto itself" (*Age of Desire*, p. 106).

100. I have in mind Hawthorne's *House of the Seven Gables* (1851), Poe's "Fall of the House of Usher" (1839), and Melville's *Pierre Or, The Ambiguities* (1852). The Melville revival (championed by Carl Van Vechten, D. H. Lawrence, and Lewis Mumford) was well underway by the late 1920s.

101. Groves and Ogburn, *American Marriage and Family Relationships*, p. 80. Alexander has observed that the family in O'Neill's oeuvre is often represented as "the original cause of all causes" ("Psychological Fate," p. 933).

102. See Von Wiegand, "Quest of Eugene O'Neill," p. 31.

103. Coontz, *Social Origins*, p. 1. Martha Bower describes O'Neill's research interests and his process of composing *A Touch of the Poet* and *More Stately Mansions* in *Eugene O'Neill's Unfinished Threnody*, pp. 9–86.

104. Cott, *Bonds of Womanhood*, p. 69. Also see Ryan, *Cradle of the Middle Class*.

105. "The doctrine of the private family as the center of morality and personal identity," writes Stephanie Coontz, "was established by a middle class that had retreated from larger ethical concerns" (*Way We Never Were*, p. 101). Coontz also notes that the word this class frequently used to describe its aims was "decency."

106. Grimké, *Letters on the Equality of the Sexes*; Smith-Rosenberg, "The Female World of Love and Ritual," in *Disorderly Conduct*, pp. 53–76.

107. Foucault, *History of Sexuality*, p. 109.

108. Ariès, *Centuries of Childhood*, pp. 40, 386, 413. Also see Ariès, "Family and the City," p. 32; Pfister, *Production of Personal Life*, pp. 2–5, 49–56; and Kovel, *Age of Desire*, p. 119.

109. Samuel Schmalhausen developed the implications of O'Neill's critique of *Mansions'* capitalist-psychological family by insisting that this privatized "pathological" unit be understood as a political structure that can be altered: "It is a vicious circle (a vicious family circle): there is no breaking out of it except by a pretty drastic

transformation of the competitive system in the direction of communism, under the socializing and liberating influence of which the members of a family will be enticed into larger and more human loyalties than an acquisitive and exploitative regime can encourage" ("Family Life," p. 286).

110. Eric Bentley's reading of the psychologization of relations in *Mansions* focuses more on O'Neill's biography: "One wonders if one of the factors bringing him to abandon the cycle and burn parts of what he had already written was the realization that he could not break out of the closed circle of his own adolescence, and that therefore his dramatic history of his country would turn out to be only an unbroken series of disguised portraits of his parents, his brother and himself" ("Touch of the Adolescent," p. 403). For some astute thoughts on the increasing privatization of the subject matter and the scenes of modern drama see Raymond Williams, *Sociology of Culture*, pp. 170–71.

111. See some of the reviews in Jordan Y. Miller's *Playwright's Progress*, pp. 133–37. Interestingly, Thomas R. Dash of *Women's Wear Daily* dissented from the raves, saying O'Neill's final play was not up to the standard set by *Strange Interlude* and *Mourning* and that it was more therapeutic than theatrical.

112. Coontz, *Way We Never Were*, pp. 31–37. Also see Elaine Tyler May's *Homeward Bound*, esp. pp. 183–207, and Arlene Skolnick's *Embattled Paradise*, esp. pp. 49–74.

113. Jameson, *Marxism and Form*, p. 27.

Chapter 2

1. Over the last fifteen or so years a growing number of distinguished anthropologists have questioned conventional humanist and "psychobiological" assumptions about the "universality" of emotions and of depth. Their cross-cultural work has led them to view the implantation of particular emotions inside the self as a social and ideological inscription. "What might be most productive," Lila Abu-Lughod and Catherine Lutz propose, "would be to begin by tracing the genealogy of 'emotion' itself, so that, in an enterprise analogous to Foucault's (1978) critical investigation of the production of sexuality in the modern age, we might consider how emotions came to be constituted in their current form, as physiological forces, located within individuals, that bolster our sense of uniqueness and are taken to provide access to some kind of inner truth about the self" ("Introduction," p. 6). In her groundbreaking final essay, the late Michelle Rosaldo challenged commonsensical Western notions of depth as a "precultural," " unknowable preserve of psychic privacy" ("Toward an Anthropology of Self and Feeling," p. 138). In 1939 Norbert Elias, the brilliant historical sociologist, studied the transition from the Middle Ages to the Renaissance court and suggested a connection between the cultural production of depth (self-as-manager-of-drives) and the increasing social need of courtiers to control their behavior and appearance (*Power and Civility*, pp. 229–319)—an argument based on a belief in "precultural" Freudian instincts that are acted upon by culture (the "civilizing" process). But Rosaldo contends that many cultures do not produce a notion of self that foregrounds the premise of controls or constraints: "For Ilongots—and, I suggest, for many of the relatively egalitarian peoples in the

world—there is no social basis for a problematic that assumes need for controls, nor do individuals experience themselves as having boundaries to protect or holding drives and lusts that must be held in check if they are to maintain their status or engage in everyday cooperation" ("Toward an Anthropology of Self and Feeling," p. 148). Rodney Needham draws attention to the fact that "the sheer numbers of words and phrases by which languages denote such [inner] states are highly variable" and concludes: "To the extent that inner states may be discriminable as universal natural resemblances, they are in the province of physiology. If inner states are inferred from social expressions, they are social facts like other social facts" ("Inner States as Universals," pp. 68, 76). Paul Heelas points out that different cultures locate emotional depth in different organs (e.g., heart, liver, stomach), that it is not uncommon for non-Western cultures to view emotions as "external agencies which invade or possess people," and that many non-Western cultures place little or no cultural value on imagining "emotions of the private self" ("Emotion Talk Across Cultures," pp. 244–45, 247, 260). Catherine Lutz observes that many non-Western cultures that she and other anthropologists have studied do not deploy constructs of depth with the aim of individualizing the self:

> Psychodynamic theories posit that the psychic depths hold causal priority, that they can be reached, and that they constitute the "really real." Other ethnotheories vary on this epistemological point; the Ifaluk [of Micronesia], for example, are unsure about the accessibility of "the insides" of other people. On the one hand, "We cannot see our insides," they say, and that is reason enough not to worry about that aspect of the unknown. On the other hand, "our insides," in their view, are not private in the way that Taiwanese and Americans see them as private; the privacy of Taiwanese insides is a result of the polluting/shameful qualities they are seen to have . . . , the privacy of American insides arises in part from the extent to which the contents of consciousness are seen as sacred, individualizing markers of the self. ("Depression and the Translation of Emotional Worlds," p. 72)

Anthropologists, sociologists, historians, and cultural theorists, in particular, are starting to grasp that "To thine own self be true" is indeed a highly variable culturally and ideologically produced notion.

2. Vernant, "History and Psychology," in *Mortals and Immortals*, p. 262.

3. Schmalhausen, *Why We Misbehave*, p. 100.

4. Peterson, *Melody of Chaos*, pp. 8–11, 17.

5. See Richard Johnson, "What Is Cultural Studies Anyway?" pp. 44, 45, 61. I am also stimulated by the insights of historian of psychology Nikolas Rose, who argues, "The 'self' does not pre-exist the forms of its social recognition" (*Governing the Soul*, p. 218).

6. O'Neill visited Jelliffe to " 'talk things over.' According to Dr. Jelliffe's widow, Belinda, O'Neill was not 'deeply psychoanalyzed' but, rather, received therapeutic help for a variety of specific reasons" (Gelb and Gelb, *O'Neill*, p. 565). For information about the copy of *Psychoanalysis and the Drama*, see Nethercot, "Psychoanalyzing of Eugene O'Neill: P. P. S.," p. 42.

7. Gelb and Gelb, *O'Neill*, p. 595.

8. Sheaffer, *Son and Artist*, pp. 188–89.

9. Alexander, "Psychological Fate," p. 924.

10. Boni and Liverwright, O'Neill's publisher till 1933, was the "first publisher to promote the writings of Freud in America" (Gelb and Gelb, *O'Neill*, p. 396).

11. Hoffman, *Freudianism*, p. 91.

12. Gelb and Gelb, *O'Neill*, p. 595. When the young Joseph Freeman was advised by his friend Horatio Winslow to be psychoanalyzed (Winslow's analysis had left him depoliticized), Freeman responded: " 'But it may kill my poetry,' I said, feeling at the time that it was better to suffer in poetry than to be happy in prose" (*American Testament*, p. 190). By contrast, Floyd Dell wrote that he elected to be psychoanalyzed "not for any particular neurotic difficulty but because I thought it might be helpful to me in my love life and literary work" (quoted in Hoffman, *Freudianism*, p. 56). Also see Leslie Fishbein's discussion of the politics of the linkage between art and neurosis in *Rebels in Bohemia*, p. 185. Hamilton too, observes Sheaffer, feared that an exhaustive analysis of O'Neill might help O'Neill the individual but reroute the creative juices of the playwright (*Son and Artist*, p. 189). By the late 1910s and 1920s it was not uncommon for the writing of literature to be understood as a fundamentally psychological practice—a notion that has its modern origins in nineteenth-century romanticism and middle-class fiction. See Raymond Williams's chapter "The Romantic Artist" in *Culture and Society*, pp. 48–64. On the ideology of the artist-as-autonomous-self, also see Burger, *Theory of the Avant-Garde*. On the emergence of the notion that literary writing should be read as symptomatic of "the psychological conflicts of an author," see White, *Uses of Obscurity*, p. 4. In late-nineteenth-century Britain, White observes, "genius" was beginning to be appreciated as "a disease of the nerves" (p. 46).

13. Tridon, *Psychoanalysis and Love*, pp. 216, 218.

14. Sheaffer, *Son and Playwright*, pp. 351, 396. Sheaffer concludes that for O'Neill writing operated "as a safety valve . . . for the aggression, self-hatred and guilt encased within him" (p. 155). Psychological discourse both encodes and values writing such as O'Neill's as a symptom. Thus Dr. Philip Weissman, "specialist in the psychiatric aspects of the creative process," analyzes the oedipal tensions in O'Neill's *Desire Under the Elms* (1925) as O'Neill's "unconscious autobiography" (quoted in Gelb and Gelb, *O'Neill*, p. 538). Weissman considered the origins of O'Neill's "amazing amount of psychoanalytic insight" to be wholly personal or familial rather than broadly cultural (*Creativity in the Theater*, pp. 113–45).

15. Armstrong and Tennenhouse, "Representing Violence," pp. 5–9.

16. Quoted in Sheaffer, *Son and Playwright*, p. 481. See OS, 3: Leo A. Marsh, " 'Anna Christie' at the Vanderbilt," *New York Evening Telegraph*, Nov. 24, 1921: "As is usual with Mr. O'Neill's plays, 'Anna Christie' deals with the sea but more especially with the psychology of the human mind." Also see OS, 5: William G. Stiegler, "Uncertainty of New Star's Fate," *Cincinnati Times Union*, Sept. 30, 1922. Stiegler categorizes *The Hairy Ape* as a "study of morbid psychology." For a review of critics in the 1920s and 1930s who linked O'Neill's work to psychoanalysis, see Nethercot, "Psychoanalyzing of Eugene O'Neill" (Part One), pp. 243–46. Also see Nethercot's "Psychoanalyzing of Eugene O'Neill" (Part Two). On the basis of the criticism he reviewed, Nethercot concludes: "The majority of [O'Neill's] critics felt

that his capture by the school of 'modern psychology,' conscious or unconscious, had not, with some provocative exceptions, eventuated in his improvement as a playwright" (p. 357). Yet the sources quoted by Nethercot in Part One of his article seem mixed (favorable responses to O'Neill's psychoanalytic leanings coming from such luminaries as Joseph Wood Krutch, Ludwig Lewisohn, Lewis Mumford, Brooks Atkinson, Walter Prichard Eaton, and Gilbert Gabriel).

17. Quoted in Sheaffer, *Son and Artist*, p. 159. In some pop psychology texts neurosis was touted as a sign of individuality, creativity, and distinction. "Submit to being called a neurotic," advised Dr. Bisch exuberantly in *Be Glad You're Neurotic*: "All the greatest things we know have come to us from neurotics" (p. 229).

18. See Dardis's chapter on O'Neill in *The Thirsty Muse*. Dardis describes one much-written about episode in 1918, when O'Neill was drunk in a Greenwich Village restaurant holding forth on Ibsen. When his wife Agnes Boulton whispered that they might return to their hotel, O'Neill—in the words of Boulton—"got to his feet, gave me a push backward, leaned toward me, swinging as hard as possible with the back of his hand and hit me across the face. Then he laughed, his mouth distorted with an ironic grin." The only friend who helped Agnes was Stella Ballantine, who took her back to her hotel. After recounting this, Dardis comments: "Such episodes became a regular part of her life; they became the price of living with a *literary genius*" (emphasis supplied) (pp. 223–24).

19. O'Neill, "Memoranda on Masks," reprinted in *Unknown O'Neill*, p. 406.

20. " 'Literature,' " Jane Tompkins reminds us, "is not a stable entity but a *category* whose outlines and contents are variable" (*Sensational Designs*, p. 190). See Tompkins's discussion of the psychologization of the "literary" and canon formation, pp. 196–201. O'Neill noted in 1942 that his plays are written to "hit the subconscious as well as the conscious" (*Selected Letters*, p. 532).

21. Jelliffe and Brink, *Psychoanalysis and the Drama*, pp. iii, 1. See Brecht, "Theatre for Pleasure or Theatre for Instruction," in *Brecht on Theatre*, pp. 69–77.

22. Eastman, "Exploring," p. 748. O'Neill, "Memoranda on Masks," reprinted in *Unknown O'Neill*, p. 406.

23. Seabury, *Unmasking*, p. xv.

24. Jelliffe and Brink, *Psychoanalysis and the Drama*, p. 2.

25. This too is the ideological strategy of industrial psychology, which was established after World War I and institutionalized in personnel departments in the late 1920s.

26. Jelliffe and Brink, *Psychoanalysis and the Drama*, p. 75.

27. Hopkins, *How's Your Second Act?*, pp. 24, 19, 21, 16.

28. On Freudian aesthetics, see Sievers, *Freud on Broadway*, p. 18. See Bentley's "Theatre and Therapy" (1969) for his reflections on the actual similarities between a theatrical performance and group therapy. As he notes, the Living Theatre in the 1950s and 1960s tried to radicalize the concept of theatre-as-group therapy.

29. Macgowan, *Theatre of Tomorrow*, pp. 248, 264. Even George Cram Cook, a founder and leader of the Provincetown Players who, with Susan Glaspell, satirized psychoanalysis in *Suppressed Desires* (1915), regarded theatre as "a laboratory of human emotions." Quoted in Helen Deutsch and Stella Hanau, *Provincetown*, p. 26.

30. Cheney, *The New Movement in Theatre*, pp. 36, 31, 34. On the European "new theatre," also see Cheney's *Art Theatre* (1917).

31. O'Neill's remarks about *"Anna Christie"* are in *Conversations*, p. 74. See TGPB, 79: Richard Watts, "Realism Doomed, O'Neill Believes," *New York Herald Tribune*, Feb. 2, 1928. O'Neill wrote in "Memoranda on Masks": "With his old—and more than a bit senile!—standby of realistic technique, [the dramatist] can do no more than, at best, obscurely hint at it through a realistically disguised surface symbolism, superficial and misleading" (*Unknown O'Neill*, p. 406). In addition see O'Neill's "Strindberg and the Theatre" (1924): "The old 'naturalism'—or 'realism' if you prefer . . . no longer applies. It represented our Fathers' daring aspirations toward self-recognition by holding the family Kodak up to ill-nature. . . . We have endured too much from the banality of surfaces" (*Unknown O'Neill*, p. 387). Michael Manheim argues that O'Neill's psychological plays were "deeper" than the nineteenth century's melodramas: "O'Neill could use with ease the melodramatic tricks he learned from his father, but he used them strictly to achieve effects, and frequently satiric ones, not as important serious attributes of his plays" (*Eugene O'Neill's New Language of Kinship*, pp. 3–4). But Kurt Eisen offers a refreshing reevaluation of how O'Neill's interest in melodrama and his modernism were integrated in *The Inner Strength of Opposites*.

32. See Thomas J. Ferraro's *Ethnic Passages*, p. 90. Ferraro quotes Henry Roth on the importance of this modernist trinity and suggested to me its pertinence to my argument.

33. O'Neill, *Conversations*, pp. 74, 80.

34. O'Neill, *Selected Letters*, pp. 390, 408.

35. Havelock Ellis noted the following about hysteria in 1918: "[The] key often lay far back and forgotten in the patient's history, and when skilfully used, with knowledge and insight, the patient's medical history acquired not only psychological significance, but something of the interest of a novel. . . . Freud's art is the poetry of psychic processes which lie in the deepest and most mysterious recesses of the soul" (quoted in Hale, *Freud and the Americans*, p. 431). John Burnham, a major contributor to the history of the "new psychology," has very perceptively suggested that the keen interest early-twentieth-century intellectuals took in socialist theory prepared them to think in terms of a subtextual self. The socialists' subtextual self was typically motivated by class and economic interests, and constituted by history, politics, and culture (see Burnham, "The New Psychology," p. 121). Psychoanalysis, by contrast, both privatized and sexualized depth. By the 1920s, intellectuals and artists who had been converted to the privatized, psychoanalytic notion of depth and to modernism's aesthetic of depth would often classify the socialist idea of the subtextual self as superficial propaganda.

36. Sheaffer, *Son and Playwright*, p. 481.

37. Schmalhausen, *Why We Misbehave*, p. 99.

38. In "The Sexual Revolution" (1929), Schmalhausen again singled out O'Neill for staging depth: "The surgical analysis of the innermost depths of human nature is by all odds the most unique literary development of an age that can love Gorki and Freud and O'Neill" (pp. 435–36).

39. Bisch, *Be Glad You're Neurotic*, p. 22; Schmalhausen, "Sexual Revolution," pp. 435–36.

40. Hale, *Freud and the Americans*, pp. 397–98.

41. Henry F. May, *End of American Innocence*, pp. 233, 235. Also see Hale, *Freud and the Americans*, p. 399. On the rapid acceptance of Freud in bohemian intellectual circles, also consult Fishbein, *Rebels in Bohemia*, pp. 83–93.

42. Hale, *Freud and the Americans*, pp. 398–99; Tom Lutz, *American Nervousness*.

43. See Hoffman, *Freudianism*, esp. p. 47; Burnham, "New Psychology: From Narcissism to Social Control," esp. pp. 361, 354.

44. Burnham observes: "In the twenties the authors of the rapidly proliferating literature of the new psychology changed the emphasis from self-improvement to self-justification; they moved from the progressive idea of service to the postwar idea of discovering one's wants, needs, and desires . . . and gratifying them" ("New Psychology: From Narcissism to Social Control," p. 397; also see pp. 373–74). Also see Burnham, "Psychiatry, Psychology and the Progressive Movement," pp. 461–65. The professionalization and psychiatrization of social work in the 1920s transformed its earlier progressive project—to ameliorate the world—into a therapeutic project of psychological adaptation. Roy Lubove writes: "In embracing psychiatry, social workers undoubtedly acquired a more sophisticated awareness of the subtle ties and ambiguities of personality, but in the process they undermined their capacity to promote institutional change and deal effectively with the problems of mass deprivation in an urban society. Psychiatry . . . deflected the social worker's attention from the social and cultural environment and from relevant insights provided by the social sciences" (*Professional Altruist*, p. 117). Burnham discusses the relevance of Lubove's thesis in "New Psychology: From Narcissism to Social Control."

45. Tridon, *Psychoanalysis and Love*, p. 42.

46. See Morawski and Hornstein, "Quandary of the Quacks," pp. 106–33. The authors observe that the popularity of psychological discourse in the 1920s blurred the boundary between professional "experts" and laypersons, and that some psychologists sought to reassert the distinction between expert and layperson.

47. See Burnham, *How Superstition Won and Science Lost*, pp. 89, 95.

48. Consult Burnham, "New Psychology," p. 117 (not to be confused with Burnham's "New Psychology: From Narcissism to Social Control").

49. Bogard, *Contour in Time*, p. 297.

50. Audiences recognized *Strange Interlude*'s "understanding of human drives" because they had encountered this understanding in the no-longer-new "new psychology" that appeared in books, magazines, and newspapers everywhere. Pop psychologists had for years educated many of O'Neill's auditors and readers as "laymen." Hale writes:

> By far the largest number of Americans—the millions of readers of *Everybody's, McClure's, Ladies' Home Journal, American Magazine, Good Housekeeping*—knew Freud as the creator of a new scientific miracle of healing that had vague, yet insistent sexual elements. Despite the broad dissemination of some knowledge of psychoanalysis, books by Freud and by the American analysts were read by very few people. No psychoanalytic book sold more than one-tenth of the 900,000

copies that qualified a book as a best seller in the period from 1910 to 1919. (*Freud and the Americans*, p. 430)

Burnham notes that by the mid-1920s psychoanalysis had become a "general intellectual phenomenon" promoted by American intellectuals ("New Psychology," p. 121). Bentley's discussion of middlebrow "psychologism" is in "Life and Hates of Eugene O'Neill," pp. 34, 38, 39. Also see his caustic and perceptive remarks on the "watered-down Freudianism" and "sex talk of the subintelligentsia"—a group that lionized O'Neill for creating "characters [who] are blown up with psychological gas" ("Trying to Like O'Neill," pp. 156–57).

51. See Henry F. May, *The End of American Innocence*, p. 235. Hale observes about popular psychoanalysis: "The element of economic discipline was especially clear in advice to parents to bring up males who would successfully compete. Instincts, sexual and aggressive, were not to be suppressed but directed" (*Freud and the Americans*, p. 407).

52. Coleman and Commins, *Psychology*, p. 230.

53. Bisch, *Be Glad You're Neurotic*, p. 230. See James Thurber's marvelous parodic review of Bisch's book, "Peace, It's Wonderful." Thurber diagnoses Bisch, quite rightly to my mind, as "an italicizing multiple-interrogator" (p. 13).

54. See Ernest Jones, *The Last Phase*, p. 29.

55. Quoted in Peter Gay, *Freud*, p. 568; for Freud's views on American culture, which are similar to O'Neill's, see pp. 566–71.

56. Freeman, *American Testament*, p. 117.

57. Foucault, *History of Sexuality*, p. 69.

58. I am indebted to Indira Karamcheti for this parenthetical aside.

59. Bisch, *Be Glad You're Neurotic*, p. 45; Hamilton and Macgowan, *What Is Wrong with Marriage*, p. 1.

60. Henry F. May notes that because psychoanalysis posited an "inner history," it "was drafted into the defense of the spirit" in the 1910s (*End of American Innocence*, p. 234).

61. "Freud is as much, and as directly, a product of the machine age as Henry Ford," V. F. Calverton recognized in "Sex and the Social Struggle" (1929): "It is not the psychoanalysts, who have suddenly discovered that the world began in sex . . . but the conditions of the modern world which have made psychoanalysis into a popular doctrine, and turned it from an individual therapeutic into a social panacea" ("Sex and Social Struggle," pp. 280, 283).

62. Eastman, "Exploring," p. 741.

63. Coleman and Commins, *Psychology*, p. 194. On *True Story* magazine see Burnham, "New Psychology: From Narcissism to Social Control," p. 368. On O'Neill's background as an altar boy, his Catholic training, and the resonances of Catholic confession in his plays, see Raleigh's informative essay, "Last Confession."

64. We see overtly in the 1920s what Michel Foucault described as a "literature ordered according to the infinite task of extracting the depths of oneself, in between the words, a truth which the very form of the confession holds out like a shimmering mirage." Nineteenth-century scientific discourse and psychoanalysis, Foucault adds, "altered the scope of confession; it tended no longer to be concerned solely with what

the subject wished to hide, but what was hidden from itself" (*History of Sexuality,* pp. 59, 66). For a perceptive analysis of the relationship between nineteenth-century British fiction and the historical shift discussed by Foucault, see Armstrong's "History in the House of Culture" in *Desire and Domestic Fiction,* esp. pp. 186–202. On the psychologization of late-nineteenth-century British writing-as-confession, see White, *Uses of Obscurity,* esp. p. 45.

65. Coleman and Commins, *Psychology,* p. 193. "Have yourself psychoanalyzed," Floyd Dell advised the young Joseph Freeman. "Confession has always been good for the soul; now we have a scientific confessional whose catharsis liberates us from the tyranny of our unconscious fears and taboos" (*American Testament,* p. 244).

66. For members of the late 1960s kibbutz studied by Bruno Bettelheim—where "personal emotions seem impossible to have"—confession does not reveal the same sexualized "self" whose therapeutic positioning drew comment from Commins and Coleman (*Children of the Dream,* p. 262). Bettelheim also notes: "Comrades . . . cannot show deep personal feelings. . . . When emotions do break through, they are understated and quickly suppressed" (p. 261).

67. Quoted in Hoffman, *Freudianism,* p. 264. Psychoanalytic confession—unmasking one's desire—was represented by Max Eastman (when not writing for *The Masses!*) as an upper-class commodity that everybody who read *Everybody's Magazine* might aspire to purchase. Eastman writes: "[Psychoanalysis] is becoming so popular a form of treatment with those who can afford to make a business of being sick that they are paying from two to five hundred dollars a month to have their souls analyzed" ("Exploring," p. 743).

68. Crothers, *Expressing Willie, Nice People, 39 East,* p. 30.

69. O'Neill, *Unknown O'Neill,* p. 406.

70. On the history of late-nineteenth-century middle-class white-collar workers see Blumin, *Emergence of the Middle Class,* pp. 259–97. Bruce McConachie offers a brilliant analysis of the rise of the business class and its consolidation of "respectable" theatre (1845–70) in *Melodramatic Formations,* pp. 157–257. Between the early 1890s and 1930, almost two-thirds of the recipients of bachelor degrees from the University of Chicago took up professional occupations. Only "24 percent of the recipients' fathers were professionals," writes Martin Sklar (*United States as a Developing Country,* p. 172).

71. Ehrenreich and Ehrenreich, "The Professional-Managerial Class," pp. 9.

72. See Ehrenreich, *Fear of Falling,* p. 15.

73. Weinstein, *Corporate Ideal in the Liberal State,* p. ix.

74. Sklar, *United States as a Developing Country,* p. 171. For a good discussion of the professional-managerial class and the emergence of modernist authors in America, see Strychacz, *Modernism, Mass Culture, and Professionalism,* pp. 1–44.

75. For example, when James Oppenheim's *Seven Arts* (one of America's most important "little magazines") maintained its critique of America's involvement in World War I, its patron, Mrs. Rankine, withdrew her funds (Hoffman et al., *Little Magazine,* p. 92).

76. Sklar, *United States as a Developing Country,* pp. 144–45; Stearns, *America and the Young Intellectuals,* p. 155.

77. Allen, *Only Yesterday*, pp. 228–29.

78. Ohmann, *Politics of Letters*, p. 79.

79. O'Neill, *Selected Letters*, p. 169.

80. See OS, 3, which contains James Whittaker, "O'Neill Has First Concrete Heroine: 'Anna Christie' Triumphs Over Environment," *New York Daily News*, Nov. 13, 1921. He added: " 'Anna Christie' and 'The Straw' are speculations. Eugene O'Neill, himself, is the buy."

81. Ehrenreich, *Fear of Falling*, p. 11.

82. De Voto, "Minority Report," p. 3 (also see pp. 4 and 16). For an overview of the Guild's history see Bigsby, *Critical Introduction*, pp. 120–58.

83. Helburn, *Wayward Quest*, pp. 3, 27.

84. Langner, *Magic Curtain*, pp. 172, 447.

85. Ibid., pp. 118, 122. On Langner and Wertheim's subsidy, see Poggi, *Theater in America*, pp. 123–24.

86. On the Guild Theatre's cost see Poggi, *Theater in America*, p. 127. The "Gobelin tapestries" are discussed by Atkinson, *Broadway*, pp. 218–19. Malcolm Goldstein, with Harold Clurman's views in mind, refers to the "damning tastefulness" of the Guild Theatre (*Political Stage*, p. 104).

87. Helburn, *Wayward Quest*, p. 199.

88. Eaton, *Theatre Guild*, pp. 127, 48, 5, 125. For leftist opinions of the Theatre Guild, see Blake, *Awakening of the American Theatre*, p. 6, and Flexner, *American Playwrights*, p. 311.

89. Clurman, *Fervent Years*, p. 23.

90. Discussed in William Leach, "Strategists of Display," p. 123.

91. Clurman, *Fervent Years*, p. 24.

92. See Wainscott, *Staging O'Neill*, p. 242.

93. Percy Hammond profiled the Guild's audiences as the "upper class of drama lovers." See TGPB, 79: Hammond quoted in Anon., " 'Marco Millions,' O'Neill Drama Is Praised by New York Critics," *Minneapolis Journal*, Jan. 29, 1928, and (for an account of Kahn and Reinhardt) John Anderson, "O'Neill's One Act Play Opens: 'Strange Interlude' Profound Drama of Subconscious," *New York Evening Journal*, Jan. 31, 1928.

94. See Rubin, *Making of Middlebrow Culture*, on the Book-of-the-Month Club (pp. 93–147) and on the Literary Guild (pp. 95, 96, 100, 105, 343). For two brilliant accounts of the emergence of middlebrow/highbrow theatres and of the role these theatres played in shaping "business class" consciousness in the second half of the nineteenth century, see Lawrence Levine's *Highbrow/Lowbrow*, esp. pp. 1–81, and Bruce McConachie's *Melodramatic Formations*, pp. 157–257.

95. On Sherwood Anderson as a white-collar author see Christopher P. Wilson, *White Collar Fictions*, pp. 163–206. Wilson's study is a superb class analysis of late-nineteenth-century white-collar authors. See his fine theoretical introduction, pp. 1–21.

96. See Atkinson, *Broadway*, p. 221 (on Jolson), and TGPB, 137: Atkinson, "Trade Practice," *New York Times*, Sept. 17, 1933.

97. Quoted in Eaton, *Theatre Guild*, p. 105.

98. See TGPB, 79.

99. See TGPB, 106: Anon., "Theatre Guild Fights Boston Ban By Radio," *Paw-tucket Times*, Sept. 20, 1929.

100. See TGPB, 106: Eaton quoted in Anon., "Ban on O'Neill Play Continues," *New Bedford Standard*, Sept. 19, 1929.

101. TGPB, 106: Anon., "Ministers Denounce Interlude," *Boston Post*, Sept. 23, 1929.

102. See Foucault, *History of Sexuality*, p. 130.

103. Helburn, *Wayward Quest*, pp. 229–30.

104. Lears, "From Salvation to Self-Realization," pp. 3, 7–8. Also see Lears, *No Place of Grace*, pp. 3–58.

105. Fox and Lears, "Introduction," p. xii.

106. See Ohmann, "Turn-of-the-Century Magazine Fiction," pp. 32, 38, 72, and "Charting Social Space," pp. 51–52.

107. Tom Lutz, *American Nervousness*, p. 6.

108. Quoted in Hedges, "Afterword," p. 40.

109. I am grateful to Keather Kehoe, a student in my O'Neill seminar, for suggesting that Gilman's piece may have caused such a stir because it was written by a woman, whereas O'Neill's study of a "neurotic" woman was more acceptable because it was authored by a man.

110. " 'I believe,' the cry of the ascetic, lost precedence to 'one feels,' the caveat of the therapeutic. And if the therapeutic is to win out, then surely the psychotherapist will be his secular spiritual guide" (Rieff, *Triumph of the Therapeutic*, pp. 20, 25). Rieff's guiding premise is: "As culture changes, so do the modal types of personality that are their bearers" (p. 2).

111. Susman, " 'Personality' and the Making of Twentieth-Century Culture," in *Culture as History*, pp. 271–85. Also see Karen Halttunen's discussion of the shift from character to personality in "From Parlor to Living Room," pp. 182, 187–88. Augustus Thomas's popular *Witching Hour*, first produced in 1907, is fascinating historically because its concerns are both with character (a word repeatedly invoked by the characters) and with a still unfathomed psychological depth that expresses itself through telepathy, hypnotism, and fixations. Thomas's melodrama thus bears signs both of a nineteenth-century culture of character and a more modern culture of personality and depth. This mass-cultural, often literary discourse of depth addressed what Fox and Lears characterize as feelings of "weightlessness" experienced by the university-trained professionals and managers of liberal corporate America ("Introduction," p. xiii).

112. I borrow this term from Stuart Ewen and Elizabeth Ewen's *Channels of Desire*, p. 228.

113. On psychological engineering (p. 133) and "psycho-technology" (a quote from the psychologist Robert Yerkes, p. 143) see Kerry Buckley's biography of Watson, *Mechanical Man*. Also see O'Donnell, *Origins of Behaviorism*, pp. 179–208, and Birnbaum, "Behaviorism in the 1920's," pp. 15–30.

114. See O'Donnell, "Origins of Behaviorism," p. 546, on behaviorism and habits. John Burnham discusses the accent on establishing control in "On the Origins of Behaviorism," p. 149. For an excellent discussion of the significance of the control of

surfaces and the marketing of self in twentieth-century American capitalism, see Stuart Ewen, *All Consuming Image*, pp. 14, 16, 22, 37, 67, 84. I take the term "impression management" from Buckley, *Mechanical Man*, p. 146. On consumer psychology, see Bowlby, *Shopping with Freud*, esp. pp. 95–96, 113. For interesting primary texts on sales psychology and impression management, consult Mears, *Salesmanship for the New Era*, esp. p. 45, and Dunn, *Scientific Selling and Advertising*, p. xxiii.

115. See Buckley, *Mechanical Man*, esp. pp. 81, 133, 146, 176.

116. See Berman, "Jealousy Farcified," p. 287.

117. The elaborate costumes reminiscent of a fashion show and the elegant sets also reinforced this message. On the production of *Marco Millions*, see Wainscott, *Staging O'Neill*, pp. 201–18, and on Lunt see pp. 217–18.

118. On Nietzsche see Trilling, *Sincerity and Authenticity*, p. 138.

119. My thoughts on psychoanalysis and its standardization of desire were shaped in conversation with Laura Wexler. Robert Bellah et al. examine how the corporate ethos and the business relationship between therapist and client mesh in terms of management strategies: "Therapy enables us to 'handle' our feelings more effectively and therefore manage others' responses to us more successfully in business and social life" (*Habits of the Heart*, p. 124; see also pp. 127–29). Ideologically, therapy stresses both the primacy of feelings and the importance of managing them.

120. Fielding, *Caveman*, p. xiv.

121. Page numbers refer to Glaspell, *Plays*.

122. Under the new psychoanalytic regime, Freeman wrote that "repression" rather than "sex" is categorized as the "sin"—you are a "sinner" if "you suffer from suppressed desires" (*American Testament*, p. 159).

123. In the 1930s, historian Caroline Ware suggested that Greenwich Villagers of the 1920s produced a hidden, conflicted "self" to stand in place of a culture that was "disintegrating": "[Psychoanalysis] either fostered or erected the individual as a psychological entity into an end in himself" (*Greenwich Village*, p. 263). Thinking along similar critical lines, Fredric Jameson notes: "The most influential formal impulses of canonical modernism have been strategies of inwardness, which set out to reappropriate an alienated universe by transforming it into personal styles and private languages: such wills to style have seemed in retrospect to reconfirm the very privatization and fragmentation of social life against which they meant to protest" (*Fables of Aggression*, p. 2). Anita Loos's amusing novel *"Gentlemen Prefer Blondes"* (1925), like *Suppressed Desires*, has a charmingly parodic anti-"psychological" edge. The unsophisticated Lorelei Lee, when touring Vienna, is sent to "Dr. Froyd," a psychoanalyst who is frustrated by her lack of neurotic symptoms and repressions; he advises her "to cultivate a few inhibitions and get some sleep" so she will dream (p. 158). This anti-"psychological" bent is also present in Loos's autobiography (1966), in which she muses: "Eugene O'Neill would have reveled in Grandma, although she was so little given to self-pity that she wouldn't have provided his particular talent with much dialogue. She never blamed her predicament on Fate, Karma, an outraged God, or even a jubilant Devil, and apparently felt that the best thing to do about the matter was to keep her mouth shut. But, with an

apology to Mr. O'Neill, I honor Grandma as a more bona fide heroine than his disgruntled and loquacious ladies" (*A Girl Like I*, p. 11). I thank Kate Gordon for suggesting that I read Loos.

124. Freeman, *American Testament*, p. 158; also see pp. 300–301 on psychoanalysis "opening new depths for the poet to explore." Mabel Dodge, who wrote descriptions of her own experience with psychoanalytic therapy for the Hearst chain of newspapers, was also shrewdly aware that she was enmeshed in the cultural production of new and by no means unproblematic categories of selfhood (a production, however, that could retain traditional gender roles for men-in-power and women-who-listened): "With these analysts one has to be so careful," she wrote in *Lorenzo in Taos* (1932); "one has to weigh everything lest one give them more than they can swallow and they turn and rend one for it! Unless one fits oneself into their systems and formulas so that they can pigeon-hole one into a type or a case, they grow puzzled or angry or sad" (quoted in Lasch, *The New Radicalism*, p. 139). A. A. Brill was her psychoanalyst at the time; she had previously seen Jelliffe.

125. See TGPB, 79: Gabriel, "Last Night's First Night," *New York Sun*, Jan 31, 1928.

126. Dell, "Speaking," p. 53. At the turn of the century neurasthenia also had been coded as "a marker of status and social acceptability," according to Tom Lutz. But psychoanalysis, not prescribing rest cures for women or trips out West for men, was able to draw more members of the professional-managerial class into "the ranks of the therapized" (*American Nervousness*, pp. 286, 6).

127. Oppenheim, *Behind Your Front*, p. v.

128. "The accusation of always seeing things black has been hurled against the best of them in all countries—Ibsen, Strindberg, Hauptmann, Andreyev, who not— so I am in good company. It is a very obvious criticism to make, especially in this 100% optimistic country" (O'Neill, *Selected Letters*, p. 646). Nietzsche, too, fueled O'Neill's and many other intellectuals' philosophical discontent with American optimism and materialism in the 1910s. It was unlikely, of course, as O'Neill himself probably sensed, that anything like a Black Purge would be organized by the state against Nietzschean playwrights who rallied professionals and managers to buy season tickets to dramas that preached depth and assailed American optimism. Henry F. May points out that some of Nietzsche's works were translated as early as 1896, and that the translation of the complete works was published in 1909–13. Nietzsche, like Freud, was used (and misused) by various intellectuals and writers to further a critique against "puritanism" and "optimism" already underway: "Superficially . . . Nietzsche had something in common with American predilections. Emersonian self-confidence, captain-of-industry ruthlessness, seemed to some Americans to be suggested by the doctrine of the Superman. Nietzsche, however, had hated what he saw as the land of dollar-chasing democracy" (*End of American Innocence*, pp. 206–7). Many scholars have pointed out that Nietzsche and Strindberg were two of the most important intellectual artistic influences on O'Neill. May's work suggests, by implication, that we might think about the cultural reasons for this influence. Also see Fishbein on Nietzsche in O'Neill: "His plays argue consistently that the worst failure of the capitalist state is its spiritual sterility" (*Rebels in Bohemia*, p. 37).

129. "To the economic interpreter [the nineteenth-century puritan] was pure

exploiter," observed Hoffman, "to the psychoanalytic historian a repressed and harried creature, whose acts had placed the nation under the black pall of a national repression" (*Freudianism*, p. 260). Eric Bentley notes: "It is such an achievement for an American to overcome the official optimism of the country that he tends to think his hard-won pessimism must sound original and daring. In Europe pessimism is taken for granted, and optimism—as when a European writer joins the Communist party—is a 'daring' gesture" ("Touch of the Adolescent," pp. 396–97).

130. Hoffman, *Twenties*, pp. 198–99. In the mid-1920s, writes Freeman, the literary intelligentsia considered it tasteful "to talk about Coolidge's 'silence' as the expression of a 'complex,'" but "it was dull and social-workerish to discuss his agrarian policy" (*American Testament*, p. 459).

131. In Philip Rieff's appraisal, the therapeutic ethos "rebelled" against "moral demand systems," "the compulsion of culture," and "communal purpose," thus bringing about a revolution "more Freudian than Marxist, more analytic than polemic, more cultural than social" (*Triumph of the Therapeutic*, pp. 20, 21, 23).

132. Christopher Caudwell wrote in the 1930s that Freudian psychologists

> never advance beyond the view-point of the "individual in civil society." Whether they study primitive man or lay down general laws of the soul, it is always with ideas formulated from a bourgeois psyche studying other bourgeois psyches, and so the instincts play always the part of splendid and free brutes, crippled by the repressions of a cruel culture. It is true that to-day the system of production relations is crippling man's splendid powers, but Freudian "libido" in bondage to "repression" is a very inadequate myth to convey this reality. It is a pale subjective reflection of the vital objective reflection of the vital objective situation. (*Studies and Further Studies in a Dying Culture*, pp. 188–89)

The assumptions of radical intellectuals were sometimes recast by this psychoanalytic notion of culture. In "A Psycho-Analytic Confession" (1920), published in the pro-socialist *Liberator*, Floyd Dell placed his conscious self, sympathetic to the Russian revolution, in contention with his unruly, middle-class unconscious. "I am not responsible for the vagaries of my Unconscious," he cautions; "it is a wayward thing, always thinking the wrong thoughts." Dell's unconscious judges the Soviet regime to be both too dogmatic and too enamored with the work ethic. His unconscious unashamedly prefers a large house and a million dollars and is summarily reprimanded by Dell for displaying "bourgeois tendencies." His unconscious retorts: "I do not wish to wallow in luxury. I wish only to lead a happy and artistic life" ("Confession," pp. 15, 16). Dell's unconscious is a suburbanized, middle-class depth suspicious of the prohibitions of culture in general. On the issue of Dell's commitment to socialism, see Cargill, *Intellectual America*. Cargill quotes Michael Gold's appraisal of Dell's libidinous, bohemian style of socialism: "At all times he had a distaste for reality, for the strong smells and confusions of the class struggle. He had none of the contacts with workingmen and strikes and battles that John Reed had. He was a Greenwich Village playboy. Even in those days his main interests were centered in the female anatomy" (p. 658). Yet Cargill himself concludes that "so far as Socialism is concerned, [Dell] has repeatedly turned his steps back to his idol. . . . [Socialism] has a sort of insistency in most of his books" (pp. 658–59).

133. Eastman writes: "People of neurotic constitution are just people who have never broken away from the family situation. They are still dominated in all that they do and feel by a repressed love, or a repressed hate, toward mother, or father, or nurse, or sister, or brother—a passion which possessed them when they were little children. What we call a 'nervous' person is a grown-up infant" ("Mr.—er—er—Oh! What's his name?" p. 96). Lasch describes this curious shift in the construct of adulthood: "Instead of seeing the child as an undeveloped adult [e.g., the way colonial Americans viewed children], one now saw the adult as an undeveloped child" (*New Radicalism*, p. 86).

134. Fielding, *Caveman*, pp. xi–xii. Only our "culture and education," observes Eastman, puts restraints on "the instinctive impulses of the savage" ("Exploring," p. 749). In "Mental Healing" (1922), Arthur Legge Jr. figured the unconscious as "zoological gardens, with all the keepers on strike. . . . the only hope for peace for the unfortunate patient is for the Psychoanalyst to open the cages and set their inhabitants free" (quoted in Hoffman, *Freudianism*, pp. 67–68).

135. Morton Peck, "Psychoanalysis and Humankind," p. 127.

136. O'Neill, *Selected Letters*, p. 391. Also see Barton, "You Can't Fool Your Other Self," pp. 11–13, 68. Barton describes the significance of his interview with psychoanalyst A. A. Brill as follows: "The purpose of this interview is to introduce you to this other self of yours. It might well be entitled 'Dr. Jekyll, Meet Mr. Hyde' " (p. 11). Pop psychology simultaneously pathologized and romanticized the Dr. Jekyll self as Mr. Hyde.

137. See Stocking, *Victorian Anthropology*, pp. 186–237, esp. p. 229. Also see Burrow, *Evolution and Society*, p. 276, Houghton, *Victorian Frame of Mind*, pp. 54–58, Kuklick, *The Savage Within*, Kuper, *The Invention of Primitive Society*, and Birken, *Consuming Desire*, esp. pp. 80–81.

138. See Fielding, *Caveman*, pp. 215–16. The postwar period saw the beginnings of industrial psychology, which was institutionalized as personnel department psychology by the late 1920s. In 1920 Dr. E. E. Southard of Harvard suggested that the "emotional tone of the revolutionary [trade unionist] is almost always unpleasant" because he somehow suffers "a state of felt passivity" ("Trade Unionism and Temperament," p. 297). For a discussion of the role played by psychologists in personnel departments in the late 1920s, see Gillespie, "Hawthorne Experiments and the Politics of Experimentation," pp. 11–37. And for a brilliant analysis of modern uses of the discourse of primitivism, see Torgovnick, *Gone Primitive*: "Somewhere at the periphery of Euro-American versions of the primitive lurk class tensions. To eradicate one set of polarities (male/female, higher/lower class, primitive/civilized) is to threaten them all" (p. 167). Also consult Cargill's chapter on "The Primitivists" in *Intellectual America*, pp. 311–98.

139. Although psychoanalysis had been viewed as a contribution to progressive political thought in the 1910s by Dell, Eastman, and others (particularly in the context of agitation for birth control and women's rights), by the 1920s it was often deployed to supplant radical critique. Freudian liberation, observes Freeman, "was becoming the prerogative not of the radical critics who had preached it as the wish-dream of poverty, but of the middle classes who practiced it as the privilege of

wealth." In this climate, bolshevism was allegorized as "a neurotic manifestation of the Oedipus complex" (*American Testament*, pp. 236, 275).

140. Hopkins, *How's Your Second Act?*, p. 25.

141. See O'Neill's letter to Martha Sparrow (October 12, 1929): "I have read only two books of Freud's, 'Totem and Taboo' and 'Beyond the Pleasure Principle.'" Quoted in Nethercot, "Psychoanalyzing of Eugene O'Neill" (Part One), p. 248.

142. See Cargill, *Intellectual America*, p. 703. Cargill derogated *Strange Interlude* as "a dramatized textbook of all the neuroses discoverable by psychoanalysis" (p. 706).

143. Volosinov, *Freudianism*, pp. 90–91.

144. O'Neill, *Selected Letters*, p. 390.

145. Alexander, "Psychological Fate," p. 927; Sheaffer, *Son and Artist*, 371; Thompson, *Anatomy of Drama*, p. 392. Cargill, however, praised the psychoanalytic dimension of *Mourning* and argued "that O'Neill has surpassed the ancient dramatists on the score of motivation and here again [*The Hunted*] he has done it with the aid of Freudian psychology" (*Intellectual America*, p. 714).

146. The "new psychology" expanded Fraina's concept of the scope of revolution: "Psychology will give us a vision of the new humanity" ("Socialism and Psychology," pp. 10–12).

147. They were dubbed the "sex boys" by some members of the Left (a Left that, by the late 1920s, had become principally concerned with criticizing economic contradictions). See Paul Buhle'e entry on *Modern Quarterly/Modern Monthly* in Buhle, Buhle, and Georgakas, eds., *Encyclopedia of the American Left*, pp. 482–83. Calverton and Schmalhausen "continued the 1910s feminist dialogue (virtually abandoned by the rest of the Left afterward) with historical materialism" (p. 482).

148. Calverton, "Sex and the Social Struggle," pp. 282–83.

149. Calverton, *Sex Expression*, p. 308. In somewhat tortured prose, Schmalhausen also suggested that what we now think of as depth may be a sociohistorical aberration of selfhood. "When the bubbling creative energies of men and women will have been for many years dedicated to radically humanistic goals,—the egocentric ferocity of sex desire in competitive and exploitative social systems, in which the vicious anarchic blind impulses to dominance and conspicuous consumption work their evil sovereignty, no longer permitted to function—sex will almost inevitably find its reasonable and dignified place, in the harmoniously socialised scheme of 'things'" ("War of the Sexes," p. 286). Schmalhausen went so far as to argue that the key to the social psychological study of the American capitalist self was not in bringing to light his or her suppressed desires, but in the analysis of the culturally produced narcissistic ego (America was a culture of narcissism that cultivated possessive individualists) ("Psycho-Analysis and Communism," p. 68).

150. Kantorovitch, "Social Background of the New Psychology," p. 45. Schmalhausen added that the "vast . . . wreckage of human nature" wrought by contemporary capitalism made necessary the "newer psychologies" that preached depth and marketed therapies ("Psycho-Analysis and Communism," p. 68). He also wrote: "It is high time that our psychologists and psychiatrists, most particularly our psychologists, stopped being lackeys and lickspittles of the rich, and in scientific and scholarly mood, loving humanity and truth more than competitive show-off and exhibi-

tionistic prestige, devoted their fine minds and marvelous experience to studying the wreckage wrought by our crazy social system" ("Family Life," p. 296). A psychological mystification of the social origins and possibilities of "human nature" was requisite to the survival of the system.

151. Schmalhausen, "War of the Sexes," p. 267. The "biologic plausibility of . . . stereotyped patterns," he asserts, relies on the "sheer illusion of antiquity" ("War of the Sexes," p. 267). Once one grasps that the self is social and historical rather than universal or natural, then it is apparent that this self can be transformed in revolutionary ways: "When the instinct psychologists speak of human nature what they mean can be more accurately described as human institutions, customs, habits, values" ("Psycho-Analysis and Communism," p. 66).

152. The quote is taken from Calverton, *American Literature*, p. 8. Also see Slochower, *Literature and Philosophy between the World Wars*: "What was an 'instinct' of acquisitiveness with Marco Polo becomes neurosis with Nina and Lavinia. What was simple reasoning with him becomes tortured self-analysis" (p. 253).

153. Kovel, *Age of Desire*, pp. 125–26.

154. See Zaretsky, *Capitalism, the Family, and Personal Life*, p. 62.

155. Kovel, *Age of Desire*, p. 128. Kovel also notes that capitalism "creates an awareness of neurosis as it creates an awareness of self generally" (p. 128).

156. Bentley points out that what drew middlebrow audiences to O'Neill's psychological dramas of the 1920s and early 1930s was not "the nihilistic view of life, which did not come home to men's business and bosoms, but merely . . . the rhetoric of psychologism. . . . Much of the talk in scene after scene was close enough to the talk at the cocktail party before the show" ("The Life and Hates of Eugene O'Neill," pp. 46–47). What Bentley terms psychologism, then, had become the jargon of members of the business class who took an interest in culture. F. Scott Fitzgerald's Nick Carraway in *The Great Gatsby* (1925) and William Dean Howell's Basil March in *A Hazard of New Fortunes* (1890) are both urban professionals, but Carraway's (modernist) alienation is encoded as *deep*. I thank Thomas J. Ferraro for suggesting this comparison.

157. I am grateful to Sarah Winter for this formulation.

158. Trilling, "Eugene O'Neill," p. 16. See OS, 1: Louis Sherwin, "Belasco, And the Little Theatres: Signs That the Pocket Playhouses Have Come to Stay." Sherwin writes in the late 1910s: "[The little theatres] are taking nothing away from the Broadway theatres because the public they attract had long ceased to visit the Broadway theatres." These audiences constitute what Trilling calls the "intellectual middle class." Also see OS, 1: Anon., from the *Seattle Post Intelligence*, May 26, 1918: "Of course, the cardinal thing that makes the existence of the Washington Square Players possible is their dauntless courage in giving expression to thoughts that are taboo on the conventional stage."

159. See Ehrenreich's comments in *Fear of Falling* on the difficulty of determining class boundaries, pp. 11–12, 13.

160. Hughes, then a Columbia student, saw *"Anna Christie"* and *The Hairy Ape*. See Rampersad, *I, Too, Sing America*, p. 55.

161. See TGPB, 127: Charles Collins, "Fourteen Episodes of Tragedy Is Critics View of 'Electra,' " *Chicago Daily Tribune*, Feb. 16, 1932. On the Board of Managers'

internecine conflicts see Langner, *Magic Curtain,* p. 160, and Simonson, *Part of a Lifetime,* p. 74.

162. See OS, 2: Anon., "An American Tragedy," *New York Literary Digest,* Feb. 28, 1920, p. 33. Also see OS, 3: Earle Dorsey, "Footlights: O'Neill's Choice of Stage Themes Excites Reaction," *Washington Herald,* Jan. 22, 1922. "Within thirty days," writes Dorsey about *Beyond the Horizon,* "O'Neill was acclaimed as the master dramatist and his strong, blighting potions—concocted of sorrow, misfortune, fear, despair and the inscrutable workings of destiny—were hailed as the supreme ant-acid for the national joy juice." But, he concludes: "The tonic air of the republic calls for neither the cloying saccharinity of Pollyanna nor the god-baited madness of an O'Neill tragedy."

163. See OS, 3. From the *New York World,* Nov. 6, 1921.

164. James O'Neill, quoted in Bentley, "Life and Hates of Eugene O'Neill," p. 33.

165. O'Neill, *"As Ever, Gene,"* p. 64. On Nathan and the emergence of the "professional critic" see John Finnegan's excellent "Foreword" to *"As Ever, Gene,"* pp. 10–11.

166. O'Neill, *Selected Letters,* p. 247.

167. Sheaffer, *Son and Artist,* p. 174. Also see O'Neill's letter on this subject to Marthe Carolyn Sparrow (October 1929), reprinted in Halfmann, *Eugene O'Neill,* pp. 84–85.

168. In his 1927 letter to Krutch, he wrote that he was intrigued by the "Behavioristic" theories and is "sort of half in one camp and half in the other." As I noted in Chapter 1, his 1943 letter to James T. Farrell made a distinction between the power of Irish psychological insights (in reference to James Joyce's *Ulysses*) and the insights of psychoanalysis. See O'Neill, *Selected Letters,* pp. 247, 545.

169. Bentley quotes from an interview in which Malcolm Cowley recounted that O'Neill praised Wilhelm Stekel's *Disguises of Love* for containing "enough case histories . . . to furnish plots to all the playwrights who ever lived." Bentley's argument about *Strange Interlude* and O'Neill's other psychological plays is that "case histories spin the plot" ("Life and Hates of Eugene O'Neill," p. 40). O'Neill enrolled in George Pierce Baker's workshop at Harvard in 1914–15 and later supported the founding of Baker's Yale School of Drama in the 1920s. Thus O'Neill participated in the academic professionalization of the dramatist (even as his troubled family life and adventures at sea provided him with another set of antiprofessional credentials). His competitive stance in relation to the increasing professionalization of psychological knowledge is in fact characteristic of the professional, as described by historian Burton J. Bledstein: "The professional person absolutely protected his precious autonomy against all assailants, not in the name of an irrational egotism but in the name of a special grasp of the universe and a special place in it" (*Culture of Professionalism,* p. 92). On the nineteenth-century origins of professionalism, also see Robert Wiebe's chapter "A New Middle Class," in *Search for Order* (pp. 111–32). Also consult Magali Sarfatti Larson's brilliant *Rise of Professionalism,* especially the chapter entitled "The Rise of Corporate Capitalism and the Consolidation of Professionalism," pp. 135–58.

170. See TGPB, 80: Krutch, "A Modern Heroic Drama," *New York Herald Tribune,* March 11, 1928, section 12, pp. 1–2 and Krutch, "Is 'Strange Interlude' America's Greatest Play?" *Jewish Daily Forward,* 1928. Also see Atkinson's review of *Mourn-*

ing, in which he commended O'Neill for lifting "his tragedy out of the miasma of petty emotions to the imperial plane of inevitable things" (TGPB, 125: "Tragedy Becomes O'Neill," *New York Times*, Nov. 1, 1931, VIII 1, p. 1).

171. O'Neill, *Eugene O'Neill at Work*, p. 214.

172. In his "Memoranda on Masks" O'Neill partly describes the modern psychological drama of the "inner man" in "age-old" spiritual language: "a drama of souls" (*Unknown O'Neill*, p. 406).

173. Commins, *O'Neill-Commins Correspondence*, p. 136.

174. On the conversion motif, see Lee, "Evangelism and Anarchy in *The Iceman Cometh*."

175. Bisch, *Be Glad You're Neurotic*, pp. ix, 4, 41.

176. Seabury, *Unmasking*, p. xvi.

177. Oppenheim, *Behind Your Front*, p. v.

178. Schneider, "The Iceman Cometh," p. 29.

179. O'Neill, "Theatre We Worked For," p. 257.

180. The words are Virginia Floyd's, who did a masterful job of editing O'Neill, *Eugene O'Neill at Work*, p. 268.

181. Harold Bloom notes that "Hickey is slain between right and right" ("Introduction," pp. 5–6): it is "right" to unmask, and it is "right" to appreciate that denial can be life-sustaining. Both unmasking and denial can be simultaneously therapeutic and destructive.

182. O'Neill, "Theatre We Worked For," p. 257.

183. Quoted in White, *Uses of Obscurity*, p. 62.

184. In 1929 Krutch criticized "the new psychology" because "its penetrating analysis of the influence of desire upon belief" has threatened "beneficent delusion and serves to hold the mind in a steady contemplation of that from which it would fain escape" (*Modern Temper*, p. 19).

185. O'Neill, *Eugene O'Neill at Work*, p. 268.

186. Quoted in Croswell Bowen, "The Black Irishman," in O'Neill, *Conversations*, p. 222.

187. Arthur Miller, "On Social Plays," in *Theatre Essays*, p. 62.

188. See TGPB, 217: John Mason Brown, "Seeing Things: All O'Neilling," *Saturday Review of Literature*, Nov. 19, 1946, pp. 26–29. "O'Neill's characters," Brown writes in his review of *Iceman*, "have almost always dared to look beyond their relations with their neighbors and sought to find their place in the universe" (p. 26).

189. Brecht, *Brecht on Theatre*, p. 101.

190. O'Hara, *Today in American Drama*, p. 24.

191. When *Strange Interlude*, O'Neill's smash hit of 1928, was revived in 1963 by the Actors' Studio, one critic charged, "It should have been left with the historians" (Shannon, *American Irish*, p. 268). This was after O'Neill's reputation as America's greatest playwright had been firmly reestablished by José Quintero's late-1950s productions of *Long Day's Journey* and *Iceman*, and by Sidney Lumet's 1962 all-star film of *Long Day's Journey*. The 1963 production did receive some excellent reviews. Frederick C. Wilkins, a discriminating O'Neill scholar, wrote an enthusiastic review of the 1985 British revival of *Strange Interlude* (produced in New York City), starring Glenda Jackson as Nina.

192. W. K. Wimsatt's provocative (but mainly ahistorical) effort to describe the representation of a "concrete universal" which can make literature seem "individual"—and great (for Wimsatt)—at one point turns to Shakespeare's portrait of Falstaff as a "rounded character" who possesses not just a "bigger bundle of attributes" than some other characters but a "crowning complexity of self-consciousness" (pp. 78–79). It might be argued that some of O'Neill's characters in *Iceman* and the four Tyrones in *Long Day's Journey* are the result of years of practice in crafting a psychological realism that gives us an understanding of the "universal" (the "human") through the "concrete" details of character. But such an argument would run the risk of ignoring the fact that O'Neill's sense of what constitutes psychological realism was founded on historically and ideologically specific notions of the universal, of the human, and of "complexity of self-consciousness."

193. Schneider, "Iceman Cometh," p. 29.

194. Krutch's *Modern Temper* (1929) represents Russian communists as "primitives" who are too uncivilized to require culture to make despair seem meaningful (they refuse "even in [their] art to concern [themselves] with the psychology of the human soul") (p. 249). Because they regard human ills as primarily "social in character," Russian communists forget that the "more fundamental maladjustments . . . subsist, not between men and society, but between the human spirit and the natural universe" (p. 242). Hence the key problem for them is not the use of culture to create illusions (O'Neill's pipe dreams) that will help make the civilized consciousness of "despair" seem "meaningful" (or deep), but rather the more mundane ("primitive") problem of the equal distribution of wealth. Their belief in this social program, he concludes, is both their strength and their naiveté.

Chapter 3

1. O'Neill, *Selected Letters*, p. 73.
2. Gelb and Gelb, *O'Neill*, p. 120. Latimer is quoted in Clark, *Eugene O'Neill*, p. 25.
3. Sheaffer, *Son and Playwright*, p. 239.
4. O'Neill, *Poems*, p. 48.
5. Ibid., p. 46.
6. See ibid., pp. 13, 31.
7. Gelb and Gelb, *O'Neill*, p. 276.
8. Sheaffer, *Son and Playwright*, p. 344. Robert K. Sarlós describes the Players: "United by their disenchantment, and nourished by such diverse sources as Plato's *Republic* and Thoreau's 'Civil Disobedience,' the ideas of Marx and Veblen, Freud and Nietzsche, Maria Montessori and the communitarian movement—this intensely creative group moved toward a communal writing and staging of plays" ("Jig Cook and Susan Glaspell," p. 251).
9. Waterman writes of the Players: "The members all claimed to be Socialists, but not to the extent that they relinquished their faith in democracy" (*Susan Glaspell*, p. 53). But also see Sarlós's "Jig Cook and Susan Glaspell," for a more specific profile: "Not all members of the group were either conscious political leftists or dedicated artistic and social iconoclasts. . . . alongside those who embodied rebellion in all aspects of creative and private life were others who worked, lived, and raised their

children in harmony with values of Main Street America" (p. 251). Yet radical ideas were indisputably "in the air" on Macdougal Street in the 1910s. Emily Hahn captures some of the bohemian spirit of Greenwich Village in the 1910s and 1920s in *Romantic Rebels*, pp. 231–60.

10. For background on Socialist intellectuals in the mid-1910s and for a (much needed) positive reassessment of the radicalism of *The Masses*, see Eugene E. Leach, "Radicals of *The Masses*."

11. See Folsom, "Education of Michael Gold." Gold, in fact, did a brief stint at Harvard.

12. For background on the founding of the Provincetown group, see Deutsch and Hanau, *Provincetown*, pp. vii, 8, 16, 29–31. On the Paterson silk workers' pageant see Cosgrove, "From Shock Troupe to Group Theatre," p. 265.

13. Sheaffer, *Son and Playwright*, p. 407.

14. Bentley, "Life and Hates of Eugene O'Neill," p. 35.

15. Sheaffer, *Son and Playwright*, pp.167–68.

16. O'Neill, *Poems*, p. 1.

17. Ibid., p. 37. Alexander points out in her acute critique of O'Neill's ballad and his other statements on the subject that the poet "assumes that poor food and overwork are not sufficient to dim the sailor's love for his work, whereas the over-concern for his own physical needs is" ("Social Critic," p. 393).

18. O'Neill, *Conversations*, p. 10.

19. Edmund Wilson, "Case of an Author," in *American Jitters*, p. 307.

20. O'Neill, *Conversations*, p. 53.

21. Gelb and Gelb, *O'Neill*, p. 147.

22. Sheaffer, *Son and Playwright*, p. 279.

23. See Von Wiegand, "Quest of Eugene O'Neill," p. 12. Sheaffer's own accent on crude, flavorsome sailor talk makes his praise read like a travel ad.

24. See OS, 1: M. C. D., "Drama: Little Plays and Little Theatres," *The Nation* (June 22, 1918). O'Neill's seafaring dramas were also taken as "adventure," and, implicitly, as proof of the playwright's masculinity. See OS, 1: Anon., "Plays of the Sea: Five Short Tragedies by Eugene O'Neill," *Brooklyn Eagle* (June 13, 1919).

25. O'Neill's *Glencairn* plays were generally categorized by critics as "American," not as radical. See OS, 2: St. John Ervine, "Literary Taste in America," *The New Republic* (Oct. 6, 1920): 147.

26. Gold, *Strike!*, p. 19.

27. In the spring of 1931 Odets began the draft of a play originally titled "The Melancholic Gorillas," a script that—as Margaret Brenman-Gibson notes—"echoes O'Neill's *The Hairy Ape*" in its preoccupation with "the romantic artist's despair that he does not belong in the world" (*Clifford Odets*, p. 186).

28. Von Wiegand, "Quest of Eugene O'Neill," p. 12.

29. Ranald, *Eugene O'Neill Companion*, pp. 724–25.

30. I thank Arthur ("Trace") Smith for his superb, untitled essay on *The Hairy Ape*, written for my advanced seminar, "The Cultural Production of the Psychological Self: Eugene O'Neill."

31. O'Neill, *Selected Letters*, p. 161.

32. Ibid., p. 522.

33. Hopkins, *Reference Point*, p. 47.

34. Again I draw on the words of "Trace" Smith's seminar essay.

35. See OS, 5: Stephen Rathburn, "Eugene O'Neill's 'Hairy Ape' Is One of the Most Vital Plays of the Season," *New York American*, April 20, 1922. After noting that O'Neill does not seem to subscribe to the worldview of the Fifth Avenue marionettes, the Socialist, or members of the IWW, he asks: "wither . . . is the *Hairy Ape* tending? . . . Evidently Mr. O'Neill lacks faith in the power of association for the purpose of alleviating human conditions and solving seemingly insoluble problems of life." For an extremely sophisticated reading of *The Hairy Ape* that broaches other issues pertaining to class, acting sytles, and autobiography, see Julia Walker's "Character, Commodity Fetishism, and the Origins of Expressionism on the American Stage," her Duke University Ph.D. dissertation-in-progress.

36. In 1933 Hughes wrote to O'Neill and other authors to enlist their help in raising funds for the legal defense of the Scottsboro Boys. In his letter to O'Neill, Hughes praised "the beauty you had given [blacks] in your writing" (quoted in Rampersad, *I, Too, Sing America*, p. 283). When *All God's Chillun* came under fire by black critics for promoting rather than retarding racism and fears surrounding intermarriage, Du Bois defended O'Neill for "bursting through" prejudice (quoted in Duberman, *Paul Robeson*, pp. 65–66). He came to the playwright's defense after O'Neill wrote in praise of Du Bois as a writer and a leader, a testimony read aloud at a dinner in honor of Du Bois in April 1924 in New York City (reprinted in Halfmann, *Eugene O'Neill*, p. 33).

37. Gregory, "Drama of Negro Life," p. 157.

38. An anonymous critic for *The Messenger* complained that " 'Emperor Jones' " is thought to be the "most desirable vehicle for presenting the Negro to the white world," and that "Broadway will not countenance [seeing] the Negro [in] a serious, dignified, classical drama" ("Who's Who," p. 394). More recently, John R. Cooley suggested that *The Emperor Jones* be considered not as serious but as "mock-serious" (*Savages and Naturals*, p. 69).

39. James Weldon Johnson, *Black Manhattan*, p. 184. After criticizing *All God's Chillun* for pulling back from a critique of racism, Johnson noted: "The play ran for several weeks, and Paul Robeson increased his reputation by the restraint, sincerity, and dignity with which he acted a difficult role" (p. 196).

40. Fauset, "Gift of Laughter," pp. 167, 165.

41. Locke, "New Negro," p. 3.

42. Regarding *Opportunity*, see Lewis, *When Harlem Was in Vogue*, p. 113. On the *Crisis* competition see Johnson and Johnson, *Propaganda and Aesthetics*, p. 44. O'Neill wrote a very warm and gracious letter to W. E. B. Du Bois on September 24, 1924, thanking him for inviting him to judge the *Crisis* playwrights and regretting that their paths had not yet crossed (Du Bois, *Correspondence of W. E. B. Du Bois*, pp. 294–95).

43. Lewis, *When Harlem Was in Vogue*, p. 115.

44. The sailor keeps to himself, chanting a "negro" (1:31) song to keep the sharks at bay. His (perhaps symbolic) "impediment of speech" (1:31) may have something to do with the impediment posed by the only people with whom he can converse.

45. Sheaffer, *Son and Artist*, p. 140.

46. Ibid., p. 135. O'Neill also said: "There is prejudice against the intermarriage of whites and blacks, but what has that got to do with my play? I am never the advocate of anything in any play" (quoted in Duberman, *Paul Robeson*, p. 58). An anonymous critic writing for *The Crisis* praised Charles Gilpin's performance in *The Emperor Jones* in similar terms: "[He] has transcended race and country. His playing in 'The Emperor Jones' is a universal appeal" ("Men of the Month," p. 172).

47. Gelb and Gelb, *O'Neill*, p. 886. Paul Robeson very much agreed with O'Neill's self-appraisal. His published comments about O'Neill radiate with the warmth of a friendship that was well established in the mid-1920s. Writing for the *Daily World* in 1974, Robeson referred to "Gene O'Neill" as one of his "dear [Provincetown Players] friends," and praised the playwright's "belief in the 'Oneness of Mankind' " (*Paul Robeson Speaks*, pp. 482, 483). Robeson starred in *The Emperor Jones* not only in the 1920s, but *after* his political and intellectual endorsement of socialism as a political cause in the 1930s. Defending *All God's Chillun Got Wings* in 1924, he depicted O'Neill as "a broad, liberal-minded man" who "has had Negro friends and appreciated them for their true worth" (*Paul Robeson Speaks*, p. 71).

48. O'Neill, *Selected Letters*, p. 500. Paul Robeson, however, starred in a London production of *The Hairy Ape* in May 1931. Perhaps O'Neill found this particular "white" working-class role suitable for a black actor (with a law degree from Columbia and a Phi Beta Kappa key from Rutgers). A London reviewer protested: "One cannot help thinking that here is something which has to do with racial consciousness and the oppression of the negro" (quoted in Duberman, *Paul Robeson*, pp. 148–49).

49. Hazel Carby is right to insist that one must recognize "whiteness, not just blackness, as a racial categorization" (*Reconstructing Womanhood*, p. 18). It would have been interesting to see how an all-black cast would have handled, and ironized, Seth's frustrations with the "nigger cook's" independent ways: "That's what we get for freein' 'em!" (2:897). I am grateful to Keather Kehoe for introducing me to the term "whiteface."

50. See Roediger, *Wages of Whiteness*, p. 18. Also see Lott, "Love and Theft," p. 27. In his celebration of Du Bois, written in April 1924, O'Neill portrayed himself "as one whose own ancestors struggled against intolerance and prejudice" (reprinted in Halfmann, *Eugene O'Neill*, p. 33). Ridgely Torrence's *Three Plays for a Negro Theatre* was received with great acclaim in April 1917. An article in *The Crisis* quotes Torrence's views on why blacks are so dramatic (interestingly, his explanation seems to be both historical and biological) and why the black "race" is like the Irish "race":

It is life under slavery, with its intense but seemingly hopeless longings for liberty, that produced in it a certain epic spirit. . . . In modern life, the Negro comes face to face with many tragedies, unknown to the Anglo-Saxon. And then, of course, his natural buoyancy of disposition produces a wealth of comedy which all the world has now learned to love. The parallel of all this with the Irish race and its national drama, made a deep impression on me. I wanted to make the experiment, and try to contribute something, if I could, to a possible Negro drama, as vital and as charming as the Irish. ("New Negro Theatre," p. 80)

I thank my student Adam Hirsch for bringing part of this quote to my notice.

51. Roediger, *Wages of Whiteness*, pp. 88–90.

52. See Lawrence W. Levine, *Black Culture and Black Consciousness*, pp. 301–4. I thank Ashraf Rushdy for reminding me of Levine's discussion of black humor. On stereotypes of the Irish as blunderers, also see Knobel, *Paddy and the Republic*, p. 91.

53. Knobel, *Paddy and the Republic*, pp. 88–90.

54. See Keller, *Art and Politics of Thomas Nast*. I appreciate Jean-Christophe Agnew's suggestion that I look at this work.

55. See Barkan, *Retreat of Scientific Racism*, pp. 199–200.

56. For a discussion of the Houston riots see Lewis, *When Harlem Was in Vogue*, pp. 9–10. Jacqueline Jones's superb *Labor of Love, Labor of Sorrow* recounts the pressures on southern black families who sought their "dream" in the North in the early decades of this century (pp. 152–95).

57. Du Bois wrote: "We return fighting" (Lewis, *When Harlem Was in Vogue*, p. 15). Black leaders were furious at the War Department's segregation of blacks who trained to be officers and felt that their preparation would be below the standard of that given to whites (ibid., p. 9). In *Scribner's* magazine in 1899, Theodore Roosevelt maintained that the "racial weakness" of blacks would prevent them from taking command as officers (Gates, "Trope of a New Negro," p. 138).

58. Lewis, *When Harlem Was in Vogue*, p. 3. Also see Huggins, *Harlem Renaissance*, p. 55.

59. *The Crisis* estimated that "77 Negroes were lynched during the year 1919, of whom 1 was a colored woman and 11 were soldiers" ("Lynching Industry, 1919," p. 183). On the high incidence of lynching of blacks in the late nineteenth and early twentieth centuries, see Slotkin, "Apotheosis of the Lynching," pp. 1–2.

60. These two cartoons appeared in the context of an article written by the "Editors" of *The Messenger* entitled, "The Cause of and Remedy for Race Riots." In addition to citing the history of slavery, and economic, class, and political inequality as causes, the editors also discussed racial prejudices promulgated and reinforced by "stage and screen" (p. 21). Gates, "Trope of a New Negro," pp. 147–48.

61. Domingo, "New Negro," p. 145.

62. See James Weldon Johnson, *Black Manhattan*, p. 249.

63. Ibid., p. 256 (comparison between Garvey and Jones), pp. 254–55 (on Garvey). A. Philip Randolph discusses whites who derogated Garvey as "the Negro King" ("Garveyism," p. 251).

64. See Martin, *Literary Garveyism*, pp. 117–18. In 1938 Robeson characterized the 1933 film as a "failure" because it deviated so much from O'Neill's script and downplayed the dramatic build-up provided by drums in the theatre (*Paul Robeson Speaks*, p. 122).

65. See Huggins, *Harlem Renaissance*, pp. 264, 267. Cooley relates the name Brutus to Brute (*Savages and Naturals*, p. 69). In *Crisis*, Jessie Fauset defended Charles Gilpin's performance in (not the script of) *The Emperor Jones*: "Many theatre goers . . . could not distinguish between the artistic interpretation of a type and the deliberate travestying of a race, and so their appreciation was clouded" (quoted in Martin, *Literary Garveyism*, p. 117).

66. Dennison, *Scandalize My Name*, pp. 357, 358, 360, 363.

67. Barnes, "Negro Art and America," pp. 19, 20; Rogers, quoted in Dyer, *Heavenly Bodies*, pp. 74–75.

68. Huggins, *Harlem Renaissance*, p. 91. In *Masks and Demons* (1923), Kenneth Macgowan and Herman Rosse link the mask with a therapeutic release of "primitive" impulses that they associate with blackness: "The end of the mask is Drama. When a man puts on a mask he experiences a kind of release from his inhibited and bashful and circumscribed soul. He can say and do strange and terrible things and he likes it. When Al Jolson puts on black-face he becomes a demoniac creature, privileged in his humor, insensate in his vitality; without the burnt cork, something of his possession is gone" (p. xii).

69. Huggins, *Harlem Renaissance*, p. 254. This is Huggins's description of the ambivalent white response—fascination and dread—to "blackface" minstrels. Along these lines see Phyllis Rose's illuminating remarks about racism, racialism, primitivism, and exoticism in the context of the 1920s, in her biography of Josephine Baker, *Jazz Cleopatra*, pp. 36, 43–45.

70. See Samelson, "From Race Psychology to Studies in Prejudice," esp. pp. 265–68.

71. See four reviews contained in OS, 4: Anon., "No Color Line in Art," *Philadelphia Inquirer*, Nov. 24, 1921; Anon., " 'The Emperor Jones' At Parson's Tomorrow: Eugene G. O'Neill's Play Dealing with Negro Psychology and Interpreted by Charles S. Gilpin, Colored Actor, will open Three Day's Engagement" (the reviewer calls it a "weird play of negro psychology"); Anon., "First Night," *Washington Post*, Dec. 18, 1921; and Hubert H. Harrison, "With the Contributing Editor," May 26, 1921.

72. *The Crisis* quotes in *praise* Kenneth Macgowan's New York *Globe* review of the play: "Such a cry of the primitive being as I have never seen in the theatre" ("Men of the Month," p. 172).

73. In *The Crisis* of February 1924, Raymond O'Neil compared "the Russian's sensuous acceptance of life" to the black's "robust, passionate, sensuous" nature, and contrasted both with the Anglo-Saxon American's "paralyzing and extirpation of his sensuous nature and emotions." He argued that this is why black actors must "guard" against the "Americanization" of their creativity ("Negro in Dramatic Art," pp. 155–57). After seeing Robeson perform in 1924, George Jean Nathan generalized, "The Negro is a born actor, where the white man achieves acting." Nathan's "professional" (his term) appraisal is that Robeson's "thoroughly eloquent, impressive, and consuming" acting is more an expression of his inner racial nature than an intellectual or artistic achievement (quoted in Hoyt, *Paul Robeson*, p. 46). Perhaps with Robeson in mind, Joseph Wood Krutch also commended the black actor's "instinctive sense for participation in an emotion larger than his comprehension" (quoted in Duberman, *Paul Robeson*, p. 65). In 1935 Robeson wrote, "To the African, dancing, singing and acting are not separate and divorced from life as they are among Western people." "This," he added, "gives his stage performance a naturalness and ease comparable with that of the Russian, and, when disciplined, gives his playing a power extremely moving to those used to the artificiality of the West" (*Paul Robeson Speaks*, p. 98). For a smart analysis of black female blues singers of the 1920s and "how mass production mass-produced the black female as sexual subject"

through the discourse of primitivism (which was aligned with psychoanalysis), see du Cille, "Blues Notes on Black Sexuality," pp. 426–29.

74. From Hughes's *The Big Sea* (1940), quoted in Cooley, *Savages and Naturals*, p. 70.

75. James Weldon Johnson, *Black Manhattan*, pp. 182–83.

76. Quoted in Lewis, *When Harlem Was in Vogue*, p. 92.

77. Gilpin said of O'Neill and the play: "Mr. O. made a breach in those walls [of discrimination against blacks in the theatre] by writing a play that had in it a serious role for a Negro. . . . But what next? If I were a white, a dozen opportunities would come to me as a result of a success like this. But I'm black" (quoted in Gelb and Gelb, *O'Neill*, p. 448).

78. Quoted in ibid., p. 449. In the mid-1920s Robeson regarded *The Emperor Jones* as one of *"the* great plays," and viewed the drama in universal terms: "Jones's emotions are not primarily Negro, but human." He remained loyal to O'Neill in his public statements. But in 1939, when he was scheduled to revive the play in White Plains, New York, he told an interviewer that he would expurgate demeaning racial epithets or refuse to "play in it" (*Paul Robeson Speaks*, pp. 70, 128).

79. O'Neill, *Selected Letters*, pp. 177, 409.

80. McKay had worked as a porter, a longshoreman, and a railroad waiter. He wrote, possibly with O'Neill as well as other white writers in mind: "When I came to write about the low-down Negro, I did not have to compose him from an outside view. Nor did I have to write a pseudoromantic account, as do bourgeois persons who become working-class for a while and work in shops and factories, whose inner lives are closed to them" (quoted in Fishbein, *Rebels in Bohemia*, p. 191).

81. McKay, "Black Star," p. 25. In 1970 Woodie King and Ron Milner tried to describe a black theatre that would not be what McKay terms "a mere comic grotesque," and added: "[Broadway] is a contented fat white cow. If you can slip in and milk her for a minute—well, then, more power to you, black brother. But . . . it's a weird price she's asking" ("Evolution of a People's Theatre," pp. viii–x). Gilpin (McKay's "black star") may have paid that "weird price."

82. Stebbins, "Hollywood's Imitation of Life," pp. 22, 10.

83. Von Wiegand, "Quest of Eugene O'Neill," p. 15. O'Neill's gold prospecting trip to Honduras in 1909 left him with the impression that "the natives are the lowest ignorant bunch of brainless bipeds that ever polluted a land and retarded its future" (*Selected Letters*, pp. 19–20).

84. Stebbins, "Hollywood's Imitation of Life," p. 23.

85. In *The Messenger*, Rogers praised O'Neill for "chasing the [interracial marriage] question into the open," but he muted his sharper critique: "The play itself . . . takes one into an almost unreal atmosphere, stressing certain racial reactions rather than depicting the general truth, at least as the writer knows it" ("Critical Excursions and Reflections," p. 116). Also see James Weldon Johnson's discussion of *All God's Chillun* in *Black Manhattan*. A. B. Budd, writing for the *Afro-American*, considered the play unbelievable: "To see a big, respectable and cultured character as the slave of a slim, depraved and silly white woman isn't the kind of enjoyment calculated to make up a good evening's entertainment" (quoted in Gilliam, *Paul Robeson: All-American*, p. 38). William Pickens, of the NAACP, averred that "the Ku

Klux [Klan] would pay to have such a play as this put on" (quoted in Duberman, *Paul Robeson*, p. 65).

86. Lott, "Love and Theft," p. 27.

87. Dawley, *Struggles for Justice*, p. 234.

88. It is likely that most corporate and government leaders were not put at ease when the railroad union came out for the Plumb Plan, which advocated government ownership of railroads in part managed by workers, or when the miners sought the nationalization of mines.

89. On the "red scare" see Dawley, *Struggle for Justice*, pp. 218–53, and Allen, *Only Yesterday*, pp. 45–75.

90. From Palmer's "The Case Against the Reds" (1920), excerpted in Baritz, *Culture of the Twenties*, pp. 76, 78. For an extreme example of hysteria about what red revolution would do to the American family and gender roles, see Saloman, *Red War on the Family*.

91. Indeed, *The Hairy Ape* was reviewed (as a play showing the political "awakening" of Yank) in the same issue of the Socialist daily, the *New York Call*, that printed a scathing critique of Palmer and his raids. See Anon., "The Plays That Pass— O'Neill's 'The Hairy Ape' a Powerful Tragedy of Today," *New York Call*, March 12, 1922, p. 4, and Lawrence Todd, "Palmer 'Red Raids' Lawless, Senate Probers Declare," *New York Call*, March 12, 1922, p. 1.

92. Allen, *Only Yesterday*, p. 61.

93. Freeman, *American Testament*, p. 255.

94. Allen, *Only Yesterday*, p. 227.

95. "Where Are the Pre-War Radicals?" pp. 565, 564, 563.

96. O'Neill is quoted in Sheaffer, *Son and Playwright*, p. 463.

97. Sheaffer, *Son and Artist*, p. 603.

98. Monterrey is quoted in O'Neill, *Conversations*, p. 220. O'Neill's 1930s and 1940s media image as the well-dressed "professional" playwright no doubt had something to do with Carlotta Monterrey, whom he wedded in 1929. She made the aristocratic Deborah Harford in *More Stately Mansions* (1939) seem unpretentious by comparison. Monterrey was anti-Semitic (as O'Neill also could be in some letters), detested Franklin Roosevelt as an American Stalin, and was dubbed a Tory by Eugene Jr. On Monterrey's anti-Semitism see Commins, *O'Neill-Commins Correspondence*, p. 69, and O'Neill, *"Theatre We Worked For,"* pp. 196–97. On O'Neill's anti-Semitic remarks, see O'Neill, *"Theatre We Worked For,"* pp. 110, 148. For Monterrey as Tory and her remarks about FDR as Stalin, see Sheaffer, *Son and Artist*, pp. 561–62. As my argument unfolds in this chapter it will be clear how thoroughly I disagree with Monterrey's narrow notion of the scope of politics. My own approach to all of O'Neill's plays is closer to Clifford Odets's premise that every play is "propaganda for one thing or another. . . . Every artist is a partisan" ("All Drama Is Propaganda," pp. 13–14). Or as the theoretician Augusto Boal put it more recently: "All theater is necessarily political, because all the activities of man are political and theater is one of them" (*Theatre of the Oppressed*, p. ix). Also see Gardener, "Theatre," p. 28. "Work in the theatre may be art or it may not be. Whether or not it is art, it is bound to contain its element of propaganda." Brecht wrote in 1947: "Nobody can stand above the warring classes for nobody can stand above the human

race. Society cannot share a common communication system so long as it is split into warring classes. Thus for art to be 'unpolitical' means only to ally itself with the 'ruling' group" (*Brecht on Theatre*, p. 196).

99. Bowen, "Black Irishman," in O'Neill, *Conversations*, p. 222.

100. Jordan Y. Miller's *Playwright's Progress: O'Neill and the Critics* is an important resource for O'Neill scholars. It reprints reviews of O'Neill's plays from the early Provincetown productions to the 1960s. None of the leftist reviews and articles I will be discussing in this chapter was reprinted in Miller's collection. Miller's *Eugene O'Neill and the American Critic*, an indispensable checklist of reviews, articles, and books about O'Neill, indicates that Miller was indeed aware of much of this leftist criticism. Still, Miller did not cite a number of important reviews and articles published in the *Socialist Call*, the *Daily Worker*, and *New Theatre*. His checklist omits reference to commentaries by V. F. Calverton, Francis Wattles, Michael Blankfort, and John Howard Lawson. Ulrich Halfmann's *Eugene O'Neill* and John H. Houchin's *Critical Response to Eugene O'Neill* also reprint many significant reviews and articles, but these books, like Miller's, do not adequately represent the views of critics on the Left, especially those critics writing in the 1930s.

101. Scholars interested in this field are fortunate to have Zaretsky's brief but brilliant overview, *Capitalism, the Family, and Personal Life*.

102. See ibid., pp. 64–68, and Stoehr, ed., *Free Love in America*.

103. In their vociferous "social purity" campaign against prostitution, for example, mainstream Socialists easily imagined "woman as the [economic] victim of capitalist degradation," but they could not entertain the notion of woman as an active, sexually independent "subject in her own right" (Mari Jo Buhle, *Women and American Socialism*, p. 254).

104. Ibid., p. 257. Buhle adds: "The claim for Socialism as a stage of civilization rather than a mere economic arrangement increasingly lacked conviction" (p. 284).

105. Ibid., pp. 268, 272.

106. "How the revolution in mass culture, especially in heterosexual relations, might produce the right constituency and setting for the final assault upon capitalism—no one would hazard a guess so literal and direct as the socialist congressional majority or a workers' factory council" (ibid., p. 267).

107. Zaretsky, *Capitalism, the Family, and Personal Life*, pp. 95–96, 91.

108. Important exceptions to this trend were the wide-ranging political critiques of personal life written by Schmalhausen, Calverton, and contributors to their *Modern Quarterly* and their many anthologies.

109. Freeman, *American Testament*, p. 267. The themes of *Welded* and *Strange Interlude* bear out Zaretsky's contention, that "sex was 'liberated' (i.e., it became a commodity, an ideology, and a form of 'leisure'), but men and women were not" (*Capitalism, the Family, and Personal Life*, pp. 93, 94).

110. Berger et al., *Ways of Seeing*, p. 154. Also see Stuart Ewen's chapter "Mobilizing the Instincts" in *Captains of Consciousness*, pp. 31–39.

111. Zaretsky, *Capitalism, the Family, and Personal Life*, p. 82.

112. O'Neill, *Conversations*, p. 61. A few months after the premiere of *The Hairy Ape*, the pages of *The Liberator* reported the bloody battle between the Southern Illinois Coal Company and striking workers. "On June 21st," writes Freeman, "a

group of unarmed strikers approached the mine; they wanted to persuade the operators and the strikebreakers to abandon the work. . . . The superintendent and the gunman opened fire. Two strikers were killed. Early next morning hundreds of [armed] miners from all over the country marched on the mine. . . . Nineteen scabs and three strikers were killed" (*American Testament*, p. 245).

113. See Paul Buhle, *Marxism in the United States*, pp. 115–16. Also see Lasch, *American Liberals and the Russian Revolution*.

114. Quoted in Aaron, *Writers on the Left*, pp. 410–11.

115. Gold (who became a key editor of the *New Masses*) and his colleagues, observes Aaron, "refused to tolerate the personal or ideological vagaries of the pioneers who had prepared the way for a sterner faith" (ibid., p. 217). The split between Gold and Dell can be found in the pages of *The Liberator*. See Eastman's introductory editorial in *The Liberator*, in which he enunciates a comprehensive notion of revolution. *Class*: "It will fight in the struggle of labor. It will fight for the ownership and control of industry by the workers, and will present vivid and accurate news of the labor and socialist movements in all parts of the world." *Gender*: "It will stand for the complete independence of women—political, social and economic—as an enrichment of the existence of mankind." *Antiracist*: "It will assert the social and political equality of the black and white races, oppose every kind of racial discrimination, and conduct a remorseless publicity campaign against lynch law." *Sexual Emancipation*: "It will oppose laws preventing the spread of scientific knowledge and birth control" (Editorial, p. 3). But also see Cosgrove, "From Shock Troupe to Group Theatre": "In the early 1920's the links between workers and intellectuals were a strange mix of anarchists, socialists, syndicalists and romantic idealists, and were generally unclear about their commitment to the working class. With the emergence of a Marxist vanguard within 'Greenwich Village intellectual-ism,' the interaction between worker and intellectual became more clear and productive" (p. 265).

116. Gold, "Defense of Agitprop," p. 5.

117. Zaretsky, *Capitalism, the Family, and Personal Life*, p. 91. Calverton, who was excoriated on numerous grounds by the editors of the *New Masses* in 1933, endeavored—as we have seen—to integrate his radical critiques of the social and the psychological in his books and essays from the early 1920s to his death in 1940. See Buhle, Buhle, and Georgakas, *Encyclopedia of the American Left*. Paul Buhle's entry on Calverton notes: "He could not accept the discipline of the Communist Party—which would have meant the loss of his editorial freedom, if not the journal [*Modern Quarterly*] itself—and he could find no other movement more appropriate for his project. . . . By the Depression, Calverton's envisioned 'revolutionary cultural-ism' had already lost ground to neo-traditional Marxist economism" (p. 483). It would be a distortion, however, to suggest that the sectarian Left had wholly neglected the personal. Freeman, for instance, who led the *New Masses* assault on Calverton, was similar to Calverton and Dell in his efforts to politicize his reading of the personal, and he maintained a self-consciously ambivalent interest in psychoanalysis throughout the 1920s and 1930s (an interest originally sparked by Dell). Also see Paul Buhle, *Marxism in the United States*: "Greenwich Village, *The Masses*, Jack Reed and the Ashcan School had all brought hope because they seemed effec-

tively to bridge the gap between intellectual and industrial life. The contact had been brief and unsustained. A terrible price would be paid for the loss, which by this time epitomized the dilemma of American radicalism" (p. 117).

118. In the 1960s, with the establishment of the New Left, the Women's Liberation movement, and the cultural studies movement in Britain, the personal was again recognized as a necessary political and cultural object of study. Perhaps no one has expressed the political importance of this linkage more incisively than Stuart Hall. Dialectical thinking, he explains, must take for its critique "cultural and subjective dimensions," and must recognize not only that gender is constructed and "deployed politically" in ways which must be delineated, but that "social practices," "forms of domination," and even the "politics of the Left" are "inscribed in and to some extent secured by sexual identity and positioning" ("Meaning of New Times," pp. 128–29).

119. On the historical and philosophical background of the European anarchist movement, see James Joll's classic, *The Anarchists*.

120. O'Neill, *Selected Letters*, p. 474; Goldman, *Social Significance of Modern Drama*, pp. 3, 2.

121. Frazer, *E. G. and E. G. O.*, p. 17.

122. "Can you dig up for me any English translations of Bakounine, Kropotkin—or any book of Emma's—which gives as clear a picture of the structure & workings of society if this Anarchist utopia came to be?" (Commins, *O'Neill-Commins Correspondence*, p. 179). O'Neill may have used this material for his sketch of Simon's utopian concepts in *More Stately Mansions*, or as background for the anarchist theme in *The Iceman Cometh* (1940), or for "The Visit of Malatesta," a sketch for a play about the illustrious Italian anarchist Enrico Malatesta (first recorded in his notebook on January 4, 1940).

123. "Benjamin Tucker once said to me," wrote Hutchins Hapgood, "that Terry is the only uncompromising Anarchist he knew in America" (Hapgood, "Case of Terry," p. 6).

124. Deutsch and Hanau, *Provincetown*, p. 29.

125. O'Neill, *Selected Letters*, p. 233.

126. Tucker, *Instead of a Book*, p. 15. O'Neill's interest in Individualist anarchism was also stimulated by Max Stirner's *Ego and His Own* (1845), which, as Sheaffer notes, "took on the State, the Press, Parents, Family Life, Morality, Education, Liberalism, Socialism, Communism, Christianity, all religions . . . in favor of individualism inviolate" (*Son and Playwright*, p. 122).

127. Quoted in Marsh, *Anarchist Women*, p. 54. Marsh also quotes Victor Yarros, who in Tucker's *Liberty* in 1888 wrote: "When I speak of a man and woman's making a home, I mean that he is to provide the means and she is to take care of the domestic affairs" (p. 54).

128. Coryell, "Value of Chastity," p. 278.

129. Coryell, "Marriage or Free Union, Which?" p. 577.

130. Goldman, "Traffic in Women," in *Red Emma*, p. 149. Eschewing both wedlock and motherhood, Goldman refused to imagine herself as "an object to be taken and owned" (quoted in Frazer, *E. G. and E. G. O.*, p. 19). Adopting a comprehensive view of what constitutes revolution, Hippolyte Havel reasoned in 1908: "The prob-

lem of the sexes is too closely related to other social problems; its solution lies in entire social regeneration" ("Literature," p. 330).

131. Marsh, *Anarchist Women*, p. 49.

132. De Cleyre, "They Who Marry Do Ill," pp. 508–9.

133. Goldman, "Jealousy: Causes and a Possible Cure," in *Red Emma Speaks*, pp. 170–72.

134. Occasionally *Mother Earth* brought to light a tradition of feminist criticism that unpacked the social dimension of women's psychological positioning within this sexual binary opposition. It reprinted Mary Wollstonecraft's "Women and Property," for example, to offer historical and theoretical perspectives on the domestic production of specific kinds of feminine personalities within relations dominated by male owners. "Whilst [women] are absolutely dependent on their husbands they will be cunning, mean, and selfish," wrote Wollstonecraft, "and the men who can be gratified by the fawning fondness of spaniel-like affection have not much delicacy, for love is not to be bought." Wollstonecraft advocates wedlock only if it is a relationship between comrades. The tone of her plea, nonetheless, indicates who holds the power: "Would men but generously snap our chains, and be content with rational fellowship instead of a slavish obedience, they would find us more observant daughters, more affectionate sisters, more faithful wives, more reasonable mothers—in a word, better comrades" ("Woman and Property," pp. 580–81).

135. As historian Margaret Marsh put it: "The chief difference between [anarchist-feminists] and their counterparts in the socialist movement and in mainstream feminist organizations was the extreme lengths to which they carried their repudiation of traditional views about the nature of womanhood" (*Anarchist Women*, p. 4). In 1906 Goldman attacked in strong anarchist terms faith in the ballot and argued that fundamental emancipation for women relies on jettisoning sexual difference ("Tragedy of Woman's Emancipation," p. 18).

136. Goldman, *Social Significance of Modern Drama*, p. 25.

137. Goldman was familiar with psychoanalysis. She had heard Freud lecture in Vienna in 1895 and also attended one of his lectures at Clark University in 1909. Goldman, like Freud, was critical of the inimical effects of sexual repression on women, not least because this repression restrained women from engaging fully in intellectual, professional, and cultural pursuits. For a brief discussion of Goldman's interest in Freud's views on women and repression see Gifford, "American Reception of Psychoanalysis." Gifford, librarian of the Boston Psychoanalytic Institute, seems to overstate Goldman's interest in Freud. Quoting from a letter from Goldman to Frank Heiner (July 24, 1934), Alice Wexler notes, "Although [Goldman] admired Freud personally, she was critical of psychoanalysis, seeing in it 'nothing but the old confessional'" (*Emma Goldman*, p. 295). Wexler points out that Goldman's thinking on the matter of sexuality was shaped in reference to her reading of Havelock Ellis, Edward Carpenter, and Nickolai Chernyshevsky (*Emma Goldman*, p. 48), among others. Also see Falk, *Love, Anarchy and Emma Goldman*. Falk discusses Goldman's lecture, "Sex: The Great Element for Creative Work" (1911): "Her lecture on sex countered the Freudian notion that creativity was linked to sexual repression: 'the creative spirit is not an antidote to the sex instinct, but a part of its forceful expression'" (p. 160). In addition see Drinnon, *Rebel in Paradise*. Drinnon,

in reference to Freud, notes that Goldman "always maintained that sex is a dominant force," but also that "she rightly rejected attempts to reduce all the complex forces acting on her to the rather simple-minded explanation of pure sex" (p. 22).

138. Marsh, *Anarchist Women*, p. 94.

139. Goldman, *Social Significance of Modern Drama*, p. 35. Calverton was thinking along the same track as O'Neill's Olga Tarnoff and Emma Goldman in *Bankruptcy of Marriage* (1928): "While man in the past has learned to conquer many of the material forces of nature, and at the present time is hastening into a period where he will learn to conquer the evils that have grown out of the private possession of property, he is only at the foothills in his attempt to conquer love" (p. 328).

140. O'Neill, *Selected Letters*, pp. 39, 41.

141. Marsh observes: "In the period from Haymarket until World War I, anarchists were directly responsible for only three violent confrontations with American society. . . . most anarchists never saw a bomb, let alone threw one" (*Anarchist Women*, p. 8).

142. O'Neill's original title for the play was *The Second Engineer*. In the late twenties he disparaged it when interviewed by Barrett Clark: "The plays I wrote for [Prof. Baker] were rotten. The long one was a rambling thing about a seaman's and fireman's strike" (*Eugene O'Neill*, p. 39).

143. Quoted in Frazer, *E. G. and E. G. O.*, p. 17.

144. See Gillespie, "Hawthorne Experiments and the Politics of Experimentation," pp. 114–37.

145. "We were not supposed to be jealous," wrote Freeman of 1920s bohemia. "Such primitive feelings were 'bourgeois prejudices'. . . . anything you didn't like was 'bourgeois' " (*American Testament*, p. 405).

146. O'Neill, *Eugene O'Neill at Work*, p. 279.

147. Alexander, "Social Critic," p. 396. Larry espouses the universalizing ideology of "Man" that Brecht's political theatre sought to dismantle by "alienating" (defamiliarizing) the spectator's view of characters and their motivations: "We must be able to portray the human without treating it as 'eternally human' " (*Brecht on Theatre*, p. 250). The response Brecht strived to elicit from his audience was not "That's great art" because the play shows one that the "sufferings of this man . . . are inescapable," but rather "That's great art" because I now realize that his sufferings "are unnecessary" (p. 71).

148. Havel added: "The fiercer the combat between the old and the new worlds, the more intensely will their ideals find expression in the literature of the time" ("Literature," p. 329). His faith in the prophetic and disruptive possibilities of art was shared by Goldman, who argued that "many radicals as well as conservatives fail to grasp the powerful message of art [because] . . . the average radical is as hidebound by mere terms as the man devoid of all ideas. 'Bloated plutocrats,' 'economic determinism,' 'class consciousness,' and similar expressions sum up for him the symbols of revolt. But since art speaks a language embracing the entire gamut of human emotions, it often sounds meaningless to those whose hearing has been dulled by the din of stereotyped phrases" (*Social Significance of Modern Drama*, p. 1).

149. Havel, "Literature," p. 330.

150. Havel, "Brothers Karamazov," pp. 56, 57. Both Havel and O'Neill shared a high regard for Ibsen. In 1907 the young O'Neill, like Lucy Ashleigh, was captivated with Ibsen's *Hedda Gabler*—he saw it ten times (Sheaffer, *Son and Playwright*, pp. 121–22). In the periodical *The Road to Freedom* (1924–32), which he edited in the 1920s, Havel argued that Ibsen's comprehensive radicalism "foreshadowed" anarchism ("Iconoclast," p. 5).

151. Havel, "Faith and Record of Anarchists," p. 367.

152. Gold, "Eugene O'Neill's Early Days in the Old 'Hell-Hole,' " p. 8.

153. Frazer, *E. G. and E. G. O.*, p. 92.

154. Ibid., p. 98.

155. O'Neill, *Selected Letters*, p. 511. *The Web*, one of O'Neill's first plays, is an obvious blend of social realism and naturalism—urban poverty and prostitution crush a young mother. But even in this early effort, in one of the final stage directions, O'Neill assigns causality to "*the ironic life force*" (1:28). In 1941 he denigrated *"Anna Christie"* in comparison to *The Iceman Cometh*: "[The former] is a play written about characters and a situation—not about characters and life" (*Selected Letters*, p. 522).

156. O'Neill, *"As Ever, Gene,"* p. 205.

157. O'Neill, *Conversations*, p. 18.

158. O'Neill, *Selected Letters*, p. 158.

159. O'Neill, *Conversations*, p. 27.

160. Ibid., p. 61.

161. Arthur Gelb and Barbara Gelb suggest just how privileged some members of this "we" and this "every one" were in their reconstruction of the opening night of *The Hairy Ape* at the Provincetown Playhouse on March 9, 1922: "The curtain fell . . . and the theatre resounded to the applause of first-nighters. Dressed in evening clothes, carrying gold-headed walking sticks, borne by chauffeur-driven limousines, the cream of the theatregoing aristocracy had sat on the rude wooden benches of the little theatre, stunned by the elemental force of the play. Also in attendance was the full complement of Broadway critics" (*O'Neill*, p. 498).

162. Life in the 1920s was not prosperous for all. "The mass of Americans, workers and farmers, were not invited to the prosperity party," Freeman reminds us. "But the middle classes were," and as "literary spokesmen" they sometimes gave the world the impression of 120 million Americans roaring through the twenties on a spending spree (*American Testament*, pp. 340–41).

163. O'Neill, *Eugene O'Neill at Work*, p. 378. "O'Neill's characters," writes Eric Bentley, ". . . being American adolescents, want to be loved, and they don't really want anything else. They only misbehave when they don't get love. Hatred itself seems only the product of this failure. . . . All too often they only want to be loved by Mom. . . . From which it can be seen how near O'Neill's life-worship comes to death-worship: sex leads back to the womb" ("Touch of the Adolescent," pp. 400–401).

164. Sheaffer, *Son and Artist*, p. 517.

165. In an appraisal of O'Neill in 1954, John Howard Lawson, the Socialist dramatist and theoretician of theatre, quoted from his eulogy of Dreiser: Lawson pledges "to him and to one another that we shall make the kind of world for which

he lived and died." He then adds ruefully: "No one can say that of O'Neill. It is an inherent part of the tragedy that he would not even have wished to have it said" ("Tragedy of Eugene O'Neill," p. 18).

166. Dell, *Intellectual Vagabondage*, pp. 246, 249.

167. Ibid., p. 249. The artist who invokes "life" or "fate" is "modern." At least this appears to be the implication of Edmund's argument with his father, Tyrone, in *Long Day's Journey*. Edmund explains that he is laughing "at life. It's so damned crazy." Tyrone responds with a "*growl*": "More of your morbidness! There's nothing wrong with life. It's we who—(*He quotes*) 'The fault, dear Brutus, is not in our stars, but in ourselves that we are underlings'" (3:810–11). Tyrone's belief in agency is, perhaps, insufficiently "psychological." O'Neill may have thought of himself as juggling both points of view. Also see Raymond Williams's remarks on O'Neill's privatized ideology of life, in reference to *Mourning Becomes Electra*: "Life itself is fate . . . which is again the inherently destructive family. . . . What matters, clearly, is the imposed pattern, which has the effect of conferring a sense of inevitability on what, as experience, was and could otherwise be seen as a series of living choices. The pattern comes from the consciousness of the isolate, rationalised by reference to modern psychology and to the Greeks" (*Modern Tragedy*, p. 118).

168. O'Neill, *"As Ever, Gene,"* p. 188.

169. O'Neill, *Selected Letters*, p. 69.

170. Atkinson, *Broadway*, p. 195.

171. See TGPB, 79: Nichols, "The New Play," *New York World*, Jan. 31, 1928.

172. See Poggi, *Theater in America*, pp. 114–17. Eric Bentley situates O'Neill's increasing absorption with "Big Themes" in the context of the establishment of reviewers (the "subintelligentsia"):

A writer like O'Neill does not give [the subintelligentsia] the optimism of an "American century" but he provides profundities galore, and technical innovations, and (as he himself says) Mystery. . . . [The subintelligentsia] are seen daily at the Algonquin and nightly at Sardi's. They don't all like O'Neill, yet his "profound" art is inconceivable without them. O'Neill doesn't like *them*, but he needs them, and could never have dedicated himself to "big work" had their voices not been in his ears telling him he was big. The man who could not be bribed by the Broadway tycoons was seduced by the Broadway intelligentsia. ("Trying to Like O'Neill," p. 155)

Interestingly, in the second half of the nineteenth century "spirituality" became a central theme of plays (as well as a characteristic of acting styles) that helped distinguish "business-class" theatres from working-class playhouses. See Lawrence Levine's *Highbrow/Lowbrow*, pp. 13–168, and Bruce McConachie's *Melodramatic Formations*, pp. 231–57.

173. See Sarlós, *Jig Cook and the Provincetown Players*, pp. 138–46, and Deutsch and Hanau, *Provincetown*, pp. 60–93.

174. O'Neill, *Selected Letters*, p. 424. In 1921 Macgowan saw psychoanalysis as providing both "content" and direction for the theatre of the future; but he also predicted, "As imaginative and spiritual values enter the drama of our life, 'psychology' will partially go out." "Spiritual issues," he wrote, "[are] a little deeper" (*The-*

atre of Tomorrow, p. 263). O'Neill's *The Great God Brown, Lazarus Laughed,* and *Days Without End* made Macgowan's "theatre of tommorow" the theatre of today.

175. Quoted in Bogard, *Contour in Time,* p. 350. In 1928 he wrote Macgowan that an autobiographical series of plays he was planning would "be one of those timeless Big Things" (*"Theatre We Worked For,"* p. 177). Boal's critique of romanticism is also applicable to O'Neill's 1920s and early 1930s preoccupation with spiritual solutions: "It was an attempt to solve in the field of the spirit the problems facing men in society" (*Theatre of the Oppressed,* p. 75).

176. O'Neill, *Selected Letters,* p. 311.

177. Nathan, quoted in Blankfort, "Facing the New Audience" (June 1, 1934), p. 11.

178. Bogard, *Contour in Time,* pp. 60–61. Along these lines, Bogard views O'Neill as a "muddled radical," as if the ideological tensions in *The Personal Equation* were unique to O'Neill and somehow represent his personal failure to unmuddle his thoughts.

179. Bigsby, *Critical Introduction,* pp. 67, 116, 117.

180. O'Neill, *Conversations,* p. 35.

181. See Wainscott, *Staging O'Neill,* pp. 117–18.

182. As Flexner remarked in her critique of *The Hairy Ape,* O'Neill treats "what is essentially a social as a philosophical problem." Yank's "not belonging" is dramatized as the consequence of his existential condition rather than his class position. "What really drives the Yanks of the world into morbid depression and madness? The loss of their jobs through overproduction and mechanization, industrial accidents, long hours, and low wages. . . . What might easily account for [Yank's] confusion and mental collapse—the terrible conditions in the stokehole—bad ventilation, the speed-up, the long hours of back-breaking toil—are to Yank a source of pride" (*American Playwrights,* pp. 149, 151). Likewise, in *Dynamo,* O'Neill reduces the dynamo, "the highest expression of the machine age, to a religious and sexual symbol, when clearly the problem today is the practical one of mastering the machine before it destroys us, of constructing a rational society which will benefit instead of suffering from the advance of science!" (p. 181).

183. These are the sort of the critical and aesthetic presuppositions that Patrick Brantlinger criticized when reflecting on his own ideological reprogramming as a literary critic-in-training: "Great literature, my own education taught me, is not about public life or politics; it is instead about experiences, values of private lives, usually 'refined' individuals (lyric romantic poetry, portraits of the artist, remembrances of things past, etc.)" (*Crusoe's Footprints,* p. 155). When the "chaos of experience" and "the rich inwardness of personal life" are categorized as the only fitting subjects for "great literature" and unbiased literary criticism, we are observing—as Terry Eagleton insists—the production of a political aesthetic and set of values whose ideological agenda is in part to shrink the concept of the political (*Literary Theory,* p. 197). As Alan Sinfield observes about the modernist construction of the "'modern condition'": "What we actually suffer under is corporate capitalism, produced by economic, political and military power, and by choices made by people in history. By investing the alleged modern condition with a romanticism of extremity, writers and critics discourage political analysis. Modernism is offered

as standing at the brink, daring to stare into the abyss so that the rest of us can only gasp. The situation is too urgent for such self-indulgence" (*Literature, Politics and Culture*, p. 201).

184. Sillen, "Confusion Has Class Character," p. 10.

185. Freeman, *American Testament*, pp. 600–601.

186. O'Neill, *Selected Letters*, p. 206. O'Neill's advice about "flesh & blood propaganda" resembles Havel's criticism that Upton Sinclair's *Moneychangers* failed to portray "psychological definiteness." His counsel also bears the stamp of Sheldon Cheney's profile of the new *liberal* "dramatists of thought": "Because they are true to their own time, the general spirit of their plays is humanitarian, or even socialistic in the best sense of the word; but they are never propagandist. They have kept their viewpoint as artists of the theatre: so they do not preach, but they make the audience feel; they remember that true art carries an intellectual stimulus only through emotional suggestion, and not by direct statement" (*New Movement in the Theatre*, pp. 35–36).

187. In his capacity as a director of the Experimental Theatre, Inc., O'Neill wrote Macgowan on September 8, 1925, the following about Maxwell Anderson's *Outside Looking In*: "I've read it. It's all right—good enough stuff, turned out well enough, meriting success—but, so it seems to me, with no depth." Then he goes on to question why they are producing such a play: "Let's be honest and either give up the ghost or give up pretending to mean anything new or deep or significant." By comparison he praises Gold's *Fiesta* (produced by the Provincetown Players in 1929) as having "real atmosphere and truth" (*Selected Letters*, p. 198).

188. Ibid., p. 308. O'Neill no doubt would have agreed with many of Max Eastman's criticisms of "crude shouts for propaganda" (p. 5) and "slogan-sabotage" (p. 79) in *Art and the Life of Action*: "It is . . . dangerous to forget that the aim of a rational revolution is not to drive men into a mould, but to set them free, within the new economic conditionings, to live what lives they please" (p. 81). But Eastman, unlike O'Neill, was committed to changing "economic conditionings."

189. Seiler, "Workers' Theatre," p. 17. Middle-class political playwrights were also classified as artless by mainstream critics. Nathan writes:

> In "We, the People," Elmer Rice confected a propaganda diatribe of various phases of American injustice. It failed of all conviction because its examples were uniformly and unremittingly of the hit-'em-in-the-jaw, steam-shovel school. If, bribed with a sufficient number of authentic beers the critic had been wheedled into writing the same basic play, he would have made it infinitely more convincing and effective by completely reversing the propaganda scheme, that is, by ironically arguing the absurdity of the charges of injustice, the full truth of which would at all times be doubly apparent to and impressed upon the auditors. ("Educating the Drama," p. 2)

190. Kline, "Writing for Workers' Theatre," p. 23.

191. O'Neill, *Selected Letters*, p. 486. Thousands of letters written by the down-and-out to Franklin and Eleanor Roosevelt make it agonizingly clear that masses of people during the Depression worried at length about "stuff" such as being "saved." "Mr Roosevelte," wrote one correspondent in December, 1935, "I am In nead Bad

Please help me I have 7 children and is Sick all the time one of my children is Sick and has Ben for a lonetime and I have no under clothes for none of the famiely we cant harly hide I Self with top cloths. . . . please help me please" (quoted in McElvaine, *Down and Out in the Great Depression*, p. 158). Of course, it is uncertain what O'Neill actually meant by "saved," writing from the seclusion of Tao House, where he spent the last years of the Depression drafting his cycle.

192. Freud, *Civilization and Its Discontents*, pp. 59–61.

193. O'Neill's *Marco Millions*, which satirized capitalist acquisitiveness and did not dramatize "depth," was sometimes reviewed as superficial. Robert Littell of the *Post* wrote in 1928: "The eleven scenes show is, in ABC's which can be read a mile away, the contrast between western money-grabbing and Eastern wisdom, between materialism and idealism, between the dollar and the dream" (quoted in Sheaffer, *Son and Artist*, p. 281).

194. Gabriel Miller writes that the more "ecstatic" mainstream reviews of Clifford Odets's *Awake and Sing!* (1935) "proclaimed Odets better than O'Neill." Interestingly, leftist critics "were harder on the play" (*Clifford Odets*, p. 30).

195. Seaver, "O'Neill, Grown Safe," p. 5. Yet in the 1930s, Alexander Tairov, director of the Kamerny, a renowned Soviet dramatic troupe touring America, held that O'Neill tears away "the gilt and gaudy trappings from the contemporaneous Western European and American cultures, and with an unparalleled profundity and truthfulness he reveals the irreconcilable conflicts and cataclysms concealed in these civilizations" (quoted in Sheaffer, *Son and Artist*, p. 380).

196. Cole and Lawson, "Two Views on Eugene O'Neill," pp. 62, 61. Lawson represents *Iceman* as "a confused lament for a society which O'Neill sees as doomed" ("Tragedy of Eugene O'Neill," p. 8). On the contrary, *Iceman* classifies the Big Problem as the Life that dooms us all. Arthur Miller writes: "It was O'Neill who wrote about working-class men, about whores and the social discards and even the black man in a white world, but since there was no longer a connection with Marxism in the man himself, his plays were never seen as the critiques of capitalism that objectively they were" (*Timebends*, p. 229). There are many ways of "writing about" the working class, "whores," and "even the black man," however; the subjects themselves do not make the politics of their representation self-evident. Miller may recognize that O'Neill is criticizing capitalism, but if O'Neill classified the problem as "life"—what *are* the implications?

197. O'Neill, *Selected Letters*, p. 168. "The tragedy is the inner tragedy of the proletarian soul," wrote Robbins. "No talk about class-consciousness or orderly revolution can help Yank" ("I. W. W. on the Stage," p. 2). Robbins could have made a more convincing case that no talk about class consciousness by Yank's Socialist mate, Long, and no discussion of "orderly revolution" by members of the I. W. W. will convert (or reconvert) O'Neill. In his correspondence with Alexander Berkman, O'Neill noted that "since the production of my *Hairy Ape* in Moscow they seem to regard me as a pure proletarian writer," thus hinting that the Muscovites were much mistaken (*Selected Letters*, pp. 233). In 1922 Floyd Dell argued that Mike Gold, his fellow editor of *The Liberator*, was blinded to thinking critically about *The Hairy Ape* because of his "*bourjooi*" Communist romance with the stokehole (the "real"). Gold had romanticized O'Neill's play for its dramatization of the "deep

spirit of revolt that burns even in the American workingman." Parodying Gold, Dell rewrites O'Neill's script: when the heiress stands transfixed by Yank in the stoke-hole, she would be "delighted" with, rather than "horrified" by his presence, and would croon—"The darling!" Dell irreverently recasts Gold, the radical editor, as the admiring heiress: "He has come back from the stoke-hole talking about how beautiful Strength and Steam and Steel and Noise and Dirt are. If so, I say, why abolish capitalism?" Rejecting this "bourjooi" pose on behalf of the proletarian, Dell acknowledges his own class outlook as that of a self-critical bourgeois "tourist" and advises Gold to do the same (Dell, "Explanations and Apologies," p. 26). Gold is quoted in a *Liberator* review, April 26, 1922. Even Freeman, who was more sympa-thetic to Gold than was Dell, recognized that Gold's stained stetson, stinking three-cent cigars, and sooty shirts were " 'proletarian' props," just as Dell's "sideburns and opera cape" served as his bohemian costume (*American Testament*, p. 257).

198. Coleman, "Lobby and Aisle," p. 11; Lawson, "Tragedy of Eugene O'Neill," p. 8. Also see Montville Morris Hansford's interview with O'Neill in 1930. Hansford tried to account for O'Neill's turning away from the "real": the playwright aban-doned socialism for the "climbing notion"; he "likes to bask in an easy chair as much as anybody" (O'Neill, *Conversations*, p. 90).

199. Sillen, "Iceman Cometh," p. 11.

200. Geddes, *Melodramadness of Eugene O'Neill*, pp. 7, 44. For Geddes's views on radical theatre see his *Towards a Revolution in the Theatre* (1933) and *Beyond Trag-edy* (1930). For good overviews of 1920s and 1930s leftist writings on theatre and drama, see Ira A. Levine, *Left-Wing Dramatic Theory in the American Theatre*, and McDermott, "Propaganda and Art." Also see Goldstein, *Political Stage*, Himelstein, *Drama Was a Weapon*, Pells, "Rise and Fall of Workers Theatre," in *Radical Visions*, Smiley, *Drama of Attack*, Taylor, *People's Theatre in Amerika*, Jay Williams, *Stage Left*, and Rabkin, *Drama and Commitment*.

201. See Herbert Kline's profile of Charmion Von Wiegand in *New Theatre and Film*, p. 50. Joseph Freeman, Von Wiegand's husband, first introduced her to Kline as "the daughter of Karl Von Wiegand" (who was a "war-mongering" yellow jour-nalist for the Hearst chain). Freeman's own political reading of his wife and his apparent treatment of her as a passive object are bizarre. After listening to Von Wiegand's views on playwrights ranging from Lawson to O'Neill, Kline writes: "I thought her remarks were brilliant and asked Joe Freeman why he didn't *have her* write for the *New Masses* [where Freeman was an editor]. He said that *she wasn't that political*" (emphasis supplied). Von Wiegand's criticisms of O'Neill belie her husband's appraisal. Freeman dedicated *American Testament* to "Charmion."

202. Von Wiegand, "Quest of Eugene O'Neill," p. 13.

203. John Gassner, writing for *New Theatre*, reconsidered O'Neill in the ideologi-cal context of a little theatre movement (centered in Greenwich Village) that sanc-tioned "quixotic" modes of "rebellion" deemed appropriate as a pastime for the "introspective" middle class ("Playreader on Playwrights," p. 9). For background on *New Theatre* magazine see Kline, *New Theatre and Film*. Kline reprints some of the most interesting pieces originally published in *New Theatre*. Von Wiegand, who also published her critiques of O'Neill in *New Theatre*, is more precise than the liberal Gassner about how the terms of this middle-class uprising work to contain it:

"The postwar period in the United States witnessed a revolt of the secure and increasingly prosperous middle-class intelligentsia from the conformity, ugliness, and standardization of Main Street." Yet O'Neill's early "flight" into the working class *never involved a break with bourgeois society.*" This is because O'Neill called his "windmill" conformity, convention, materialism, standardization—life ("Quest of Eugene O'Neill," pp. 12–13, 31). The stereotypical romantic starving artist (John Brown) in O'Neill's *Bread and Butter* (1914) who refuses to conform to bourgeois conventions and materialism is left with only his art as a recourse. When he does marry back into his social class, his only way out is a romance with death. John Brown's (suicidal) tilt at the windmill, as Von Wiegand would say, never really broke with bourgeois ideology. Leftist critics often focused on the class position of O'Neill's audiences and reviewers as a way of understanding the class-based character of his themes. In 1934, Lawson vented his spleen at the "well-to-do audience for whom [O'Neill] writes" and the "shallow attitudes of bourgeois critics," all of whom demand "well-written [plays] . . . free of the embarrassing curse of propaganda" ("Towards a Revolutionary Theatre," p. 7). Writing in the same vein, Mike Gold argued that the "despair" of *Iceman* should be read as an intellectual luxury purchased by "the middle-aged, comfortable Theatre Guild audience" ("Eugene O'Neill's Early Days," p. 8).

204. Blankfort, "Facing the New Audience—Part II," p. 14. Sillen, likewise, interpreted the depth of *Iceman* as "decay" ("Iceman Cometh," p. 11).

205. An ideological symptom of bourgeois theatre, then, is that it narrowly represents the psychological in order to reproduce bourgeois subjectivity in certain forms. This construct of the psychological, while seeming nonpartisan (and scientific), serves as propaganda—a "function . . . of which capitalism is not wholly unaware" (Lawson, "Towards a Revolutionary Theatre," p. 6).

206. Seaver, "O'Neill, Grown Safe," p. 55. Lawson, again connecting O'Neill's aesthetic to a specific construction of the psychological, argued: "Broadway is sick because it represents a sick bourgeoisie; the tawdriness of its productions reflects the psychology of a dull and blasé audience" ("Towards a Revolutionary Theatre," p. 6). Geddes assessed the split self of John Loving in *Days Without End* as a dramatization of depth that could be better grasped as a class specific aberration of humanity: "Neuroticism, despair, self-deception . . . O'Neill here affirms a way of life" (Geddes, "End of O'Neill," p. 27).

207. Lawson, "Towards a Revolutionary Theatre," p. 7. Blankfort too criticized the psychological as a production of class subjectivity that is ideologically potent because of its capacity to dissolve the category of class. His criticism of Joan Crawford–style socialite films is equally applicable to *Welded*, *Strange Interlude*, and *Mourning Becomes Electra*: "Out of this specious liaison with the upper class, a fiction is created that beneath their trappings the wealthy are just as human and even more troubled than the poor and the poor ought to be glad they're poor" ("Facing the New Audience—Part II," p. 15). Von Wiegand argued that O'Neill's white-collar psychological dramas reveal not the timeless unconscious, but more exactly "the outlines of a neurotic pattern common to the petty bourgeois 'intelligentsia'" ("Quest of Eugene O'Neill," p. 16).

208. Blake, *Awakening of the American Theatre*, p. 7. Also see OS, 5: Florence

Wattles, "The Socialist and the Ape," *New York Call*, June 4, 1922. Wattles's review of *The Hairy Ape* criticizes the *politics* of O'Neill's representation of an antipolitical, individualist worker. "This ape . . . has no class philosophy. He is a rampant individualist. The class struggle doesn't 'belong.' It has no place in his individualistic mind. He is a deficient individualist in a hostile world, determined to force his way to the top and demonstrate the mean—of his strength and his power to destroy."

209. Calverton, "Theatre," p. 97.

210. Flexner, *American Playwrights*, p. 29.

211. Geddes, *Left Turn for American Drama*, p. 12.

212. Lawson, "Towards a Revolutionary Theatre," p. 6.

213. Geddes, "End of O'Neill," p. 27.

214. Blankfort, "Facing the New Audience—Concluded," p. 25.

215. Lawson, "Towards a Revolutionary Theatre," p. 7.

216. Von Wiegand, "Quest of Eugene O'Neill," p. 31.

217. Alexander, "Social Critic," p. 403.

218. Clurman, *Fervent Years*, p. 23.

219. O'Neill, *Selected Letters*, p. 409.

220. Commins, *O'Neill-Commins Correspondence*, p. 136. O'Neill's description of *Ah, Wilderness!* as a simple "comedy" that does not set out to "spoof" the period (as did *Marco Millions*) echoes Marco Polo's notion of the escapism provided by a good play: "Just take it easy and enjoy a good wholesome thrill or a good laugh and get your mind off things until it's time to go to bed" (2:431). Of course, we are meant to interpret Marco's view as shallow. This is precisely the "amusement-racket" kind of play that O'Neill refused to write for the bourgeoisie.

221. See Van Laan, "Singing in the Wilderness," p. 105. For a very different reading of the play, which contends that O'Neill mainly affirms the middle-class-we-have-lost, see Ellen Kimbel, "Eugene O'Neill as Social Historian."

222. Freeman explains that in the 1920s psychoanalytic therapy socialized many "bohemian writers and artists" to interpret their "romantic rebellion" as adolescent: "Adolescent revolt against paternal authority, clothing itself in literary and political symbols, was but the repudiation of conventional mores under the pressure of a normal sensuality in conflict with an abnormal conscience. Once that conflict was resolved, once sensuality and conscience were reconciled, the road was open for the return of the prodigal to the bourgeois fold" (*American Testament*, p. 276).

223. "April, 1932," writes Blake, "marked the beginning of a new period. From then on the workers' theatre appealed directly to the skilled craftsmen of the professional theatre and little theatre for theatrical aid" (*Awakening of American Theatre*, p. 26).

224. That year the Shock Troupe of the Workers' Laboratory Theatre (about thirteen members) performed their mobile agitprop plays before approximately 100,000 workers (Cosgrove, "From Shock Troupe to Group Theatre," pp. 268, 271–72). Also see Friedman, "Brief Description of the Workers' Theatre Movement," and McDermott, "Workers' Laboratory Theatre."

225. Gassner, *Masters of the Drama*, p. 665.

226. Clurman writes: "O'Neill . . . I believe, didn't read or see the play, but . . . felt that Paul Green and a new group merited a hearing" (*Fervent Years*, p. 52).

227. Helburn, *Wayward Quest*, pp. 224, 222. Also see Langner, *Magic Curtain*, p. 250.

228. Sheaffer, *Son and Playwright*, p. 116.

229. See Alexander, *Tempering of Eugene O'Neill*, pp. 101–7.

230. Commins, *O'Neill-Commins Correspondence*, p. 210.

231. See the Baker-O'Neill correspondence in Yale University's Manuscripts and Archives (Sterling Memorial Library), box 8, folders 168–70. Baker's letter to O'Neill was written on May 5, 1926 (folder 168). O'Neill's response was sent on May 21, 1926 (folder 168). A Yale University News Statement, issued on November 8, 1931, trumpeted the presentation of Edmond Quinn's bust of O'Neill to Baker: this "comes at a time when O'Neill's new play, 'Mourning Becomes Electra,' has won critical acclaim at the high point of his career" (folder 170). Yale had invested in O'Neill-the-dropout, O'Neill-the-maverick.

232. See Veblen, *Theory of the Leisure Class*, p. 237. Interestingly, *Ah, Wilderness!* here may have been influenced by Lawson's *Roger Bloomer* (1923), in which one sober midwest father advises his son to attend Yale because it's really a "business institution" (p. 36) (as opposed to state colleges—"too many Socialists!" [p. 22]; this comment made by a Yale man). O'Neill saw *Roger Bloomer* in 1923: "The play . . . carried its study of adolescence to the extent of being adolescently badly written and thereby bored me, for I came expecting to see something. However, the evening was made well worth while for me by the performance of the actor who played the Yale man" (*Selected Letters*, p. 181).

233. Ohmann, *Politics of Letters*, pp. 32, 39. Also see Freeman: "My friends and I entered Columbia University in 1916. The more we learned there, the wider became the gap between us and the ghetto. We were the products of an economic process whereby those who had the means went on to the professions" (*American Testament*, p. 81).

234. O'Neill, *Eugene O'Neill at Work*, p. 40. For a superb analysis of universities as centers that trained professionals to build corporate America, and for an account of how turn-of-the-century university presidents acted "in the manner of captains of industry," see Larson, *Rise of Professionalism*, p. 150–53.

235. See Sheaffer, *Son and Artist*, p. 209. For information on the Harkness gifts to Yale, see Bergin, *Yale's Residential Colleges*, pp. 19–25, 128. On October 29, 1931, George Pierce Baker invited Harkness to attend the production of *Bound East for Cardiff* and *The Emperor Jones* on the night the bust of O'Neill was to be presented to Baker (Yale University, Manuscripts and Archives [Sterling Memorial Library], box 8, folder 179).

236. Commins, *O'Neill-Commins Correspondence*, p. 217.

237. D'Emilio and Freedman, *Intimate Matters*, pp. 182, 201.

238. Lindsey and Evans, *Revolt of Youth*, p. 127. Also see G. Stanley Hall, *Adolescence*. In his chapter, "Adolescent Love," Hall endowed sex with depth—the solution to the meaning of life. "Sex is the most potent and magic open sesame to the deepest mysteries of life, death, religion, and love. It is, therefore, one of the cardinal sins against youth to repress healthy thoughts of sex at the proper age, because thus the mind itself is darkened and its wings clipped for many of the higher intuitions,

which the supreme muse of common sense at this psychologic moment ought to give" (p. 109).

239. Foucault, *History of Sexuality*, p. 130.

240. Flexner, *American Playwrights*, pp. 306–7.

241. Allen, *Only Yesterday*, pp. 98, 88.

242. Raymond Williams introduces the concept of "incorporation" in the context of his discussion of Antonio Gramsci's idea of hegemony. Incorporation is the manifestation of hegemonic power that "at once produces and limits its own forms of counter-culture" (*Marxism and Literature*, p. 114).

243. See Ryan, *Womanhood in America*, pp. 156–57.

244. Paul Buhle, *Marxism in the United States*, pp. 177, 173.

245. O'Neill, *Eugene O'Neill at Work*, p. 242.

246. Sheaffer, *Son and Artist*, p. 442.

247. Ibid., p. 480. For detailed discussions of O'Neill's work on the cycle see Martha Bower's fascinating *Eugene O'Neill's Unfinished Threnody*.

248. Sheaffer, *Son and Artist*, p. 480.

249. See TGPB, 217: Anon., "Guild to Do Two More O'Neill's," *New York Herald Tribune*, Dec. 28, 1945.

250. Vernant, "History and Psychology," in *Mortals and Immortals*, p. 268.

251. I am alluding here to the title of Richard Sennett and Jonathan Cobb's superb study, *Hidden Injuries of Class*.

252. See Alexander, *Tempering of Eugene O'Neill*, p. 22.

253. Brecht, *Brecht on Theatre*, p. 79.

254. On the Federal Theatre Project see *Federal Theatre Magazine* (1935–39), *Theatre Arts Monthly* (1935–39), McDermott, "Living Newspaper as a Dramatic Form," Buttitta and Witham, *Uncle Sam Presents*, Flanagan, *Arena*, Houseman, *Run-through*, O'Connor and Brown, *Free, Adult, Uncensored*, Mathews, *Federal Theatre*, Goldstein, *Political Stage*, Himelstein, *Drama Was a Weapon*, and Rabkin, *Drama and Commitment*.

Chapter 4

1. The original "stage" for this play was Hutchins Hapgood's house in Provincetown. But the play was revived by the Provincetown Players when they actually had a stage, and by many "little theatre" groups across the country in the 1910s and 1920s.

2. For a good brief comparison between O'Neill and Glaspell (which posits parallels between *The Hairy Ape* and Glaspell's *The Verge*) see Ben-Zvi, "Glaspell and O'Neill: The Imagery of Gender," pp. 22–27. Ann E. Larabee suggests links between *The Emperor Jones* and *The Verge* in her sophisticated analysis, " 'Meeting the Outside Face to Face,' " pp. 80–82. Veronica Makowsky offers an excellent critical overview of feminist themes in Glaspell's plays from *Trifles* to *The Verge* in *Susan Glaspell's Century of Women*, pp. 59–82.

3. For a discussion of O'Neill's representation of women in *The Iceman Cometh*, *Long Day's Journey Into Night*, and *A Moon for the Misbegotten*, see Ann C. Hall, "A

Kind of Alaska," pp. 17–53. Hall's approach is informed by psychoanalysis as well as feminist theory.

4. See Barker-Benfield, *Horrors of the Half-Known Life,* p. 196.

5. Smith-Rosenberg, "Davy Crockett as Trickster," in *Disorderly Conduct,* pp. 90–108; see esp. p. 90. Also see Nissenbaum, *Sex, Diet, and Debility.*

6. See Smith-Rosenberg, "Sex as Symbol," 212–47.

7. Tom Lutz, *American Nervousness 1903,* p. 28.

8. Quoted in ibid., pp. 287–88. Another prominent spokesman for this emancipation, department store owner John Wanamaker, hailed the America of 1906 as a "Land of Desire" in which advertising "EDUCATES DESIRE" (quoted by William Leach in "Strategists of Display," p. 102).

9. Lynn Fontanne starred as Nina Leeds in the original Theatre Guild production of *Strange Interlude.* She felt that O'Neill had overpsychologized Leeds: "She gave herself to those soldiers because she wanted to. She liked a lot of sex. She didn't feel sorry for them. I didn't ever feel that O'Neill made her a tragic figure. I don't think he knew the first thing about women" (quoted in Sheaffer, *Son and Artist,* p. 275).

10. Psychological studies of sexual practices like G. V. Hamilton's *Research in Marriage* (1929)—for which O'Neill was a subject—"discovered" that married women had engaged in masturbation, premarital sex, extramarital sex, same-sex relations, oral sex, and anal sex. "By 1918," historian Mary Ryan observes, "23 percent of the more prestigious American periodicals endorsed the doctrine that sexual release was psychologically healthy for both sexes. By 1928, 40 percent of the mass magazines concurred" (*Womanhood in America,* p. 156). Ryan suggests that the rise of corporate capitalism contributed to this new sexual economy: "The intensive capital accumulation required by industrialization was completed and corporate financing methods had become so sophisticated that private saving, be it of cash or semen, was no longer of great economic significance" (p. 154).

11. Lindsey and Evans, *Revolt of Youth,* p. 130.

12. Freud, *Sexuality and the Psychology of Love,* p. 25.

13. Although the sublimation or displacement of desire makes "civilization" possible, according to Freudian psychoanalytic theory, desire is nonetheless imagined as the essence of pre-"civilized" ("primitive") depth.

14. Sennett, *Fall of Public Man,* p. 7.

15. Tom Lutz, *American Nervousness 1903,* p. 286.

16. Consult Stuart Ewen's chapter on the 1920s advertising industry, "Mobilizing the Instincts," in *Captains of Consciousness,* pp. 31–39. Both pop psychologists and advertising corporations profited from "mobilizing the instincts" (and sometimes worked together to do so).

17. Ryan, *Womanhood in America,* p. 162. Also see Agnes Miles, *The Neurotic Woman.* Miles discusses contemporary feminist sociological "labelling" studies that examine how women's "depression" is produced in specific terms by psychiatric discourse: "There is no medical condition called unhappiness or socio-behavioural problem, and the category that doctors can easily make up is that of neurotic disorders. 'Depression', 'anxiety' or simply 'neurosis' can all be used to explain the prescription of a minor tranquilliser or sedative" (p. 9). Labels such as "depression"

stand in place of an analysis of the "condition [that] brought about the illness in the first place" (p. 12).

18. The photograph is reprinted in Barbara Gelb's informative essay, "Eugene O'Neill in Provincetown," p. 312.

19. Trimberger, "New Woman and the New Sexuality," pp. 111, 113. On free love and jealousy, also consult Fishbein, *Rebels in Bohemia*, pp. 94–99. On Mabel Dodge see Lasch's chapter "Mabel Dodge Luhan: Sex as Politics," in *New Radicalism*, pp. 104–40.

20. See Rudnick, "New Woman": "One could argue that the amount of attention and energy paid to women's sexual freedom, by both men and women, ultimately worked to undermine the fight for women's economic, intellectual, and political equality" (p. 78). Also see June Sochen, *New Woman*.

21. On Bryant's play see Matthews, "New Psychology and American Drama," p. 156. See Buhle, Buhle, and Georgakas, *Encyclopedia of the American Left*. Virginia Gardner's entry on Bryant observes: "She graduated from the University of Oregon in 1909, married a Portland dentist and with him raised Persian cats. When John Reed came to visit his mother in Portland they met, and within weeks she went to New York City at his urging." She later married Reed. Gardner notes that Bryant was an accomplished journalist (scooping Reed on the first accounts of the Russian Revolution), and that her book *Six Months in Russia* won much praise (p. 114).

22. For biographical background see Sarlós, "Jig Cook and Susan Glaspell," p. 254; Sochen, *New Woman*, pp. 21–23; and Waterman, *Susan Glaspell*.

23. Boulton, *Part of a Long Story*, p. 179.

24. See Sarlós, "Jig Cook and Susan Glaspell," p. 258. On the context of their relationship see Sarlós, *Jig Cook and the Provincetown Players*. Also see Glaspell's book on Cook, *Road to the Temple*.

25. Sarlós, "Jig Cook and Susan Glaspell," p. 252. Also see Fishbein's discussion of "The New Paganism" in *Rebels in Bohemia*, pp. 41–48, 54.

26. We see signs of similar plotting in *Welded* (1924). At first puzzled by Michael Cape's anxiety and self-absorption, "Woman," the prostitute, gradually figures it out: "What's eaten you. (*then with a queer sort of savage triumph*) Well, I'm glad one of youse guys got paid back like you oughter" (2:264). By the end of her session with Michael, however, she too is reduced to (psychosexual) "servitude" by the plot. Woman knows that her pimp will abuse her, "coin" or no "coin," and she has, so she claims, "loin[ed] to like it." In *A Touch of the Poet* (1939), Nora and Sara Melody also affirm female solidarity with one another, but curiously so, by rationalizing emotional "servitude" to men as a mode of affective self-aggrandizement. Assenting to her mother's "wisdom," Sara concludes: "[a woman's man] doesn't count at all, because it's love, your own love, you love in him, and to keep that your pride will do anything. . . . It's love's slaves we are, Mother, not men's" (3:263). This "wisdom" is belied by Nora's distressingly servile role as a reflection for her husband's ego—an ego made confident from having a wife to push around. "I'm the only one in the world he knows nivir sneers at his dreams!" (3:256).

27. O'Neill, *Selected Letters*, p. 163.

28. See Cott, *Grounding of Modern Feminism*, pp. 38–39.

29. There was considerable interest in theatre among Heterodites. The Socialist trade unionist Rose Pastor Stokes (*The Woman Who Wouldn't*) and Paula Jakobi (*The Chinese Lady*) tried their hand at playwriting. Many Heterodites, such as Eastman, Rauh, Stokes, Glaspell, Rheta Childe Dorr, Lou Rogers, Henrietta Rodman, Florence Woolston Seabury, and Charlotte Perkins Gilman were committed to socialist change. Rauh, just a few years before channeling her energies into directing and performing in several of O'Neill's Provincetown plays, wagered a friend that "the United States would be a socialist republic" by the early 1920s. Grace Potter, a Freudian psychoanalyst, Beatrice Hinkle, a Jungian psychoanalyst, and Leta Hollingsworth, a psychologist, were Heterodites who no doubt brought the significant developments in 1910s and 1920s psychological discourse to bear on the group's consciousness raising efforts. See Schwarz, *Radical Feminists of Heterodoxy*, p. 35. Also see Rudnick, "New Woman," p. 73.

30. Early in her career Glaspell shared O'Neill's interest in the figure of the mask (indeed, she may have played a role in getting O'Neill to think about masks). See her book of short stories, *Lifted Masks* (1912). Glaspell's play *Inheritors* (1924) also shows an interest in the family at different phases in history, something O'Neill would take up in the mid-1930s in his efforts to write his epic eleven-play cycle. Martha Bower, in *Eugene O'Neill's Unfinished Threnody*, examines O'Neill's creation of many strong, independent female characters and his numerous weak male characters in his notes and drafts of his cycle.

31. Glaspell did, however, win a Pulitzer Prize for her play *Alison's House* in 1930. For a critical overview of Glaspell, see Bigsby, "Introduction."

32. Long, "Eugene O'Neill," review of Barrett Clark's *Eugene O'Neill*, pp. 84–85. During the first years of his marriage with Boulton, O'Neill dismissed *Now I Ask You* as superficial—"not my sort of stuff, but it's a damn good idea for a popular success" (recommending that Agnes "fix it up"). Boulton, *Part of a Long Story*, p. 192.

33. Gerstenberg, *Overtones*, in *One-Act Plays*, pp. 37, 39.

34. All quotes from *Trifles* and *Woman's Honor* are taken from Glaspell, *Plays*.

35. Hamilton and Macgowan, *What Is Wrong with Marriage*, p. 65.

36. Collected in the OS, 1: Anon., "Washington Square Players," *New York Tribune*, May 26, 1919. Judith L. Stephens situates *Trifles* in the context of Progressive Era plays by women and argues that Glaspell's play "both challenged and reinforced the dominant gender ideology of the period" ("Gender Ideology and Dramatic Convention," p. 291). I would suggest, however, that *Trifles* challenges more than it accommodates established gender roles because Mrs. Hale and Mrs. Peters are so obviously in an initial phase of their feminist awakening. The play does not simply leave "the system . . . intact," it suggests why this system can remain intact (hence its political value as a play). Also see Karen F. Stein's brief but excellent feminist reading of the play, "Women's World of Glaspell's *Trifles*."

37. Like cultural historian Richard Johnson, Claire questions "the social life of subjective forms . . . and the different ways in which human beings *inhabit* them" ("What Is Cultural Studies Anyway?" pp. 62–63). What Glaspell's heroine is moving toward is the critical consciousness sketched by Adrienne Rich: "When we become acutely, disturbingly aware of the language we are using and that is using

us, we begin to grasp a material resource that women have never before collectively attempted to repossess" ("Power and Danger," in *On Lies, Secrets, and Silence*, p. 247).

38. For some overviews of *The Verge* in the context of Glaspell's plays, see Ben-Zvi, "Susan Glaspell and Eugene O'Neill: The Imagery of Gender," pp. 22–27; Ben-Zvi, "Susan Glaspell and Eugene O'Neill," pp. 21–29; Christine Dymkowski, "On the Edge," pp. 91–105.

39. Rich, "Valediction Forbidding Mourning," p. 137.

40. Clearly, I disagree with Sochen's conclusion about the politics of Glaspell's dramas: "Susan Glaspell interpreted the woman's problem as essentially an individual, personal one, not a social one" (*New Woman*, p. 43).

41. Ohmann, *Politics of Letters*, p. 84.

42. Sievers, *Freud on Broadway*, pp. 70–71. If Sievers had said that Claire has a conscious wish to be other than "woman," he would have been nearer the mark. Indeed, Claire possesses some of the characteristics of the form-breaking, androgynous New Woman of the 1910s and 1920s described by Smith-Rosenberg in "The New Woman as Androgyne" in *Disorderly Conduct*, pp. 245–96.

43. For sophisticated psychoanalytic discussions of the kinds of feminist issues raised by *The Verge*, see the chapters "Woman's Desire" (pp. 85–132) and "Gender and Domination" (pp. 183–218) in Benjamin, *Bonds of Love*, and the chapters "Rich Girl" (pp. 86–107), "Desire and the Family" (pp. 108–32), and "The Mending of Sarah" (pp. 202–27) in Kovel, *Age of Desire*. Both Benjamin and Kovel situate their readings of the "psychological" and of desire in a social and ideological matrix. Also see Jameson's "Pleasure: A Political Issue," which occasionally draws on psychoanalytic theory, yet also is critical of the ahistorical assumptions of psychoanalysis.

44. Quinn, *History of the American Drama*, 2:211.

45. Quoted in Sochen, *New Woman*, p. 42.

46. Quoted in Schwarz, *Radical Feminists of Heterodoxy*, p. 3. The response of reviewers was decidedly mixed. Critics such as Percy Hammond, Kenneth Macgowan, Alexander Woolcott, and J. Rankin Towse were dismissive of the play's complexity, whereas other critics—Stephen Rathburn, Maida Castellun, Frank Shay, Ludwig Lewisohn—rallied to its defense (reviews of *The Verge* are described and discussed by Papke, *Susan Glaspell*, pp. 64–69, 142–47). Ludwig Lewisohn, in *The Nation*, suggested that most reviewers were not up to Glaspell's level and that she "has a touch of that vision without which we perish" ("Drama: 'The Verge,'" pp. 708, 709).

47. O'Neill, *Selected Letters*, p. 103.

48. Berger et al., *Ways of Seeing*, pp. 46–47. The advertising industry intensified the sexualization of women as objects of desire to sell products. "Throughout the twenties," notes Stuart Ewen, "a noticeable proportion of magazines depicted [women] looking into mirrors" (*Captains of Consciousness*, p. 177). Also see the chapters "The Culture of Beauty in the Early Twentieth Century" (pp. 202–25) and "The History of Woman and Beauty since 1921" (pp. 271–91) in Banner, *American Beauty*.

49. Along these lines, Martha Roth writes: "The sexual appeal of a performing woman begins with the fact that she is on display. This makes her sexually available

to any man, in fantasy and often in fact. . . . I want to see new images [on stage]. I want women in performance to take off the masks of the male imagination" ("Notes toward a Feminist Aesthetic," pp. 8, 12).

50. O'Neill, *Poems*, pp. 26–27.

51. Glaspell's critique of feminine forms is taken up by artist Barbara Kruger in many of her representations in the 1980s. I have in mind, in particular, a close-up photograph of a woman's face with fur growing on it (the wolfwoman), with the superimposed caption: "I will not become what I mean to you" (*We Won't Play Nature to Your Culture*, p. 30). Also see "I am your immaculate conception" (p. 38) and "We are the future of ritual cleansing" (p. 42).

52. In some plays O'Neill makes such patterns and forms visible as problems at the same time that he reproduces them. The stage directions that describe Deborah Harford, for example, pathologize her as she pathologizes herself. First the "praise": "*One cannot believe, looking at her, that she has ever borne children. There is something about her perversely virginal.*" On the same page, the pathology: Deborah is "*astonishingly youthful, with only the first tracing of wrinkles about the eyes and mouth, a foreshadowing of sagging flesh under the chin, and of scrawniness in the neck*" (3:314–15). As Deborah ages, O'Neill's portraiture takes on vindictive shades:

> Her small immature, girlish figure has grown so terribly emaciated that she gives the impression of being bodiless, a little, skinny, witch-like, old woman, an evil god-mother conjured to life from the page of a fairy tale, whom strong sunlight would dissolve, or a breath of reality disperse into thin air. Her small, delicate oval face is haggard with innumerable wrinkles, and so pale it seems bloodless and corpse-like, a mask of death, the great dark eyes staring from black holes. She is dressed in white, as ever, but with pathetically obvious touches of calculating, coquettish feminine adornment. (3:503)

53. O'Neill, *Selected Letters*, p. 148.

54. Boulton, *Part of a Long Story*, pp. 48, 46–47, 256.

55. Ibid., p. 180.

56. O'Neill, *Poems*, p. 16.

57. See Withers, "Artistic Women and Women Artists."

58. See Showalter, "Representing Ophelia," pp. 83–84.

59. Ibid., p. 89.

60. Showalter, *The Female Malady*, pp. 60, 81.

61. Showalter, "Representing Ophelia," p. 86.

62. Sheaffer, *Son and Playwright*, pp. 384–85. Sheaffer suggests that "Mrs. Keeney is the earliest image of Ella O'Neill in her son's writings" (p. 385).

63. O'Neill, *Eugene O'Neill at Work*, p. 290.

64. Black, "Ella O'Neill's Addiction," p. 24. Black writes: "Although withdrawal symptoms of 'the abstinence syndrome' are intense for only 2 or 3 days, and are 'generally milder than the dramatic depictions of cold-turkey withdrawal,' the symptoms may persist for 6 months or longer" (p. 24).

65. For a discussion of Sanger's contribution to the sexualization of motherhood, and of Progressive and Socialist narratives of prostitution, see Mari Jo Buhle, *Women and Socialism*, pp. 272, 254. Curiously, the guidelines for censorship in

Boston, which resulted in the banning of *Strange Interlude* in 1929, included taboo-ing "the portrayal by performers of either sex of a dope fiend" (see TGPB, 106: Karl Schriftgiesser, *Boston Evening Transcript*, Sept. 21, 1929).

66. Levy, *Other Women*, p. 127.

67. The first O'Neill scholar who suggested provocative parallels between *Hamlet* and *Long Day's Journey* as well as some links between Mary and Fat Vi was Normand Berlin in his 1979 essay "Ghosts of the Past," p. 318. For a more extensive and fascinating discussion of O'Neill's debt to and use of Shakespeare, see Berlin's 1993 study, *O'Neill's Shakespeare*, esp. pp. 187–224. Also see some of the connections Alexander establishes among Fat Vi, Mary Tyrone, and the prostitute Cybel in *The Great God Brown* (*Eugene O'Neill's Creative Struggle*, pp. 66–67). I developed the rudiments of my own reading of Mary and Fat Vi as a graduate student at the University of London in 1977–78. Bentley's remarks about Eugene probably apply equally well to his brother Jamie: "He was very much an Irishman, and the Virgin Mother composed an image he could not do without. He liked to use the phrase, 'God the Mother.' Otherwise, in the works of O'Neill, femininity is found largely in whores" ("The Life and Hates of Eugene O'Neill," p. 31). Bentley's observation and *Long Day's Journey* raise interesting questions about *who* Eugene and Jamie were sleeping with—on a substitutive level—when they engaged prostitutes. Who was it they were simultaneously loving *and* despising in bed?

68. Bogard, *Contour in Time*, p. 433.

Afterword

1. See Wainscott, *Staging O'Neill*, p. 288. Also see Sands, "O'Neill's Stage Directions."

2. See TGPB, 217: John Mason Brown, "Seeing Things: All O'Neilling," *Saturday Review of Literature* 39 (Oct. 19, 1949): 26.

3. See TGPB, 125: Anon., "Dr. Hauptmann Hails U. S. Idea of 'Be Yourself,' " *New York Herald Tribune*, March 17, 1932.

4. See TGPB, 124: Ben Washer, "O'Neill Says Europe Will Seek Theatrical Guidance Here Soon," *New York World-Telegram*, May 22, 1931.

5. See Nathan, "Theatre," p. 243. Nathan reserves some commendation for the New York theatre and lavishes much praise on O'Neill.

6. Sheaffer, *Son and Artist*, p. 364.

7. Clark, *Eugene O'Neill*, p. 5; Raleigh, *Plays of Eugene O'Neill*, p. 243.

8. This is the title of Atkinson's chapter on O'Neill in *Broadway*, pp. 191–205.

9. I owe this point to Leonard Tennenhouse.

10. See Foucault, "Subject and Power," p. 213.

11. See Stallybrass, "Shakespeare, the Individual, and the Text," p. 593.

12. Sinfield, *Alfred Tennyson*, p. 66. Other provocative readings on the complex history of "the individual" include Raymond Williams's essay on "Individual" in *Keywords*, pp. 133–36; Armstrong and Tennenhouse, *Imaginary Puritan*, esp. pp. 17–18, 161–62, and 171–72; Morris, *Discovery of the Individual 1050–1200*, esp. pp. 1–19; Kendrick, *Milton*, esp. pp. 55–77; Lukes, *Individualism*; Warner, "Thoreau's Bottom"; Caudwell, *Studies and Further Studies in a Dying Culture*, esp. pp. 158–

228; Moore, *Status of the Individual in East and West*; Probyn, *Sexing the Self*, esp. pp. 1–31.

13. See C. B. Macpherson's classic, *Political Theory of Possessive Individualism*.

14. See Gillian Brown, *Domestic Individualism*.

15. See Zaretsky, *Capitalism, the Family, and Personal Life*, Armstrong, *Desire and Domestic Fiction*, Gillian Brown, *Domestic Individualism*, and Pfister, *Production of Personal Life*. The emergence of the middle-class psychological self in the nineteenth century complicates Warren Susman's use of the word "character" to describe the reproduction of subjectivity before the advent of modern consumer culture. Not only was the second half of the nineteenth century a consumer culture (see Lears, "Beyond Veblen: Rethinking Consumer Culture in America"), mid-nineteenth-century fiction was already concerned with "depth," even when it represented it through a discourse of sentiment and character (see Pfister, *Production of Personal Life*, pp. 27–28, 54–56). Thus it is not surprising that many reviewers and critics have compared O'Neill's psychological plays to the overheated psychological fictions of Hawthorne, Poe, and Melville (see for example Raleigh's *Plays of Eugene O'Neill*, pp. 243–83). Susman and other historians who have helped us understand the importance of the concept of character in the nineteenth century have made invaluable contributions, but the term does not encompass the various forms that middle-class subjectivity could take.

16. See Raymond Williams's discussion of the word "individual" in *Keywords*, pp. 133–36.

17. In a daring speculative essay, "The Romantic Construction of the Unconscious," Catherine Belsey argues that the potential radicalism of psychoanalysis resides in the challenge it poses to the modern bourgeois ideology that the self is sovereign, fixed, unitary, and—ideally—in control of itself, and that this self can therefore be held individually responsible for its "free" choice of commodities, government officials, cultural meanings, and economic practices (pp. 75–76). By contrast, psychoanalysis exposes a "split subject, no longer master in its own house" (p. 59). She traces the construction of a romantic discourse of the unconscious and the fragmented, out-of-control self back to the political "crises of the 1790s" and their manifold cultural and intellectual ramifications in the first half of the nineteenth century. I am somewhat skeptical of the "challenge" either the romantic or the psychoanalytic ideology of the split self actually posed to the bourgeois hegemony. Their "de-centered" or nonunitary notions of selfhood have usually remained very much *within* the ideological field of "the individual"—despite the not-always-clear, fairly recent efforts of Lacanian and feminist-Lacanian theorists to criticize assumptions about the autonomous self. Romantic, psychoanalytic, and pop psychological imaginings of the "de-centered" self usually give more credence to the idea that the self is mysteriously and unfathomably "individual" at a historical phase when—for a range of economic, political, and sociological reasons—at least some members of the bourgeoisie entertained doubts about the autonomy of their individuality and the "freedom" of the choices that were made available to them. It can be argued that the discourse of the unconscious, fragmented self became a modern, therapeutic bourgeois ideology of self that—perhaps because of its individualized "radicalism"—*supplemented*, even as it challenged, an older bour-

geois ideology of selfhood that continues to be popular (it is still going strong in the United States), but is constantly under strain.

18. Arthur Miller, *Timebends*, p. 228. See the Soviet critic Alexander Anikst's "Preface to Russian Translations of O'Neill." Anikst links O'Neill's plays to the writings of Dreiser, Lewis, Faulkner, Hemingway, Fitzgerald, and Wolfe, arguing that "each of them, in his own way, expressed deep concern about man's fate in an advanced industrial society during an imperialist era. Unquestionably, their greatest service to American literature was the exposure of flagrant social contradictions . . . in bourgeois civilization." However, in the next sentence he claims that "what is most important in their work is the rich and many-faceted depiction of the psychology of twentieth-century man." He sees this as implicitly radical: "The social significance of their novels and dramas cannot be defined by the degree to which they accepted the progressive social movements of their time." They challenged "bourgeois reality" by asking: "Why was the American way of life so unbearable? What brought about constant spiritual crises?" Anikst does not offer details about the radicalism of their answers. He concludes: "They portrayed not abstract social forces but concrete people exposing the depths of their emotions" (pp. 154–55). Anikst seems to take "depth" as an ahistorical given and interprets its exposure as O'Neill's Dostoyevsky-like radicalism. Another Soviet critic, Maya Koreneva, also takes this approach: "In defining these plays as 'psychological studies,' I do not mean in the least that they are devoid of social significance. . . . The depth and originality of O'Neill's insights are, in fact, the result of his highly critical attitude toward American society" ("One Hundred Percent American Tragedy," p. 150). What we must gauge are the contradictory historical and ideological effects that the "psychological" produced as an implicitly "radical" bourgeois discourse.

19. Lukàcs, *Meaning of Contemporary Realism*, p. 84. I thank Christina Crosby for bringing Lukàcs's discussion of O'Neill to my attention.

20. One reviewer of *The Hairy Ape* applauded this grandstand-of-detachment approach and outlined its political implications. See OS, 5: Heywood Broun, "It Seems to Me," *New York World*, April 30, 1922: "[O'Neill] sympathizes no more with Yank than with the Cockney [Long, the Socialist] or with Fifth Avenue dummies [the wealthy churchgoers]. Not only does he not sympathize individually, but even less does he take any one's cause. If he is a revolutionary he never lets the fact interfere with his plays. What O'Neill has to say is not that the human race ought to be improved but that it cannot be. That it cannot be improved, by himself or by a reformer, alternately disgusts and amuses him. And that is his propaganda, such as it is." In reference to *More Stately Mansions*, Eric Bentley describes O'Neill's theoretical dead end: "America, it seems, is blamed for having missed the opportunity of giving humanity a fresh start and creating an earthly paradise. Yet the fact of this failure is also presented as proof that human nature is perverse and evil, in which case the opportunity to make a fresh start never existed" ("Touch of the Adolescent," p. 396).

21. See Raymond Williams's discussion of what might be termed the complacent pessimism of "liberal tragedy": "The identification of the false society . . . [becomes] part of one's own desires, so that it can no longer be meaningfully opposed, or even bitterly challenged by death, but has simply to be confirmed, forgiven, and lived

with, in our separate and isolated suffering" (*Modern Tragedy*, p. 105). Also see Julie Adam's perceptive description of O'Neill's radical pessimism in *Versions of Heroism in Modern Drama*, pp. 122–23, 127. In addition, consult Tom F. Driver's astute discussion of O'Neill's pessimism and his "Thanatos-romanticism" in "On the Late Plays of Eugene O'Neill."

22. For examples of excellent cultural approaches to O'Neill see Von Wiegand's "Quest of Eugene O'Neill," Flexner's *American Playwrights*, Alexander's "Eugene O'Neill as Social Critic" and "Psychological Fate" (both published in the early 1950s), Bentley's "Life and Hates of Eugene O'Neill," "Touch of the Adolescent," and "Trying to Like O'Neill," and Raleigh's *Plays of Eugene O'Neill*, especially his chapter "The Form," pp. 171–238. Scholars of O'Neill's work and of American theatre in general can learn much from recent provocative studies of nineteenth-century American theatre, such as McConachie's *Melodramatic Formation* (also see his essay "Using the Concept of Cultural Hegemony to Write Theatre History"), Lott's *Love and Theft*, Levine's *Highbrow/Lowbrow*, and Allen's *Horrible Prettiness*.

23. Raymond Williams, *Marxism and Literature*, p. 131. Also see Williams's discussion of nineteenth- and twentieth-century "liberal tragedy," especially his remarks on its location of individualism in "individual psychology" and on its "structure of feeling" (which shifts from a focus on the self against society to the self against the self) (*Modern Tragedy*, pp. 87–88, 99–100, 105).

24. Eagleton, *Ideology*, p. 149.

Aaron, Daniel. *Writers on the Left: Episodes in American Literary Communism.* New York: Harcourt, Brace & World, 1961.

Abu-Lughod, Lila, and Catherine A. Lutz. "Introduction: Emotion, Discourse, and the Politics of Everyday Life." In Catherine A. Lutz and Lila Abu-Lughod, eds., *Language and the Politics of Emotion.* Cambridge: Cambridge University Press; Paris: Editions de la Maison des Sciences de l'Homme, 1990.

Adam, Julie. *Versions of Heroism in Modern Drama: Redefinitions by Miller, Williams, O'Neill and Anderson.* London: Macmillan, 1991.

Alexander, Doris. "Eugene O'Neill as Social Critic." In Oscar Cargill, N. Bryllion, and William J. Fisher, eds., *O'Neill and His Plays: Four Decades of Criticism.* New York: New York University Press, 1961.

———. *Eugene O'Neill's Creative Struggle: The Decisive Decade, 1929–1933.* University Park, Penn.: Pennsylvania State University Press, 1992.

———. "Psychological Fate in *Mourning Becomes Electra.*" *PMLA* 68 (December 1953): 923–34.

———. *The Tempering of Eugene O'Neill.* New York: Harcourt, Brace & World, 1962.

Allen, Frederick Lewis. *Only Yesterday: An Informal History of the Nineteen-Twenties.* New York: Harper, 1931.

Allen, Robert. *Horrible Prettiness: Burlesque and American Culture.* Chapel Hill: University of North Carolina Press, 1991.

Altick, Richard D. *Lives and Letters: A History of Literary Biography in England and America.* New York: Knopf, 1969.

Anderson, Michael, ed. *Approaches to the History of the Western Family, 1500–1914.* London: Macmillan, 1980.

Anikst, Alexander. "Preface to Russian Translations of O'Neill." In Horst Frenz and Susan Tuck, eds., *Eugene O'Neill's Critics: Voices from Abroad.* Carbondale: Southern Illinois University Press, 1984.

Anthony, Katharine. "The Family." In Harold E. Stearns, ed., *Civilization in the United States: An Inquiry by Thirty Americans.* New York: Harcourt, Brace, 1922.

Arent, Arthur. *One-Third of a Nation.* In *Federal Theatre Plays.* New York: Random House, 1938.

Ariès, Philippe. *Centuries of Childhood: A Social History of Family Life.* Translated by Robert Baldick. New York: Vintage, 1962.

———. "The Family and the City in the Old World and the New." In Virginia Tufte and Barbara Myerhoff, eds., *Changing Images of the Family.* New Haven: Yale University Press, 1979.

Armstrong, Nancy. *Desire and Domestic Fiction: A Political History of the Novel.* New York: Oxford University Press, 1987.

Armstrong, Nancy, and Leonard Tennenhouse. *The Imaginary Puritan: Literature, Intellectual Labor, and the Origins of Personal Life.* Berkeley: University of California Press, 1992.

———. "The Literature of Conduct, the Conduct of Literature, and the Politics of Desire: An Introduction." In Nancy Armstrong and Leonard Tennenhouse, eds., *The Ideology of Conduct: Essays on Literature and the History of Sexuality*. New York: Methuen, 1987.

——. "Representing Violence, or 'How the West Was Won.' " In Nancy Armstrong and Leonard Tennenhouse, eds., *The Violence of Representation: Literature and the History of Violence*. London: Routledge, 1989.

Atkinson, Brooks. *Broadway*. New York: Macmillan, 1970.

Atkinson, Brooks, and Albert Hirschfeld. *The Lively Years 1920–1973*. New York: Association Press, 1973.

Atkinson, Jennifer McCabe. *Eugene O'Neill: A Descriptive Bibliography*. Pittsburgh: University of Pittsburgh Press, 1974.

Banner, Lois. *American Beauty*. New York: Knopf, 1983.

Baritz, Loren, ed., *The Culture of the Twenties*. Indianapolis: Bobbs-Merrill, 1970.

Barkan, Elazar. *The Retreat of Scientific Racism: Changing Concepts of Race in Britain and the United States between the World Wars*. Cambridge: Cambridge University Press, 1992.

Barker-Benfield, G. J. *The Horrors of the Half-Known Life: Male Attitudes toward Women and Sexuality in Nineteenth-Century America*. New York: Harper Colophon, 1976.

Barlow, Judith. "O'Neill's Many Mothers: Mary Tyrone, Josie Hogan, and Their Antecedents." In Shyamal Bagchee, ed., *Perspectives on O'Neill: New Essays*. Victoria, B.C.: English Literary Studies, University of Victoria, 1988.

Barnes, Albert C. "Negro Art and America." In Alain Locke, ed., *The New Negro*. 1925. Rpt. New York: Atheneum, 1980.

Barrett, Michele, and Mary McIntosh. *The Anti-Social Family*. London: Verso, 1982.

Barton, Bruce. "You Can't Fool Your Other Self." *American Magazine* 91 (September 1921): 11–13, 68.

Bellah, Robert N., Richard Madsen, William M. Sullivan, Ann Swidler, Steven M. Tipton. *Habits of the Heart: Individualism and Commitment in American Life*. Berkeley: University of California Press, 1985.

Belsey, Catherine. "The Romantic Construction of the Unconscious." In Francis Barker, Peter Hulme, Margaret Iversen, and Diana Loxley, eds., *Literature, Politics and Theory: Papers from the Essex Conference 1976–84*. London: Methuen, 1986.

Benjamin, Jessica. *Bonds of Love: Psychoanalysis, Feminism, and the Problem of Domination*. New York: Pantheon, 1988.

Bentley, Eric. "The Life and Hates of Eugene O'Neill." In *Thinking about the Playwright: Comments from Four Decades*. Evanston: Northwestern University Press, 1987.

——. "Theatre and Therapy." In *Thinking about the Playwright: Comments from Four Decades*. Evanston: Northwestern University Press, 1987.

——. "A Touch of the Adolescent." In *What is Theatre? Incorporating the Dramatic Event and Other Reviews 1944–1967*. New York: Atheneum, 1968.

——. "Trying to Like O'Neill." In Jordan Y. Miller, ed., *Playwright's Progress: O'Neill and the Critics*. Chicago: Scott, Foresman, 1965.

Ben-Zvi, Linda. "Susan Glaspell and Eugene O'Neill." *Eugene O'Neill Newsletter* 6 (Summer-Fall 1982): 21–29.

———. "Susan Glaspell and Eugene O'Neill: The Imagery of Gender." *Eugene O'Neill Newsletter* 10 (Spring 1986): 22–27.

Berger, John. *And Our Faces, My Heart, Brief as Photos*. New York: Pantheon, 1984.

Berger, John, Sven Blomberg, Chris Fox, Michael Dibb, and Richard Hollis. *Ways of Seeing*. Harmondsworth, Middlesex: Penguin, 1979.

Bergin, Thomas G. *Yale's Residential Colleges: The First Fifty Years*. New Haven: Yale University, 1983.

Berlin, Normand. "Ghosts of the Past: O'Neill and Hamlet." *Massachusetts Review* 22 (Summer 1979): 312–23.

———. *O'Neill's Shakespeare*. Ann Arbor: University of Michigan Press, 1993.

Berman, Louis. "Jealousy Farcified." *New Review: A Critical Survey of International Socialism* 3 (November 1, 1915): 287.

Bettelheim, Bruno. *The Children of the Dream*. Toronto: Macmillan, 1969.

Bigsby, C. W. E. *A Critical Introduction to Twentieth-Century American Drama*. Vol. 1, *1900–1940*. Cambridge: Cambridge University Press, 1982.

———. "Introduction." In C. W. E. Bigsby, ed., *Plays by Susan Glaspell*. Cambridge: Cambridge University Press, 1987.

———. "A View from East Anglia." *American Quarterly* 41 (March 1989): 128–32.

Birken, Lawrence. *Consuming Desire: Sexual Science and the Emergence of a Culture of Abundance, 1871–1914*. Ithaca, N.Y.: Cornell University Press, 1988.

Birnbaum, Lucille C. "Behaviorism in the 1920's." *American Quarterly* 7 (Spring 1955): 15–30.

Bisch, Louis, M.D. *Be Glad You're Neurotic*. New York: McGraw-Hill, 1946.

Black, Stephen A. "Ella O'Neill's Addiction." *Eugene O'Neill Newsletter* 9 (Spring 1985): 24–26.

Blake, Ben. *The Awakening of the American Theatre*. New York: Tomorrow Publishers, 1935.

Blanchard, Phyllis. *The Child and Society: An Introduction to the Social Psychology of the Child*. New York: Longman's, Green, 1928.

Blanchard, Phyllis, and Carlyn Manasses. *New Girls for Old*. New York: Macauley, 1930.

Blankfort, Michael. "Facing the New Audience: Sketches toward an Aesthetic for the Revolutionary Theatre." *New Theatre* (June 1, 1934): 11–12.

———. "Facing the New Audience: Sketches toward an Aesthetic for the Revolutionary Theatre—Part II." *New Theatre* (July-August 1934): 14–15.

———. "Facing the New Audience: Sketches toward an Aesthetic for the Revolutionary Theatre—Concluded." *New Theatre* (December 3, 1934): 25–27.

Bledstein, Burton. *The Culture of Professionalism: The Middle Class and the Development of Higher Education in America*. New York: Norton, 1976.

Bloom, Harold. "Introduction." In Harold Bloom, ed., *Eugene O'Neill's The Iceman Cometh*. New York: Chelsea House, 1987.

Bloom, Steven F. "Empty Bottles, Empty Dreams: O'Neill's Use of Drinking and Alcoholism in *Long Day's Journey Into Night*." In James J. Martine, ed., *Critical Essays on Eugene O'Neill*. Boston: G. K. Hall, 1984.

Blumin, Stuart M. *The Emergence of the Middle Class: Social Experience in the American City, 1760–1900*. Cambridge: Cambridge University Press, 1989.

Boal, Augusto. *The Theatre of the Oppressed*. Translated by Charles A. McBride and Maria-Odilia Leal McBride. New York: Theatre Communications Group, 1985.

Bogard, Travis. *Contour in Time: The Plays of Eugene O'Neill*. Rev. ed. New York: Oxford University Press, 1988.

Boulton, Agnes. *Part of a Long Story*. Garden City, N.Y.: Doubleday, 1958.

Bourdieu, Pierre. *The Field of Cultural Production: Essays on Art and Literature*. New York: Columbia University Press, 1993.

Bower, Martha Gilman. *Eugene O'Neill's Unfinished Threnody and Process of Invention in Four Cycle Plays*. Lewiston, N.Y.: Edwin Mellen Press, 1992.

Bowlby, Rachel. *Shopping with Freud*. London: Routledge, 1993.

Brantlinger, Patrick. *Crusoe's Footprints: Cultural Studies in Britain and America*. New York: Routledge, 1990.

Brecht, Bertolt. *Brecht on Theatre: The Development of an Aesthetic*. Edited and translated by John Willett. New York: Hill and Wang, 1964.

Brenman-Gibson, Margaret. *Clifford Odets: American Playwright. The Years from 1906 to 1940*. New York: Atheneum, 1981.

Briffault, Robert. *The Mothers: A Study of the Origins of Sentiments and Institutions*. 3 vols. New York: Macmillan, 1927.

Brittan, Arthur. *The Privatised World*. London: Routledge & Kegan Paul, 1978.

Brodhead, Richard H. *The School of Hawthorne*. New York: Oxford University Press, 1986.

———. "Sparing the Rod: Discipline and Fiction in Antebellum America." *Representations* 21 (Winter 1988): 67–96.

Brougham, John. *A Recollection of O'Flannigan and the Faeries*. New York: Samuel French, 1856.

Brown, Dorothy M. *Setting a Course: American Women in the 1920s*. Boston: G. K. Hall, 1987.

Brown, Gillian. *Domestic Individualism: Imagining Self in Nineteenth-Century America*. Berkeley: University of California Press, 1990.

Buckley, Kerry W. *Mechanical Man: John Broadus Watson and the Beginnings of Behaviorism*. New York: Guilford Press, 1989.

Buhle, Mari Jo. *Women and American Socialism, 1870–1920*. Urbana: University of Illinois Press, 1981.

Buhle, Mari Jo, Paul Buhle, and Dan Georgakas. *Encyclopedia of the American Left*. New York: Garland, 1990.

Buhle, Paul. *Marxism in the United States: Remapping the History of the American Left*. Rev. ed. London: Verso, 1991.

Burger, Peter. *Theory of the Avant-Garde*. Translated by Michael Shaw. Minneapolis: University of Minnesota Press, 1984.

Burgess, Ernest. "The Family as a Unity of Interacting Personalities." *The Family* 7 (March 1926): 3–9.

Burnham, John C. *How Superstition Won and Science Lost: Popularizing Science and Health in the United States*. New Brunswick, N.J.: Rutgers University Press, 1987.

——. "The New Psychology." In Adele Heller and Lois Rudnick, eds., *1915, The Cultural Moment: The New Politics, the New Woman, the New Psychology, the New Art, and the New Theatre in America.* New Brunswick, N.J.: Rutgers University Press, 1991.

——. "The New Psychology: From Narcissism to Social Control." In John Braeman, Robert H. Bremmer, and David Brody, eds., *Change and Continuity in Twentieth-Century America: The 1920's.* Columbus: Ohio State University Press, 1968.

——. "On the Origins of Behaviorism." *Journal of the History of the Behavioral Sciences* 4 (April 1968): 143–51.

——. "Psychiatry, Psychology and the Progressive Movement." *American Quarterly* 12 (Winter 1960): 457–65.

Burrow, J. W. *Evolution and Society: A Study in Victorian Social Theory.* Cambridge: Cambridge University Press, 1966.

Buttitta, Tony, and Barry Witham. *Uncle Sam Presents: A Memoir of the Federal Theatre, 1935–1939.* Philadelphia: University of Pennsylvania Press, 1982.

Calhoun, Arthur W. *A Social History of the American Family.* 3 vols. 1917–19. Rpt. New York: Barnes & Noble, 1960.

Calverton, Victor Francis. *American Literature at the Crossroads.* Seattle: University of Washington Bookstore, 1931.

——. *The Bankruptcy of Marriage.* New York: Macaulay, 1928.

——. "Sex and the Social Struggle." In Victor Francis Calverton and Samuel D. Schmalhausen, eds., *Sex in Civilization.* London: George Allen & Unwin, 1929.

——. *Sex Expression in Literature.* New York: Boni & Liverwright, 1926.

——. "The Theatre: Season 1931–1932 in Review." *Modern Quarterly* 6 (Summer 1932): 95–97.

Canby, Henry Seidel. "Sex and Marriage in the Nineties." *Harper's* 169 (1934): 427–36.

Carby, Hazel V. *Reconstructing Womanhood: The Emergence of the Afro-American Woman Novelist.* New York: Oxford University Press, 1987.

Cargill, Oscar. *Intellectual America: Ideas on the March.* New York: Macmillan, 1941.

Cargill, Oscar, N. Bryllion, and William J. Fisher, eds. *O'Neill and His Plays: Four Decades of Criticism.* New York: New York University Press, 1961.

Caspar, Scott. "Constructing American Lives: The Cultural History of Biography in Nineteenth-Century America." Ph.D. diss., Yale University, 1992.

Caudwell, Christopher. *Studies and Further Studies in a Dying Culture.* New York: Monthly Review Press, 1971.

"The Cause of and Remedy for Race Riots." *The Messenger* (September 1919): 14–21.

Cheney, Sheldon. *The Art Theatre.* Rev. ed. New York: Knopf, 1925.

——. *The New Movement in Theatre.* 1914. Rpt. Westport, Conn.: Greenwood Press, 1977.

Clark, Barrett H. *Eugene O'Neill: The Man and His Plays.* New York: McBride, 1929.

Clurman, Harold. *The Fervent Years: The Story of the Group Theatre and the Thirties.* 1945. Rpt. New York: Hill and Wang, 1957.

Cole, Lester, and John Howard Lawson. "Two Views on O'Neill." *Masses and Mainstream* 7 (June 1954): 56–63.

Coleman, Loyd Ring, and Saxe Commins. *Psychology: A Simplification.* New York: Boni & Liverwright, 1927.

Coleman, McAlister. "Lobby and Aisle." *New York Socialist Call,* November 21, 1936.

Commins, Dorothy, ed. *"Love and Admiration and Respect": The O'Neill-Commins Correspondence.* Durham, N.C.: Duke University Press, 1986.

Cooley, John R. *Savages and Naturals: Black Portraits by White Writers in Modern American Literature.* Newark: University of Delaware Press, 1982.

Coontz, Stephanie. *The Social Origins of Private Life: A History of American Families, 1600–1900.* London: Verso, 1988.

——. *The Way We Never Were: American Families and the Nostalgia Trap.* New York: Basic Books, 1992.

Coryell, John R. "Marriage or Free Union, Which?" *Mother Earth* 2 (February 1988): 566–78.

——. "The Value of Chastity." *Mother Earth* 8 (November 1913): 273–78.

Cosgrove, Stuart. "From Shock Troupe to Group Theatre." In Raphael Samuel, Ewan MacColl, and Stuart Cosgrove, *Theatres of the Left, 1880–1935: Workers' Theatre Movements in Britain and America.* London: Routledge & Kegan Paul, 1985.

Cott, Nancy F. *The Bonds of Womanhood: Woman's Sphere in New England, 1780–1835.* New Haven: Yale University Press, 1977.

——. *The Grounding of Modern Feminism.* New Haven: Yale University Press, 1987.

Cronin, Harry. *Eugene O'Neill, Irish and American: A Study in Cultural Context.* New York, Arno Press, 1976.

Crothers, Rachel. *Expressing Willie, Nice People, 39 East.* New York: Brentano's, 1924.

Dardis, Tom. *The Thirsty Muse: Alcohol and the American Writer.* New York: Ticknor & Fields, 1989.

Dawley, Alan. *Struggles for Justice: Social Responsibility and the Liberal State.* Cambridge: Harvard University Press, 1991.

De Cleyre, Voltarine. "They Who Marry Do Ill." *Mother Earth* 2 (January 1908): 500–511.

Delany, Paul. *British Autobiography in the Seventeenth Century.* London: Routledge & Kegan Paul, 1969.

Dell, Floyd. "Explanations and Apologies." *The Liberator* 5 (June 1922): 25–26.

——. *Intellectual Vagabondage: An Apology for the Intelligentsia.* New York: George H. Doran, 1926.

——. "A Psycho-Analytic Confession." *The Liberator* 3 (April 1920): 15–19.

——. "Speaking of Psycho-Analysis: The New Boon for Dinner Table Conversationalists." *Vanity Fair* 5 (December 1915): 53.

D'Emilio, John, and Estelle Freedman. *Intimate Matters: A History of Sexuality in America.* New York: Harper & Row, 1988.

Demos, John. "Introduction: Family History's Past Achievements and Future Prospects." In Jean E. Hunter and Paul T. Mason, eds., *The American Family: Historical Perspectives.* Pittsburgh: Duquesne University Press, 1991.

———. "Oedipus and America: Historical Perspectives on the Reception of Psychoanalysis in the United States." *Annual of Psychoanalysis* 6 (1978): 23–28.

———. *Past, Present, and Personal: The Family and the Life Course in American History.* New York: Oxford University Press, 1986.

Dennison, Sam. *Scandalize My Name: Black Imagery in American Popular Music.* New York: Garland, 1982.

Deutsch, Helen, and Stella Hanau. *The Provincetown: A Story of the Theatre.* 1931. Rpt. New York: Russell & Russell, 1972.

De Voto, Bernard. "Minority Report." *Saturday Review of Literature* 15 (November 21, 1936): 3, 4, 16.

Ditzion, Sidney. *Marriage Morals and Sex in America: A History of Ideas.* New York: Bookman, 1953.

Domingo, W. A. "A New Negro and a New Day." *The Messenger* 2 (November 1920): 144–45.

Drinnon, Richard. *Rebel in Paradise: A Biography of Emma Goldman.* Chicago: University of Chicago Press, 1961.

Driver, Tom F. "On the Late Plays of Eugene O'Neill." In John Gassner, ed., *O'Neill: A Collection of Critical Essays.* Englewood Cliffs, N.J.: Prentice-Hall, 1964.

Duberman, Martin Bauml. *Paul Robeson.* New York: Knopf, 1988.

Du Bois, W. E. B. *The Correspondence of W. E. B. Du Bois.* Vol. 1, *Selections, 1877–1934.* Edited by Herbert Aptheker. Amherst: University of Massachusetts Press, 1973.

du Cille, Ann. "Blues Notes on Black Sexuality: Sex and the Texts of Jessie Fauset and Nella Larsen." *Journal of the History of Sexuality* 3 (1993): 418–44.

Dunn, Arthur. *Scientific Selling and Advertising.* New York: Harper, 1922.

Dyer, Richard. *Heavenly Bodies: Film Stars and Society.* New York: St. Martin's Press, 1986.

Dymkowski, Christine. "On the Edge: The Plays of Susan Glaspell." *Modern Drama* 31 (March 1988): 91–105.

Eagleton, Terry. *Ideology: An Introduction.* London: Verso, 1991.

———. *Literary Theory: An Introduction.* Minneapolis: University of Minnesota Press, 1983.

Eastman, Max. *Art and the Life of Action with Other Essays.* New York: Knopf, 1934.

———. Editorial. *The Liberator* 1 (March 1918): 3.

———. "Exploring the Soul and Healing the Body." *Everybody's Magazine* 23 (June 1915): 741–50.

———. "Mr.—er—er—Oh! What's his name?" *Everybody's Magazine* (July 1915): 95–103.

Eaton, Walter Prichard. *The Theatre Guild: The First Ten Years.* New York: Brentano's, 1929.

Ehrenreich, Barbara. *Fear of Falling: The Inner Life of the Middle Class.* New York: Harper Perennial, 1990.

Ehrenreich, Barbara, and John Ehrenreich. "The Professional-Managerial Class." In Pat Walker, ed., *Between Labor and Capital.* Boston: South End Press, 1979.

Eisen, Kurt. *The Inner Strength of Opposites: O'Neill's Novelistic Drama and the Melodramatic Imagination*. Athens: University of Georgia Press, 1994.

Elias, Norbert. *Power and Civility*. Vol. 2 of *The Civilizing Process*. Translated by Edmund Jephcott, New York: Pantheon, 1982.

Engel, Edwin A. *The Haunted Heroes of Eugene O'Neill*. Cambridge: Harvard University Press, 1953.

Ewen, Stuart. *All Consuming Image: The Politics of Style in Contemporary Culture*. New York: Basic Books, 1984.

——. *Captains of Consciousness: Advertising and the Social Roots of Consumer Culture*. New York: McGraw-Hill, 1976.

Ewen, Stuart, and Elizabeth Ewen. *Channels of Desire: Mass Images and the Shaping of American Consciousness*. New York: McGraw-Hill, 1982.

Falk, Candace. *Love, Anarchy and Emma Goldman*. New York: Holt, Rinehart and Winston, 1984.

Falk, Doris. *Eugene O'Neill and the Tragic Tension*. New Brunswick, N.J.: Rutgers University Press, 1958.

Fass, Paula. *The Damned and the Beautiful: American Youth in the 1920's*. New York: Oxford University Press, 1977.

Fauset, Jessie. "The Gift of Laughter." In Alain Locke, ed., *The New Negro*. 1925. Rpt. New York: Atheneum. 1980.

Fechter, Charles. *Monte Cristo (James O'Neill's Version)*. In Barrett H. Clark, ed., *Favorite Plays of the Nineteenth Century*. Princeton: Princeton University Press, 1943.

Ferraro, Thomas J. *Ethnic Passages: Literary Immigrants in Twentieth-Century America*. Chicago: University of Chicago Press, 1993.

Fielding, William J. *The Caveman within Us: His Peculiarities and Powers; Enlist His Aid for Health and Efficiency*. New York: E. P. Dutton, 1925.

Fishbein, Leslie. *Rebels in Bohemia: The Radicals of "The Masses," 1911–1917*. Chapel Hill: University of North Carolina Press, 1982.

Flanagan, Hallie. *Arena*. New York: Duell, Sloan, and Pearce, 1940.

Flexner, Eleanor. *American Playwrights 1918–1938: The Theatre Retreats from Reality*. New York: Simon and Schuster, 1938.

Floyd, Virginia, ed., *Eugene O'Neill: A Worldview*. New York: Frederick Ungar, 1979.

——. *The Plays of Eugene O'Neill: A New Assessment*. New York: Frederick Ungar, 1985.

Flynn, Joyce. "A Complex Causality of Neglect." *American Quarterly* 41 (March 1989): 123–27.

Folsom, Michael B. "The Education of Michael Gold." In David Madden, ed., *Proletarian Writers of the Thirties*. Carbondale: Southern Illinois Press, 1968.

Foucault, Michel. *An Introduction*. Vol. 1 of *The History of Sexuality*. New York: Vintage, 1980.

——. "The Subject and Power." In Hubert L. Dreyfus and Paul Rabinow, eds., *Beyond Structuralism and Hermeneutics*. Chicago: University of Chicago Press, 1983.

——. "What Is an Author?" In Paul Rabinow, ed., *The Foucault Reader*. New York: Pantheon, 1984.

Fox, Richard Wightman, and T. J. Jackson Lears. "Introduction." In Richard Wightman Fox and T. J. Jackson Lears, eds., *The Culture of Consumption: Critical Essays in American History, 1880–1980.* New York: Pantheon, 1983.

Fraina, Louis. "Socialism and Psychology." *New Review: A Critical Survey of International Socialism* 3 (May 1, 1915): 10–12.

Frazer, Winifred. *E. G. and E. G. O.: Emma Goldman and "The Iceman Cometh."* Gainesville: University Presses of Florida, 1974.

Freeman, Joseph. *An American Testament: A Narrative of Rebels and Romantics.* New York: Farrar & Rinehart, 1936.

Freud, Sigmund. *Civilization and Its Discontents.* New York: Norton, 1961.

——. *Sexuality and the Psychology of Love.* Edited by Philip Rieff. New York: Collier, 1963.

——. *Totem and Taboo: Some Points of Agreement between the Mental Lives of Savages and Neurotics.* Translated by James Strachey. New York: Norton, 1950.

Friedman, Daniel. "A Brief Description of the Workers' Theatre Movement of the Thirties." In Bruce A. McConachie and Daniel Friedman, eds., *Theatre for Working Class Audiences in the United States, 1830–1980.* Westport, Conn.: Greenwood Press, 1985.

Gadlin, Howard. "Private Lives and Public Order: A Critical View of the History of Intimate Relations in the United States." In George Levinger and Harold Rausch, eds., *Close Relationships: Perspectives on the Meaning of Intimacy.* Amherst: University of Massachusetts Press, 1977.

Gainor, J. Ellen. "A Stage of Her Own: Susan Glaspell's *The Verge* and Women's Dramaturgy." *Journal of American Drama and Theatre* 1 (Spring 1989): 79–99.

Gardener, William. "The Theatre." *New Masses* (January 1934): 28.

Gassner, John, ed. *Eugene O'Neill: A Collection of Critical Essays.* Englewood Cliffs, N.J.: Prentice-Hall, 1964.

——. *Masters of the Drama.* 1949. Rpt. New York: Dover, 1954.

——."A Playreader on Playwrights." *New Theatre* (October 1934): 9–11.

Gates, Henry Louis, Jr. "The Face and Voice of Blackness." In Guy C. McElroy, ed., *Facing History: The Black Image in American Art 1710–1940.* San Francisco: Bedford Arts, 1990.

——. "The Trope of a New Negro and the Reconstruction of the Black." *Representations* 24 (Fall 1988): 129–55.

Gay, Peter. *Freud: A Life for Our Time.* Garden City, N.Y.: Doubleday, 1988.

Geddes, Virgil. *Beyond Tragedy: Footnotes on the Drama.* Seattle: University of Washington Bookstore, 1933.

——. "The End of O'Neill." *New Masses* (February 6, 1934): 27.

——. *Left Turn for American Drama.* Brookfield, Conn.: Brookfield Players, 1934.

——. *The Melodramadness of Eugene O'Neill.* Brookfield, Conn.: Brookfield Players, 1934.

——. *Towards a Revolution in the Theatre.* Brookfield, Conn.: Brookfield Players, 1933.

Gelb, Arthur, and Barbara Gelb. *O'Neill.* Rev. ed. New York: Harper & Row, 1987.

Gelb, Barbara. "Eugene O'Neill in Provincetown." In Adele Heller and Lois Rudnick, eds., *1915, The Cultural Moment: The New Politics, the New Woman, the*

New Psychology, the New Art, and the New Theatre in America. New Brunswick, N.J.: Rutgers University Press, 1991.

Gerstenberg, Alice. *The One-Act Plays*. New York: Brentano's, 1921.

Gifford, Sanford. "The American Reception of Psychoanalysis, 1908–1922." In Adele Heller and Lois Rudnick, eds., *1915, The Cultural Moment: The New Politics, the New Woman, the New Psychology, the New Art, and the New Theatre in America*. New Brunswick, N.J.: Rutgers University Press, 1991.

Gillespie, Richard. "The Hawthorne Experiments and the Politics of Experimentation." In Jill G. Morawski, ed., *The Rise of Experimentation in American Psychology*. New Haven: Yale University Press, 1988.

Gilliam, Dorothy Butler. *Paul Robeson: All-American*. Washington, D.C.: New Republic Book Co., 1976.

Glaspell, Susan. *The Inheritors: A Play in Three Acts*. London: Ernest Benn, 1924.

——. *Lifted Masks*. New York: Frederick A. Stokes, 1912.

——. *Plays*. Boston: Small, Maynard, 1920.

——. *The Road to the Temple*. New York: Frederick A. Stokes, 1941.

——. *The Verge: A Play in Three Acts*. Boston: Small, Maynard, 1922.

Glazer, Nathan, and Daniel P. Moynihan. *Beyond the Melting Pot: The Negroes, Puerto Ricans, Jews, Italians, and Irish of New York City*. Cambridge: MIT Press, 1970.

Gold, Michael. "Defense of Agitprop." *Daily Worker* (March 27, 1934): 5.

——. "Eugene O'Neill's Early Days in the Old 'Hell-Hole.'" *Daily Worker Supplement* (October 27, 1946): 8.

——. "Strike! A Mass Recitation." *New Masses* (July 1926): 19–21.

Goldman, Emma. *Red Emma Speaks: Selected Writings and Speeches*. Edited by Alix Kates Shulman. New York: Random House, 1972.

——. *The Social Significance of Modern Drama*. 1914. Rpt. New York: Applause, 1987.

——. "The Tragedy of Woman's Emancipation." *Mother Earth* 1 (March 1906): 9–18.

Goldstein, Malcolm. *The Political Stage: American Drama and Theater of the Great Depression*. New York: Oxford University Press, 1974.

Goodwin, Donald W., M.D. *Alcohol and the Writer*. Kansas City: Andrews and McMeel, 1988.

Gramsci, Antonio. *Selections from Prison Notebooks*. Edited and translated by Quintin Hoare and Geoffrey Nowell Smith. New York: International Publishers, 1971.

Greeley, Andrew M. *The Irish Americans: The Rise to Money and Power*. New York: Harper & Row, 1981.

——. *That Most Distressful Nation: The Taming of the American Irish*. Chicago: Quadrangle Books, 1972.

Gregory, Montgomery. "The Drama of Negro Life." In Alain Locke, ed., *The New Negro*. 1925. Rpt. New York: Atheneum, 1980.

Griffen, Clyde. "Reconstructing Masculinity from the Evangelical Revival to the Waning of Progressivism: A Speculative Synthesis." In Mark Carnes and Clyde Griffen, eds., *Meanings for Manhood: Constructions of Masculinity in Victorian America*. Chicago: University of Chicago Press, 1990.

Grimké, Sarah. *Letters on the Equality of the Sexes and the Conditions of Women.* 1838. Rpt. New York: Burt Franklin, 1979.

Groves, Ernest, and William Fielding Ogburn. *American Marriage and Family Relationships.* New York: Henry Holt, 1928.

Guarneri, Charles. *The Utopian Alternative: Fourierism in Nineteenth-Century America.* Ithaca, N.Y.: Cornell University Press, 1991.

Habermas, Jurgen. *The Structural Transformation of the Public Sphere: An Inquiry into a Category of Bourgeois Society.* Translated by Thomas Burger. Cambridge: MIT Press, 1993.

Hahn, Emily. *Romantic Rebels: An Informal History of Bohemianism in America.* Boston: Houghton Mifflin, 1967.

Hale, Nathan G., Jr. *Freud and the Americans: The Beginnings of Psychoanalysis in the United States, 1876–1917.* New York: Oxford University Press, 1971.

Halfmann, Ulrich. *Eugene O'Neill: Comments on the Drama and the Theater.* Tubingen: Gunter Narr Verlag Tubingen, 1987.

Hall, Ann C. *"A Kind of Alaska": Women in the Plays of O'Neill, Pinter, and Shepard.* Carbondale: Southern Illinois Press, 1993.

Hall, G. Stanley. *Adolescence: Its Psychology.* Vol. 2. New York: D. Appleton, 1905.

Hall, Stuart. "Cultural Studies and the Centre: Some Problematics and Problems." In *Culture, Media, Language: Working Papers in Cultural Studies, 1972–79.* London: Hutchinson and CCCS, 1980.

——. "The Meaning of New Times." In Stuart Hall and Martin Jacques, eds., *New Times: The Changing Face of Politics in the 1990s.* London: Lawrence & Wishart, 1989.

Halttunen, Karen. "From Parlor to Living Room: Domestic Space, Interior Decoration, and the Culture of Personality." In Simon J. Bronner, ed., *Consuming Visions: Accumulation and Display of Goods in America, 1880–1920.* New York: Norton, 1989.

Hamilton, G. V. *A Research in Marriage.* New York: Albert & Charles Boni, 1929.

Hamilton, G. V., and Kenneth Macgowan. *What Is Wrong with Marriage.* New York: Albert & Charles Boni, 1929.

Hapgood, Hutchins. "The Case of Terry." *Revolt* 1 (February 19, 1916): 6.

Havel, Hippolyte. "The Brothers Karamazov." *Mother Earth* 8 (April 1913): 55–60.

——. "The Faith and Record of Anarchists." *Mother Earth* 6 (February 1912): 367–71.

——. "An Iconoclast." *Road to Freedom* 5 (October 1928): 5.

——. "Literature: Its Influence upon Social Life." *Mother Earth* 3 (October 1908): 329–31.

Hedges, Elaine R. "Afterword." In Charlotte Perkins Gilman, *The Yellow Wallpaper.* Brooklyn: Feminist Press, 1973.

Heelas, Paul. "Emotion Talk Across Cultures." In Rom Harré, ed., *The Social Construction of Emotions.* Oxford: Basil Blackwell, 1986.

Helburn, Theresa. *A Wayward Quest: The Autobiography of Theresa Helburn.* Boston: Little, Brown, 1960.

Heller, Adele, and Lois Rudnick, eds. *1915, The Cultural Moment: The New Politics, the New Woman, the New Psychology, the New Art, and the New Theatre in America.* New Brunswick, N.J.: Rutgers University Press, 1991.

Henderson, Robbin, Pamela Fabry, Adam David Miller, eds. *Ethnic Notions.* Berkeley: Berkeley Art Center, 1982.

Herbert, Christopher. *Culture and Anomie: Ethnographic Imagination in the Nineteenth Century.* Chicago: University of Chicago Press, 1991.

Herbert, T. Walter. *Dearest Beloved: The Hawthornes and the Making of the Middle-Class Family.* Berkeley: University of California Press, 1993.

Hicks, Granville. *The Great Tradition: An Interpretation of American Literature since the Civil War.* New York: Macmillan, 1933.

Himelstein, Morgan. *Drama Was a Weapon: The Left-Wing Theatre in New York, 1929–1941.* New Brunswick, N.J.: Rutgers University Press, 1963.

Hinden, Michael. *Long Day's Journey Into Night: Native Eloquence.* Boston: Twayne, 1990.

Hinkle, Beatrice. "The Chaos of Modern Marriage." *Harper's* 152 (December 1925): 1–13.

——. *The Re-creating of the Individual: A Study of Psychological Types and Their Relation to Psychoanalysis.* New York: Harcourt, Brace, 1923.

Hoffman, Frederick J. *Freudianism and the Literary Mind.* Baton Rouge: Louisiana State University Press, 1945.

——. *The Twenties: American Writing in the Postwar Decades.* New York: Viking, 1955.

Hoffman, Frederick J., Charles Allen, and Carolyn F. Ulrich. *The Little Magazine: A History and a Bibliography.* Princeton: Princeton University Press, 1946.

Hopkins, Arthur. *How's Your Second Act?: Notes on the Art of Production.* New York: Samuel French, 1931.

——. *Reference Point.* New York: Samuel French, 1948.

Houchin, John H., ed. *The Critical Response to Eugene O'Neill.* Westport, Conn.: Greenwood Press, 1993.

Houghton, Walter E. *The Victorian Frame of Mind, 1830–1870.* New Haven: Yale University Press, 1957.

Houseman, John. *Run-through: A Memoir.* New York: Curtis Books, 1972.

Howard, Ronald L. *A Social History of American Family Sociology, 1865–1940.* Edited by John Mogey. Westport, Conn.: Greenwood Press, 1981.

Howard, Sidney. *The Silver Cord.* In *The Theatre Guild Anthology.* New York: Random House, 1936.

Hoyt, Edwin P. *Paul Robeson: The American Othello.* Cleveland: World Publishing Co., 1967.

Huggins, Nathan. *Harlem Renaissance.* New York: Oxford University Press, 1971.

Jameson, Fredric. *Marxism and Form: Twentieth-Century Dialectical Theories of Literature.* Princeton: Princeton University Press, 1974.

——. "Pleasure: A Political Issue." In *Syntax of History.* Vol. 2 of *The Ideologies of Theory: Essays, 1971–1986.* Minneapolis: University of Minnesota Press, 1988.

Jelliffe, Smith Ely, and Louise Brink. *Psychoanalysis and the Drama.* Washington, D.C.: Nervous and Mental Disease Publishing Company, 1922.

Johnson, Abby, and Ronald Mayberry Johnson. *Propaganda and Aesthetics: The Literary Politics of African-American Magazines in the Twentieth-Century.* Amherst: University of Massachusetts Press, 1991.

Johnson, James Weldon. *Black Manhattan*. New York: Arno Press, 1968.

Johnson, Richard. "What Is Cultural Studies Anyway?" *Social Text* 16 (1986): 38–80.

Joll, James. *The Anarchists*. New York: Grosset & Dunlap, 1964.

Jones, Ernest. *The Last Phase*. Vol. 3 of *The Life and Work of Sigmund Freud*. New York: Basic Books, 1957.

Jones, Jacqueline. *Labor of Love, Labor of Sorrow: Black Women, Work, and the Family from Slavery to the Present*. New York: Vintage, 1986.

Jones, Robert Edmond. *The Dramatic Imagination: Reflections and Speculations on the Art of the Theatre*. Rpt. New York: Theatre Arts, 1992.

——. *Towards a New Theatre: The Lectures of Robert Edmond Jones*. Edited by Delbert Unruh. New York: Limelight, 1992.

Kantorovitch, Haim. "The Social Background of the New Psychology." *Modern Quarterly* 4 (January-April 1927): 42–51.

Keller, Morton. *The Art and Politics of Thomas Nast*. New York: Oxford University Press, 1968.

Kendrick, Christopher. *Milton: A Study in Ideology and Form*. New York: Methuen, 1986.

Kett, Joseph. "Adolescence and Youth in Nineteenth-Century America." In Theodore K. Rabb and Robert I. Rotberg, eds., *The Family in History: Interdisciplinary Essays*. New York: Harper Torchbooks, 1971.

Kimbel, Ellen. "Eugene O'Neill as Social Historian: Manners and Morals in *Ah, Wilderness!*" In James J. Martine, ed., *Critical Essays on Eugene O'Neill*. Boston: G. K. Hall, 1984.

King, Woodie, and Ron Milner. "Evolution of a People's Theater." In Woodie King and Ron Milner, eds., *Black Drama Anthology*. New York: New American Library, 1977.

Kirchwey, Freda, ed. *Our Changing Morality*. New York: Albert and Charles Boni, 1930.

Kline, Herbert, ed. *New Theatre and Film 1934 to 1937: An Anthology*. San Diego: Harcourt, Brace, Jovanovich, 1985.

——. "Writing for Workers' Theatre." *New Theatre* (December 1934): 22–23.

Knobel, Dale T. *Paddy and the Republic: Ethnicity and Nationality in Antebellum America*. Middletown, Conn.: Wesleyan University Press, 1986.

Koreneva, Maya. "One Hundred Percent American Tragedy: A Soviet View." In Virginia Floyd, ed., *Eugene O'Neill: A World View*. New York: Frederick Ungar, 1979.

Kovel, Joel. *The Age of Desire: Reflections of a Radical Psychoanalyst*. New York: Pantheon, 1981.

——. *The Radical Spirit: Essays on Psychoanalysis and Society*. London: Free Association Books, 1968.

Kruger, Barbara. *We Won't Play Nature to Your Culture*. London: Institute of Contemporary Arts; Basel: The Kunsthalle, 1984.

Krutch, Joseph Wood. *The Modern Temper: A Study and a Confession*. New York: Harcourt, Brace, 1929.

Kuklick, Henrika. *The Savage Within: The Social History of British Anthropology, 1885–1945*. Cambridge: Cambridge University Press, 1991.

Kuper, Adam. *The Invention of Primitive Society: Transformations of an Illusion.* London: Routledge, 1988.

Kuttner, Alfred B. "Nerves." In Harold E. Stearns, ed., *Civilization in the United States: An Inquiry by Thirty Americans.* New York: Harcourt, Brace, 1922.

Langner, Lawrence. *The Magic Curtain: The Story of a Life in Two Fields, Theatre and Invention by the Founder of the Theatre Guild.* New York: Dutton, 1951.

Larabee, Ann E. " 'Meeting the Outside Face to Face': Susan Glaspell, Djuna Barnes, and O'Neill's *The Emperor Jones.*" In June Schlueter, ed., *Modern American Drama: The Female Canon.* Rutherford, N.J.: Fairleigh Dickinson University Press, 1990.

Larson, Magali Sarfatti. *The Rise of Professionalism: A Sociological Analysis.* Berkeley: University of California Press, 1977.

Lasch, Christopher. *The American Liberals and the Russian Revolution.* New York: Columbia University Press, 1962.

———. *The New Radicalism in America [1889–1963]: The Intellectual as Social Type.* New York: Knopf, 1965.

Lawrence, D. H. *Studies in Classic American Literature.* New York: Viking Press, 1972.

Lawson, John Howard. *Roger Bloomer: A Play in Three Acts.* New York: Thomas Seltzer, 1923.

———. *Theory and Technique of Playwriting.* New York: Hill and Wang, 1960.

———. "Towards a Revolutionary Theatre: The Theatre—The Artist Must Take Sides." *New Theatre* (June 1, 1934): 6–7.

———. "The Tragedy of Eugene O'Neill." *Masses and Mainstream* 7 (March 1954): 7–18.

Leach, Eugene E. "The Radicals of *The Masses.*" In Adele Heller and Lois Rudnick, eds., *1915, The Cultural Moment: The New Politics, the New Woman, the New Psychology, the New Art, and the New Theatre in America.* New Brunswick, N.J.: Rutgers University Press, 1991.

Leach, William. "Strategists of Display and the Production of Desire." In Simon J. Bronner, ed., *Consuming Visions: Accumulation and Display of Goods in America, 1880–1920.* New York: Norton, 1989.

Lears, T. J. Jackson. "Beyond Veblen: Rethinking Consumer Culture in America." In Simon J. Bronner, ed., *Consuming Visions: Accumulation and Display of Goods in America, 1880–1920.* New York: Norton, 1989.

———. "From Salvation to Self-Realization: Advertising and the Therapeutic Roots of the Consumer Culture, 1880–1930." In Richard Wightman Fox and T. J. Jackson Lears, eds., *The Culture of Consumption: Critical Essays in American History, 1880–1900.* New York: Pantheon, 1983.

———. *No Place of Grace: Antimodernism and the Transformation of American Culture, 1880–1920.* New York: Pantheon, 1981.

Lee, Robert C. "Evangelism and Anarchy in *The Iceman Cometh.*" In Harold Bloom, ed., *Eugene O'Neill's The Iceman Cometh.* New York: Chelsea House, 1987.

Levine, David, Leslie Page Moch, Louise A. Tilly, John Modell, and Elizabeth Pleck.

Essays on the Family and Historical Change. Edited by Leslie Page Moch and Gary D. Stark. College Station: Texas A & M University Press, 1983.

Levine, Ira A. *Left-Wing Dramatic Theory in the American Theatre*. Ann Arbor: UMI Research Press, 1985.

Levine, Lawrence W. *Black Culture and Black Consciousness: Afro-American Thought from Slavery to Freedom*. New York: Oxford University Press, 1977.

———. *Highbrow/Lowbrow: The Emergence of Cultural Hierarchy in America*. Cambridge: Harvard University Press, 1988.

Levy, Anita. *Other Women: The Writing of Class, Race, and Gender, 1832–1898*. Princeton: Princeton University Press, 1991.

Lewis, David Levering. *When Harlem Was in Vogue*. New York: Knopf, 1981.

Lewisohn, Ludwig. "Drama: 'The Verge.' " *The Nation* 113 (December 14, 1921): 708–9.

Lindsey, Ben B., and Wainwright Evans. *The Companionate Marriage*. New York: Boni & Liverwright, 1927.

———. *The Revolt of Youth*. New York: Boni & Liverwright, 1925.

Locke, Alain, ed. *The New Negro*. 1925. Rpt. New York: Atheneum, 1980.

Long, Walter. "Eugene O'Neill." *Modern Quarterly* 4 (January-April 1927): 83–85.

Loos, Anita. *"Gentlemen Prefer Blondes": The Illuminating Diary of a Professional Lady*. New York: Grosset & Dunlap, 1925.

———. *A Girl Like I*. New York: Viking Press, 1966.

Lott, Eric. *Love and Theft: Blackface Minstrelsy and the American Working Class*. New York: Oxford University Press, 1993.

———. "Love and Theft: The Racial Unconscious of Blackface Minstrelsy." *Representations* 39 (Summer 1992): 23–50.

Lubove, Roy. *The Professional Altruist: The Emergence of Social Work as a Career, 1880–1930*. Cambridge: Harvard University Press, 1965.

Lukàcs, Georg. *The Meaning of Contemporary Realism*. Translated by John Mander and Necke Mander. London: Merlin Press, 1963.

Lukes, Steven. *Individualism*. New York: Harper & Row, 1973.

Lutz, Catherine A. "Depression and the Translation of Emotional Worlds." In Arthur Kleinman and Byron Good, eds., *Culture and Depression: Studies in the Anthropology and Cross-Cultural Psychiatry of Affect and Disorder*. Berkeley: University of California Press, 1985.

Lutz, Tom. *American Nervousness 1903: An Anecdotal History*. Ithaca, N.Y.: Cornell University Press, 1991.

"The Lynching Industry, 1919." *The Crisis* 19 (February 1920): 183–86.

Lynd, Robert S., and Helen Merrell Lynd. *Middletown: A Study in Modern Culture*. 1929. Rpt. New York: Harcourt, Brace & World, 1956.

Macgowan, Kenneth. *The Theatre of Tomorrow*. New York: Boni & Liverwright, 1921.

Macgowan, Kenneth, and Herman Rosse. *Masks and Demons*. New York: Harcourt, Brace, 1923.

Macpherson, C. B. *The Political Theory of Possessive Individualism: Hobbes to Locke*. Oxford: Oxford University Press, 1962.

Makowsky, Veronica. *Susan Glaspell's Century of American Women: A Critical Interpretation of Her Work*. New York: Oxford University Press, 1993.

Manheim, Michael. *Eugene O'Neill's New Language of Kinship*. Syracuse: Syracuse University Press, 1982.

Marsh, Margaret S. *Anarchist Women 1870–1920*. Philadelphia: Temple University Press, 1981.

Martin, Tony. *Literary Garveyism: Garvey, Black Arts and the Harlem Renaissance*. Dover, Mass.: The Majority Press, 1983.

Mathews, Jane DeHart. *The Federal Theatre, 1935–1939: Plays, Relief, and Politics*. Princeton: Princeton University Press, 1967.

Matthews, Fred. "The New Psychology and American Drama." In Adele Heller and Lois Rudnick, eds., *1915, The Cultural Moment: The New Politics, the New Woman, the New Psychology, the New Art, and the New Theatre in America*. New Brunswick, N.J.: Rutgers University Press, 1991.

May, Elaine Tyler. *Great Expectations: Marriage and Divorce in Post-Victorian America*. Chicago: University of Chicago Press, 1980.

———. *Homeward Bound: American Families in the Cold War Era*. New York: Basic Books, 1988.

———. "Myths and Realities of the American Family." In Antoine Prost and Gerard Vincent, eds., *Riddles of Identity in Modern Times*. Vol. 5 of *A History of Private Life*, edited by Philippe Ariès and Georges Duby. Translated by Arthur Goldhammer. Cambridge: Harvard University Press, 1991.

May, Henry F. *The End of American Innocence: A Study of the First Years of Our Own Time, 1912–1917*. 1959. Rpt. Chicago: Quadrangle, 1964.

McConachie, Bruce A. *Melodramatic Formations: American Theatre and Society, 1820–1870*. Iowa City: University of Iowa Press, 1992.

———. "Using the Concept of Cultural Hegemony to Write Theatre History." In Thomas Postlewait and Bruce A. McConachie, eds., *Interpreting the Theatrical Past: Essays in the Historiography of Performance*. Iowa City: University of Iowa Press, 1989.

McDermott, Douglas. "The Living Newspaper as Dramatic Form." *Modern Drama* 7 (May 1965): 82–94.

———. "Propaganda and Art: Dramatic Theory and the Great Depression." *Modern Drama* 11 (May 1968): 73–81.

———. "The Workers' Laboratory Theatre: Archetype and Example." In Bruce A. McConachie and Daniel Friedman, eds., *Theatre for Working Class Audiences in the United States, 1830–1980*. Westport, Conn.: Greenwood Press, 1985.

McElvaine, Robert S., ed. *Down and Out in the Great Depression: Letters from the "Forgotten Man."* Chapel Hill: University of North Carolina Press, 1983.

McKay, Claude. "A Black Star." *The Liberator* 4 (August 1921): 25.

Mears, Charles W. *Salesmanship for the New Era*. New York: Harper, 1929.

"Men of the Month." *The Crisis* 21 (February 1921): 171–72.

Meyer, Donald B. *The Positive Thinkers: A Study of the American Quest for Health, Wealth, and Personal Power from Mary Baker Eddy to Norman Vincent Peale*. Garden City, N.Y.: Doubleday, 1965.

Meyer, Michael. *Strindberg*. New York: Random House, 1985.

Miles, Agnes. *The Neurotic Woman: The Role of Gender in Psychiatric Illness*. New York: New York University Press, 1988.

Miller, Arthur. *The Theatre Essays of Arthur Miller*. Edited by Robert A. Martin. New York: Viking Press, 1978.

——. *Timebends: A Life*. New York: Grove Press, 1987.

Miller, Gabriel. *Clifford Odets*. New York: Continuum, 1989.

Miller, Jordan Y. *Eugene O'Neill and the American Critic: A Biographical Checklist*. Hamden, Conn.: Archon, 1973.

——. *Playwright's Progress: O'Neill and the Critics*. Chicago: Scott, Foresman, 1965.

Miller, Kerby A. *Emigrants and Exiles: Ireland and the Irish Exodus to North America*. New York: Oxford University Press, 1985.

Mintz, Steven. *A Prison of Expectations: The Family in Victorian Culture*. New York: New York University Press, 1983.

Mintz, Steven, and Susan Kellogg. *Domestic Revolutions: A Social History of Family Life*. New York: Free Press, 1988.

Moore, Charles A., ed. *The Status of the Individual in East and West*. Honolulu: University of Hawaii Press, 1968.

Morawski, Jill G., and Gail A. Hornstein. "Quandary of the Quacks: The Struggle for Expert Knowledge in American Psychology, 1890–1940." In J. Brown and A. K. Keuren, eds., *The Estate of Social Knowledge*. Baltimore: Johns Hopkins University Press, 1991.

Morris, Colin. *The Discovery of the Individual 1050–1200*. New York: Harper & Row, 1973.

Mowrer, Ernest. *The Family: Its Organization and Disorganization*. Chicago: University of Chicago Press, 1932.

Murray, Christopher. "O'Neill and 'The Ultimate Wound': An Essay on Tragedy." In Edward L. Shaughnessy, *Eugene O'Neill in Ireland: The Critical Reception*. Westport, Conn.: Greenwood Press, 1988.

Nathan, George Jean. "Educating the Drama." *American Spectator* 1 (July 1933): 2.

——. "The Theatre." In Harold E. Stearns, ed., *Civilization in the United States: An Inquiry by Thirty Americans*. New York: Harcourt, Brace, 1922.

Needham, Rodney. "Inner States as Universals: Sceptical Reflections on Human Nature." In Paul Heelas and Andrew Lock, eds., *Indigenous Psychologies: The Anthropology of the Self*. London: Academic Press, 1981.

Nethercot, Arthur A. "The Psychoanalyzing of Eugene O'Neill." [Part One.] *Modern Drama* 3 (Winter 1960): 242–56.

——. "The Psychoanalyzing of Eugene O'Neill." [Part Two.] *Modern Drama* 3 (February 1961): 357–72.

——. "The Psychoanalyzing of Eugene O'Neill: P. P. S." *Modern Drama* 16 (June 1973): 35–48.

"The New Negro Theatre." *The Crisis* 14 (June 1917): 80–81.

Nicholson, Linda. *Gender and History: The Limits of Social Theory in the Age of the Family*. New York: Columbia University Press, 1986.

Nissenbaum, Stephen. *Sex, Diet, and Debility in Jacksonian America: Sylvester Graham and Health Reform*. Westport, Conn.: Greenwood Press, 1980.

O'Connor, John, and Lorraine Brown, eds. *Free, Adult, Uncensored: The Living History of the Federal Theatre Project.* Washington, D.C.: New Republic Books, 1978.

O'Donnell, John Michael. "The Origins of Behaviorism: American Psychology, 1870–1920." Ph.D. diss., University of Pennsylvania, 1979.

——. *The Origins of Behaviorism: American Psychology, 1870–1920.* New York: New York University Press, 1985.

O'Hara, Frank Huburt. *Today in American Drama.* Chicago: University of Chicago Press, 1939.

O'Higgins, Harvey. *The Secret Springs.* New York: Harper, 1920.

O'Neil, Raymond. "The Negro in Dramatic Art." *The Crisis* 27 (February 1924): 155–57.

O'Neill, Eugene. *"As Ever, Gene": The Letters of Eugene O'Neill to George Jean Nathan.* Edited by Nancy L. Roberts and Arthur W. Roberts. Rutherford, N.J.: Fairleigh Dickinson Press, 1987.

——. *Conversations with Eugene O'Neill.* Edited by Mark W. Estrin. Jackson: University Press of Mississippi, 1990.

——. *Eugene O'Neill at Work: Newly Released Ideas for Plays.* Edited by Virginia Floyd. New York: Frederick Ungar, 1981.

——. *Eugene O'Neill Work Diary 1924–1943,* 2 vols. Edited by Donald Gallup. New Haven: Yale University Library, 1981.

——. *Poems 1912–1944.* Edited by Donald Gallup. New York: Ticknor & Fields, 1980.

——. *Selected Letters of Eugene O'Neill.* Edited by Travis Bogard and Jackson R. Bryer. New Haven: Yale University Press, 1988.

——. *"The Theatre We Worked For": The Letters of Eugene O'Neill to Kenneth Macgowan.* Edited by Jackson R. Bryer with Ruth M. Alvarez. New Haven: Yale University Press, 1982.

——. *The Unknown O'Neill: Unpublished or Unfamiliar Writings of Eugene O'Neill.* Edited by Travis Bogard. New Haven: Yale University Press, 1988.

Odets, Clifford. "All Drama Is Propaganda." *Current Controversy* (February 1936): 13–14.

Ohmann, Richard. "Charting Social Space." Unpublished manuscript, Wesleyan University, 1992.

——. *The Politics of Letters.* Middletown, Conn.: Wesleyan University Press, 1987.

——. "Turn-of-the-Century Magazine Fiction." Unpublished manuscript, Wesleyan University, 1992.

Oppenheim, James. *Behind Your Front.* New York: Harper, 1928.

Papke, Mary E. *Susan Glaspell: A Research and Production Sourcebook.* Westport, Conn.: Greenwood Press, 1993.

Peck, Martin W., M.D. "Psychoanalysis and Humankind." *The Survey* 64 (May 1, 1930): 127–30, 165–67.

Pells, Richard. *Radical Visions and American Dreams: Culture and Social Thought in the Depression Years.* New York: Harper & Row, 1973.

Perrot, Michelle, ed. *From the Fires of Revolution to the Great War.* Vol. 4 of *A History of Private Life,* edited by Philippe Ariès and Georges Duby. Translated by Arthur Goldhammer. Cambridge: Harvard University Press, 1990.

Perry, Lewis. *Childhood, Marriage, and Reform: Henry Clark Wright, 1797–1870*. Chicago: University of Chicago Press, 1980.

Peterson, Houston. *The Melody of Chaos*. New York: Longmans, Green, 1931.

Pfister, Joel. "The Americanization of Cultural Studies." *Yale Journal of Criticism* 4 (Spring 1991): 199–229.

——. *The Production of Personal Life: Class, Gender, and the Psychological in Hawthorne's Fiction*. Stanford: Stanford University Press, 1991.

Poggi, Jack. *Theater in America: The Impact of Economic Forces, 1880–1967*. Ithaca, N.Y.: Cornell University Press, 1968.

Probyn, Elspeth. *Sexing the Self: Gendered Positions in Cultural Studies*. New York: Routledge, 1993.

Quinn, Arthur Hobson. *A History of the American Drama: From the Civil War to the Present Day*. Vol. 2, *From William Vaughn Moody to the Present Day*. New York: Harper & Brothers, 1927.

Rabkin, Gerald. *Drama and Commitment: Politics in the American Theatre of the Thirties*. Bloomington: Indiana University Press, 1964.

Raleigh, John Henry. "Communal, Familial, and Personal Memories in O'Neill's *Long Day's Journey Into Night*." *Modern Drama* 31 (1988): 63–72.

——. "The Irish Atavism of *A Moon for the Misbegotten*." In Virginia Floyd, ed., *Eugene O'Neill: A World View*. New York: Frederick Ungar, 1979.

——. "The Last Confession: O'Neill and the Catholic Confessional." In Virginia Floyd, ed., *Eugene O'Neill: A World View*. New York: Frederick Ungar, 1979.

——. "O'Neill's *Long Day's Journey Into Night* and New England Irish-Catholicism." In John Gassner, ed., *Eugene O'Neill: A Collection of Critical Essays*. Englewood Cliffs, N.J.: Prentice-Hall, 1964.

——. *The Plays of Eugene O'Neill*. Carbondale: Southern Illinois University Press, 1965.

Rampersad, Arnold. *I Dream a World*. Vol. 2 of *The Life of Langston Hughes* (1941–1967). New York: Oxford University Press, 1988.

——. *I, Too, Sing America*. Vol. 1 of *The Life of Langston Hughes* (1902–1941). New York: Oxford University Press, 1986.

Ranald, Margaret Loftus. *The Eugene O'Neill Companion*. Westport, Conn.: Greenwood Press, 1989.

Randolph, A. Philip. "Garveyism." *The Messenger* 6 (September 1921): 248–52.

Rapp, Rayna, and Ellen Ross. "The Twenties Backlash: Compulsory Heterosexuality, the Consumer Family, and the Waning of Feminism." In Amy Swerdlow and Hanna Lessinger, eds., *Class, Race, and Sex: The Dynamics of Control*. Boston: G. K. Hall, 1983.

Reed, Ruth. *The Modern Family*. New York: Knopf, 1929.

Rich, Adrienne. *On Lies, Secrets, and Silence: Selected Prose 1966–1978*. New York: Norton, 1979.

——. "A Valediction Forbidding Mourning." In *The Fact of a Doorframe: Poems Selected and New 1950–1984*. New York: Norton, 1984.

Rieff, Philip. *The Triumph of the Therapeutic: Uses of Faith after Freud*. New York: Harper & Row, 1966.

Robbins, R. "The I. W. W. On the Stage: Eugene O'Neill's 'The Hairy Ape' A Truly Inspired and Socially Significant Play." *Industrial Solidarity* (April 8, 1922): 2.

Robeson, Paul. *Paul Robeson Speaks: Writings, Speeches, Interviews 1918–1974.* Edited by Philip S. Foner. New York: Brunner/Mazel, 1978.

Roediger, David R. *The Wages of Whiteness: Race and the Making of the American Working Class.* London: Verso, 1991.

Rogers, J. A. "Critical Excursions and Reflections." *The Messenger* 6 (April 1924): 107, 111, 116.

Rosaldo, Michelle Z. "Toward an Anthropology of Self and Feeling." In Richard A. Shweder and Robert A. LeVine, eds., *Culture Theory: Essays in Mind, Self, and Emotion.* Cambridge: Cambridge University Press, 1984.

Rose, Nikolas. *Governing the Soul: The Shaping of the Private Self.* London: Routledge, 1990.

Rose, Phyllis. *Jazz Cleopatra: Josephine Baker in Her Time.* New York: Vintage, 1991.

Rosenberg, Charles E., ed. *The Family in History.* Philadelphia: University of Pennsylvania Press, 1975.

Roth, Martha. "Notes toward a Feminist Performance Aesthetic." *Women and Performance: Journal of Feminist Theory* 1 (Spring/Summer 1983): 5–14.

Rothman, David. *The Discovery of the Asylum: Social Order and Disorder in the New Republic.* Boston: Little, Brown, 1971.

Rubin, Joan Shelley. *The Making of Middlebrow Culture.* Chapel Hill: University of North Carolina Press, 1992.

Rudnick, Lois. "The New Woman." In Adele Heller and Lois Rudnick, eds., *1915, The Cultural Moment: The New Politics, the New Woman, the New Psychology, the New Art, and the New Theatre in America.* New Brunswick, N.J.: Rutgers University Press, 1991.

Ryan, Mary P. *The Cradle of the Middle Class: The Family in Oneida County, New York, 1790–1865.* Cambridge: Cambridge University Press, 1981.

———. *The Empire of the Mother: American Writing about Domesticity.* New York: Harrington Park Press, 1985.

———. *Womanhood in America: From Colonial Times to the Present.* New York: New Viewpoints, 1979.

Saloman, Samuel. *The Red War on the Family.* New York: Beckwith, 1922.

Samelson, Franz. "From 'Race Psychology' to 'Studies in Prejudice': Some Observations on the Thematic Reversal in Social Psychology." *Journal of the History of the Behavioral Sciences* 14 (1978): 265–78.

Samuel, Raphael, Ewan MacColl, and Stuart Cosgrove. *Theatres of the Left 1880–1935: Theatre Movements in Britain and America.* London: Routledge & Kegan Paul, 1985.

Sands, Jeffrey Elliott. "O'Neill's Stage Directions and the Actor." In Richard F. Moorton Jr., ed., *Eugene O'Neill's Century: Centennial Views on America's Foremost Tragic Dramatist.* Westport, Conn.: Greenwood Press, 1991.

Sanger, Margaret. *Happiness in Marriage.* Rpt. Fairview Park, N.Y.: Maxwell Reprint Co., 1969.

Sarlós, Robert Karoly. *Jig Cook and the Provincetown Players: Theatre in Ferment.* Amherst: University of Massachusetts Press, 1982.

——. "Jig Cook and Susan Glaspell: Rule Makers and Rule Breakers." In Adele Heller and Lois Rudnick, eds., *1915, The Cultural Moment: The New Politics, the New Woman, the New Psychology, the New Art, and the New Theatre in America.* New Brunswick, N.J.: Rutgers University Press, 1991.

Sartre, Jean-Paul. *Search for a Method.* Translated by Hazel E. Barnes. 1963. Rpt. New York: Vintage, 1968.

Saxton, Alexander. *The Rise and Fall of the White Republic: Class Politics and Mass Culture in Nineteenth-Century America.* London: Verso, 1990.

Scanlan, Tom. *Family, Drama, and American Dreams.* Westport, Conn.: Greenwood Press, 1978.

Schmalhausen, Samuel D. "Family Life: A Study in Pathology." In Victor Francis Calverton and Samuel D. Schmalhausen, eds., *The Intimate Problems of Modern Parents and Children.* New York: Macaulay, 1930.

——. "Psycho-Analysis and Communism." *Modern Quarterly* 6 (Summer 1932): 62–68.

——. "A Psychological Analysis of Socialism." *Modern Quarterly* 5 (November-February 1928–1929): 61–72.

——. "The Sexual Revolution." In Victor Francis Calverton and Samuel D. Schmalhausen, eds., *Sex in Civilization.* London: George Allen & Unwin, 1929.

——. "The War of the Sexes." In Samuel D. Schmalhausen and Victor Francis Calverton, eds., *Woman's Coming of Age: A Symposium.* New York: Horace Liverwright, 1931.

——. *Why We Misbehave.* New York: Macaulay, 1928.

Schneider, Isidor. "The Iceman Cometh." *New Masses* 61 (October 29, 1946): 28–30.

Schwarz, Judith. *The Radical Feminists of Heterodoxy.* Lebanon, N.H.: New Victoria Publishers, 1982.

Seabury, David. *Unmasking Our Minds.* New York: Boni & Liverwright, 1925.

Seaver, Edwin. "O'Neill, Grown Safe, Given Nobel Award." *Daily Worker* (November 13, 1936): 5.

Seiler, Conrad. "Workers' Theatre: A Criticism." *New Theatre* (June 1, 1934): 17.

Sennett, Richard. "Destructive Gemeinschaft." In Robert Bocock, Peter Hamilton, Kenneth Thompson, and Alan Walton, eds., *An Introduction to Sociology.* Brighton: Harvester, 1980.

——. *The Fall of Public Man: On the Social Psychology of Capitalism.* New York: Vintage, 1978.

Sennett, Richard, and Jonathan Cobb. *The Hidden Injuries of Class.* New York: Vintage, 1973.

Shannon, William V. *The American Irish.* New York: Macmillan, 1966.

Shaughnessy, Edward L. *Eugene O'Neill in Ireland: The Critical Reception.* Westport, Conn.: Greenwood Press, 1988.

Shea, Daniel B., Jr. *Spiritual Autobiography in Early America.* Princeton: Princeton University Press, 1968.

Sheaffer, Louis. *O'Neill: Son and Artist.* Boston: Little, Brown, 1973.

——. *O'Neill: Son and Playwright.* New York: Paragon House, 1968.

Shorter, Edward. *The Making of the Modern Family.* New York: Basic Books, 1975.

Showalter, Elaine. *The Female Malady: Women, Madness, and Culture in England, 1830–1980*. New York: Pantheon, 1986.

———. "Representing Ophelia: Women, Madness, and the Responsibility of Feminist Criticism." In Patricia Parker and Geoffrey Hartman, eds., *Shakespeare and the Question of Theory*. New York: Methuen, 1985.

———, ed. *These Modern Women: Autobiographical Essays from the Twenties*. Old Westbury, N.Y.: The Feminist Press, 1978.

Sievers, W. David. *Freud on Broadway: A History of Psychoanalysis and the American Drama*. New York: Hermitage House, 1955.

Sillen, Samuel. "Confusion Has Class Character." *Daily Worker* (April 7, 1946): 10.

———. "The Iceman Cometh." *Daily Worker* (October 14, 1946): 11.

Simmel, George. "Sociability." In Donald E. Levine, ed., *On Individuality and Social Forms*. Chicago: University of Chicago Press, 1971.

———. "The Isolated Individual Dyad." In Mike Brake, ed., *Human Sexual Relations: Towards a Redefinition of Sexual Politics*. New York: Pantheon, 1982.

Simonson, Lee. *Part of a Lifetime: Drawings and Designs 1919–1940*. New York: Duell, Sloan and Pearce, 1943.

———. *The Stage Is Set*. New York: Harcourt, Brace, 1932.

Sinfield, Alan. *Alfred Tennyson*. Oxford: Basil Blackwell, 1986.

———. *Literature, Politics and Culture in Postwar Britain*. Oxford: Basil Blackwell, 1989.

Sirjanaki, John. *The American Family in the Twentieth Century*. Cambridge: Harvard University Press, 1953.

Sklar, Martin. *The United States as a Developing Country: Studies in United States History in the Progressive Era and the 1920's*. Cambridge: Cambridge University Press, 1992.

Skolnick, Arlene. *Embattled Paradise: The American Family in an Age of Uncertainty*. New York: Basic Books, 1991.

Slochower, Harry. *Literature and Philosophy between the World Wars: The Problem of Alienation*. New York: Citadel, 1964.

Slotkin, Richard. "Apotheosis of the Lynching: The Political Uses of Symbolic Violence." *Western Legal History* 6 (Winter/Spring 1993): 1–15.

Smiley, Sam. *The Drama of Attack: Didactic Plays of the American Depression*. Columbia: University of Missouri Press, 1972.

Smith, Susan Harris. "Generic Hegemony: American Drama and the Canon." *American Quarterly* 41 (March 1989): 112–22.

Smith-Rosenberg, Carroll. *Disorderly Conduct: Visions of Gender in Victorian America*. New York: Oxford University Press, 1986.

———. "Sex as Symbol in Victorian Purity: An Ethnohistorical Analysis of Jacksonian America." *American Journal of Sociology* 84 (Special Summer Supplement, 1978): 212–47.

Sochen, June. *The New Woman: Feminism in Greenwich Village, 1910–1920*. New York: Quadrangle Books, 1972.

Southard, E. E., M.D. "Trade Unionism and Temperament: Notes upon the Psychiatric Point of View in Industry." *Mental Hygiene* 4 (April 1920): 281–300.

Stallybrass, Peter. "Shakespeare, the Individual, and the Text." In Lawrence Grossberg, Cary Nelson, and Paula Treichler, eds., *Cultural Studies*. New York: Routledge, 1992.

Stearns, Harold E. *America and the Young Intellectual*. 1921. Rpt. Westport, Conn.: Greenwood Press, 1973.

———, ed. *Civilization in the United States: An Inquiry by Thirty Americans*. New York: Harcourt, Brace, 1922.

Stebbins, Robert. "Hollywood's Imitation of Life." *New Theatre* (June 1935): 8–10.

Stein, Karen F. "The Women's World of Glaspell's *Trifles*." In Helen Krich Chinoy and Linda Walsh Jenkins, eds., *Women in American Theatre: Careers, Images, Movements*. New York: Crown Publishers, 1981.

Stephens, Judith. "Gender Ideology and Dramatic Convention in Progressive Era Plays, 1890–1920." In Sue-Ellen Case, ed., *Performing Feminisms: Feminist Critical Theory and Theatre*. Baltimore: Johns Hopkins University Press, 1990.

Stearns, Peter N. *Jealousy: The Evolution of an Emotion in American History*. New York: New York University Press, 1989.

Stocking, George W., Jr. *Victorian Anthropology*. New York: Free Press, 1987.

Stoehr, Taylor. *Free Love in America: A Documentary History*. New York: AMS Press, 1979.

Strychacz, Thomas. *Modernism, Mass Culture, and Professionalism*. New York: Cambridge University Press, 1993.

Susman, Warren. *Culture as History: The Transformation of American Society in the Twentieth Century*. New York: Pantheon, 1984.

Taylor, Karen Malpede. *People's Theatre in Amerika*. New York: Dream Book Specialists, 1973.

Thomas, Augustus. *The Witching Hour*. New York: Samuel French, 1916.

Thompson, Alan Reynolds. *The Anatomy of Drama*. 1946. Rpt. Freeport, N.Y.: Books for Libraries Press, 1968.

Thurber, James. "Peace, It's Wonderful." *Saturday Review of Literature* 25 (November 21, 1936): 13.

Tompkins, Jane. *Sensational Designs: The Cultural Work of American Fiction, 1790–1860*. New York: Oxford University Press, 1985.

Torgovnick, Marianna. *Gone Primitive: Savage Intellects, Modern Lives*. Chicago: University of Chicago Press, 1990.

Tridon, André. *Psychoanalysis and Love*. New York: Brentano's, 1922.

Trilling, Lionel. "Eugene O'Neill." In Harold Bloom, ed., *Eugene O'Neill: Modern Critical Views*. New York: Chelsea House, 1987.

———. *Sincerity and Authenticity*. London: Oxford University Press, 1974.

Trimberger, Ellen Kay. "The New Woman and the New Sexuality: Conflict and Contradiction in the Writings and Lives of Mabel Dodge and Neith Boyce." In Adele Heller and Lois Rudnick, eds., *1915, The Cultural Moment: The New Politics, the New Woman, the New Psychology, the New Art, and the New Theatre in America*. New Brunswick, N.J.: Rutgers University Press, 1991.

Tucker, Benjamin. *Instead of a Book: By a Man Too Busy to Write One*. 1897. Rpt. New York: Haskell House, 1969.

Van Laan, Thomas. "Singing in the Wilderness: The Dark Vision of O'Neill's Only Mature Comedy." In Harold Bloom, ed., *Eugene O'Neill: Modern Critical Views.* New York: Chelsea House, 1987.

Veblen, Thorstein. *The Theory of the Leisure Class.* 1899. Rpt. New York: New American Library, 1953.

Vernant, Jean-Pierre. *Mortals and Immortals: Collected Essays.* Edited by Froma Zeitlen. Princeton: Princeton University Press, 1991.

Volosinov, V. N. *Freudianism: A Critical Sketch.* Edited by I. R. Titunik and Neal H. Bruss. Translated by I. R. Titunik. Bloomington: Indiana University Press, 1987.

Von Wiegand, Charmion. "The Quest of Eugene O'Neill." *New Theatre* (September 1935): 12–17, 30–32.

Wainscott, Ronald H. *Staging O'Neill: The Experimental Years, 1920–1934.* New Haven: Yale University Press, 1988.

Waldau, Roy S. *Vintage Years of the Theatre Guild, 1928–1939.* Cleveland: The Press of Case Western Reserve University, 1972.

Walker, Julia. "Character, Commodity Fetishism, and the Origins of Expressionism on the American Stage." Ph.D. diss., Duke University, in progress.

Ware, Caroline. *Greenwich Village, 1920–1930: A Comment on American Civilization in the Post-War Years.* Boston: Houghton Mifflin, 1935.

Warner, Michael. "Thoreau's Bottom." *Raritan* 11 (Winter 1992): 53–79.

Waterman, Arthur E. *Susan Glaspell.* New York: Twayne, 1966.

Watson, Steven. *Strange Bedfellows: The First American Avant-Garde.* New York: Abbeville Press, 1991.

Weedon, Chris. *Feminist Practice and Poststructuralist Theory.* New York: Basil Blackwell, 1987.

Weinstein, James. *The Corporate Ideal in the Liberal State: 1900–1918.* Boston: Beacon, 1968.

Weissman, Philip. *Creativity in the Theater: A Psychoanalytic Study.* New York: Basic Books, 1965.

Wexler, Alice. *Emma Goldman: An Intimate Life.* New York: Pantheon, 1984.

"Where Are the Pre-War Radicals?" *Survey Graphic* 55 (February 1926): 556–66.

White, Allon. *The Uses of Obscurity: The Fiction of Early Modernism.* London: Routledge, 1981.

Whittemore, Reed. *Whole Lives: Shapers of Modern Biography.* Baltimore: Johns Hopkins University Press, 1989.

"Who's Who." *The Messenger* 4 (April 1922): 394.

Wiebe, Robert H. *The Search for Order, 1877–1920.* New York: Hill and Wang, 1967.

Wilkins, Frederick C. Review of *Strange Interlude. Eugene O'Neill Newsletter* 9 (Spring 1985): 46–49.

Williams, Jay. *Stage Left.* New York: Scribner, 1974.

Williams, Raymond. *Culture and Society, 1780–1950.* Harmondsworth, Middlesex: Penguin, 1963.

——. *Keywords: A Vocabulary of Culture and Society.* New York: Oxford University Press, 1976.

——. *Marxism and Literature.* New York: Oxford University Press, 1978.

——. *Modern Tragedy*. Stanford: Stanford University Press, 1966.

——. *The Sociology of Culture*. New York: Schocken, 1981.

Wilson, Christopher P. *White Collar Fictions: Class and Social Representation in American Literature, 1885–1925*. Athens: University of Georgia Press, 1992.

Wilson, Edmund. *The American Jitters: A Year of the Slump*. 1932. Rpt. Freeport, N.Y.: Books for Libraries Press, 1968.

——. *The Twenties*. Edited by Leon Edel. New York: Farrar, Strauss and Giroux, 1975.

Wimsatt, W. K. *The Verbal Icon*. Lexington: University Press of Kentucky, 1967.

Wishy, Bernard. *The Child and the Republic: The Dawn of Modern Child Nurture*. Philadelphia: University of Pennsylvania Press, 1968.

Withers, Josephine. "Artistic Women and Women Artists." *Art Journal* 35 (Summer 1976): 330–36.

Wollstonecraft, Mary. "Woman and Property." *Mother Earth* 9 (August 1916): 578–81.

Zaretsky, Eli. *Capitalism, the Family, and Personal Life*. New York: Harper Colophon, 1979.

Aaron, Daniel, 142
Abbey Theatre, 30
Abu-Lughod, Lila, 239–40 (n. 1)
Advertising industry, 79, 140–41
Alexander, Doris, 41, 93–94, 151–52, 168, 181
Allen, Frederick Lewis, 71, 138, 180
Althusser, Louis, 219, 227–28 (n. 28)
American Pipe Dream, 102, 139, 185
American Mercury, 76, 138
American Spectator, 72–73
American theatre, 6, 142, 217, 218–19
Anarchism: *The Iceman Cometh* and, 102, 150, 151, 152–53, 154; O'Neill and, 107, 142–44, 151, 153; *Abortion* and, 144; anarchist-feminists, 144, 145–46, 148, 149, 153, 154; and violence, 148, 269 (n. 141); *Now I Ask You* and, 149
Anderson, Sherwood, 61–62, 76
Animal Crackers (film), 10–11
Arent, Arthur: *One-Third of a Nation*, 185
Ariès, Philippe, 22, 46
Armstrong, Nancy, 57–58, 245–46 (n. 64), 285–86 (n. 12)
Art, 71, 163
Artists, 10, 57, 70–71, 227 (n. 24)
Atkinson, Brooks, 76–77, 88, 159, 219
Atlantic Monthly, 76, 79

Baker, George Pierce, 21, 146, 161, 173–74
Barnes, Albert, 130
Barrett, Mary, 232–33 (n. 30)
Barton, Bruce, 79–80
Behaviorist psychology, 80, 98–99
Belsey, Catherine, 286–87 (n. 17)
Benny, Jack, 10
Bentley, Eric, 250–51 (n. 129); on O'Neill, 64, 99, 234 (n. 38), 270

(n. 163), 271 (n. 172); on *Glencairn* cycle, 109
Berger, John, 201, 236 (n. 76), 265 (n. 110)
Berkman, Alexander, 143, 274–75 (n. 197)
Bettelheim, Bruno, 232–33 (n. 30), 233 (n. 34), 238 (n. 92)
Bigsby, C. W. E., 161, 228 (n. 31), 247 (n. 82)
Biography, 22, 232 (n. 28)
Birth control movement, 140
Bisch, Louis, 55–56, 57, 62, 66–67; *Be Glad You're Neurotic*, 65, 100
Blackface minstrel shows, 123, 129, 136
Blacks, 260 (n. 50); *Moon of the Caribbees* and, 112; O'Neill and, 121, 123, 133–35, 136–37, 259 (n. 36); *The Dreamy Kid* and, 121, 124; as actors, 121, 130, 134, 259 (n. 38), 262–63 (n. 73); racism and, 122–24, 132–34, 135, 136; in race riots, 124–25; in World War I, 124–25, 261 (n. 57); *The Emperor Jones* and, 125–26, 128–32, 135, 136; Harlem Renaissance, 126–28; *All God's Chillun Got Wings* and, 135–36; lynching of, 261 (n. 59)
Blake, Ben: *The Awakening of American Theatre*, 167
Blankfort, Michael, 166, 168, 276 (n. 207)
Blast, 143
Bledsoe, Jules, 131–32
Blitzstein, Marc: *Cradle Will Rock*, 118
Boal, Augusto, 264–65 (n. 98)
Bogard, Travis: on O'Neill's works, 8, 17–18, 161, 229 (n. 3); on *Welded*, 32, 35; on *Strange Interlude*, 64; on *Long Day's Journey Into Night*, 215

Boston, Mass.: *Strange Interlude*
banned in, 77, 78, 97, 160, 226
(n. 12); police strike, 137; *Desire
Under the Elms* banned in, 142–43
Boucicault, Dion, 30
Boulton, Agnes (pseud. Eleanor Rand),
242 (n. 18); divorce from O'Neill, 8,
36; marriage to O'Neill, 32–33, 39,
55, 108, 205–6; *The Guilty One*,
33; and O'Neill and Glaspell, 192,
194–95, 206; *Part of a Long Story*,
205
Bourdieu, Pierre, 229 (n. 6)
Bowen, Croswell, 139
Bowlby, Rachel, 248–49 (n. 114)
Boyce, Neith: *Constancy*, 191
Boyd, Ernest, 72
Brantlinger, Patrick, 272–73 (n. 183)
Brecht, Bertolt, 41, 59, 103, 185, 264–
65 (n. 98), 269 (n. 147)
Bridges, William, 128
Brink, Louise, 61; *Psychoanalysis and
the Drama*, 55, 58–60
Brisbane, Arthur, 140
Brodhead, Richard H., 226–27 (n. 16),
233 (n. 34)
Brougham, John, 30
Broun, Heywood, 287 (n. 20)
Brown, John Mason, 217
Bryant, Louise, 108, 191, 192, 281
(n. 21); *The Game*, 191
Bryer, Jackson R., 8
Buhle, Mari Jo, 140
Buhle, Paul, 181, 266–67 (n. 117)
Burnham, John, 243 (n. 35), 244
(n. 44)
Byron, George Gordon, Lord: *Childe
Harold*, 11, 12, 183, 204

Cabell, James Branch, 72
Calverton, V. F., 67, 94–95, 167, 236
(n. 80), 266–67 (n. 117)
Capitalism, 189, 219; *More Stately
Mansions* and, 25, 42–45, 47,
158–59, 182; psychoanalysis and,
65; *The Hairy Ape* and, 69–70;

O'Neill and, 80, 221; *Mourning
Becomes Electra* and, 87; *Desire
Under the Elms* and, 91; *The Iceman
Cometh* and, 102; *A Touch of the
Poet* and, 182–84
Capitalist class, 69
Carby, Hazel V., 260 (n. 49)
Cargill, Oscar, 93
Carlin, Terry, 143
Carlyle, Thomas: *French Revolution*,
172, 173
Carnegie, Dale, 79–80
Caspar, Scott, 232 (n. 28)
Catholicism, 17, 19, 83, 102, 158, 160,
207, 209–10, 234 (n. 45)
Caudwell, Christopher, 251 (n. 132)
Challenger, 128
"Character," culture of, 169
Chekhov, Anton, 166, 185, 221
Cheney, Sheldon: *The New Movement
in the Theatre*, 60, 273 (n. 186)
Children, psychological influence of
family on, 22–25, 29, 41, 56, 231
(n. 24), 232–33 (n. 30)
Clark, Barrett, 9, 195, 207, 218, 221
Class structure, 69, 90, 110, 120,
168
Cleyre, Voltarine de, 145
Clurman, Harold, 76, 168, 172, 181,
183; *The Fervent Years*, 75–76
Coleman, Loyd Ring, 65, 67; *Psychol-
ogy: A Simplification*, 56
Coleman, McAlister, 165
Commins, Saxe: on O'Neill and pri-
vacy, 23; *Obituary*, 56; *Psychology:
A Simplification*, 56; friendship with
O'Neill, 56–57, 143; on psycho-
analysis, 65, 67; O'Neill's letters to,
99, 143, 169, 173, 177
Communism, 142, 160, 164
Confession discourse, 67–69
Consumer culture, 28–29, 78–79, 189
Cook, George Cram ("Jig"), 107, 149,
191; *Suppressed Desires*, 14, 84–85,
87, 188, 195; *Athenian Women*, 143;
marriage to Glaspell, 192

Family: *Mourning Becomes Electra* and, 5–6, 40–43, 47, 93; history of family life, 15–16, 23–24, 54, 228–29 (n. 1), 231 (n. 24), 231–32 (n. 25); O'Neill's views on, 16, 22, 32, 48, 229 (n. 2); psychological influence on children, 22–25, 29, 41, 56, 231 (n. 24), 232–33 (n. 30); "hothouse family," 23, 26, 41, 54, 235–36 (n. 70); "oedipal family," 25, 41–42, 54, 93, 235–36 (n. 70); "psychological family," 28–29, 32, 47–49, 51, 54–55; "pathological family," 37; *More Stately Mansions* and, 42–45, 46–47, 48–50, 93

Farrell, James T., 31

Fathers, 24, 25, 93

Fauset, Jessie, 121

Fechter, Charles: *Monte Cristo*, 18

Federal Theatre Project, 118, 123, 164, 185

Feminism, 140, 145, 190; Glaspell and, 14, 192–93, 194, 199, 201; anarchist-feminists, 144, 145–46, 148, 149, 153, 154; O'Neill and, 194, 202

Fielding, William J.: *The Caveman Within Us*, 88, 89

Fishbein, Leslie, 244 (n. 41), 250 (n. 128)

Fitzgerald, M. Eleanor, 143

Flaubert, Gustave: *Madame Bovary*, 231 (n. 24)

Flexner, Eleanor, 167, 183, 272 (n. 182)

Floyd, Virginia, 28, 102

Fontanne, Lynn, 77, 280 (n. 9)

Foucault, Michel, 46, 66, 67, 78, 179, 229 (n. 6), 245–46 (n. 64)

Fox, Richard Wightman, 248 (nn. 105, 111)

Fraina, Louis (pseud. Lewis Corey), 94

Frank, Waldo: "Joyful Wisdom," 68

Frazer, Winifred, 142, 153–54

Freeman, Joseph, 140, 162–63, 181; on psychoanalysis, 66, 86, 241 (n. 12), 249 (n. 122), 277 (n. 222); *American Testament*, 85–86; marriage to Von Wiegand, 166, 275 (n. 201)

Freiligrath, Ferdinand: "Revolution," 172

Freud, Sigmund, 71; O'Neill's denial of influence by, 5, 40–41, 98, 99; American receptiveness to, 7, 26, 63, 244–45 (n. 50); invention of psychoanalysis, 7, 31, 60; and aesthetics of depth, 60; and pop psychology, 63, 64, 65–66; and "primitives," 88, 89; *Totem and Taboo*, 89, 91; *Civilization and Its Discontents*, 164; and sexual "revolt of youth," 180–81, 189–90. *See also* Pop psychology; Psychoanalysis

Garvey, Marcus, 129

Gassner, John, 171, 275–76 (n. 203)

Gates, Henry Louis, 126–28

Geddes, Virgil, 167, 183, 184; *The Melodramadness of Eugene O'Neill*, 166; "The End of O'Neill," 168

Gelb, Arthur and Barbara, 16, 110, 270 (n. 161)

Gerstenberg, Alice: *Overtones*, 195–96

Gilman, Charlotte Perkins, 138; "The Yellow Wallpaper," 79, 199

Gilpin, Charles, 121, 130, 132, 133–34

Glaspell, Susan, 191–92, 203, 206; *Suppressed Desires*, 14, 84–85, 87, 188, 195; influence on O'Neill, 14, 149, 188, 190, 194–95; and feminism, 14, 192–93, 194, 199, 201; *Trifles*, 14, 195, 196–97, 282 (n. 36); *Woman's Honor*, 14, 197–98; *The Verge*, 14, 198–202, 205, 206, 213, 215; in Provincetown Players, 107, 143, 195; marriage to Cook, 192

Gold, Mike (Irving Granich), 151, 181; *Ivan's Homecoming*, 108; *Strike!*, 118; "Defense of Agitprop," 142; criticisms of O'Neill, 142, 153, 274–75 (n. 197); *Fiesta*, 163; *Hoboken Blues*, 163; O'Neill's letter on propaganda to, 163, 164, 184

Goldman, Emma, 97, 180; advocacy of anarchism, 107, 149, 220; *The Social Significance of Modern Drama*, 142, 145, 154–55; O'Neill and, 142–43, 171; critiques of gender roles, 144, 145, 178–79; *The Personal Equation* and, 146, 147; *The Iceman Cometh* and, 153–54; and psychoanalysis, 268–69 (n. 137)

Gramsci, Antonio, 227–28 (n. 28)

Granich, Irving. *See* Gold, Mike

Great Depression, 42, 83, 110, 169, 172, 273–74 (n. 191)

Green, Paul: *The House of Connelly*, 171

Greenwich Village Theatre, 91, 96

Gregory, Montgomery, 121

Group Theatre, 75, 76, 168, 171–72

Groves, Ernest: *American Marriage and Family Relationships*, 29

Guild Theatre, 74–75

Hale, Nathan, 63

Hall, G. Stanley, 278–79 (n. 238)

Hall, Stuart, 227–28 (n. 28), 267 (n. 118)

Halttunen, Karen, 248 (n. 111)

Hamilton, Gilbert V., 67; *What Is Wrong with Marriage*, 37–38, 41, 56, 197, 215; *A Research in Marriage*, 56; treatment of O'Neill's drinking, 56, 229–30 (n. 7)

Hapgood, Hutchins, 107, 191, 201

Harlem Renaissance, 126–28

Harper's, 56

Harper's Weekly, 124

Harrigan, Edward, 30

Harrison, William Greer: *O'Neill, or the Prince of Ulster*, 26

Hart, Moss, 16

Hauptmann, Gerhart, 218

Havel, Hippolyte, 143, 151–53, 154, 273 (n. 186); "The Brothers Karamazov," 152; "The Faith and Record of Anarchists," 152; "Literature: Its Influence upon Social Life," 152, 269 (n. 148)

Hawthorne, Nathaniel, 7–8, 41, 226 (n. 14), 226–27 (n. 16)

Heelas, Paul, 239–40 (n. 1)

Helburn, Theresa, 73, 74, 76, 77, 78, 171–72

Hepburn, Katharine, 208

Herbert, T. Walter, 231 (n. 24)

Heterodoxy club, 194, 201, 282 (n. 29)

Hicks, Granville, 37

Hinkle, Beatrice, 36

Hoffman, Frederick J., 57, 87–88

Hopkins, Arthur, 60, 61, 120; *How's Your Second Act?*, 60, 90

Hornstein, Gail A., 244 (n. 46)

"Hothouse family," 23, 26, 41, 54, 235–36 (n. 70)

Howard, Sidney: *The Silver Cord*, 237 (n. 90)

Hudson Dusters, 96–97

Huggins, Nathan, 129

Hughes, Langston, 97, 121, 131, 132

Ibsen, Henrik, 31, 61, 64, 155, 162, 181, 221; *Hedda Gabler*, 204, 270 (n. 150)

Individualism, 70, 71–72, 84, 97–98, 219–21, 222–23

Industrial revolution, 46

Industrial Solidarity, 165

Industrial Workers of the World (IWW), 118, 137, 138, 165

Intellectuals, 70–71, 85, 138

Ireland, 26, 29–30

Irish Americans, 17, 18, 26–27, 29–31, 54, 123–24, 183, 231 (n. 22), 234 (n. 43)

Jackson, Josephine A.: *Outwitting Our Nerves*, 65

Jameson, Fredric, 50, 249–50 (n. 123)

Jazz, 130

Jazz Singer (film), 76

Jelliffe, Smith Ely, 61; *Psychoanalysis and the Drama*, 55, 58–60

Mencken, H. L., 138
Messenger, 126, 128
Middle class, 96, 162, 167, 270
  (n. 162); and preoccupation with
  psychology, 7, 49–50; and family
  roles, 24, 49; and consumer culture,
  78, 79; *Moon of the Caribees* and,
  112, 114; and women's roles, 113,
  177–78, 188, 207; anarchist critiques
  of, 142, 150; *The Iceman Cometh*
  and, 151; *Ah, Wilderness!* and,
  168–70, 177–78, 179, 180–81; and
  individualism, 219, 220. *See also*
  Professional-managerial class
Millay, Edna St. Vincent, 192
Miller, Arthur, 16–17, 102, 221, 274
  (n. 196)
Mintz, Steven, 231 (n. 24)
Modernism, 61–62, 71, 78, 221, 272–
  73 (n. 183)
Modern Quarterly, 94, 95
Monterrey, Carlotta, 8; marriage to
  O'Neill, 36, 39; and politics, 139,
  264–65 (n. 98)
Morawski, Jill G., 244 (n. 46)
Mother Earth, 142, 144, 152, 172, 177,
  268 (n. 134)
Mothers, 237 (n. 90); childrearing
  responsibility, 23, 24, 25; cult of
  motherhood, 25, 47, 233–34 (n. 37);
  mother-son relationships, 37–39, 40,
  238 (n. 96); "mother complex," 40
Mullett, Mary, 155–56, 166

Nast, Thomas, 124
Nathan, George Jean, 11, 72–73, 138,
  273 (n. 189); on O'Neill's works, 97,
  226 (n. 8); O'Neill's letters to, 154,
  161, 164, 203; on American theatre,
  218; on black actors, 262–63 (n. 73)
National Theatre, 123
Naturalism, 103, 109
Needham, Rodney, 239–40 (n. 1)
"Negro psychology," 130–31
Neurasthenia, discourse of, 79, 189,
  190

New London, Conn., 27–28
New London *Telegraph*, 106, 107
New Masses, 100–101, 104, 141–42,
  181
New Theatre, 164, 166, 171
"New Woman," 191
New York Call, 107, 212
New York Drama League, 133
New York *World*, 78
Nichols, Dudley, 5, 7, 159–60
Nicholson, Linda, 228–29 (n. 1)
Nietzsche, Friedrich, 82, 102, 250
  (n. 128)
Nobel Prize, 6, 73, 165

O'Casey, Sean: *The Plow and the
  Stars*, 164; *The Stars Turn Red*, 164
Odets, Clifford, 164, 221, 264–65
  (n. 98); *Waiting for Lefty*, 118
"Oedipal family," 25, 41–42, 54, 93,
  235–36 (n. 70)
Oedipus complex, 26, 40, 43, 93
O'Faolain, Sean: *The Great O'Neill*, 31
Ogburn, William: *American Marriage
  and Family Relationships*, 29
O'Hara, Frank: *Today in American
  Drama*, 103
Ohmann, Richard, 72, 79, 174, 199
O'Neill, Eugene: photographs of, 1–4,
  8–9, 10, 113; artistic influences
  on, 4, 30, 31, 64, 250 (n. 128), 270
  (n. 150); denial of influence by
  Freud, 5, 40–41, 98, 99; awarded
  Pulitzer Prizes, 6, 49, 138; given
  honorary doctorate from Yale, 6, 72,
  173–74; awarded Nobel Prize, 6, 73,
  165; protests against notoriety, 8;
  divorce from Agnes Boulton, 8, 36;
  autobiographical references in plays,
  11, 12, 16, 17–18, 32–33, 205, 229
  (n. 3), 241 (n. 14); preoccupation
  with self-image, 11, 13; biographies
  of, 13–14, 16–18, 32, 48, 50; and
  radical politics, 14, 70, 106, 107, 108,
  138–39, 141, 142–44, 150–51, 154,
  160; Glaspell's influence on, 14, 149,

188, 190, 194–95; influence of family on, 15–16, 22, 23–24, 25, 26, 29; influence on theatre, 16–17, 72, 217–19; childhood and adolescence, 20–21; marriage to Kathleen Jenkins, 21; college education, 21, 146, 173, 255 (n. 169); early career, 21–22, 263 (n. 83); obsession with privacy, 23; and Irish heritage, 26, 28, 30–31; marriage to Agnes Boulton, 32–33, 39, 55, 108, 205–6; divorce from Kathleen Jenkins, 36; marriage to Carlotta Monterrey, 36, 39; therapy for alcoholism, 55, 56, 229–30 (n. 7); psychoanalytic diagnosis of, 55–56, 57–58; friendship with Saxe Commins, 56–57, 143; role in Theatre Guild, 73, 74, 77, 79; poetry, 106–7, 109; in Provincetown Players, 107, 108, 195; affair with Louise Bryant, 108; and black actors, 121, 134; as actor, 121–22; opposition to racism, 123, 133–35; homes owned by, 138; and political theatre, 154, 155–56, 162–64; and "Big Themes," 160–61, 162, 185, 271 (n. 172); leftist criticisms of, 164–68, 184–85; destruction of manuscripts, 182; neurological tremor, 182; and feminism, 194, 202; and "trappings of theatre," 203–5, 209, 215

WORKS:

—*Abortion*, 144, 175–76

—*Ah, Wilderness!*, 176, 204, 220; depiction of middle-class family, 27, 168–70, 180–81; O'Neill on, 99, 169; leftist criticism of, 168, 181; depth in, 169, 170, 179–80; and radical politics, 169, 170–71, 172–73, 177; and femininity, 177–79, 189

—*All God's Chillun Got Wings*, 121, 123, 135–36, 263–64 (n. 85)

—"*Anna Christie*," 60, 103; O'Neill on, 61, 110, 203, 215; awarded Pulitzer Prize, 138

—"Ballad of the Seamy Side," 109, 110

—*Beyond the Horizon*, 97, 159, 160; awarded Pulitzer Prize, 138

—*Bound East for Cardiff*, 108–9, 111, 115, 195

—*Bread and Butter*, 97, 275–76 (n. 203)

—*Days Without End*, 83–84, 141, 160, 196

—*Desire Under the Elms*, 91–92, 93, 96, 141, 160, 197; O'Neill on, 61, 98; banned in Boston, 142–43

—*Diff'rent*, 188–89

—*The Dreamy Kid*, 121, 124

—*Dynamo*, 161, 272 (n. 182)

—*The Emperor Jones*, 136, 160, 259 (n. 38); depictions of blacks, 121, 125–26, 128–29, 132; film version, 129, 134; as "negro psychology," 130–31; black audiences and, 131–32; leftist criticisms of, 134–35; Robeson on, 263 (n. 78)

—*Fog*, 97, 156–57

—"Fratricide," 107, 148, 170, 171

—"Free," 109, 110

—*Glencairn* cycle, 108–9, 110, 137, 164, 165

—*The Great God Brown*, 96, 141, 196; father-son rivalry in, 25; use of masks, 58, 62, 82, 206; depth in, 81–83

—*The Hairy Ape*, 60, 115–21, 160, 270 (n. 161), 272 (n. 182); and class structure, 69–70, 89, 118, 119, 120; leftist responses to, 118, 119, 165, 274–75 (n. 197); and politics, 118–19, 120, 137–38, 164, 276–77 (n. 208); O'Neill on, 120, 156, 161–62, 165, 274–75 (n. 197); Irish stereotypes in, 124

—*The Iceman Cometh*, 2, 172, 221, 274 (n. 196); and marital relations, 38, 39–40; psychological depth in, 100–101, 103–4, 150, 226 (n. 8); O'Neill on, 101–2; National Theatre

production of, 123; and racism, 136;
and anarchist politics, 143, 150–51,
152, 153–54; leftist responses to,
153, 166
—*Ile*, 195, 204, 210, 211
—*In the Zone*, 86, 108–9, 111–12
—*Lazarus Laughed*, 58, 141, 174
—*Long Day's Journey Into Night*,
220; and theatre as cultural force,
14, 188, 205, 207–8, 215; connections to O'Neill's family in, 16, 17,
18, 20, 21, 27, 229 (n. 4), 230 (n. 11);
Irishness in, 17, 26, 31–32, 231
(n. 22); mother-child relations in,
24, 25, 37, 202–3; and the making of
the psychological family, 29, 30, 31,
48, 49, 51; awarded Pulitzer Prize,
49; popularity of, 49, 50; pop psychology in, 101, 103–4; and anarchist politics, 105–6; on "life," 157–
58, 205, 222, 271 (n. 167); film version, 208; Ophelia figure, 208–10,
211
—"The Long Tale," 107
—*The Long Voyage Home*, 103,
108–9, 111
—*Marco Millions*, 25, 80–81, 95, 97,
174, 220, 274 (n. 193)
—"Memoranda on Masks," 58, 69, 243
(n. 31)
—*A Moon for the Misbegotten*, 101,
105, 175, 202; connections to
O'Neill's family in, 16, 17, 24, 26;
and mother-child relations, 37, 38;
on "life," 157
—*The Moon of the Caribees*, 103,
108–9, 112–14, 154
—*More Stately Mansions*, 26, 185;
critique of capitalism, 25, 42–45, 47,
158–59, 182; and the making of the
psychological family, 42–45, 46–47,
48–50, 93; and women, 45–46, 201;
O'Neill's intended destruction of,
182; and individualism, 220, 221
—*Mourning Becomes Electra*, 1, 17,
56, 123, 141, 218; psychological

family in, 5–6, 40–43, 47, 93;
O'Neill on depth of, 5–6, 61; popularity of, 50; and pop psychology, 87,
93–94, 96, 97, 103–4; women in,
144–45, 202
—*Now I Ask You*, 149–50, 194, 204
—*The Personal Equation*, 142, 146–
49, 161, 201–2
—"Sentimental Stuff," 202
—*Servitude*, 193–94, 204–5
—*Strange Interlude*, 61, 141, 196;
interior monologues, 4, 5, 11, 67,
68–69; psychological "depth" in,
4–5, 62, 64, 77–78, 79, 84, 92–93,
166, 187–88, 222; O'Neill on, 4–5,
98, 225–26 (n. 7); critical responses
to, 5, 64, 77–78, 86, 99, 103, 159–60,
166, 180; awarded Pulitzer Prize, 6;
financial success of, 6, 64, 77, 226
(n. 12); Marx Brothers' parody of,
10–11; popularity of, 50, 64, 67;
and pop psychology, 56, 64–65,
69, 103–4, 163; and professional-
managerial class, 65, 69, 95, 96, 222;
Theatre Guild production, 76, 77,
95; banned in Boston, 77, 78, 97,
160, 226 (n. 12); and primitivism,
88, 89; and women, 94, 189
—"Strindberg and the Theatre," 243
(n. 31)
—*A Tale of Possessors, Self- dispos-
sessed*, 182, 220, 221
—*Thirst*, 121–23
—"Tomorrow," 86
—*A Touch of the Poet*, 15, 26, 204,
281 (n. 26); psychological depth in,
11–12, 185; on "life," 158, 185; critique of capitalism, 182–84
—"Upon Our Beach," 106–7, 175
—*The Web*, 214, 270 (n. 155)
—*Welded*, 112, 141, 281 (n. 26); autobiographical references in, 32–33;
psychological dyad, 33–35, 57; and
marriage, 35, 36–37; on "life," 35,
90, 156; and class differences, 89–90,
96; on motherhood, 213

O'Neill, Eugene, Jr., 21, 61, 134, 169, 173

O'Neill, James, 215; acting career, 18–19, 209; death of, 19, 20, 210; and Irish heritage, 26, 27–28, 124; on *Beyond the Horizon*, 97

O'Neill, James, Jr. ("Jamie"), 20, 21, 24–25, 210

O'Neill, Mary Ellen Quinlan ("Ella"), 27, 207, 208, 210, 215; marriage and childbirth, 19–20; as mother, 20, 24–25

O'Neill, Oona, 16, 26

O'Neill, Shane Rudraighe, 16, 26, 123

Ophelia figure, 208–9, 210, 211, 213

Oppenheim, James, 86; *Night*, 86; *Behind Your Front*, 86–87, 100

Opportunity, 121

Optimism, critique of, 87

Palmer, Mitchell A., 137

Palmer raids, 137, 165

"Pathological family," 36, 37

Patriarchy, 24, 36, 45

Patten, Simon: *The New Basis of Civilization*, 189

Peters, Paul, 167

Peterson, Houston, 54

Pfister, Joel: *The Production of Personal Life*, 7, 41, 286 (n. 15); "The Americanization of Cultural Studies," 228 (n. 28)

Pilgrim, James, 30

"Pipe dreams," 102–3, 104, 136

Poe, Edgar Allan, 7, 8, 41

Political theatre, 162–63, 164, 167

Politics, 13, 139, 163

Pop psychology: in literary criticism, 7; O'Neill's dramatization of, 14, 54–55, 64, 103–4; and women's sexuality, 36, 39, 146, 180–81; professional-managerial class and, 55, 80, 222; *Strange Interlude* and, 56, 64–65, 69, 103–4, 163; and artists, 57; and theatre, 59–60; and literature, 62; and psychoanalysis, 63–64,

65–66; and neurosis, 66–67, 96, 222; and discourse of confession, 67–69; *Mourning Becomes Electra* and, 87, 93–94, 96, 97, 103–4; and primitivism, 88–89, 120; *The Hairy Ape* and, 120. *See also* Freud, Sigmund; Psychoanalysis

Primitivism, 88–89, 92, 131

Princeton University, 21, 72, 173

Professional-managerial class, 55; formation of, 69, 70; as characters in O'Neill plays, 69, 80, 82–83, 95, 97; cultural interests of, 71–72, 73, 74, 78, 79; and depth psychology, 80, 81, 84, 87–88, 90, 96, 166; as audience for O'Neill, 83, 96, 97, 120, 176–77, 222. *See also* Middle class

Progressive Era, 63, 70

Prostitution, 212, 214

Provincetown Players, 56, 96, 194, 195; production of *Suppressed Desires*, 84, 188; and socialist politics, 107–8; production of O'Neill plays, 122, 160

Psychiatric treatments, 49

Psychoanalysis, 50, 65, 286–87 (n. 17); influence on O'Neill, 6, 98–99; invention of, 7, 60; and "oedipal family," 25, 41, 54; popularity in America, 54, 63, 86, 244–45 (n. 50); and artists and intellectuals, 57, 66, 243 (n. 35); therapeutic function of drama, 58–61, 97; role of confession in, 67–68; *Suppressed Desires* and, 84–85, 195; critiques of, 85–86, 93–96; professional-managerial class and, 87–88; and death drive, 164; women and, 190, 195–96, 268–69 (n. 137). *See also* Freud, Sigmund; Pop psychology

Psychoanalytic Review, 55

"Psychological capital," 7–8, 53–54, 104

"Psychological family," 28–29, 49–50, 54; O'Neill's depictions of, 12, 31, 32, 37, 42, 47–49, 51, 55